COMMUNISM IN AFRICA

COMMUNISM
IN AFRICA

By

FRITZ SCHATTEN

London

GEORGE ALLEN & UNWIN LTD

RUSKIN HOUSE . MUSEUM STREET

FIRST PUBLISHED IN 1966

PRINTED IN GREAT BRITAIN
10 *on* 11 *point Ehrhardt type*
BY C. TINLING AND CO., LTD
LIVERPOOL, LONDON AND PRESCOT

CONTENTS

Chapter I

THE AFRICAN REVOLUTION

THE twentieth century is witnessing yet another revolution. A gigantic, elementary upheaval beyond anything previously known: the emancipation of a whole continent from historical darkness and political formlessness. This new eruption is changing not only the face of Africa but that of the whole world. Since the beginning of the modern era the history of the world has been dominated by fewer and fewer powers, and at first it seemed that a 'monopoly' had been established. From time to time the balance may have shifted slightly between the big Powers and their groups of alliances, and the pattern of individual loyalties may have changed a little, but the basic structure always remained the same. Even after the Second World War, which led to the development of great Powers with their allies and satellites, nothing changed fundamentally; instead, as Robert Strausz-Hupé wrote in 1948:[1] 'this balance of power lost none of its validity and merely took on a more subtle significance.' The tension between the two international poles after the Second World War determined world political development after 1945, and led to the establishment of a *status quo* which appeared to be permanent and unalterable.

Since 1960, however, we can see the beginning of a fundamental and decisive change in world affairs: the revolutionary upheaval in Africa, the emancipation of the African continent, and its emergence from the status of a mere passive object of the great European Powers to that of a potential individual actor on the world stage, constitute a development that has suddenly enhanced the importance of these States. Previously they had swung indecisively this way and that between the Eastern and Western blocs, while never being really strong enough to act effectively as a 'third force'. If this group of neutral or non-aligned Powers, now being tremendously reinforced by the new African countries, is ever in a position to act independently and with determination, and is able to maintain its independence and to strengthen internal solidarity, then a completely new international situation will develop. It can, for example, operate as a 'new majority' in the United Nations and the specialized agencies and even out-vote the 'old Powers' in matters exclusively concerning them—a possibility underlined by events at the United Nations since the autumn of 1960, and especially demonstrated during the sessions in 1962 and 1963. It was not incidental that the presidents of the General Assembly's 17th, 18th and 19th sessions came from the three 'emergent' continents: from Asia (1962), Latin America (1963) and Africa (1964).

Again, if either the West or the East should succeed in influencing this process and win even some of the Afro-Asian Powers over to its side, the consequences would be equally far-reaching. Such a shift in Power relationships would automatically change the *status quo*—as the Cuban example demonstrated for Latin America—and the struggle between liberty and totalitarianism would enter a new, more dynamic phase. As events in recent years have clearly shown, such a shift in the balance of power in Asia could be brought about only by military means and with great difficulties. Both East and West are thus concentrating their efforts to a far greater extent on Africa, a continent whose spiritual and political liability, vacillation and vehemence seem to offer ideal conditions for the exercise of both ideological and practical influence on the part of the great Powers.

Thus practically overnight Africa has become an area of international importance; quite suddenly a vast continent, which only yesterday seemed an out-of-the-way region, has acquired enormous political significance. As far as Europe and America were concerned, Africa was until very recently regarded as a sort of primeval, heathen, mysterious and magical nature reserve. It was a favourite area for the investigations of zealous archaeologists, anthropologists and ethnologists; a promising field of endeavour for missionaries of all denominations; an ideal background for big-game hunters, globe-trotters, adventurers, charlatans, reformers and ordinary business men. This vast continent, the last to be explored and to be carved into colonies (a process which ended only at the beginning of the twentieth century) seemed like an unchanging *terra incognita*, an unformed world patiently awaiting the arrival and civilizing influence of the White Man, who alone could rescue it from primitive backwardness. During the last two thousand years the traditional European picture of Africa hardly changed; the Dark Continent was still, as in the days of the Roman Empire, regarded as just the southern coast of the Mediterranean. And as such it represented both an exclusion of, and a task for Europe.

An Africa against, or even without, Europe, was unthinkable. The only alterations permitted in this picture were carefully calculated to create a future European–African partnership within the framework of an enormous, compact 'Eurafrica'. The very name of this artificial construction, which has frequently come up for discussion during the past twenty years, reflects the idea of European primacy. That this is no accident can be seen from the views expressed by Dietrich Westermann, who might be described as the Nestor of international Africanism. Referring to the Eurafrican ideal he declared:

'That is the decisive factor today: the lives of individuals and communities flow together, but in every case inevitably along lines marked out by whites, and people's destinies depend on how they come to terms with this experience.'[2]

This assumption of superiority, this demand for white domination, which up to a few years ago determined European colonial policy, is the chief factor for understanding European–African relationships right down to the present. This attitude emerged unaltered from the chaos of the Second World War and still dominated the European outlook as late as January 1944. At the Brazzaville conference, which took place under the aegis of de Gaulle, it was solemnly declared that 'the aims of French colonial policy exclude any idea of autonomy and any possible future self-government for the colonies'.[3] And in the same year Arthur Creech-Jones, the British Colonial Secretary in the Labour Government, announced:

'Great Britain stands firmly in her colonies and cannot withdraw. And I for one do not think she should withdraw. We have obligations towards these colonial areas and we must continue our policy of constructive trusteeship.'[4]

Thus the provision of the Atlantic Charter, promising self-determination to the dependent colonial areas, remained a dead letter, although the various Powers continued to pay lip-service to it. The African policy of the Western Powers remained conservative, even reactionary. During the Second World War hundreds of thousands of Africans fought and many of them died on the battle-fields of Europe and North Africa for the ideas of democracy and liberty; in return for their efforts they were not, however, given independence, but 'practical equality'. 'Assimilation' became the keyword of colonial policy; the colonial areas were to be integrated into the Motherland. London talked of 'partnership' and Paris talked of 'one hundred million Frenchmen'. The *Lex Caracalla* of 7 May 1946 assured all 'French peoples' that

'From 1 January 1946 onwards all the peoples of French overseas territories, including Algeria, will enjoy exactly the same rights, as citizens, as Frenchmen living in the Motherland.'[5]

Referring to this period, Maurice Violette, former Governor-General of Algeria, later declared:

'I am still in favour of the policy of assimilation . . . I feel that it would be possible to bring the whole population (of Algeria) in great swathes into a French unity, and that in this way France would become the greatest *Mohammedan* Power in the world. It was a grand dream—and one I thought worthy of my country—to desire one heart beating for France from the North Sea to the Congo'.[6]

Ideas such as these led to the formation of the *Union Française*, established by proclamation of the Fourth Republic on 27 October 1947 and France still clung to this dream long after Tunisia and Morocco were lost and even after the *loi-cadre* of 1956, which granted 'internal autonomy' in order to counteract the danger of a coloured African movement for external independence. During the first Constituent Assembly of the Fourth Republic, Pierre Cot, presenting the draft of the new Constitution to the Assembly, announced: 'The Colonial Empire is dead!' But in 1959 there were still official posters from Paris on walls in the French Ivory Coast territory, lyrically praising the idea of French hegemony:

'Africa! We have devoted the energy and inventiveness of so many generations to her, and we have carried the idea of our power and grandeur to her so that now she bears our indelible stamp! Under our protection and our leadership her advance in the coming years and the coming centuries will be steady, prosperous and profound!'[7]

However, the death-knell of colonialism had already tolled in Africa and it was to the accompaniment of such grandiloquent phrases that the French colonial empire, with all its 'power and grandeur', slid into liquidation. The first phase of this process of dissolution began in the Maghreb. Libya attained independence in 1951, and Morocco, Tunisia and the former Anglo-Egyptian Sudan followed suit in 1956. Then, only a few months later nationalism began to spread over the Dark Continent. On 6 March 1957, a date of historic importance, the British colony formerly known as the Gold Coast became Ghana, the first independent black African nation of the twentieth century—110 years after the foundation of the West African State of Liberia. And with Ghana—synonym for a great pre-colonial Negro State—came a programme for the liberation of the whole African continent, a programme which Europe could not ignore.

De Gaulle came to power as 'the Saviour of France', and of African France too, after the chaos of the Algerian revolt of May 1958. He immediately recognized the challenge of Ghana and realized that her influence was spreading throughout West Africa. His response was the far-reaching plan for a 'Communauté Française', which provided that the French African possessions should remain 'with limited sovereignty' in a community with the Motherland. However sensible and attractive the proposal appeared, it was too late for half-measures. On 28 September 1958 Guinea rejected the Constitution of the Fifth Republic and thus the 'Communauté Française'. Sékou Touré, 'the elephant of African nationalism', had successfully canvassed for an overwhelming 'No!' vote in de Gaulle's referendum. On hearing the dismayed comments from Paris, Dakar, Bamako, Abidjan, and other capitals of the French Community, the rebel of Conakry proudly and mockingly answered:

'If they say in the Ivory Coast, in the Sudan or in Senegal that Guinea is lost because she chose liberty, then let them say it. I promise you that within two months we shall be showing the others the way . . .'[8]

Touré, and not de Gaulle, was proved right. Guinea exercised a magnetic attraction: within a few weeks Conakry, the capital of Guinea, developed into a new centre of anti-colonial agitation even outdoing Accra, the capital of Ghana. Within a few months Conakry became the new secular Mecca to which radical nationalists from all over Africa flocked and listened in quasi-religious ecstasy to the gospel of 'secession from Europe' which they carried back to their native lands. Even the moderates in the *Communauté* were soon gazing with fascination at Guinea. In his Conakry residence Touré received delegations and ambassadors from all over the world. During his first journey abroad as president he was received in Washington, at the UNO headquarters, and in London, Bonn, Moscow and Prague. Meanwhile the African leaders of the French Community had to content themselves with their role of administrators in what was still, in fact if not in name, colonial territory. Their position deteriorated as the stirring slogans from Conakry and Accra strengthened opposition within their own territories and at the same time their own ambitions and desire for independence remained unsatisfied. If they wanted to save face they would have to allow the dynamic propaganda to carry them along too. It is characteristic of the psychological dilemma which this created for the *Communauté* that it was 'the best African friends of France' who were the first to demand that the *Communauté* should 'adapt itself to the new situation'. Speaking in Abidjan on behalf of Houphouet-Boigny, the president of the Ivory Coast Republic, Mamadou Coulibaly, the Speaker in Parliament, declared:

'The formula of the "reformed Communauté" will no longer deceive anyone overseas. It's just another veneer stuck over the old one, but the old worm-eaten timber is still underneath . . . The "reformed Communauté" which is supposed to meet the requirements of the new world situation appears to have just about as much chance of survival as the old one . . .'[9]

Two years after the establishment of the *Communauté Française*, which had been planned to give colonialism a breathing space in

Africa, the constitutional scaffolding collapsed. In order to prevent 'an all-African Guinea' or perhaps even a Dien Bien Phu in the desert and the torrid jungle of the Dark Continent, Paris gave member-states their freedom. A new framework was drawn up and a 'modified Communauté' on the lines of the British Commonwealth was planned; but no one was deceived, it was a very ephemeral structure, a phantasmagoria without a solid basis.

Thus 1960 became, as the extremists had prophesied, Africa's Year: within a few months seventeen African countries—the Cameroons, Togoland, Senegal, the Sudan, Mali, Madagascar, the Belgian Congo, the French Congo, Somalia, Upper Volta, the Ivory Coast, Dahomey, Niger, Chad, the Central African Republic, Gabon, Mauritania—became independent. In London the Colonial Office hastened to keep up with the breakneck pace and hurriedly announced the dates on which Sierra Leone, Nigeria, and Tanganyika were to achieve their independence. Leaders of other African territories were urgently invited to confer with the Colonial Secretary at Lancaster House to work out a time-table for the independence of their countries and by now Great Britain has granted independence to all her African territories with the exceptions of Southern Rhodesia, Basutoland, Bechuanaland and Barotseland.

Thus, at a date far earlier than even the most enthusiastic supporters of African nationalism would have dared to prophesy, the end of white colonial dominance over the Dark Continent became a certainty. Portugal and Spain may try to ignore the writing on the wall, but it can only be question of time before they are compelled to bow before the inevitable. A series of revolutionary factors precipitated the whole process, as history develops its own dynamic. Nothing can now hold it up: neither reason nor moderation, nor the dream of a *grande nation* embracing the continents, nor any humanitarian ideal of a multiracial partnership and brotherhood. Such things are nothing but shifting sands on which the last bastions of white colonialism in Africa hope to rest.

Belgium, in particular, has been given good reason to know this. Belgium was guilty of terrible cruelties and atrocities in the Congo (Roger Casement described them in detail in 1903), but gradually she adopted a policy of enlightened paternalism, which was supported by the Church and by business interests. Planning was very long-term indeed. Belgium carefully graded her economic and educational reforms. Nothing was to be hurried, there was time, plenty of time, and above all there were no political or educational ambitions among the natives which had to be considered.

While Britain and France steadily furthered educational schemes in their colonial territories and established a narrow pyramid of educated Africans fairly quickly, and while more and more coloured students were to be seen at the Sorbonne and the London School of Economics, the Belgian authorities stuck rigidly to their old horizontal plan: all the 'primitive children of the Congo' were to be taught the three R's at once and anything that went further was rejected as premature and likely to endanger the grand plan. The idea of encouraging the development of a native élite who could take over the administration was not a matter of practical politics—it was no more than a theoretical possibility for the far-distant future.

Certainly up to the early 1950s Belgian calculations met with a good deal of approval in Europe. British and French travellers to the Belgian Congo usually found more to praise than to blame and, in particular, were inclined to regard the educational and social policy of the Belgians as eminently sensible. Some urged their own governments to regard Belgian policy as a prime example of enlightened colonial policy.

Faced with such unsolicited admiration, the Belgian Government certainly saw no reason to worry or to revise its tried and trusted Congo policy—particularly as young King Baudouin was welcomed by his African subjects in the Congo with tremendous enthusiasm. Though the waves of nationalism were beating high in other parts of Africa, they seemed at a low ebb in the Belgian Congo. In the summer of 1958 a Belgian official in Leopoldville declared smugly to the author:

'In many parts of Africa anti-white and anti-European passions are rising, but there is no danger of any such thing in the Congo. And we shall certainly not make the mistakes that other colonial powers have made. Belgium has no plans for meeting the demands of native politicians. But the future prospects are all the more promising.'[10]

How far away that future was thought to be can be judged from discussions that took place in Brussels on the African policy of the Belgian Government. Deeply impressed by what was happening in the Maghreb and in Ghana, anti-colonial intellectuals and left-wing politicians in Paris and London gave colonialism a life-span of ten, or at a maximum fifteen, years in Africa. That was in 1955. But the Belgian opposition was far more optimistic in its estimate of the remaining life-span of colonialism. For example, in 1955 the Belgian colonial historian, van Bilsen, a critic of his country's colonial policy, drafted a '*Plan de trente ans pour l'Emancipation de l'Afrique Belge*'. In other words, even the opponents of Belgium's colonial policy in the Congo assumed that any radical change in the immediate future was out of the question. It would take thirty years to establish a basis for Congolese autonomy: 1985—not a moment earlier!

In fact, the life-span of Belgian colonialism in the Congo was just three, and not thirty, years from that date. The picture of 'the sleeping Congo', painted by both white and black, proved to be false. In January 1959 the first and only violent insurrection of the natives took place in Leopoldville; from then on '*Uhuru!*' (Swahili for 'freedom')—the battle cry of African nationalism—resounded throughout the Congo. Incredulous horror seized the Belgian settlers, technicians and officials in the Congo, while the politicians in Brussels were overcome with dismay, although the first news of the revolt had actually been joked about as 'the false report of the year'. Belgian smugness, not to say frivolity, about colonial affairs disappeared. A panic ensued and paternalist illusions were abandoned overnight. Until then Belgians had regarded the Congo as 'the most secure investment for our future', but now they found themselves sharing the opinion of Disraeli that 'the wretched colonies are a millstone round our neck'. The sooner that millstone was jettisoned the better and without previous warning King Baudouin used the fateful word 'independence'. Once this was done Belgium herself advanced the date again and again and a year later—on 24 January 1960—the Brussels Round-Table Conference fixed the date for lowering the Belgian flag in Africa as 30 June 1960, less than six months later. African nationalism had won a lightning victory and Brussels dropped the Congo—as one Belgian publicist put it—'like a hot brick'. We all know the result.

The speed at which Africa won its liberty, and at which Europe retreated from the African continent, is unequalled in history. How very different was the evolution in Asia. The withdrawal of European colonialism from Asia was also accompanied by violent and protracted upheavals, but there had been warnings of the coming struggle. As early as 1835 Lord Macaulay prophesied that it would not be long before India would be lost to the British Crown. The final phase of the struggle for independence in India lasted for forty years if we take 1909, the year in which the radical wing of the Congress Party put forward the demand for complete independence, as its beginning. Mahatma Gandhi started *Satyagraha*, the movement for 'passive resistance until victory', in 1919. From 1927 the Congress Party demanded independence with growing insistence. Britain felt compelled to grant home rule to Ceylon as early as 1931, but it was only in 1947 that the island attained dominion status. The national-revolutionary movement in Indo-China goes back to the days of the Chinese revolution of 1911, but it was not until 1954 that it was finally successful, after various changes of front and repeated partition of the Secession States. The Philippines were first shaken by a nationalist revolt as early as 1898 when the United States took over the islands from Spain. From 1916, the national-revolutionary movement harassed the United States forces by protracted guerilla warfare. Resistance flared up again in 1932 and only in 1946 were the islands able to celebrate the attainment of their independence. Reformist groups first put forward a nationalist programme for Indonesia in 1908; they increased their activity during the First World War and consolidated their position with the foundation of Sukarno's National Party in 1927. However it was not until 1945 that they approached their objective and after Dutch and British intervention their triumph came in 1950.

The modern Asian nationalist movement thus has a long and impressive tradition and its ultimate victory was the result of a struggle waged over a long period of time. The African nationalist movement, on the other hand, has no such tradition: it drew up its demands virtually out of nothing and gained them in an incredibly short time. The fact is that everything went too fast for them. Men who are now determined opponents of 'half-solutions' and who look with contempt on those who still think in terms of assimilation and integration only yesterday thought in that way themselves and rejected the path of nationalism. Ferhat Abbas, former head of the provisional government of the Republic of Algeria, is a case in point. In 1937, in his book *Beyond Nationalism*, he wrote:

'If I had created the Algerian nation I would be a nationalist, and I should see no reason to blush for that . . . But I did not create it. I turned to history, to the living and the dead. I visited the cemeteries. You cannot build on dust and wind. We have got rid of the mist and spectres once and for all, and we are determined to throw in our lot irrevocably with the great work of French construction in our country. Six million Mohammedans live in a territory that has been French for a hundred years. They live in holes, go barefoot and in rags, and they have not enough to eat. Our aim is to turn this mass of starvelings into a modern society . . . We want to educate them to human dignity so that they will become worthy of being called Frenchmen.'[11]

You can find statements by many African native leaders who had similar ideas regarding their own people.

The reasons for this sudden change in the African situation and for the African upheaval itself are extremely complicated. African and non-African factors merge into each other and it often seems impossible to separate the important from the subsidiary. But again and again we shall be brought back to the fact that the westernization of Africa, the awakening of the continent, and its colonization—as distinct from its colonial conquest—did not start until the beginning of this century and did not become really effective until after the First World War. Apart from one or two early attempts the same is true of the missionary work to convert Africa to Christianity. As against this, a French Jesuit, Alexandre de Rhodes, was in Indo-China at the beginning of the seventeenth century. Within a few years an Annamite Catechism was available and by 1660 there were French bishops in Siam, Cochin-China and Tonkin. Moreover, Asiatic religions gradually adapted themselves to the general process of spiritual and intellectual enlightenment. In Africa the situation was very different; as the Nigerian leader Doctor Nnamdi Azikiwe suggests in his book, *Renascent Africa*, published in London in 1937, that until quite recently African society was culturally stagnant (apart from the period of classical antiquity in Ethiopia and 'the immortal achievements of our ancestors in Negro Africa', for example, during the Middle Ages when Songhai flourished).

Azikiwe is himself a Methodist and he feels that the Christian mission is an important factor in the advance of Africa.

It can, of course, be argued that only one out of seven of the 220 million native inhabitants of Africa is a Christian, but this reliance on statistics is deceptive. Whoever reads the biographies of the leaders of present-day Africa will constantly come across Christian influences.

In their political writings many African leaders have stressed the liberating and encouraging effect of the Christian message, which they compared favourably with the fatalism of the primitive religions of Africa.

There is, of course, something else in the Christian message which is of great importance to Africans: 'All men are children of God, and all men are equal before God, whether black or white'. This is the teaching of Christianity and the missionaries took it with them to Africa, where the newly converted natives took it up with religious fervour. It was not long before they discovered that in practice this equality operated only within their own community, while many ostensibly Christian whites refused to recognize them as Christian brothers.

From here it is only a short step to the sectarian adaptations of Christianity which arise in Africa from time to time and in which Christian influences merge with survivals of old African nature religions. Soon after the First World War a movement known as Kimbanguism arose in the Congo and developed into the *Mission des Noires*. After the Second World War it came to the fore again and played quite an important role in the tragic events in the Congo in 1960 as well as in 1964. Its founder, Simon Kimbangu, was born in 1889, became a Baptist and in 1921, 'thanks to the grace of God', was, so he claims, 'entrusted with the divine mission' of freeing his black brothers. He adopted the title of Ngunza, which means Messiah. The sect he founded grew rapidly and even won supporters from African missionaries, partly because Kimbangu was clever enough to use the traditional deep respect of Africans for their ancestors as a cornerstone of his creed. Kimbangu frequently had 'revelations' from his own ancestors and finally announced that he had been instructed to sever all connections with the white man's Church and to establish 'the Kingdom of the Black Saviour' on earth. With this the white man, and particularly the white missionary, became superfluous. To Kimbangu and his followers the white man was comparable to the Egyptians and Philistines who had threatened Israel, the Jews who crucified Jesus, and the Romans. The white man was now 'the instrument of Satan' and it was the duty of the black man to destroy him. The Belgian authorities put Kimbangu under lock and key, but if they had hoped that this would destroy his political influence they were mistaken. Kimbangu was regarded as a martyr and even worshipped as the Messiah who would return to drive out the white heathen and liberate his faithful black followers: 'God has sent us Simon Kimbangu. He is to us what Moses was to the Jews, Jesus to the Gentiles and Mohammed to the Arabs.'

Kimbanguism has now developed into a militant, aggressive religion of salvation. The 'Ngunzaists' aimed at establishing a strongly centralized and liberated Congo. One of their prophets advocated that 'when the Divine seizure of power takes place' the followers of the movement should treat the 'femmes-madames' of the whites like whores. It is not difficult to imagine the effect of such an Africanization of Christianity in these troubled days. Incidentally quite a number of the more radical Congo leaders have in recent years expressed their support for Kimbanguism.

The majority of African Christians, of course, regard Kimbanguism or Ngunzaism as a distortion of Christianity; however we must not lose sight of the cause of this new movement: the obvious contradiction between the idea of the equality of all men before God, preached by the Christian missionaries, and the constant discrimination practised by white against black men. The result has been an inversion of beliefs. The *Mission des Noires* now declares that the black man, and not the European, is in 'a state of Grace', that he is the vessel of God's will and is called upon to perform God's mission on earth. This mission is to wrench the mask from the face of 'the white hypocrite', to expose him as the 'instrument of the Devil', and to drive him out of 'the promised land'.[12] We are faced here with one of the negative aspects of negritude—the overcompensation of an inferiority complex that has developed, understandably enough, among many Africans, particularly among the intellectuals. At the same time, even the more moderate forms of negritude—the awakening of the national consciousness of African Negroes—represent a reaction against European colonization.

It was not only Christian missionaries who proclaimed the principle of equality; before long, equality before God was supplemented by the cry for equality before the law, while books written by white men advocated social equality as well. Students at Makerere College eagerly studied English and American history; by the age of twelve the child in the British missionary school was learning about the democratic institutions of Britain. In French missionary schools the strains of the Marseillaise were heard and the 14th of July, the day of the storming of the Bastille, was as much a national holiday in French Africa as in France. The children learnt the three great principles of the French Revolution 'Liberty, Equality, Fraternity!' in their earliest primers. These were later translated into African languages and in this way their influence spread even further. However, wrenched out of their historical context, these great political principles were often reduced to the level of propaganda slogans.

The clash which was to come was therefore inevitable: sooner or later the African arrived at the point where he could see the contradiction between the officially proclaimed principles of 1789 and the failure, or even refusal, to put them into practice which, naturally, he found intolerable. Even the *evolués*, the more educated Africans, who were willing to accept the 'ifs' and 'buts' and supported the evolutionary programmes of the colonial Powers found it difficult to get round this contradiction. For example, in a lecture delivered in November 1959 to the Royal Institute of International Affairs in London, Sékou Touré declared:

'At first many of us accepted the assimilation programme because it seemed to open up new horizons. But these horizons came no closer. The original objective was the equality of the rulers and the ruled. But only too often those Africans who, for example, got into the *Assemblée*, found their own problems farther away than ever from a solution.'[13]

It is understandable that those who were disappointed with the slow progress made in realizing this original objective began to turn to more radical measures when they discovered that all they had to do was to increase nationalist agitation and build up pressure from below and the Colonial Office would recognize that the areas in question had arrived at the necessary degree of maturity.

The upheaval in Africa can be divided into three phases. The ideological basis for emancipation was laid during the first period, which ended with the Second World War. African intellectuals came together at Lincoln University in the United States and at various European universities. In an investigation into the political awakening of the coloured people, Bernard Fonlon writes:

'The coming together of coloured students in European and American centres became of far-reaching significance. Africans who came to London, Paris and New York from the Antilles, Africa and America found each other . . . From their meeting developed a joint consciousness, a feeling of racial solidarity, and an irresistible and steadily growing force.'[14]

Such political demands as were put forward did not seek the exclusion of the colonial Powers from Africa. In those days African intellectuals were not so much interested in political independence as in the questions of domestic freedom and the political rights of the individual.

The second period was dominated by the war-time experience of Africans. In addition to the large force raised in the Maghreb (Tunisia, Morocco and Algeria), many thousands of Africans fought on the various fronts of 'the European civil war'.[15] They were mobilized to fight for democracy and liberty against a system which trampled on the fundamental rights of man. Further, they were mobilized against a régime which was waging a brutal campaign of extermination against a whole race—the Jews. This gave Africans food for thought. The demands of the African élite became more political and more radical in an atmosphere of growing bitterness. Various organizations, once mainly educational and social, quickly developed into political associations and in October 1946 African leaders in French West Africa met in Bamako and founded the *Rassemblement Démocratique Africain*. It was the first big political party on the African continent. A few months later, on 27 March 1947, an anti-colonial revolt broke out in Madagascar. Together with the Mau-Mau insurrection, this explosion shattered the hope of the European Powers that colonial unrest could be confined to Asia. The wind 'bloweth where it listeth', particularly the wind of change, and road blocks are no good against ideas. The influence of events in Asia sparked off trouble in Africa much sooner than had been expected and the slogan of equality and liberty was taken up throughout the continent.

Nevertheless, in that phase it was still possible for the colonial Powers to suppress the Madagascar revolt and to crush the Mau-Mau terror by a white counter-terror that was only gradually decreased. This brings us to the third stage of the African upheaval, which began in the mid-fifties. In this period (apart from exceptions such as South Africa and Angola) force ceased to play its former role in the defence of colonial interests; in fact it became the practice of colonial Powers to forestall threatened outbreaks of violence by making concessions—even at the ultimate price of colonial self-liquidation. The most remarkable example of this is the Congo. In other words, colonialism ceased to exist as a naked power system.

Two factors determined this change. The first, one could term 'the Dien Bien Phu experience': the catastrophic defeat suffered by the French in Indo-China, coupled with the subsequent realization that it could have been avoided by more adroit tactics, was a great shock for Europe. The military retreat of colonialism in Asia, of which Dien Bien Phu was a symbol, revealed the inability of conventional military and political measures to deal with a psychological force such as the movement for political independence by the non-white peoples. Colonialism was compelled to recognize that the time had come when force could achieve nothing. Force only led to ever more violent counter-measures and ultimately destroyed the economic basis of colonialism itself. Dien Bien Phu demonstrated that the strategic concepts of Sandhurst and St Cyr had lost their validity in colonial policy.

The second factor arose in the West itself: after the Second World War the question of liberty was given a new and even more extreme formulation and made into one of the main instruments of Western foreign policy, and one cannot condemn Nazism and Bolshevism as systems hostile to human liberty while maintaining old-style colonial policies. One cannot condemn Hitler, Stalin and Khrushchev for refusing liberty to their satellites while at the same time refusing liberty to the people of Africa and Asia: not, at least, without being accused of double standards and hypocrisy. You cannot cancel out Uganda with Hungary, or Tanganyika with Tibet.

With this we have arrived at a point which is of fundamental importance; the independence of the African peoples is not the result of an examination of conscience in the West, it is not the result of a voluntary act of repentance and a determination to follow the straight and narrow path in the future—let there be no illusions about that. It is mainly the East-West conflict that has forced the West to repair some of its errors and cure some of its own moral sores.

NOTES

[1] 'The Great Powers and the New World Order', *The Annals of the American Academy of Political and Social Science*, CCLVII (May 1958), p. 52.

[2] Dietrich Westermann, *Africans Tell of Their Lives*, quoted in Rolf Italiaander, *The New Leaders of Africa* (New York, 1961), p. v.

[3] *Conférence africaine française* (Paris, ?), p. 35. Cf. also Charles de Gaulle, *Mémoires de Guerre* (Paris, ?), II: *L'Unité*, pp. 555 ff. For English translation, see *War Memoirs of Charles de Gaulle* (New York, 1958-60), II: *Unity 1942-1944*.

[4] Quoted in T. Walter Wallbank, 'Britain's New Programme for the Colonies', *Current History*, XV (August 1948), p. 84.

[5] Quoted in Herbert Lüthy, 'Ein Kolonialreich in der Krise', *Der Monat* (Berlin), No. 14 (November 1949), p. 184.

[6] Ibid.

[7] Observed by the author during a visit to the Ivory Coast.

[8] From a speech delivered by Sékou Touré at the Cinema Vox, Conakry, 2 October 1958. Cyclostyled publication of the Government of Guinea.

[9] *Fraternité* (Abidjan), 3 June 1960.

[10] In an interview with the author, Leopoldville, 1958.

[11] Quoted in Lüthy, op. cit., p. 182.

[12] Georges Balandier, *Sociologie actuelle de l'Afrique Noire* (Paris, 1945); E. Andersson, *Messianic Popular Movements in the Lower Congo* (Uppsala, 1958).

[13] Cyclostyled text issued by the Government of Guinea (December 1959).

[14] *Afrika* (Munich), 11 November 1960, p. 439.

[15] More than 120,000 Africans in French-speaking West and Equatorial Africa were called up for war service. Cf. 'Chronique de la Communauté', *Documentation Française* (Paris), March 1960, p. 11.

Chapter II

AFRICAN CONTRASTS

LÉOPOLD SÉDAR SENGHOR, one of the leading intellectuals of the new Africa, has described 'the nation' as 'the primary reality of the twentieth century' and 'the historical inevitability of our continent'.[1] Sékou Touré, for some time the exponent of political radicalism in Africa, supplements this by saying: 'Europe can afford to abandon the idea of sovereign nationhood today because it has outgrown the national stage of its history. We have not done that yet. This is the tragedy of our situation.'[2]

The second observation is particularly interesting, partly because of the undertone of resignation and regret and partly because it is in such strong contrast to the enthusiasm with which Touré usually speaks of African nationhood. The tragedy of Africa lies in the fact that so far this idea of nationhood has dominated the thoughts of a small élite only; it has still to be turned into a concrete fact for the masses of the African people and the conditions under which this has to be done are desperately unfavourable. Even the early stages of nationhood in Africa are providing more painful than similar experiences elsewhere.

According to Ernest Renan: 'What makes a nation is not merely speaking the same language or belonging to the same ethnic group, but the fact that in the past its members have done great deeds together and aspire to do them again in the future.'[3] Writing in 1928, Salvador de Madariaga went further and argued that 'not even history, geography, religion, language and a common will are enough to constitute a nation. A nation is a psychological fact.'[4] And Cedric Dover declares:

'The solidarity of a community depends on whether there is

26

sufficient acknowledgement in its ranks of a certain number of essential values. Certain beliefs, certain patterns of behaviour and certain patterns of action must be common to all if social life is to function without friction.'[5]

If we look at African reality from this angle the difficulty becomes obvious. The common acceptance of a certain number of essential values, the great deeds done together in the past, the aspiration to do them again in the future, and the psychological fact of which de Madariaga speaks—where are they in Africa? According to Nkrumah, 'The African nation has formed itself in the struggle against colonialism', and at first sight there would seem to be something in his contention. In only a few of the African countries was there a short period prior to independence in which the nationalist slogans of the élite were taken up by the masses. This was the case in Guinea where, on 28 September 1958, a referendum showed that over ninety-five per cent of the population were opposed to de Gaulle's proposal for a 'Communauté Française'. It was also true in Ghana in 1955, when Nkrumah began the final phase of his struggle for independence, and it was also the case in Leopoldville during the January uprising of 1959. But in most of the other countries of Africa the movement for independence rested on small groups of leaders who were active, not on the masses. In the new 'model' African nations there is now, even *after* independence, very little evidence of any national solidarity. On the contrary, it would appear that the new élite have prematurely hitched their wagon to the star of the future; for the traditional leaders of African society, the tribal and paramount chiefs, have no use for such a future, while the masses of the people have little notion of what it is all about. The fact is that there is a gap of centuries between the dream of the few and the force of inertia of the many.

In the spring of 1964 a young Kenyan politician explained the internal quarrels in his country by saying:

'We had set such high hopes on our independence, but instead things only got worse, much worse. At one time there really was something like a single, united Kenya, but that's all past. The question of how best to govern, and the question of with whom we should line up in foreign affairs, has divided once more. The

Kenyans? Every tribe, every group appeals to Kenya, and each means something different. It's terrible.'

The situation in Kenya reflects the situation in Africa as a whole. The Congolese could find these words applicable to their country in exactly the same way. After its 'liberation' the former Belgian Congo was also divided 'a dozen times over'.

Even the strong African States on the west coast, such as Ghana and Guinea, are not immune to this tendency. Has Nkrumah really created an African nation in his country as he repeatedly claims? Has Touré's energetic leadership in Guinea really overcome the racial and tribal separatism formerly blamed on colonialism? During his travels in Africa the author found frequent evidence (particularly in Guinea and Ghana) of the fact that rivalries between the various ethnic groups are still as strong as ever. In Ghana the Ashanti complain of the predominance of the coastal tribes and of their own inadequate representation in the central political organizations. In Guinea the Fulani complain that they are being placed at a disadvantage by the Malinke and the Susu. And the unrest of April 1960 and the revolt of November 1961 as well as the tensions late in 1964 were really caused by tribal rivalries, although they were later exacerbated by slogans of an ideological character. Despite these things, Nkrumah and Touré are already talking of 'the United States of Africa'. The deplorable experience of the Mali Federation, proclaimed in the summer of 1960 by the leaders in Dakar and Bamako, seems to contain no warning for them. Yet the swift and inglorious collapse of the federation came as a surprise only to those who knew nothing whatever about the situation. If you ask a Senegalese taxi-driver in Dakar whether he's Sudanese or, conversely, ask a Sudanese whether he comes from Senegal, the answer will always be the same: 'Sir, do you really take me for one of that Sudanese (or Senegalese) lot?'

The gigantic artificial structure erected in the Congo fell to pieces even more quickly than the Mali Federation. Only a few days after the removal of the corset of colonialism, the whole 'Heartland of Africa', as Patrice Lumumba called it, broke into a chaos of races and tribes. Katanga, the richest province of the old Belgian Congo, refused for years to submit to the central government, rejecting the idea of national unity, while in the Kasai province the

Balubas and Luluas reverted to their old tribal enmity and terrible slaughter ensued.

The politicians of the new Africa may aim as high as they like in their dreams and projects, but at their feet are the ball and chain of the past. The pre-colonial and colonial heritage has left a crushing mortgage which is a severe burden, as is the rapid dissolution of the old social structure.

First there is the difficult question of frontiers: the present frontiers were drawn at a time when the whole continent was viewed exclusively in terms of imperial, colonial and strategic interests. The Powers taking part in the Berlin Conference of 1884, and the subsequent conference in 1885, had no idea of the ethnographic conditions of the continent whose map they light-heartedly carved up with the help of ruler and drawing-board. Races and tribes were arbitrarily joined together or torn apart. Today, seventy years later, those on whom this heritage devolves ask themselves in despair how national unity will ever develop in the face of the elementary antagonisms of race and religion.

It is not, however, merely a question of tribal disputes and racial and religious resentments and rivalries—suppressed with difficulty in the latter-day phase of colonialism—now bursting out all the more violently in the wake of de-colonization and liberation. The problem is more complicated than this. Present-day Africa is experiencing not only a political, but also a profound social, economic, and cultural revolution, and in the process traditional values are being called into question before new ones have been evolved. The fact that this process is historically inevitable and necessary does not make it any the less painful.

The actual process involved is only partially described by the terms 'liberation' or 'emancipation'. Parallel with liberation there has been general disintegration, a total dissolution of the inner structure of African society. It began when the white man seized the African continent and it was accelerated when the phase of exploration, subjugation and mere domination developed into the purer form of colonialism, that is, the imposition of European educational, social, and economic ideas on African society. With this, traditional African societies found themselves faced with systems they were unable to compete with, and the more rational European methods of dominating man and nature proved their superiority. Up to this time the African had just taken things as they came, but now, as the African publicist, Thomas Diop, points out, 'he began to ask questions'[6] and to have doubts about his traditional values.

These values related to the narrow world of the family hierarchy, the clan and the tribe, the natural community in which the African lived. In distant, out-of-the-way places such communities may still be intact and functioning effectively. All the same, large family and clan groups—usually based on the patriarchate, with a council of elders, a strict hierarchy of chiefs and medicine men, and associations of young men and girls, with their plethora of ritual instructions, exercises and obligations—this traditional structure finds itself condemned to disappear in the face of economic development, the growth of communications, the conquest of illiteracy, the increasing prestige of the African élite who have broken away from the old traditions, and the democratization of the African State.

Naturally, the old order is not giving up without a struggle. Shortly before Nigeria achieved independence the Sardauna and the Emirs in Northern Nigeria bitterly opposed the introduction of school attendance for boys and girls; they resisted the orders for Nigerianization issued from Lagos and deliberately delayed the date for their country's self-government. There have been a number of revolts by tribal chiefs in Ghana, Guinea, Uganda, Tanganyika and other countries during recent years and the new rulers had to demonstrate their power forcefully before they could be repressed.

In the Cameroons, partly as a revolt of the agricultural population against the domination of the chiefs, the so-called *Chefferie*, the peasants and artisans, small traders and merchants of the Bamileke tribe refused to pay the traditional, and often high tributes to the chiefs, something that would have been unthinkable as recently as 1950. The chiefs allied themselves with the Ahidjo Government, which is supported by the feudal North. But in the long run the upshot of this struggle, here as elsewhere, is not in doubt. More and more Africans are coming to regard the *Chefferie* as an anachronism and even the chiefs are beginning to feel that the days of their power are numbered.

The new centres in Africa are the factories, the large-scale plantations, and the industrial giants: Fria in Guinea, Edea in Cameroon, others in Katanga and Rhodesia, and above all in the towns. These centres exercise an enormous attraction which reaches into the most distant reserves of the hinterland. New values have been set up, primarily the value of money. By observing their white masters the Africans realized that money could achieve what formerly only birthright offered; money makes all men equal; and nothing can be so quickly squeezed out of the misery of the dependent, the enslaved, and the oppressed. Money makes it possible for the African to dress like the European and nowhere in the world are top hats, morning coats, patent-leather shoes, even spats, more highly thought of than among the new African élite. For money you can drink foaming beer—the turnover and profits of African breweries and of European beer exporters have risen to fantastic heights—and money affords the chance of better education (until recently some missionary schools charged fees for their pupils).

Until recently all this was to be had only by direct connection with the whites, so the flow of people into the towns and European colonial centres was increasing rapidly. *Bidonvilles*, the colonies of shacks made of petrol tins and corrugated iron, have shot up like mushrooms around the white towns. Johannesburg, Leopoldville, Douala, Lagos, Abidjan, Dakar, Salisbury and other capitals now have more than twice as many inhabitants today as twenty years ago, and the process continues in a mad, uncontrolled rush. Dilapidated, jerry-built huts of tin cans and wood spring up in the drainless streets and alleyways of these *Bidonvilles*—mud, clay, unhewn stones, ragged sacks, any kind of material goes into their making. They collapse, are rebuilt, collapse, and are rebuilt yet again. 'Fascinating Africa!', a favourite expression of the advertisements of tourist agencies and shipping lines, but one look at the grim reality of these chaotic, squalid settlements is enough to destroy all these illusions about 'the untouched land', 'virgin soil', etc. Women with swollen bellies and flaccid, hanging breasts pound their maize monotonously and squat among old packing cases and cardboard boxes, offering trifling articles for sale. Three paces away others squat for a different purpose. Scruffy, scabby children whine and bombard passers-by with demands for *cadeau* or dash, meaning alms. The great plagues of the pre-colonial era have been mastered but more civilized scourges, infectious diseases, particularly syphilis and tuberculosis, still claim large numbers of victims. Prostitution is rampant; according to conservative calculations in 1960, seven per cent of the women in the New Bell native quarter of Douala prostituted themselves. Grinding poverty and proletarianization represent the fate of the many thousands who flock to the market-places of a foreign civilization from their own savannahs and the bush, and all are drawn and fascinated by the new totem—money.

As there is not enough work for everyone, and as the training of Africans for the more complicated industrial jobs is still deficient, social tensions increase with the arrival of every person who leaves the security of his village to brave the hazards of urban life. Unemployment is steadily increasing; today those unemployed number between twenty and twenty-five per cent of the total of employable persons almost everywhere. The first African regional conference of the International Labour Organization, which took place in December 1960 in Lagos, declared that 'rural poverty and under-employment is now developing into urban unemployment and frustration.'[7]

The situation is aggravated by the fact that when an African comes into a town he is immediately confronted with both the sunny and the seamy sides of the imported European civilization; and—as a Nigerian study points out—he accepts both naïvely 'without being able to tell what is good and what is bad'. In this connection there are three things which have a particularly unfavourable influence on urban Africans: alcohol, the cinema, and pulp literature.

Alcohol has always been a companion of colonialism. According to German sources (for example, the minutes of the Reichstag of 13 March 1896) the imports of spirits into what was then the German Cameroons rose from a value of 550,000 marks in 1892 to 981,000 marks in 1894, although in that period the value of the mark remained stable. The importation of alcoholic liquor represented fifteen per cent of the total imports of the Cameroons, and thirty per cent of the total imports of Togoland.[8] In 1953, Madagascar paid twenty times more for imports of wines and spirits than for the importation of agricultural machinery. Similarly, the Ivory Coast Republic paid twice as much for imports of spirits in 1958 as for the importation of artificial fertilizers. The consequences of this excessive importation of alcohol can be seen any evening in the *Bidonvilles* of modern Africa. Beer or raw spirits can be bought at almost every corner of the slum quarters. It has been calculated that the inhabitants of the native quarter of New Bell in Douala spend up to twenty-five per cent of their income on beer and spirits. It certainly did not take Africans long to discover what an effective narcotic alcohol is for the poor. . . .

Western films are hardly a less demoralizing influence. There are many flea-pit cinemas where the programme is changed daily. They rarely if ever show anything of any real value, usually just the dregs of the American and European film markets. These films, with their strip-tease, love scenes, vice and crime, adultery, and lynchings, have a deplorable impact on a public whose ethical and social standards are even less firmly grounded than those of audiences in the West. As seen from the angle of this spurious cinematic world, which he takes for real, the naïve African cannot but regard the commandments of Christianity, which he too is called upon to keep, as plain hypocrisy. The result is that the already low moral authority of the white man is understandably being further undermined. How do the guiding principles of Christian education and training compare with this 'other reality' that Africans can see evening after evening on the cinema screen?

The situation is very much the same when one examines most of the literary imports available. If you visit African bookshops in Lagos or Salisbury in order to discover what kind of books are favoured, everywhere the answer will be the same: apart from teach-yourself manuals on English, arithmetic and geography, they are paper-backs of love and adventure, and other more or less undesirable literature besides. The windows are largely filled with trash whose coloured covers depict either half-naked women or scenes of violence and leave no doubt as to the literary level of the book. In addition, many of these bookshops have a special collection of pornographic publications imported from overseas.

This is another aspect of the Westernization of Africa, continuing at a break-neck pace, breaking down old standards, and replacing old ideals by new, and often inferior ones. It is true that modern African nationalism calls loudly for the development of a *personalité africaine*, an African consciously drawing on his own cultural and historical past and resisting foreign and outside influences. But the fact is that the true sources of African history and culture are being destroyed and buried—the imported attractions of the European world are too strong.

Even the leaders of the new élite who were the first to inscribe the slogan 'Back to Africa!' on their banners do not seem to think so. If one expected to find their loudly proclaimed adherence to their own African tradition reflected in the style, decoration, and furnishing of their houses, one would be disappointed. A visitor to the homes of the leaders of young Africa will seldom find examples of African art, collected with pride in the creative achievements of Africa past and present for their admiration. Instead, the interiors, reception and drawing rooms owe everything to London, Paris or Brussels and the various articles of furnishing have been culled from the catalogues of European firms or from the advertisement columns of European newspapers.

This is symptomatic of the deep hiatus which exists between the Africa of yesterday and of today, though to some extent the two still exist side by side. The great mass of the people and the old feudal ruling class are still closely attached to the old traditions and ignore modern innovations, but in the towns the restless, rootless, unattached proletariat and the young élite are groping their way forward into strange, extra-African spheres. The result is a split in African society and the cultural secession of the élite, a tragedy illustrated by the frank admission of President Sékou Touré of Guinea that he feels more at home with his French friends, for example, than he does with 'my older brother who has never been to school.'[9]

What kind of people belong to this new élite? Hugh and Mabel Smythe of the Department of Sociology and Anthropology of Brooklyn College, New York, went to Nigeria in 1960 to investigate the problem. Their analysis is influenced by American behaviourism and in some ways is unsatisfactory, but it declares: 'A certain number of Nigerians have studied abroad, particularly in Great Britain and the United States, and they have accumulated a wealth of first-class professional experience. Every year more and more coloured people follow their example. These are the men and women who form the new upper stratum, and very little is known about them outside Africa. The typical representative of the present-day élite is between twenty-five and forty-five years old. He came from the rural areas into the town in search of opportunities for education and work. As nationalism and politics in general are most highly developed in the towns he also took up party politics. He may very well be a member of one or other of the various chief religions of his country, animism, Christianity (chiefly in the south) or Mohammedanism (chiefly in the north), but any such religious differences will not bring him into conflict with the other members of the élite. Language is also not a factor making for separation. There are over ninety languages and dialects in Nigeria, and the essential condition for belonging to the élite is that he should be able to speak English.'[10]

The authors also provided certain illuminating figures regarding the rapid growth of this élite. For example, between the years 1938 and 1948 only 177 Nigerians had the opportunity of being educated abroad. During the next four years the number increased to 665 and by the end of 1952 there were no fewer than 2,028 Nigerians studying in Great Britain and another 334 in the United States. The authorities in Lagos calculate that the corresponding figures for 1958 were 3,000 in Great Britain and 300–400 in the United States. But in 1964 there were at least 15,000 Nigerians studying abroad.

If one takes these figures in relation to the population of Nigeria as a whole (which, as the census results of 1964 show, is 55 million) we see that by now one person out of 3,500 has received some sort of higher education, or approximately 0·030 per cent of the population; and it must be remembered that not all of these completed their studies.

In this respect Nigeria is in an exceptionally favourable position. When the former Belgian Congo became independent fewer than one hundred Congolese had had the advantage of some form of higher education. In other African States the situation will be somewhere between these two extremes, with the exception of the Portuguese colonial territories, where higher education is still difficult to attain for Africans. However, the élite does not consist exclusively of those who have had some sort of higher education. The élites include employees of the administration, particularly teachers and trade-union leaders. The size of this group in Nigeria, including university graduates, was estimated in 1963 to be 70,000, and in view of the great progress being made in this, the biggest African country, in the campaign against ignorance and illiteracy, we may assume a rapid growth in the future.

It is naturally very difficult to lay down hard and fast rules for this young élite, beyond saying that it is sharply separated from the old élite. Origins, social background, and, in particular, intellectual and professional interests, and political affiliations, all these and

35

other factors are producing a progressive differentiation in the ranks of the new élite of Africa. The fundamental differences between British and French colonial policy have also played an important role.

However, there are similarities between the two groups: the new élite is marked by a common ideological disposition, a consciousness of its historical task, the shared experience of colonial subjugation, and racial discrimination. Thus the present-day élite in Africa, which is, of course, closely connected with the national upheaval and serves, indeed, as its fermenting yeast, could hardly be conservative. This élite is constantly brought face to face with the dire consequences of colonialism: the misery and impoverishment of the masses, the startling contradiction between the vast economic resources of the African continent and the little that has been done to exploit them, the bitter heritage of the African past and the cruel economic and social dilemma of the present. This situation is so unusual and exceptional that they are literally forced to the conclusion that it cannot be remedied by ordinary means.

But what traditional examples and methods are there to solve their problems? What models, technological methods, were actually created to transform Africa into a continent of economic, social, and intellectual progress?

A liberal, moderate intellectual East African speaking in a discussion at the Second All-African Peoples' Conference declared:

'Your present-day African is a man without prejudices, without ideological ballast and without the burden of a historical past. He is of our own day and he refuses to look for the solution of his problems along the old, well-worn paths. He is not hemmed in; he is free. And this means that he is able to examine anything anywhere in the world completely without prejudice and solely from the standpoint of its usefulness to him.'[11]

But this judgement requires some modification. Most of the members of this young African élite are certainly not without prejudices, particularly where the West, democracy and capitalism are concerned. In a description of the new social strata in Africa, Jean D. Merlo, a young French sociologist who became closely acquainted with African problems as a student-priest in Paris, has the following to say about the attitude of African intellectuals:

'They reject imperialism and colonial capitalism. But first of all they distort it in order to be able to reject it. This is 'the healthy method' . . . In the same way they reject a democratic system that is simply transplanted from Europe to Africa. In their opinion liberal democracy is no use in Africa because the general political education of the population is not sufficiently advanced to allow them to give the voting paper its proper political significance.'[12]

Merlo does not examine the reasons for this attitude, but they are obvious enough. The nationally conscious, educated African sees the Western economic system primarily as an instrument of political colonialism. Such contact as he has had with it has been confined to Africa. It was at home in the colonial territories that he first heard the names of Esso, Shell, Unilever, UTC, UAC, Firestone, and so on. In his mind these concerns—and others as well—have made gigantic profits at the cost of the Africans. He compares the social standards of European directors, managers and technicians with the wages of the African workers and commercial employees, and comes to the conclusion that the whites were able to get rich because they kept the Africans in poverty. And it is, of course, a fact that for the same work performed under the same conditions, a European often receives much higher wages than an African worker. Even in the Congo where (according to a study of the International Labour Office, 30 August 1960) wages were on the whole more favourable to Africans than elsewhere, the minimum wage for European-born workers was from seven to twenty-seven times greater than the corresponding minimum wages for Africans.

In the eyes of many an African intellectual, capitalism destroys that harmony of society for which a social being must strive. At the same time he believes that such harmony existed in Africa before colonialism destroyed it. He believes that capitalism automatically produces inequality and causes social tension, and where it finds social tensions already in existence it exacerbates them. At the same time capitalism results in the formation of intensely antagonistic classes and opens the door to a reckless, anti-social rush for individual profits and power.

There is clearly an element of paradox in this. On the whole, the enlightened African rejects the old Africa with its rigid social structure, its unproductive use of labour, and its lack of efficient methods. But at the same time he makes no attempt to conceal his inner attachment to a society based essentially on the common use of the land by the tribe, the clan, and the family, and on the division of property; a society in which, in the most ideal sense, there was a 'communism', an actual communal rule. He would like to maintain or re-create this integrated, egalitarian society despite the economic revolution, which he recognizes as necessary and inevitable. His problem is whether Africa, while maintaining its communal solidarity, can achieve such economic and technological progress that it can, in fact, overcome its backwardness (by comparison with the highly industrialized countries). It is thus hardly surprising that Africans arrive at a completely different assessment of socialism and communism from that of West Europeans. The African regards the social theories of Proudhon, St Simon, Marx, Lenin, and Mao Tse-tung as promising remedies for his country, particularly as on the face of it they appeal to the communal spirit of Africans.

At this point it is not our intention to offer an analysis of the attitude this same African intellectual adopts towards the West, as distinct from the East, but it must be pointed out that the African élite find the way to socialism or communism made easy for them by a number of factors. Unlike the Europeans, and to a certain extent the Asians, Africans have come to know communism during a phase in which Russia, having left the worst barbarisms of Stalinism behind, has entered a slightly more liberal period. The uninitiated African, who has not witnessed forty-five years of communist dictatorship, but only a short and relatively peaceful phase and therefore knows little or nothing about the atrocities and mass terrorism of the twenties and the thirties in Russia, or of the days of Stalinist imperialist expansion in Central Europe, is misled by the results of 'the intensified class struggle'. In particular, he is more inclined to see the result than the methods by which it was obtained. For him the tangible result is a world power created, apparently, out of nothing, a power now able to shoot *luniks* and *sputniks* into the air, a power with a tremendous industrial potential, powerful armaments, and international prestige. To reinforce this favourable picture, he is influenced by communist propaganda that seeks to convince him that Soviet success was attained by the methods of 'real socialism' and collectivism, to the exclusion of parasitic individualism and individualistic groups.

Perhaps he is also strongly impressed by the example of the Chinese People's Republic. Here too the African is more inclined to see the end result than the methods by which it was achieved, atrocities and hecatombs of victims. And even though the achievements of the Chinese People's Republic are not yet as great as those of the Soviet Union, nevertheless they are, from his point of view, already considerable. Communist China has emancipated itself, both economically and politically, from an allegedly colonial and a preponderantly agrarian condition, despite the fact that it was hampered by the legacy of long years of civil war. At the same time Chinese communist propaganda suggests that 'real socialism' and true collectivism are even more to the fore in China than in the Soviet Union.

The effect of this can be seen from the case of Barry Diawadou, former Minister of Education in Guinea. After a visit to China he declared:

'Since my return I am quite convinced of the efficacy of Chinese methods. I was greatly impressed by the similarity of the economic problems that China has succeeded in solving and those that are now facing the peoples of Africa. In China I saw what can be done if you mobilize the vital forces of a nation. With all due regard to the difference in magnitude we now propose to do the same thing.'[13]

One can readily think of many examples that must seem like striking parallels to Africans when they compare the starting points of the economic revolutions in the Soviet Union and in Communist China with the present situation in Africa. Even those African intellectuals who are under no illusions about the seamy side of the communist world are not entirely immune to such ideas. Léopold Sédar Senghor, the Senegalese friend of France, demands, in his *Rapport sur la Doctrine et le Programme du Parti de la Fédération Africaine*, as well as in other writings and speeches, that Africans should bear 'the positive achievements of Marx' in mind. He also pleads for the application of 'the dialectical method and a comprehensive planning of the economic, social, political, and cultural process'. Although Senghor himself rejects the materialist philosophy of Marxism-Leninism, what about his less intelligent followers? Are they able to distinguish between 'the positive achievements' and the negative features? And where is the line to be drawn between what is acceptable and what is not?

Apart from the general attraction which certain orthodox, socialist economic theories hold for Africans, communism exercises one special fascination. This is the achievement of discipline, the apparent ability of the communists to give everyone his task within the general process of development, to place him where he is required, even if by force. From the standpoint of the African it looks as though everyone behind the Iron Curtain is given his own function in a sharply defined framework and that the people work together for the ultimate objective of a classless society.

Compare this admirable discipline and efficient organization of communist society with the apparent waste of manpower and material in the West! Intellectual, artistic, and creative talents are allowed to run to seed uselessly instead of being suitably employed for the benefit of society. Five, six, and even more firms compete with each other for industrial orders, whereas in the East a whole undertaking will be planned from the start by one (and of course the best one) while a staff of technicians work out a programme for executing projects in the most economical way. Thus Africans come to the conclusion that the wasteful methods of the West are not the best for their continent. We have to take this into consideration.

NOTES

[1] Report to the Constitutive Congress of the Party of African Federation (PFA), Dakar, 1 July 1959. Congress Record, p. 51.

[2] Lecture by Sékou Touré to the Royal Institute of International Affairs, London, in November 1959. Cyclostyled report issued by the Government of Guinea (December 1959).

[3] Quoted in W. R. Sharp and G. Kirk, *Contemporary International Politics* (New York, 1940), p. 113.

[4] Salvador de Madariaga, *Englishmen, Frenchmen and Spaniards* (London, 1928), p. xi.

[5] Quoted by Thomas Diop, 'Wesenszüge des Afrikaners', *Afrika* (Munich), November 1960, p. 425.

[6] Ibid., p. 424.

[7] Stenographic Minutes of the First African Regional Conference of the International Labour Organization, Lagos, December 1960.

[8] Stenographic Report of the Proceedings of the German Reichstag, 1896, II, pp. 1424-7, 1505.

[9] Lecture by Sékou Touré to the Royal Institute of International Affairs, London, in November 1959.

[10] *Afrika-heute* (Cologne, 1960), pp. 44 ff.

[11] Notes made by the author at the Second All-African Peoples' Conference, Tunis, January 1960.

[12] Jean D. Merlo, 'Probleme der jungen Elite Schwarzafrikas', *Afrika* (Munich), January 1961, p. 19.

[13] J. Jacquet-Francillon, 'En Afrique–la Chine arrive', *Le Figaro*, 25 December 1959.

Chapter III

THE AFRICAN CRISIS

So far two generations have been responsible for the African revolution. Initially, at least, both were guided by high ideals and it is only now that the third generation, which is beginning to come forward, finds itself forced to face the harsh realities of the situation. This third generation will determine which way the continent will go, what path the States will follow in their development and what economic and social ideas, doctrines and programmes will get the upper hand in this part of the world.

The first generation consisted of the prophets and dreamers. They did not and could not have had much to offer beyond splendid but rather vague ideals. At first it was little more than an appeal for the 'rise of the coloured people', and it was only later that more concrete aims emerged. Often they appealed to symbols of the past, and in this phase conceptions such as Ghana, Mali, Songhai, Malawi, Zambia and Zimbabwe developed into propaganda myths. The first signs of all this appeared in the United States in the early part of the nineteenth century when a consciousness of their origins began to grow among the slaves.

With the support of philanthropic whites, Negroes whose freedom had been purchased began to return to the land of their fathers. However, the Liberian experiment, which began on 7 January 1822 with the landing of black Pilgrim Fathers on the Pepper Coast, proved a failure. These high-minded Negroes, who felt they were returning to their ancestral home, were not always accepted by the natives as brothers; on the contrary, they were regarded as strangers and even enemies, and it was only after long and bloody struggles that they managed to establish themselves. The aftermath of this

42

conflict is still noticeable today. Far from finding their way back to an original culture in the Land of the Free, the descendants of the Negro slaves of the United States have set themselves up as a master-caste known as the Americo-Liberians and they tend to remain aloof from the natives of the hinterland. Although President Tubman, who has been uninterruptedly at the helm since 1944, has tried to reduce some of the worst inequalities under the pressure of radical changes beyond the frontiers of Liberia, the gap between the two groups remains very deep. The majority of the original native tribes still live in near-archaic conditions, while the living conditions and behaviour of the small group of Americo-Liberians resemble a caricature of life in the southern States of the United States around 1880. In fact this 'first modern African State' has nothing in common with present-day Africa and modern African statesmen and politicians cannot make use of the Liberian experiment. Kwame Nkrumah, who visited Monrovia, the capital of Liberia, in 1947 felt repelled rather than attracted by this country.

Unfortunately however, there are few useful models anywhere for the guidance of modern Africans. The first generation of African *homines novi* concentrated on the fight for independence. They assumed that this was the most difficult task. The second generation, educated, guided and enthused by the prophets and dreamers of the first, carried out this task with astonishing speed, especially once they became aware of the weakness and demoralization of colonialism, and then set about creating modern political organizations for their countries. The international situation, exacerbated by the East-West conflict, did the rest. In consequence, what had looked like the task of decades was carried out almost throughout Africa within the space of a few years. But then Africans were faced with a much harder task: the consolidation of their gains. They had to cope as well as they could with the legacy of colonialism, and to work out practical programmes for the first phase of independence—indeed, even to find half-way passable tracks through the jungle of difficulties which faced them.

The current problems demanding a solution are vast. In many, even most, parts of Africa the twentieth century and the Middle Ages rub shoulders. Fanatical enlightenment amongst the so-called *evolués* finds itself up against a no less fanatical traditionalism. As we have seen, for example, in the Congo in 1964 the deepest ignorance and obscurantism contrast directly with determined intellectualism; narrow-minded tribalism clashes with national demands; a general unwillingness to work hard takes no account of the urgent need for economic progress; mass misery mocks the pomp of feudal chiefs and the arrogance of young upstarts. In such circumstances it is not really surprising that some of the leaders of this new generation think, for the moment, only of power (and generally speaking this means personal power) and its consolidation. History offers numerous examples of the tendency of even serious, honest revolutionaries to call a halt once they have managed to seize power. For the first time they are enjoying the taste of power and it is understandable that it tends to go to their heads. Their policies veer away from their earlier promises and ideals; urgent, difficult social problems are pushed into the background, until such time as the revolution is considered to be securely safeguarded against any internal or external threats.

In Africa the temptation to behave in this way is perhaps greater because of the enormous complexity of the problems and the limited means available for their solution. The majority of the African population does not bother much about the future and certainly not about 'the nation'. There is little desire for hard work, and even less for hard work in the interest of the general welfare. Even in Guinea, where Sékou Touré managed to get the masses to start working on a voluntary construction programme (*investissement humain*), enthusiasm, self-sacrifice, and thought for the common welfare soon faded. From the standpoint of political organization Guinea is the most advanced country in Africa, but the 1963 congress of Sékou Touré's *Parti Démocratique* ended with a flood of bitter complaints about the low labour morale of the people, the lack of mass initiative, and the declining popularity of the party and its aims among the population: and this is typical. Black marketeering and corruption are flourishing, discontent and even veiled rebellion are growing.

What is a threat in Guinea is already a fact in other African countries. The victorious leaders of the second generation set out to establish absolute power, but their dictatorial and usually autocratic régimes are not particularly strong and stable. In some of the young States the writ of the government hardly extends beyond the area served by the main roads, sometimes not much beyond the government buildings in the capital. Behind the petty bureaucracy, the smug pretentiousness and arrogance of the Ministers, there is frequently uncertainty, incompetence and ignorance. Take the former Belgian Congo: after five years of independence it has still not emerged from the anarchy which marked its birth as an independent State. Unemployment figures are rising steadily, the national income, even after reunification with Katanga, is falling alarmingly. Despite currency reform the Congolese franc is still without proper backing and has no real purchasing power. Regionalism is strong and if the writ of the central government extends beyond the Boulevard de 30 Juin, it is only thanks to the support of the Casques Bleues and the United Nations civilian operations in the Congo. Trade unions, students' organizations, and the followers of the late Lumumba are constantly plotting new revolts, issuing grandiloquent manifestos and proposing new panaceas. Meanwhile the various régimes appear unconcerned. Corrupt and incompetent, they rely completely on outside help and enjoy the record of having the largest administration of any African State, absorbing ninety-two per cent of the national income.

The Congo may be an extreme case, but elsewhere in Africa similarly deplorable conditions often exist. Three factors are primarily responsible for this depressing situation. First of all the leaders of the independence movements and the mass of their followers hoped for too much from their victory over colonialism. Anyone who witnessed the final phase before 'Uhuru Day' anywhere in Africa knows that the hope and belief that a radical change would come about as soon as independence was won was deliberately and artificially inflated. Secondly, the elementary conditions needed for the formation of capital are lacking, particularly when capital is taken to include the sum of accumulated labour. This lack naturally results in a regrettable dependence on foreign capital; in fact, those African countries which were formerly under French rule have to look abroad for no less than ninety per cent of the capital they need, while other African countries need between fifty and seventy-five per cent before they can make any investments at all. Thirdly, the immediate effect of the new slogans and plans is to accelerate the breakdown of existing social structures, aggravating the explosive processes of social change.

The older generation of African nationalists are largely aware of these fundamental facts, and they know how easily a single spark could result in an explosion. But a third generation is growing up, educated not only in Africa but also in schools and universities as far apart as the United States and Red China. They are already putting forward their demands. Here and there they have already succeeded in enforcing them elsewhere, and they do not hesitate to use force if necessary.

Unlike their predecessors, this third generation were not brought up amidst dreams of sovereignty, nor were they involved in the struggle to attain it. They grew up after independence had been won, and are only interested in rapid progress. Their minimum demand is for a share of responsibility, which means a share of political power. So far this demand has been refused, sometimes quite ruthlessly, but here and there individuals or groups have succeeded in worming their way into the ruling strata thanks chiefly to nepotism or the influence of cliques. They sometimes find that the established régime is prepared to go a long way towards weakening and neutralizing their radicalism by corrupting them with material temptations. This tactic has been used very successfully in Addis Ababa where, during the past few years, intriguing and troublesome young intellectuals have been promoted from their coffee bars to lucrative administrative posts and given pompous-sounding titles with no real influence or opportunities for development. But this has been relatively easier in Ethiopia than in other African countries. In Nigeria, for example, it was calculated at the end of 1963 that the coming four years would see the return of 15,000–17,000 students after the completion of their studies and training at universities and high schools abroad. At least 3,000 of these will return to Nigeria from the countries of the Soviet bloc. But no matter where they come from, or what social ideas they bring with them, the really important question is whether suitable jobs can be found for them. Even worse, if the educational system develops at its present rate, by 1966 only sixty per cent of those who complete secondary school will have a chance of finding suitable jobs, or be able to go on to high educational institutions in Nigeria or elsewhere. Taken together with the growing mass unemployment in the towns this is producing a problem which looks insoluble.

There are already examples of difficulties created if those in power ignore these, and other, sources of tension, and occupy themselves with propaganda and power politics instead of taking the drastic measures needed. The ostensible motives may vary from case to case, but one thing runs like a red thread through all the attempts at revolt, the assassination attempts and the *coups d'état* which, in 1963 alone, took place in Tunisia, Senegal, Ghana, Mali, Somalia, Algeria, the two Congos, Togo, the Ivory Coast Republic, Chad and Dahomey, as well as the revolts in Zanzibar and Gabon, and the mutinies in Tanganyika, Kenya and Uganda early in 1964.

In all these tense situations, there is one fundamental cause which is always present: the introduction of the one-party State and one-man rule.

The theoretical justification for this state of affairs is given in negative terms. By Léopold Senghor to Modibo Keita, Kwame Nkrumah, Julius Nyerere, and Felix Houphouet-Boigny, democracy is unanimously rejected as being irreconcilable with African needs and with the given African situation. It is certainly true that the difficulties in the way of establishing a democratic society in Africa are enormous. Even in Europe and in the United States democracy is an extraordinarily complicated system which is very difficult to manage; so much so that in many instances it is only a working hypothesis. How much more difficult and complicated is it to establish in a continent where social differences are so enormous, where people live mainly in small, isolated communities, where there are hundreds of languages and dialects, where there is widespread illiteracy and no solidly established middle class, and where the inexperienced élite are desperately trying to solve the urgent tasks facing them. Furthermore, democracy as a political system is discredited owing to the fact that the oldest and greatest European democracies, Great Britain and France, were the chief representatives of colonialism in Africa.

Nevertheless, the almost wholesale condemnation of democracy in Africa is still astonishing. It is equated with anarchy and 'a struggle of all against all'. At best it is described as a luxury that young countries cannot afford. Africans claim that as it is a system in which many political parties fight each other, its adoption would rapidly lead to 'the disruption of the nation'.

I do not propose to question the cogency of many of the arguments and over-simplifications advanced against democracy. No one suggests that a political structure which allowed each little group or tribe to express itself by forming a political party would be suitable for Africa. No one wants to see the creation of dozens of political parties whose endless struggles would lead to political paralysis. But what can be, and in fact is being, more and more impatiently demanded by the people is that governments show some respect for certain elementary, democratic principles, such as freedom of speech, of the Press, and of religion, and the adoption of a system which neither excludes all traditional bodies nor ignores all regional and tribal interests in favour of unrestricted centralization and modernization.

However, this is precisely the opposite of what the second generation of élites is attempting to do in most African countries. Even in Nigeria, where a federal system of originally three (now four) regions was established, and where democracy seemed to be working, the régime has not always adhered to these elementary principles as the circumstances of the General Elections at the end of 1964 demonstrated. And the situation is, of course, worse in those countries where, right from the start, little or no attention was paid to traditional or regional interests.

Very soon after independence the rulers of Ghana, Tanganyika, Dahomey, and other countries proclaimed that the traditional social structure was 'incompatible' with the political structure of a modern State. Under the slogan of 'national concentration', chiefs and headmen were deprived of their social functions and often of their dignity and refused any representation, while differences between regions and tribes were ignored. Once in power, the leading men of the New Guard centralized the administration down to the last detail. They turned the trade unions into state organizations, and declared all opposition treasonable. They introduced, or are on the way to introducing, legislation such as the Preventive Detention Act of Ghana, which allows political rivals to be disposed of without the formality of a trial. All this is being done for the sake of 'national unity' and 'national construction'.

However, to short-circuit history is not an easy task and ironically the result of these 'unification processes' has been the opposite of what was intended. Opposition to such régimes is growing, even among former sympathizers. Trade unions which started with a keen desire to co-operate with the Government have, since being nationalized and placed under government control, suddenly become hotbeds, not only of trade-union opposition but of party-political conspiracies, as was illustrated by the Tanganyika crisis in January 1964. In the same way the gagged Press frequently manages to make its views known, while tame opposition politicians are developing from obedient yes-men into awkward opponents.

The most crucial fact for all these opposition groups is that the existing constitutions do not allow them the right of opposition. Legality is the exclusive privilege of one party and the one man. This means that the opposition is forced to conduct an illegal struggle. The lesson this teaches, as more than one African leader has had to learn, is written in blood. Regrettable as this is, it would be too easy merely to condemn those who are forced to adopt these tactics. The guilty ones are those who have hidden behind a barrier of smug decrees and savage laws, who have closed their eyes to current political realities, and who blindly devote themselves to the cult of their own personalities and power.

No matter how clever their tactics or how firm their conviction that they hold an endless lease of power, the ultimate result will always be the same. It will end, as in Togo, with the murder of the president, a man who started off with everything on his side but ignored the interests of a small, important group. It will end with the sudden overthrow of the leader, as in the former French Congo, where the Abbé Foulbert Youlou, a politician who considered himself the Lord's Anointed, wandered around in a cassock but ignored the most elementary canons of Christianity. It will end, as it did in Dahomey, with the dismissal of a president who thought himself powerful enough to act like a French governor and play off groups, tribes and politicians against each other. Or it will end, as in Ghana, with a president too scared to appear among his people for months on end and forced to live cooped up in a colonial fort behind security cordons. Everywhere the radicalization of the opposition and the adoption of extreme, sometimes violent measures is the inevitable result of authoritarianism and dictatorship practised in the name of national unity. No nation, however young and poor, is so lacking in spiritual, social and political resources that it does not wish to share in the government of the country or to criticize and think for itself. Such wishes cannot be repressed indefinitely. If these elementary human and political desires and needs are blocked, and even suppressed by violence, they will one day crystallize into demands which will finally break the restrictive structure of a one-party State. The inevitable result of a system which concentrates all power in the hands of a few, often even of one man, under the cloak of a struggle against national disunity, will be the disruption of that self-same national unity.

This will come about sooner if, in addition, the upholders of the one-party State fail to produce any stirring ideas likely to appeal to the nation, and are not able to persuade them that they really do hold out some promise for the future. But the situation is particularly unfortunate in this respect. We have already pointed out that the first and second generations in Africa concentrated their attention on gaining independence. However, the fact that this independence fell into their laps with unexpected suddenness, giving them no time to develop any broad practical plans, cannot be accepted as a valid excuse for their present attitude of despair and resignation, or for the ingenuous belief that they have completely exhausted all the possibilities open to them, so that now they concentrate exclusively on staying in power, using ideas only as a means of camouflage.

But that is the situation today and in the last resort expressions like 'African unity' and 'African socialism' are frequently empty words. African unity, in particular, is likely to remain unattainable for a very long time. Firstly, because those who proclaim its desirability regard it in terms of power politics. Men like Nasser and Nkrumah have always aimed at unity that would be in their own interests rather than in the interests of the continent. That is why the Casablanca Group (founded in 1961) rapidly degenerated into a farce. It collapsed because of the conflicting ambitions within it and because African unity is hardly possible while large areas of the continent remain in neo-colonialist dependence on France—an economic, political and military dependence planned on a long-term basis. Finally the Casablanca Group collapsed because the colonial heritage of arbitrarily divided, or united, tribes and peoples proved so burdensome that even with the best will in the world, the new rulers could do very little about it. The conflicts between Morocco and Mauritania and between Ghana and Togo, the frontier clash between Morocco and Algeria in the autumn of 1963 and the ever-present threat of open war over the Ogaden district between Ethiopia and Somalia in 1964 are not exceptional; they are merely the local symptoms of an explosive danger which exists throughout the continent and which could come to the surface at any time. The decision of the Congress for African Unity in Addis Ababa in May 1963 that existing frontiers should be recognized—a decision that was confirmed once and for all by a second congress in Addis Ababa in the following November—has never had anything but rhetorical significance. It will be called more and more into question as various régimes find it necessary to distract the attention of their people from domestic problems to higher national tasks. Algeria carried out such a manoeuvre in the autumn of 1963 when the frontier dispute with Morocco was a gift from heaven for Ben Bella's hard-pressed régime.

'Pan-Africa' and 'African unity' are no more than slogans. The noble feelings that find expression in such ideals are destroyed by egoistic dreams of power and precedence. Pan-Africa is not pursued as a practical aim requiring long, hard, solid work, but has become a fetish and a cover for very different aims.

The terms 'socialism'—and in particular, 'African socialism'—also have their ambiguities. In Tanganyika, Julius Nyerere wants to develop a kind of family organism which he calls 'Ujamaa', a Swahili term which combines the family and socialism. What Ujamaa would mean in practice is not clear. In his book, *I Speak of Freedom: a Statement of African Ideology*, Kwame Nkrumah discusses 'Ghanaian socialism' at great length, and talks of the political ideology which, according to him, inspires his Convention People's Party. He says that the CPP is both a dynamic and a socialist party, but does not explain what these terms mean. At *Parti Démocratique de Guinée* congresses, Sékou Touré eloquently defends ideas such as 'democratic centralism', 'criticism and self-criticism', 'planned economy', 'collective leadership', and 'the unity of all the toilers', but one is reminded of a juggler constantly producing rabbits out of a hat—and only imitation rabbits anyway. There is a good deal of talk about the necessity for tight governmental control 'in the first phase of socialist transformation', about the role of the one united party as the motive power in the historical process towards socialism, and about 'the special role of leading personalities' in the initial phase of that process. Words, words, words, but without any real meaning, without anything tangible or concrete to give us any idea of what is really intended.

At first the communists, keepers of the Holy Grail of 'scientific socialism', were startled and dismayed by the woolly ideas of African socialists, but they seem to have given up worrying. They entertain the well-founded hope that this African socialism will soon expose itself as a mere rhetorical façade erected by the men who hold power in Africa and that the African masses will soon see for themselves how little substance there is in the ideology of the leaders of the second generation. When this happens, they hope the masses (and in particular the up-and-coming élite of the third generation) will turn to 'real' socialism, socialism in its most logical, radical form, namely communism. Meanwhile the communists seem content to let the present rulers stew in their own juice while urgent problems of Africa pile up menacingly.

Is their calculation realistic? Has communism a good chance of gaining influence in, or even winning over, parts of this continent?

We shall examine this important question in detail.

Chapter IV

COMMUNISM, COLONIALISM, AND WORLD REVOLUTION

THE Africa policy of the communists developed rather late, and as a reaction to the genuine success of the movement for independence. The communists had no traditional, practical experience to fall back on, apart from some improvised attempts to exercise influence on the chiefly literary awakening of the coloured peoples in the twenties.[1] Against their lack of practical experience, however, they had a long tradition of theory, ready-made explanations of the phenomenon of 'colonial revolution', and theoretical solutions for it. The African problem was part and parcel of this theory. For our purposes, it is essential to take a closer look at the original communist theory of 'colonial revolution', because many of the practical steps now being taken as part of their African policy are understandable only in terms of these earlier ideological assumptions. Fortunately it is not necessary to go right back to the classic representatives of scientific socialism, Marx and Engels, since they confined their theories almost entirely to capitalism in the highly developed countries (although there are one or two chapters in Marx's *Das Kapital* that touch upon the colonial problem). The series of articles on China and India, written by Marx in 1863 for the *New York Tribune* also touch upon the subject, but only rather superficially. As far as the orthodox fathers of scientific socialism were concerned, 'the actual history of mankind' began in the industrialized countries. Industrialization produces capitalism and capitalism produces its own grave-diggers in the shape of the impoverished proletariat, who have nothing to lose but the chains which they finally cast off in a revolutionary upheaval. The famous communist manifesto of 1848 ends with the words 'Workers of the world, unite!' But although they said the world, Marx and Engels were thinking primarily of central and western Europe.

If Lenin had tried to uphold this theory inflexibly he would have found himself in an impossible dilemma, because Russia was the largest agricultural power in Europe and industrialization was only in its preliminary stages. There was no accumulation of capital and no strong proletariat. Particularly after the failure of the revolution of 1905 however, the will to power triumphed over strict loyalty to dogma. Although in his book, *Two Tactics for Social Democracy in the Democratic Revolution*, Lenin condemns 'the reactionary idea' of looking for 'the salvation of the working class in anything but the further development of capitalism', at the same time he recommends a 'tactical opening on the right', that is, a strengthening of the proletarian forces by turning to the peasantry.[2] This extension of the original sphere of communist action is of fundamental importance. By politically rehabilitating the peasantry and allowing them into an alliance with the proletariat, Lenin introduced a new basic factor into communist revolutionary movements in countries which were not sufficiently developed, economically and structurally, to comply with the original Marxist conditions for a socialist upheaval. This new departure applied not only to Tzarist Russia, but also to China, where it took on increasing importance. In fact, Mao Tse-tung's doctrine of anti-imperialist action and of 'the New Democracy' is based on the position Lenin adopted in 1905. Today, when the communists adopt similar tactics in their efforts to win over Asia and Africa, they are acting in complete accord with Lenin's own ideology.

This early solution of the central dilemma of communism was developed further during the First World War. In a discussion with Rosa Luxemburg and in his book, *Imperialism, the Highest Stage of Capitalism*, Lenin stressed the value of colonial territories for monopoly capitalism and discussed the likely political effects of the disintegration of the colonial system. He insisted that the ruling strata of the industrial States of the West were being increasingly compelled to go in for colonial expansion in order to create new markets for their goods and to obtain the raw materials they needed. In his view, the struggle for these markets and for the control of the colonial and semi-colonial peoples had become a fundamental law of monopoly capitalism.[3]

Following on this, Lenin seized on the implication that there were other ways, apart from the classic way of revolution, in which socialism could be victorious: to prise the colonies out of the capitalist economic structure, for example, would deal capitalism a fatal blow and would indirectly assist in a communist victory.[4]

With the victory of the Bolsheviks in the November Revolution of 1917 these ideas became of great practical significance. It is well known, of course, that in the first flush of victory the communists thought a chain reaction of socialist upheavals would be set up in the highly industrialized countries of the West. Their plans for extending the national into an international revolution included the East, and although at first this meant only Asiatic Russia, it was soon extended to the whole colonial and semi-colonial sphere, including Latin America and, finally, Africa; as time went on, this aspect of the world revolution began to play an increasingly important role. On 7 December 1917 Lenin, as the first Chairman of the Council of People's Commissars, and Stalin, as People's Commissar for Nationalities, issued an appeal 'to all toiling Muslims in the East' (including Africa it should be remembered). After referring to the explosive upheaval in Russia the appeal went on:

'But Russia does not stand alone in this holy cause . . . The workers and soldiers of the West are already flocking to the banner of socialism and shaking the bastions of imperialism to their foundation. And far-away India, which has been enslaved for centuries by the modern robbers of Europe, has already raised the standard of revolt, is organizing her Soviets, throwing off the hated chains of slavery and calling on the peoples of the East to fight for their freedom . . . You are not threatened with oppression by Russia and her revolutionary Government, but by robber imperialism, which has turned your countries into impoverished and exploited colonies . . . Lose no time in shaking off the chains of oppression in your countries!'[5]

Clearly the references to India were more in accordance with Bolshevik wishes than with reality, but although at the time this appeal represented little more than empty words it nevertheless documented a significant change in communist policy: the Bolsheviks were no longer pinning their hopes exclusively on the proletarian masses of the West, they were trying to draw the impoverished peasant masses of the East into the hoped-for world revolution. The theoretical importance of this appeal is that it built for the first time a strategic bridge between Europe and the Afro-Asian world and established a new connection between revolutionary forces in the West and the East.

A year later Stalin wrote in the same spirit in his book, *The October Revolution and the National Question*, declaring that

'The great world-wide significance of the October Revolution chiefly consists in the fact that it has widened the scope of the national question and converted it from the particular question of combating national oppression in Europe into the general question of emancipating the oppressed peoples, colonies and semi-colonies from imperialism.

'It has thereby erected a bridge between the socialist West and the enslaved East, having created a new front of revolutions *against* [Stalin's italics] world imperialism, extending from the proletarians of the West, through the Russian Revolution, to the oppressed peoples of the East.'[6]

At the same time, in October 1918, communists and crypto-communists from Asia, the Levant, and North Africa were meeting in Moscow to discuss the practical problems of a 'unification of the revolutionary forces of the East'. Under Soviet auspices they founded a League for the Emancipation of the East, though for the time being its operations were confined to the peoples of Asiatic Russia and the Levant. The chief interest of this league is that it was the first communist front organization for the colonial areas and its programme contained *in nuce* all the essential communist demands for an economic, social and political transformation of the under-developed countries. Particular attention should be paid to one point which has been repeated since then in innumerable communist declarations and which represents one of the main arguments of communist anti-colonial propaganda: despite cultural and technical backwardness, Afro-Asia can 'go forward over the heads of both feudalists and capitalists and advance from its pre-capitalist system to socialism without first going through the painful stage of capitalism'.[7] This formula did much to give new life and vigour to the theories first worked out by Lenin in 1905, and extended in 1916, for a 'communist theory' of colonial emancipation and it is no accident that Peking, in particular, is still working in the under-developed countries according to the programme of the early League for the Emancipation of the East.

These theories, however, remained on paper, as did the stirring appeals addressed to the West. The revolution in Germany for which Moscow hoped and worked did not take place. Likewise the longed-for upheavals in India, China and other Eastern countries failed to materialize, or were damp squibs. Thus for the time being there was no question of the much desired 'united and effective front against Western imperialism'. In this disappointing situation Lenin made a general reassessment of the world situation and of communist chances in both the West and the East. With his eye on the forthcoming Second Congress of the Communist International, he wrote his famous book, *Left-Wing Communism*, perhaps better known by its sub-title *An Infantile Disorder*.[8] The Congress met in July-August 1920 and duly adopted the new thesis laid down in this book. Henceforth it was the tactical bible of world communism.

The important questions discussed at this congress were questions of tactics, including discussions about the most profitable areas for political action. Lenin's book had settled the general question of communist tactics. He opposed dogmatic, rigid methods and he insisted on the adoption of elastic tactics. However, there was still little hope of success in the West, where capitalism was gradually re-establishing its hold, so the Second World Congress of the Comintern decided that, for the time being, there were greater prospects of success in the East. It was therefore in the East that Lenin's new tactics were to be given their first trial. The theoretical basis for this tactical experiment was provided by an original 'Draft Thesis on the National and Colonial Question' drawn up by Lenin for the World Congress and put forward by the Indian communist, Manabendra Nath Roy. Later on Roy was expelled from the Comintern as a heretic, but the Second World Congress adopted his analysis if not all his conclusions. His second and third points are particularly interesting:

'2. European capitalism draws its strength mainly not from the European industrial countries but from its colonial possessions. To keep itself in existence it needs control over the extensive colonial markets and a wide field for exploitation. Britain, the bulwark of imperialism, has been suffering for a century from over-production. Without her extensive colonial possessions, which are necessary for the sale of her goods and which at the same time represent her raw-material basis, the capitalist order in Britain would long ago have collapsed under its own weight. In turning millions of the inhabitants of Asia and Africa into slaves, British imperialism at the same time keeps the British proletariat under the dominance of the bourgeoisie.

'3. The extra profits obtained in the colonies represent one of the chief sources from which the strength of contemporary capitalism is drawn. The European working class will be able to overthrow the capitalist order only when this source is finally cut off.'[9]

Hardly any opposition was voiced at the World Congress to this thesis which placed the fulcrum of the world revolution, for the time being, not in the West but in the colonies. In fact the delegates seemed enthusiastic at the prospect of finding a way out of the blind alley in which communism found itself in the West. But even their enthusiasm could not prevent them from recognizing the enormous gap that existed between desire and reality. There were either no communist parties at all in the colonial countries, or they were very weak indeed. Manabendra Roy and a number of extremely doctrinaire communists called for the gingering-up of these groups and insisted that they be given freedom to enter into alliances with non-communist groups. Roy did not fail to point out that 'at first . . . the revolution in the colonies will not be a communist revolution', but he consoled the congress with the assurance that provided the communist advance guard put itself at the head of the colonial revolution at once it would soon be able to lead the masses along 'the correct path'. Even on the (for him) all-important agrarian question Roy was in favour of adopting cautious tactics, and the ninth point of his theses declares that it would be an error 'to try to carry out the agrarian revolution according to communist principles immediately'. At the same time he insisted that at no time should the leadership in the colonies be left 'in the hands of the bourgeois democrats'. Indeed, 'the proletarian parties' were to carry on intensive propaganda for communist ideas and form 'workers' and peasants' soviets' at the first opportunity. These soviets were to work 'in the same way as in the Soviet Republics of the more advanced capitalist countries in order to bring about the final overthrow of the capitalist régime all over the world.'[10]

Lenin, and therefore the majority of the Congress, had other views, however. Lenin was well aware that the communists in the colonial countries were not strong enough to form such workers' and peasants' soviets, and that there would consequently have to be a long transitional period leading from colonial exploitation to the 'national democratic' phase of liberation, to the seizure of power by the communists. However, even Lenin demanded that in the colonial question communist propaganda should not adopt the usual formulae in the question of national self-determination and the equality of nations.[11]

Instead of 'an empty slogan for recognition and self-determination', Lenin declared in the original draft theses that it must be made clear to the oppressed peoples that there was no salvation for them 'except through the victory of the Soviet power' and that 'only a Soviet system of society is in a position to give the nations real equality'.[12]

However, more important for the future of communist policy in the colonial and semi-colonial countries is what Lenin had to say about the co-operation of the communists with other elements. In *Left-Wing Communism: an Infantile Disorder* he had condemned as obstinate the refusals to make compromises with other, even with hostile, groups. He insisted that communists must be prepared 'to agree to all and every sacrifice, and even—if need be—to resort to various stratagems, artifices, illegal methods, to evasions and subterfuges'[13] in order to gain their ends. Lenin recommended the use of such methods for the colonial struggle too. Addressing the Second World Congress he declared:

'With regard to the backward states and nations, in which feudal or patriarchal and patriarchal-peasant relations predominate, it is particularly important to bear in mind:
First, that all Communist Parties must assist the bourgeois-democratic liberation movement in these countries;
Second, that it is necessary to wage a fight against the clergy and other influential reactionary and mediaeval elements in backward countries;

Third, that it is necessary to combat Pan-Islamism and similar trends which strive to combine the liberation movement against European and American imperialism with the attempt to strengthen the positions of the khans, the landlords, mullahs, etc;
Fourth, that it is necessary in the backward countries to give special support to the peasant movement against the landlords, against large landownership, and against all manifestations or survivals of feudalism, and strive to lend the peasant movement the most revolutionary character and to establish the closest possible alliance between the West-European communist proletariat and the revolutionary peasant movement in the East, in the colonies, and in the backward countries generally.'[14]

Now come the decisive passages which unmistakably reveal the real purpose of all these and similar manoeuvres:

'The Communist International must support the bourgeois-democratic national movements in colonial and backward countries *only on condition* [italics added] that in all backward countries the elements of future proletarian parties which are communists not only in name shall be grouped together and trained to appreciate their special tasks, viz. to fight the bourgeois-democratic movements within their own nations; the Communist International must enter into a temporary alliance with bourgeois-democracy in colonial and backward countries, but must not merge with it and must under all circumstances preserve the independence of the proletarian movement, even if in its most rudimentary form.'[15]

The delegates to the Second World Congress of the Communist International approved these plans and accepted the report of the Commission for National and Colonial Questions presented by Lenin. This document developed the existing ideological preliminaries into an integral theory governing communist penetration of the colonial world. This was what Lenin meant when he declared that the Communist International needed a *scientifically based plan* to bring the backward countries into the Soviet system 'with the aid of the proletariat of the advanced countries'. Once this was achieved then, after they had passed through a certain stage of development, they could be brought to the Soviet system 'without having to pass through the capitalist stage.'[16]

To sum up: proceeding from Lenin's theses of 1905 and 1916 and from the discussions that took place from 1917 to 1920, the Second Congress of the Communist International adopted a uniform, power-political conception of the communist colonial revolution, which is still valid today. It embraces the following points:

1. In view of the lack of communist success in the progressive countries the colonial areas offer possibilities for world-revolutionary expansion.

2. However, the proletarian forces in these areas are not yet strong enough to take independent revolutionary action. The national-revolutionary movements are under bourgeois-democratic dominance. Therefore, in this situation the communists must, *temporarily*, support the bourgeois-democratic forces, enter into an alliance with them and adopt their slogans.

3. This policy does not mean the abandonment of the ultimate communist objectives, which are the transformation of the bourgeois-democratic phase of the national-revolutionary movement into a socialist phase; and, after that, the gradual establishment of a Soviet system followed by a *direct transition to Communism*.

4. In order to extend their power and influence, the communists must maintain complete (ideological) independence within the framework of their alliance with the bourgeois-democratic forces and, at the same time, must systematically train the future elements of the proletarian parties in the spirit of Marxism-Leninism. It is the duty of all existing communist parties to give this process their full support.

If at the same time we remember that at Lenin's suggestion the Second Congress of the Communist International, for propaganda purposes, replaced the expression 'bourgeois-democratic movement' by 'national-revolutionary movement', we can see that the leading communists of our own day have contributed few new ideas to the communist theory of colonial revolution and that they are quite right when they identify their Eastern policy of the sixties with the theories of Lenin. The controversy now going on between Moscow and Peking with regard to this Eastern policy is also nothing new; it is, in fact, typical of the permanent communist dispute about methods and, in this case, the Chinese communists have taken over the more rigid views of men like Manabendra Nath Roy, who failed to recognize the value of Lenin's supple elastic tactics, ran the danger of isolating themselves by their ultra-left attitude, and robbed themselves of all influence.

A few months later, the anti-colonial principles of the Second Congress of the Communist International were taken up, for propaganda purposes, by a specifically Afro-Asian body, the First Congress of the Peoples of the East, which met in Baku in September 1920 and was attended by 1,891 delegates from thirty-two 'nations of the East', ranging from Manchuria to Morocco to South Africa. According to the report subsequently submitted to the Executive Committee of the Communist International (ECCI) by Zinoviev on 20 September 1920, only two-thirds of those present at the congress could be called communists. The others were representatives of those national-revolutionary groups—chiefly members of the intelligentsia—that were now to be deliberately wooed and won for an alliance with communism. Despite revolutionary harangues by Radek and Bela Kun, who apparently had not toed the line completely, the congress followed the intended policy. Zinoviev said frankly that in the Soviet view communism could not yet be realized in Asia and Africa. However, the time for national revolts against imperialism was at hand and the Soviet Government was ready and willing to co-operate with all the national, democratic and revolutionary forces in the colonial countries. The congress decided to form a Council of Propaganda and Action for the Peoples of the East. Its activities were largely propagandistic and it founded and published the periodical *People of the East* in Russian, Turkish, Persian and Arabic.[17]

Lenin died on 21 January 1924, long before it was possible to discover whether the colonial policy laid down by the Second Congress of the Communist International at his behest was likely to be effective. His last article, published posthumously in *Pravda*, painted the national and international position of Soviet communism in sombre rather than cheerful colours. It talked about 'the confusion in our camp' and recorded the general 'recovery of capitalism'. World revolution seemed to have drifted into a blind alley. Significantly, Lenin pinned what hope he had onto the 'unusual speed' with which the thickly peopled colonial continents were 'being dragged into the fight for emancipation', so that, '*in this respect* there cannot be the slightest shadow of doubt what the final outcome of the world struggle will be. *In this sense*, the complete victory of socialism is fully and absolutely assured.'[18]

A number of knowledgeable people regard these words as the real testament of Lenin and it is impossible not to agree with them. In any case, his successors, and in particular Stalin, have always understood the last article of the founder of Soviet socialism in this sense. The Fifth Congress of the Communist International in 1924 drew up marching orders for the world revolution 'in the East' and Stalin, who for some time had presented himself as the ideological successor of Lenin, underlined the theoretical consequences in a series of lectures delivered in April and May 1924, 'The Foundations of Leninism'. He dismissed 'the former idea' that a victory of the proletariat in Europe could take place without *a direct alliance with the liberation movement in the colonies*, denouncing it as an 'anti-revolutionary standpoint' which must be 'exposed'. He went on,

'Leninism has proved . . . that the national question can be solved only in connection with and on the basis of the proletarian revolution and that the road to victory of the revolution in the West lies through the revolutionary alliance with the liberation movements of the colonies, and dependent countries against imperialism . . . Leninism . . . recognizes the existence of revolutionary capacities in the national liberation movements of the oppressed countries, and the possibility of using these for overthrowing the common enemy, for overthrowing imperialism.'[19]

Stalin qualified his contention, however, by saying that only national-revolutionary movements whose interests did not 'clash with the interests of the proletarian movement' were to be supported in this way. Even the struggle of the Emir of Afghanistan for the independence of his country from imperialism could be regarded as a contribution to the revolutionary movement

'despite the monarchist views of the Emir and his associates, for it weakens, disintegrates and undermines imperialism . . . For the same reason, the struggle that the Egyptian merchants and bourgeois intellectuals are waging for the independence of Egypt is *objectively* [italics added] a *revolutionary* [Stalin's italics] struggle, despite the bourgeois title of the leaders of the Egyptian national movement, despite the fact that they are opposed to socialism; whereas the struggle that the British 'Labour' Government is waging to preserve Egypt's dependent position is for the same reason a *reactionary* [Stalin's italics] struggle despite the proletarian origin and the proletarian title of the members of that government.'[20]

Such words clearly show that Khrushchev's co-existence policy towards Ethiopia, Liberia, Morocco or Tunisia was not in conflict with communist tradition, but was firmly based on history and theory, and was completely in conformity with the communist strategy and tactics laid down in the twenties.

One year later Stalin introduced a new differentiation into the colonial debate. On 18 May 1925, at the fourth anniversary of the foundation of the 'Communist University of the Toilers of the East' in Tashkent, he addressed students 'from no less than fifty nations and national groups in the East' and told them that 'there are no fewer than three categories of colonial and semi-colonial countries' and that therefore specific tactics must be developed for each of them. For the first time the expression 'national bourgeoisie' was used; thenceforth it squeezed out expressions such as 'bourgeois democrats' and became a key-word of communist anti-colonialism. Stalin defined and classified the three categories according to 'the degree of consciousness of the national bourgeoisie or the proletariat', and this degree determined the communist approach.

In countries such as Morocco (Category 1) 'where the national bourgeoisie has, as yet, no grounds for splitting up into a revolutionary party . . . the task of the communist elements is to take all measures to create a united national front against imperialism'. The situation in Egypt and China (Category 2) was regarded as different: the national bourgeoisie here was already split and one wing was inclined towards 'reactionary tendencies'. Here the communists could co-operate only with the petty bourgeoisie. Finally, in countries such as India (Category 3) the compromising bourgeoisie had already gone over completely to the side of imperialism, therefore the communists must go in for independent action and an alliance with the revolutionary bourgeoisie could serve only to prepare the proletariat 'to take the leading role in the movement for freedom'. The 'hegemony of the proletariat' must be clearly safeguarded and so, too, must the alliance of the movement for freedom with the 'proletarian movement of the advanced countries'.[21]

The co-operation between the communists and the national

bourgeoisie in the first category soon became of increasing practical importance. In order to establish a broad, anti-imperialist united front the communists were even prepared to keep their manoeuvres in the background and, outwardly, to play second fiddle to bourgeois scholars, authors and politicians. This was the case in the various anti-colonial and anti-imperialist leagues, committees, etc., founded in many Western countries, which came together at the Congress against Colonial Oppression and Imperialism, held at the Palais Egmont in Brussels in February 1927, where the chief organizer and wire-puller was the German communist, Willi Münzenberg, and the finance came from the Communist International. Incidentally, the significance of this congress is exaggerated today by people who are inclined to see 'a red conspiracy' behind every move towards co-operation between communists and non-communists. A number of well-known people were present at that meeting including Jawa-harlal Nehru, Messalij Hadj, Paul-Henri Spaak, Henri Barbusse, Theodor Lessing and Madame Sun Yat-sen, and it developed into a great protest against the colonial policy of the Western powers, while by way of contrast the anti-colonialist attitude of the Soviet Union was lavishly praised.[22]

A year later the Sixth Congress of the Communist International opened in Moscow to discuss communist and anti-colonial strategy and tactics in greater detail, and Stalin's recommendations were officially adopted. The catastrophic failure of communist action in China in 1927, which was primarily the result of Stalin's policy of alliance with the national bourgeoisie, giving the Kuomintang the opportunity to crush the communist party of China for the time being, did nothing to hamper the Eastern orientation of the Comin-tern. On the contrary, in accordance with Stalin's thesis that irrespective of dogma, communism should seek out 'the weakest links in the imperialist chain' and apply to these the lever of revolu-tion, the main weight of communist activity was now increasingly concentrated on the East, where the colonial countries were des-cribed as the most vulnerable sector of the imperialist front. As there could be no question of any strong proletariat or of any 'revolutionary mass consciousness' in these areas, the Congress instructed communists to support *local bourgeois movements* every-where and to identify themselves with the developing forms of nationalism and the slogan of self-determination.[23] Ultimately, of course, the 'movements for national-revolutionary freedom' would be persuaded that there was no salvation for them, except in 'an alliance with the revolutionary proletariat and as a result of the victory of the proletarian world revolution over world imperialism.'[24] The national factor must, however, always be taken into account and special attention paid to the peasantry as well as the intelligentsia—in fact, permission was expressly given to the intelligentsia in the colonies to form the *chief cadre*.[25] The Sixth Congress again appealed to the communist parties of the metropolitan States to be active in their colonial territories, particularly as there had been no progress in this field since the Fifth Congress of the Communist International. Then, in a report presented to the congress on 30 June 1924, Manuilsky had indignantly declared, 'A year ago the Communist International issued an appeal to the colonial slaves to rise in revolt against their masters, but when this revolutionary appeal came to the notice of a local branch of the French Communist Party in Sidi-Bel-Abbes in Algeria, it adopted a resolution condemning this Communist International appeal . . . I should like to ask our French comrades what public pronouncements their Communist Party has made demanding freedom for the colonies . . . Our English comrades are no less deserving of blame. Not one of the official statements on the attitude of the British Communist Party contains any clear and unambiguous demand for the separation of the colonies from the British Empire.'[26] In the period between the two congresses the communist parties of France and Great Britain had failed to become more resolute and vigorous, so they had once again to be called to order. The Negro problem in the United States also came up for closer attention. The theses of the Sixth Congress classified Negroes into the following main groups: those in Central Africa; in the colonial and semi-colonial countries, such as Haiti; in the Union of South Africa; in North America; and in Central and South America. In future these groups should be linked and the coloured people of the United States were called upon to pay special attention to their brothers in Africa.[27] All the measures decided upon by the congress and its tactical and strategic proposals were summed up in the programme of the Sixth World Congress, which declared:

'The international proletarian revolution represents a combination of processes which differ in character and in point of time. There are purely proletarian revolutions; bourgeois-democratic revolutions developing into proletarian revolutions; national-revolutionary wars; and colonial revolutions. The world dictatorship of the proletariat comes only as the result of the (total) revolutionary process.'[28]

Although the Sixth Congress of the Communist International dealt with the colonial problem in great detail and all the delegates solemnly promised that in the future they would 'support the struggle of the colonial and semi-colonial peoples more and more effectively', all the talk and the resolutions came to nothing.

The reason for this was not entirely due to the impotence of international communism, but was rather the result of the anti-international shift that took place in the Kremlin as a result of Stalin's final victory over Trotsky, the rejection of Trotsky's programme of permanent revolution and the adoption of Stalin's thesis of '*the building up of socialism in one country alone*' (the Soviet Union). Thus the Sixth Congress of the Communist International cannot be regarded as having drawn up a new programme for regenerating communism; what it did was to provide the epilogue to a ten-year period of world revolutionary activity. From now on, communist propaganda organs everywhere were to trumpet about the 'gigantic' successes of Soviet industrialization and collectivization; finally, when the great party purge of the late thirties gutted the Comintern too, the egoistic, imperialistic Soviet-Russian interests personified by Stalin celebrated their full triumph over the interests of the world-wide proletarian revolution.

For the next twenty years, from 1928 to 1948, the colonial problem disappeared almost completely from the theoretical debates of communism. Apart from the problem of China, Stalinist foreign policy touched on Afro-Asian themes in a very pragmatic fashion and without in the least bothering about dogma or principles. The Seventh (and last) Congress of the Communist International, which took place in 1936, was completely dominated by the anti-fascist struggle (to the exclusion of the old anti-imperialism) and by the effort of forming United Fronts, People's Fronts, and other front organizations in the capitalist States. The congress dismissed the colonial problem by saying that the formation of People's Fronts was the chief task of communists. In practice these coalition manoeuvres were not based on profound ideas or principles and amounted to little more than a readiness to work together with any and every ally. A good example of United Front policy in practice is offered by the relations between the communists and Hadj Amin al Husseini, the ex-Mufti of Jerusalem, who was extremely right-wing rather than liberal. During the uprisings of 1929 and 1936, Husseini was vigorously supported by the Bolsheviks and in 1937 two communist Middle Eastern leaders, Fuad Nasr[29] and Nimr Oda, acted as his liaison officers and advisers. The attitude of the Soviet Government in the Italo-Abyssinian war was no less ambiguous. The reports of Soviet oil deliveries to Mussolini shortly before the invasion of Abyssinia have never been officially denied by the Kremlin. Finally the Russians showed little or no interest when the French authorities launched an attack on the Algerian Communist Party in 1937, a time when the communists were co-operating closely with the French socialists in the People's Front. In other words, there was no longer a clear, definite communist policy in Afro-Asian matters. The great alliance between the Soviets and the Western Powers between 1941 and 1945 resulted in the complete neglect of colonial problems by the communists; clearly, consideration for their new allies forbade any intervention in colonial affairs. It was not until Mao's success in China, the rising of the post-war anti-colonial wave in Asia and the Near East, and the gradual formation of nationalist groups in Africa, that the attention of the Russians was again—twenty years after the Sixth Congress of the Comintern—irresistibly turned towards developments in Asia and Africa. And then they found—with growing misgivings—that matters were proceeding almost completely according to their own laws and along their own channels. With this, the largely platonic premises and assumptions of the communists' Afro-Asian policy from 1918 to 1928 took on a new significance.

Zinoviev's name had been erased from all Soviet history books, but his words to the Congress of the Eastern Peoples at Baku in 1920 now became topical: 'The real revolution will develop only when the eight hundred million inhabitants of Asia are united with us, when the African continent is united with us, when we see that hundreds of millions of people are on the move'.[30] And it was just as long since Stalin had written in one of the most important declarations on Eastern strategy:

'If Europe and America may be called the front or the arena of the major battles between socialism and imperialism, the unequal nations and the colonies with their raw materials, fuel, food and vast store of manpower must be regarded as the rear, the reserve of imperialism. To win a war it is necessary not only to triumph at the front, but also to revolutionize the enemy's rear, his reserves. Hence the victory of the world proletarian revolution may be regarded as assured only if the proletariat is able to combine its own revolutionary struggle with the liberation movement of the labouring masses of the unequal nations and the colonies against the rule of the imperialists and for the dictatorship of the proletariat.'[31]

The period after the Second World War was more than ever the time for communists to put these words into action.

NOTES

[1] Cf. George Padmore, *Pan-Africanism or Communism?* (London and New York, 1956).

[2] V. I. Lenin, 'Two Tactics of Social Democracy in the Democratic Revolution', *Selected Works* (2 vols, London, 1947).

[3] In an article entitled 'Revolution in China and in Europe', published in the *New York Tribune*, 14 June 1853, Marx wrote that the day must come 'when the extension of the [colonial] markets is unable to keep pace with the extension of British manufactures, and this disproportion must bring about a new crisis with the same certainty as it has done in the past. But if one of the great markets suddenly becomes contracted, the arrival of the crisis is necessarily accelerated thereby.' (*Marx on China 1853-1860: Articles from The New York Daily Tribune* [London, 1951], p. 4.) As so often with Marx, his desire to see this happen was stronger than his understanding of the realities and possibilities of modern industrial economics.

[4] Lenin, *Collected Works*.

[5] *Izvestia*, 22 November 1917 (old Russian calendar).

[6] J. V. Stalin, *Works* (Moscow, 1952-55), IV, pp. 169-70.

[7] Quoted by K. Troyanovsky, *Moskau und der Orient* (Berlin, 1922), p. 10.

[8] Lenin, 'Left-Wing Communism, An Infantile Disorder', *Selected Works* (3 vols, Moscow, 1961), III.

[9] Ibid. (annotated by Troyanovsky).

[10] Ibid. (annotated by Troyanovsky).

[11] Speaking on this point at the Eighth Congress of the Russian Communist Party (Bolsheviks) on 18 March 1919, Bukharin declared cynically: 'Let us by all means proclaim self-determination for the European colonies, for Hottentots, Bushmen, Negroes, Indians, and the rest. It won't cost us anything.' And Piatakov, the leader of the Ukrainian Communist Party, was equally frank: 'All this talk about self-determination isn't worth a tinker's damn. It's either a diplomatic game we sometimes have to play, or—much worse—it's a game we are wrong to take seriously.' Lenin, *Selected Works* (? vols; London, ?), VIII, p. 26.

[12] Ibid., p. 14.

[13] Lenin, *Selected Works* (Moscow, 1961), III, p. 404.

[14] Lenin, *Selected Works* (London, 1947), II, p. 657.

[15] Ibid., pp. 657-8.

[16] Lenin, *Selected Works* (Moscow, 1961), III, p. 501.

[17] *Syezd Narodov Vostoka*, the stenographic minutes of the Congress of the Peoples of the East, Baku, 1-8 September 1920 (Petrograd-Moscow, 1920).

[18] Lenin, *Selected Works* (London, 1947), II, p. 854.

[19] Stalin, *Works*, VI, p. 146.

[20] Ibid., pp. 148-9.

[21] Ibid., VII, pp. 149, 151.

[22] *Das Flammenzeichen vom Palais Egmont*, the official minutes of the Brussels Congress Against Colonial Oppression and Imperialism.

[23] 'Theses and Resolutions of the Sixth World Congress of the Communist International', *International Press Correspondence* (Vienna), VIII, No. 28, p. 1670.

[24] Ibid., p. 1661.

[25] Ibid., p. 1670.

[26] 'Protokoll des V. Kongresses der Kommunistischen Internationale' (Hamburg, ?), p. 630.

[27] 'Theses and Resolutions of the Sixth Congress of the Communist International,' p. 1672.

[28] Ibid, p. 1661.

[29] Fuad Nasr was appointed General Secretary to the Communist Party of the Kingdom of Jordan, although in 1941 he had collaborated with the Nazis and broadcast over Athens Radio as the mouthpiece of Nazi Arab propaganda. Although the Mufti also collaborated closely with Hitler and Ribbentrop, he was always treated with great consideration in Soviet Middle Eastern propaganda.

[30] *Syezd Narodov Vostoka*, p. 45.

[31] Stalin, *Works*, V, p. 57.

Chapter V

STALIN—KHRUSHCHEV—MAO

The Three Paths of the 'Colonial Revolution' after 1945

THE Soviet Union emerged from the Second World War as a Great Power and as a result of the post-war communist operations in Europe communism enlarged its geo-political basis into a Socialist Camp. When the victory of Mao in China added vastly to the area under communist domination, a Socialist World System was pronounced. However, this enormous extension of communist power resulted far less from the application of original Marxist theorems than from the ruthless use of imperialist Machiavellian principles and techniques. By this time, the original communist ideology had mostly degenerated into terminology and its main function was to provide *ex post facto* ideological trimmings to give the results Marxist respectability.

Power breeds a desire for more power; the next phase of communist policy, not only in Europe, but also in Asia and the Near East, was carried out to the accompaniment of sabre-rattling and the roll of minatory drums. As the conventional methods of power politics—which have nothing to do with ideology—had produced such unexpected successes, the communists were naturally tempted to try them out on a world scale. In consequence this whole period, which reached its peak in 1950 and persisted until 1955, was remarkable for the abandonment of the usual methods of propagandist infiltration and dexterous manoeuvring, the formation of alliances, and all the other tricks and devices of communist penetration and conquest. Soon after the war, in September 1947, Zhdanov, who up to Stalin's death in 1953 was his close confidant, Zhdanov was addressed the inaugural conference of what was dubbed the done in in 1948...

71

Communist Information Bureau (Cominform) and summed up the guiding principle of communist post-war operations in the 'Two Camp' slogan: on the one hand there was the camp of the imperialist bloc under the leadership of Washington, and on the other the anti-imperialist camp under the leadership of Moscow. These two camps were declared to be in irreconcilable opposition and the rest of the world was told that it would have to choose between them. There was no middle way, no possibility of *positive neutrality*, or of any other halfway solution.[1]

This new policy had two related consequences: firstly, the bourgeois leaders of the movements for colonial independence and all bourgeois national-revolutionary groups were contemptuously dismissed, and disqualified as allies. Instead of co-operation with such people there was now to be revolutionary—that is to say primarily military or para-military—action in the colonial countries and even in those former colonies which had already attained their independence. But as the working class was still too weak to conduct independent political operations and as it was now forbidden to pursue a policy of alliance with the 'national bourgeoisie', all that remained was a policy of *military force*. The result was the armed insurrections of 1946 and 1948 in Indo-China, Burma, Malaya, the Philippines and Indonesia and in the Telengana area of India. The theoretical explanation provided for these complex processes was that the working class had now 'taken over the leading role in the struggle for national independence', pushing aside 'the treacherous bourgeoisie' and at the same time establishing the 'natural connection between the anti-imperialist struggle and the class struggle'.

The relative failure of this kind of revolution did not dismay the communists. Those responsible for communist policy refused to consider the realities of the situation and their activities were still obstinately directed towards an 'independent communist policy', which involved a *war on two fronts*, against both foreign imperialists and national imperialists. Not even the real anti-Western developments in the colonial and former colonial countries were sufficient to persuade the communists to abandon their independent tactics or, at least, to adapt them to the situation. Some years later the Persian communist Eskandari admitted:

'We have experienced great difficulties in our activities, and have made no few mistakes . . . For example, we did not support Mossadegh, who undoubtedly represented the interests of the national bourgeoisie . . . thereby isolating ourselves from the masses who followed the bourgeoisie, and not our Party.'[2]

In India, Gandhi was declared to be a 'traitor' and 'demagogue' who never had been serious in his professed intention of liberating India and abolishing the caste system. The founders of the first Indian trade unions were denounced as 'mercenaries of capitalism'. And what communists dismissed as the 'pseudo-left wing' of the Congress Party, (which was after all under the leadership of Pandit Nehru) had to put up with the reproach that it made 'revolutionary and anti-imperialist gestures' only in order to put pressure on the British imperialists and thus obtain better conditions for the collaborators.[3] A similar attitude was taken towards the Egyptian 'Wafd' movement and when King Farouk was finally deposed an official Soviet source made the following comment: 'In the night of July 22nd a reactionary group of officers in alliance with the United States seized power.'[4] In the same way the African national movement was denigrated and abused. Except for the orthodox leaders of the *Rassemblement Démocratique Africain* (Sékou Touré, Ruben Um Nyobe and Modibo Keita) they were, according to Soviet accounts, merely 'lickspittles' and 'lackeys of colonialism and imperialism'. For example, a book published in the Soviet Union in December 1954 entitled *Narody Afriki* (*The Peoples of Africa*) described Kwame Nkrumah's Convention People's Party and the first government formed by Nkrumah as 'shields behind which the reality of British imperialist dominance conceals itself'.

The tactics recommended by Lenin, Stalin, and the Comintern from the twenties onwards seemed to have been forgotten. In those days communists had been advised to aim at tactical co-operation with the national revolutionary movements, but now the line was: 'History has proved that the national bourgeoisie of the colonial and semi-colonial countries, which are attached by a thousand bonds to the feudal classes and to foreign imperialism, can never lead the national-revolutionary movement to victory. The anti-imperialist and anti-feudal revolution can be victorious only *under the leadership of the communists* and on the basis of an alliance between the workers and peasants.'[5]

In the meantime however, the colonial system was rapidly deteriorating. In Asia, North Africa, and later in the whole of Africa, the leaders of the national bourgeoisie showed very clearly that they were, in fact, quite capable of leading the national-revolutionary movement to victory on their own, without communist assistance, while the communists found themselves in increasing danger of being excluded from an important historical process and of being left behind. Peking was the first of the communist régimes to take steps to win friends in the colonial and ex-colonial countries. Even during the Korean war the leaders of the Chinese Communist Party had come to the conclusion that quite a number of the allegedly pro-imperialist governments of Asia were by no means in the pockets of the British and the Americans and that they were honestly seeking an independent line between the two big political blocs. Consequently the Chinese communists set out to woo India and the Indian Ambassador in Peking was showered with attention. A further consequence was the drawing-up of the famous 'Five Principles' of non-intervention and co-existence between the Chinese and Indian governments.

It was not until the first half of 1955 that Moscow began to revise its policy. At the time of the Bandung Conference, Russia was compelled to recognize that the statesmen of almost all the existing African and Asian States had come together (in the presence of representatives from Red China and North Vietnam, but in the absence of North Korea, the Mongolian People's Republic and the Soviet Union!) to form an oriental Third Force and to constitute themselves as an independent Power of a politico-moral nature. The 'spirit of Bandung' radiated a magic attraction amongst Afro-Asians, and threatened to drive Moscow's 'Spirit of the November Revolution' from the minds of the Afro-Asian élite. It was obviously necessary and urgent for Moscow to have second thoughts about its own anti-colonial policy.

What guiding principles have since emerged? What official declarations are available summarizing the new policy? First of all there are the policy lines drawn up in 1955 and confirmed at the Twentieth Congress of the Communist Party of the Soviet Union and at the Moscow conferences of 1957 and 1960. Among a profusion of official declarations, perhaps what was said by Idris Cox, a leading member of the British Communist Party, best sums up the

74

reasons for the change of policy. During a discussion at the Leipzig Historical Institute of the Karl Marx University in East Germany at the end of May 1949, which was attended by representatives from the Soviet Union, the satellite countries, Africa, and Asia, Idris Cox examined the role of the bourgeoisie in the national-revolutionary movement and declared that

'At the Sixth Congress of the Comintern in 1928 the perspective was that the colonies would achieve political independence only after the working class (in alliance with the peasants, petty bourgeoisie, and progressive sections of the national bourgeoisie) was in the leadership of the national-liberation movement. In practice it has been revealed since the Second World War that political independence has been achieved in India, Indonesia, Ghana and other countries under the leadership of the national bourgeoisie.'[6]

This is a frank and self-critical presentation of the dilemma in which the communists now find themselves. They cannot get out of it by saying that it was due to 'the growth of the socialist world' that imperialism was compelled to abandon its old methods of oppression, so that therefore, indirectly, it was communism after all which helped the national-revolutionary movement to victory. Communism did not, as Cox freely admitted, trigger off the national-revolutionary movement in very large areas of Asia and Africa; in reality the much-abused national bourgeoisie proved itself a stronger force than the communists. Incidentally, the negative attitude now adopted towards the decisions of the Sixth Congress of the Communist International requires no comment. Tactically, the slogans of this congress were—from the communist point of view—more cleverly formulated than most of the official communist declarations from 1945 to 1955; nowadays there is a tendency to present the ideas of this congress as the root of all evil; this is merely one of the many attempts now being made by men in the Kremlin, who were themselves responsible for the rigid, unsuccessful communist anticolonial policy of the post-war decade, to shift the burden of responsibility from their own shoulders.

This tendency first became evident at the Twentieth Congress of the Communist Party of the Soviet Union in February 1956, when Khrushchev, Otto Kuusinen, and Shepilov (who was Soviet Foreign Minister at the time) proposed the revision of the communist programme for colonial revolution. Kuusinen, an old Finnish communist and member of the Praesidium of the Central Committee, was put up to draw attention to 'the sectarian errors' of certain Soviet orientalists and publicists—though not, of course, to the errors of the communist leaders themselves. 'Under the changed conditions of the present day and now that the prestige of the Soviet Union has greatly increased,' as Kuusinen put it, there must in particular be a re-examination of the character and role of the national bourgeoisie in the colonial and semi-colonial countries.[7] Shepilov, the first speaker to refer to the special situation in Africa, struck a somewhat different note when he declared:

'Communists are in principle opponents of sectarian narrowness. They advocate that the efforts of all kinds and varieties of mass movements of the present day must be merged into an anti-imperialist stream. The great aspirations of all the downtrodden peoples of the Arab, Asian or Latin American countries, of all working people, whether they be Catholics, Protestants, followers of Buddhism or Islam, will find their realization in the struggle against social oppression, against colonialism, in the struggle for peace and democracy. Never before has the great slogan of *unity* had such active and comprehensive purport.'[8]

This statement, and the admission of Khrushchev that there was now 'an extensive zone of peace' in Asia and Africa, mark the re-opening of a protracted inter-Marxist discussion on the necessity, usefulness, and objectives of a communist policy of alliance with the national forces of the colonial and former colonial countries—on both an international and a national level.

The stages of this discussion became public on four occasions, at the two publicity meetings in the spring of 1959 devoted to an analysis of the situation and at the two Moscow conferences in 1957 and 1960.

The first two meetings took place in Moscow and Leipzig respectively. In Moscow the editorial boards of the Moscow *Mezhdunarodnaya Zhisn* (*International Life*) and of the Peking *Shi Chi Shi* (*World Culture*) held a joint meeting to discuss 'the particular characteristics of the national-revolutionary movement in the colonial and dependent countries of the East'. Specialists and journalists from the Soviet Union, from the satellite States and from the West, from Africa, and Asia took part in the meeting at the Karl Marx University in Leipzig. Chinese representatives were not present on this occasion. The subject was 'The Role of the Bourgeoisie in the National-Revolutionary Liberation Movement'. The result of these deliberations was that the national bourgeoisie was rehabilitated and declared worthy of being an ally of the communists. It was at the conference in Moscow that this was stated most clearly. The Leipzig meeting had adopted an almost defeatist attitude towards the national bourgeoisie, but the Moscow conference emphasized the practical nature of any alliances with it. Two quotations will suffice to make clear the difference of tone and attitude:

'In the present conditions of revolutionary struggle for national independence and democracy (in Africa) the social and economic development of the national bourgeoisie can be neither halted nor retarded . . . In our days imperialist plans will, in the final analysis, merely aggravate the contradictions between the oppressed peoples on the one hand, and imperialism on the other, between the national bourgeoisie in the oppressed countries and the big capitalists in the oppressor countries.'[9]

The above is a quotation from Leipzig; the tone at Moscow was different:

'The working class of the oppressed countries . . . regards the achievement of national independence merely as a stage and a necessary pre-condition for social transformations and for the subsequent development of the national and colonial revolution into the socialist revolution. As far as the national bourgeoisie is concerned, the achievement of national independence is its ultimate aim, and it consists in the establishment of their undivided rule in a sovereign State.'[10]

However, the Moscow conference, which was largely dominated by the radical theses of the Chinese, was also compelled to recognize the actual strength of the national bourgeoisie in the underdeveloped countries and even to grant it 'revolutionary possibilities' for the future. The point was made that this situation called for 'very elastic tactics but at the same time firm principles' on the part of the communist parties and the crypto-communist groups. The declaration then went on to say: 'The struggle of the working class for a *People's Democratic* solution in those countries that have already achieved their political independence does not exclude the determined exploitation of every revolutionary possibility afforded by the national bourgeoisie and the anti-imperialist movement—on the contrary, it presupposes it. The struggle demands the maximum extension and intensification of all such possibilities, and must lend the whole movement a far-reaching democratic character'.[11] For 'democratic' one must read 'communist'.

This was a clear extension of the decisions of the first Moscow conference, in November 1957, which declared:

'1. Communism recognizes the objective advantage of the Afro-Asian movement for independence because, although the existence of new, independent States does not *subjectively* facilitate the victory of communism, it *objectively* weakens imperialism;

'2. The socialist camp, as the natural partner of the new States of Asia and Africa, desires to consolidate the independence of these new States by means of improved diplomatic, economic and cultural relations, and thus free them from the pressure of Western imperialism and of Western capital;

'3. The struggle of many peoples for their national independence against colonial aggression and feudal oppression makes it necessary to form an anti-imperialist and anti-feudalist united front of the workers and peasants, the urban petty bourgeoisie, the national bourgeoisie and other patriotic and democratic forces.'[12]

These were very vague formulations and revealed the abandonment of any attempt at either an ideological analysis or a formulated strategic-tactical point of view. On the one hand this was because the examination of the situation had led to no very clear conclusions and on the other because the intention was to appeal to every possible ally in the colonial and ex-colonial countries and to avoid offending them.

Three years later, at the second conference in Moscow in November 1960, the communists formulated their objectives and intentions more clearly. They recorded that the national-revolutionary movement in the East, which had triggered off the dissolution of the system of colonial slavery, was in its historic significance 'the most important phenomenon after the rise of the socialist world system'. They went on to say:

1. The urgent tasks of national re-birth in the freed countries can be carried out 'only if a determined struggle is waged against imperialism and the remnants of feudalism and if all the patriotic forces of the nation come together in a national, democratic united front'.

2. The following measures in particular were declared necessary:

'the consolidation of political independence, agrarian reform in the interests of the peasantry, the abolition of the last vestiges of feudalism, the abolition of the economic roots of imperialist rule, the restriction and elimination of foreign monopoly undertakings in the national economy, the creation and development of national industry, the raising of living standards for the people, the demo-cratization of public life, a peace-loving foreign policy, and the development of economic and cultural relations with the socialist countries.'

The national bourgeoisie was still reproached for a strong tendency to vacillate and for various 'undemocratic' actions, but on the whole it was highly commended. For the first time since the twenties it was very definitely laid down for the communist move-ment as a whole that 'the national bourgeoisie in the colonial and dependent countries is objectively interested—in so far as it is not connected with imperialist circles—in carrying out the chief tasks of the anti-imperialist, anti-feudalist revolution'. This being so it is regarded as worthy of 'taking part in the revolutionary struggle against imperialism and feudalism and to be given a clean bill of health for the purposes of alliance.'[13]

This statement, as other passages indicate, did not involve any compromise in principle with the national bourgeoisie, but the intention was unmistakable: the ruling strata in the non-communist countries in Africa and Asia were, for the time being, to be treated with respect, granted far-reaching recognition on account of their 'progressive' behaviour, and considered worthy of both internal and external support by communism. That policy was especially applied to India in the Himalaya crisis in October 1962, but could also be observed in the Soviet wooing of Nasser and other Arab leaders in recent years. This attitude was clearly illustrated by the new description of the progressive national States as 'national democracies'. Boris Ponomarov, member of the Central Committee of the C.P.S.U. and in charge of the communist and crypto-communist parties outside the 'socialist camp', explained the specific characteristics of each 'independent national democratic State' in an article published in *Communist*, an official organ of the Party, in December 1960:

'First of all, it should most vigorously and determinedly defend its political and economic independence against the imperialists and the war bloc, and object most strongly to the establishment of military bases on its territory. Secondly, it should fight against new forms of colonialism and against the penetration of the country by imperialist capital. In particular the nation which is united in such a State must be filled with an abiding hatred of the imperialist exploiters and carry on a relentless struggle against all imperialist attempts to undermine the full independence of its own domestic and foreign policy and of its own independent path of development. Thirdly, this State must reject all dictatorial and despotic methods of government. The most widespread democratic rights and liberties will be secure in such a State, including the freedom of speech, the freedom to meet and to demonstrate, and the freedom to form political parties and other organizations. And fourthly, such a State will safeguard the possibility of introducing agrarian and other reforms, and in general measures instituting democratic and social changes, including the right of the masses of the people to take part in the formation of public policy, and so on. In such a country the broad masses of the people will be drawn into the process of building up its economy, since it will spurn foreign patronage whilst at the same time its people will be filled with a desire to overcome centuries-old backwardness, misery and lack of culture.'[14]

The first thing that strikes one about this list of ideal qualifications for a National Democracy is that it does not even mention the word 'socialist', much less 'communist', and everything is judged by *democratic* and *anti-imperialist* criteria. But is there any country anywhere that conforms to this ideal picture and fulfils all the conditions laid down by Ponomarov? Do Morocco, Ethiopia, Liberia and the United Arab Republic conform? And how far do the communists extend their 'specific characteristics'? What about Ghana and Guinea? Can they be included amongst Ponomarov's independent national democratic States? It is not easy to find clear answers to these important questions. However, the Moscow conference of 1960 did, strange to relate, inform the world that Iraq had 'successfully concluded its anti-imperialist revolt'—this at a time when Kassem was engaged in the liquidation of the communist party in Iraq! If necessary communism is apparently prepared to tolerate such behaviour. An official communist publication has this to say on the subject:

'It often happens that when the representatives of the national bourgeoisie are in power . . . they launch violent attacks against the communist parties. But even in such cases the communists continue to let their relations with such governments be guided primarily by the basic criterion of the role such governments play in the struggle against imperialism.'

In such cases the representatives of these 'anti-imperialist bourgeois governments' have to be left 'to learn by experience that they are not threatened by "the communist danger" but by the inner and outer reaction.'[15]

In the meantime—and even before Kassem was killed—Iraq has disappeared from the ranks of the national democratic States. On the other hand, in December 1961 Ivan Potekhin, the leading Soviet specialist on Africa, listed Ghana, Guinea and Mali as States entitled to be referred to as national democracies.[16] The East German publication *Einheit* lays it down that 'an important step on the way to the national democratic State is the formation of broad democratic fronts'. Indonesia is mentioned as one of the States in which such a broad united front has been formed. The article then goes on, 'a similar development towards the formation of strong national democratic fronts is taking place in Ceylon, Guinea, Ghana and Mali'.[17] The unwillingness of communist publicists to be specific in this matter, as displayed here and in other communist publications, is obviously caused by the fact that the expression 'national democracy' represents an ideal state of affairs. They dare not be specific because if they were it would in all cases restrict and reduce the significance of the term. In all probability this is why the expression is used only very rarely in the programme of the Communist Party of the Soviet Union as adopted by the Twenty-second Congress of the party in October 1961. Chapter VI of this

programme is entirely devoted to the national-revolutionary liberation movement, which the congress declared to be the most important international phenomenon since the establishment and
consolidation of the socialist camp. At the same time it warns this
movement not to be content with the achievement of political independence, but to 'end economic dependence on imperialism', build
up national industry, liquidate the vestiges of feudalism, carry out a
radical agrarian reform, pursue 'an independent and peace-loving
foreign policy', 'democratize social life', and pursue a policy of
alliance with 'all the patriotic and progressive forces of the nation'.
The 'fundamental condition for the solution of all national tasks' is
defined as 'a thoroughgoing struggle against imperialism' and its
chief bulwark, US imperialism. The young national States are
warned that they can expect only 'an intensification of social
inequality' from 'a capitalist path of development', whereas socialism
would open up brilliant future prospects for them.

Regretfully it is admitted that most of these young States have not
yet found the way to socialism, and that difficult sociological
problems, due primarily to the weakness of the working class, still
exist. For the time being, therefore, the working class in these
countries must seek alliances with the peasantry, *and with the
national bourgeoisie* which, under the circumstances, is 'objectively
interested in carrying out the fundamental tasks of the anti-
imperialist and anti-feudal revolution'. The programme goes on to
say that 'in consequence the progressive role of the national bourgeoisie and its ability to take part in the carrying out of the urgent
general national tasks are not yet exhausted'. Despite this ambiguity,
neither the programme nor the other documents of the Twenty-
second Party Congress show any tendency to write off the national
bourgeoisie. Indeed, as the leading strata of the former colonial
States they are conceded to have the ability to play an influential
part in the international field—above all in 'the solution of the central
problem of our time, the prevention of a new world war'.[18] The
section of the party congress resolution which enumerates the
'fundamental' problems of world politics returns to this aspect of
the problem. The 'final liquidation of all forms and phenomena of
colonial oppression, and the provision of real and effective help for
those peoples who have recently achieved their independence' is
listed immediately after the demand for general and complete dis-

armament. In this connection it is interesting to note that such hotly disputed and important matters as the German and Chinese questions and the reorganization of the United Nations come only after the references to the under-developed countries.[19]

Despite a great profusion of words, the Twenty-second Congress of the Communist Party of the Soviet Union did nothing to alter the fundamental Soviet line. As various statements after the congress show, Soviet communists are still in favour of eliminating ideological considerations from their relations with the under-developed countries. Generally speaking they are prepared to do without the immediate inauguration of a people's democratic, socialist policy and to aim for the time being at casting off or loosening economic and political bonds with the West and, as far as possible, at drawing the new States into an anti-imperialist front. This new attitude makes sense only if we recognize the transformation of the Soviet Union itself into a neo-bourgeois social system far removed from any communist programme and engaged in pursuing imperialist power policies—disguised perhaps by the slogan of *co-existence* but conducted essentially in the style of the bourgeois imperialist States of the nineteenth and twentieth centuries. From this standpoint, Afro-Asian States are regarded less as areas for communist infiltration than as areas to be removed, economically and politically, from the sphere of influence of the West. It is logical therefore that the Soviets pay special attention to the Congo, demanding vociferously that the colonial system be completely liquidated, because it is the biggest producer of cobalt and uranium in the world. This, too, is the reason for the friendly words to Morocco, Ethiopia, and Liberia. Although reactionary feudal conditions prevail in all these States they nevertheless enjoy at least the goodwill of the Soviet Press.

This opportunist attitude towards the Third World was certainly not adopted without internal communist opposition. The gradual abandonment by Moscow of Zhdanov's ideas of the rehabilitation of the national bourgeoisie, and the policy of co-existence and alliance with partners not really qualified for the purpose have—as numerous references and documents show—aroused the growing mistrust and undisguised opposition of Peking. In fact the Chinese Communist Party did formally append its signature to the declarations of the Moscow conferences of 1957 and 1960. It was formerly in favour of a more elastic attitude to the question of co-operation with other classes and during the period 1952 to 1957 (during which they took part in the Bandung Conference) the Chinese operated no less opportunistically towards the existing national-bourgeois régimes.

The orthodox attitude of the Chinese Communist Party, based on strict revolutionary principles, is chiefly due to the Chinese claim—in competition with Moscow—for a monopoly role in the liberation of the colonial and semi-colonial countries. Even before (and certainly after) their own seizure of power, the Chinese communists disputed the claim of the Russians that the November Revolution and the socialism of the Soviet Union represented an obligatory model for the rest of the world in the matter of emancipation and social revolution. As early as November 1949 Liu Shao-chi, in a speech to the Trade-Union Conference of Asian and Australasian countries, declared that China was the model for the colonial countries to follow. Eighteen months later Lu Ting-yi, one of Peking's leading men, went even further: the following quotations were printed in a Cominform publication; according to this source Liu Shao-chi declared unmistakably:

'The path taken by the Chinese people to defeat imperialism and its lackeys and to found the People's Republic of China should now be followed by other countries in order to achieve their national independence and allow them to establish a people's democratic régime.'[20]

The decisive passage in Lu Ting-yi's speech reads:

'The November Revolution is the classic type of a revolution in imperialist (that is to say, capitalistically developed) countries. *The Chinese revolution is the classic type of a revolution in colonial and semi-colonial countries*, and its experience is of incalculable value to the peoples of such countries.'[21]

On 16 June 1950 *Jen Min Jih Pao*, the official organ of the Communist Party of China, referring to 'Lessons of the Chinese Revolution', the joint work of Mao Tse-tung and Liu Shao-chi, wrote in the same strain:

'The experiences of the revolutionary victory of China are of great significance for the peoples of all countries who are still groaning under the dominance of imperialism and their own reactionaries. In other words, the chief characteristic of the Chinese revolution, the armed struggle, can under certain historical conditions become the common characteristic of the revolutionary development in all colonial and semi-colonial countries.'[22]

This view has been repeated in innumerable variations since then, particularly since 1959, and the speech of Liu Shao-chi to the Seventh Congress of the Communist Party of China is frequently quoted to justify the Chinese claim for a monopoly in colonial affairs. In fact, this speech, 'On the Party', is one of the fundamental documents of Chinese communism, one with which it stakes its claim to independence. In this speech Liu Shao-chi declared:

'The proletarian programme and the policy of the Chinese Communist Party differ from those of *all other parties*. It was on the basis of this programme and this policy that our party *independently* organized and carried out the anti-imperialist and anti-feudalist new democratic revolution of the Chinese people and carried out the tasks of the Chinese proletariat in the present bourgeois-democratic revolution in the widest possible sense, and secured for itself the leadership of the people's revolution, whose ultimate aim is socialism and communism.'[23]

This speech is particularly interesting because *expressis verbis*—it sets out why the Chinese communists claim the right to be the only 'true' model for the colonial and semi-colonial countries to follow. Liu stressed that the Chinese revolution took place in a 'colonial, semi-colonial and semi-feudal country' and he pointed out that 'the chief forces of our party' were concentrated in the rural areas.[24] He went on to say: 'the broad masses of the peasants represented the chief strength of our revolution'.[25] And in another passage 'the present revolution in China is essentially a peasant revolution'.[26] He also pointed out that the working class acted more as a vehicle than as an active participant, and declared:

'the lessons of Mao Tse-tung on the Chinese revolution united the Marxist-Leninist theory with the present practice of the Chinese revolution. It is communism and Marxism adapted to China. The lessons of Mao Tse-tung on the Chinese revolution represent *the further development of Marxism in the national-democratic revolution in a colonial and semi-feudal country . . .*[27] These lessons represent a great and useful contribution to the struggle for liberation of the peoples of all countries in general and the peoples of the East in particular.'[28]

After the victory of the Chinese communists in 1949 this 'specific character' of the Chinese revolution was intensified by a number of exclusively Chinese 'achievements'. Peking claims originality for the Chinese *organization of the people* (in the People's Communes for example), for the Chinese *organization of labour* (in the mass application of labour power and in the 'individual iron smelting works') and above all in *the revolutionary organization of all forces in the struggle against imperialism*. The last point is of particular importance: it refers to the Chinese thesis that complete liberation from colonialism and victory over world imperialism can be won *only by force of arms*. In his speech to the Trade-Union Conference of Asian and Australasian countries in November 1949 Liu Shao-chi made a special point of this:

'If the people of a colonial or semi-colonial country have no arms to defend themselves they have nothing at all. The existence and development of proletarian organizations and the existence and development of a national united front are *closely linked* to the existence and development of such an armed struggle. For many colonial and semi-colonial peoples this is *the only way* in their struggle for independence and liberation.'[29]

Two recent Western publications, *Problems of Communism* and the *China Quarterly*, are right to draw attention in this and other Chinese statements to the necessity of an armed struggle. Arthur A. Cohen draws attention to a study published in Peking in 1951 by Ch'en Po-ta under the somewhat cumbersome title, 'Mao Tse-tung's Theory of the Chinese Revolution and the Integration of Marxism-Leninism with the Practice of the Chinese Revolution'. Ch'en Po-ta also mentions *guerilla warfare* as a characteristic feature of the Maoist strategy of revolution.[30] The official Chinese communist writings, which recommend waging a prolonged revolutionary struggle from self-supporting communist bases in the countryside and using guerilla warfare tactics, aroused great interest after the victory of communism in China. In recent years this interest has noticeably revived and the question has received a new significance. For example, in the new edition of Mao's book, *How can China's Red Political Power Exist?*, originally written in 1928 and published as the first volume of his *Selected Works* in 1951, there is an added footnote emphasizing the applicability of the Chinese revolutionary experience to other countries in the East. The key passage in the voluminous footnote reads:

'Thus—just as the Chinese people did—all, or at least some, of the colonial peoples of the East can hold big or small base areas and maintain revolutionary régimes for a protracted period, and wage permanent revolutionary war to encircle the towns from the countryside and thus proceed gradually to take over the towns and win nation-wide victory in their respective countries.'[31]

As we shall show in connection with Chinese policy in the Cameroons, these recommendations have not fallen on deaf ears in Africa and the tactics suggested have actually been adopted, while in its controversy with Moscow the Chinese Communist Party has returned to its contention that 'all political power goes back to the barrel of a gun',[32] and stressed this revolutionary axiom in its propaganda in Africa and Asia.

We do not propose to analyse the Sino-Soviet controversy as such. It has been going on for a long time though it first came to public notice only in the preparatory phase of the second Moscow conference of November 1960. However, in order to understand Chinese policy in Africa we must at least deal with that aspect of the dispute which has arisen over communist strategy and tactics in the colonial and semi-colonial countries.

Sino-Soviet disagreement on this question first came into the open in a leading article in *Pravda* on 26 August 1960 by Yevgeni Zhukov, a member of the Soviet Academy. His arguments were clearly directed against Peking and it was obviously the Chinese communists he had in mind when he said reproachfully that there were comrades who failed to understand the role of the national bourgeoisie in the colonial and semi-colonial countries in the struggle for liberation from colonialism. He went on, 'Dogmatists and sectarians, who understand nothing of the laws of social development, suggest that the application of the Leninist principles of peaceful co-existence hampers the development of the movement for national liberation and condemns it to stagnation—a thoroughly false point of view!'

As against the Chinese Communist Party, which regards the yoke of colonialism as having been shaken off only if political as well as economic independence has been won and which therefore regards mere political sovereignty as a sham, Zhukov said: 'Only petty-bourgeois left-wingers and hopeless dogmatists can deny the importance of the fact that sovereign States have been formed in Asia and Africa, even though some of them have not yet achieved economic independence.' Zhukov grants, of course, that the proletariat represents the great counterweight to imperialism, but he points out that Lenin regarded it as quite natural that at the beginning of every national movement the (national) bourgeoisie should play a leading role and Lenin called for support of the revolutionary elements in the bourgeois-democratic national liberation movements. Zhukov made a clear distinction between the national and the social (socialist) revolution when he pointed out that the front of the 'anti-imperialist liberation movement' was much broader than that of the 'social revolution'.[33]

This article represented a clear warning to the Chinese communists not to stake everything, in sectarian fashion, on the extreme left wing but rather to pursue an elastic policy *in the present phase*, supporting the bourgeois forces 'in so far as they work for liberation from colonialism' because they represent the leading force in the anti-colonial movement.

The answer of the comrades in Peking was not long delayed: 'If we were to agree to regard the movement led by the bourgeoisie in the colonial countries as the main stream of the national-revolutionary liberation movement, and keep silent about the anti-imperialist struggle of the masses, or even treat it with contempt [the reference is, of course, to the left-wing revolutionaries], this would represent in practice an adoption of the bourgeois standpoint and run counter to Lenin's views.'[34]

In an article published on 2 November 1960 *Hung Ch'i* (*The Red Flag*), the theoretical organ of the Communist Party of China, launched a frontal attack on the Soviet standpoint. Just before the departure of the Chinese delegation led by Liu Shao-chi to the second Moscow conference, an editorial entitled 'Fundamental

Summary of the Experiences of the Victory of the Chinese People's Revolution' appeared, ostensibly in connection with the publication of the fourth volume of Mao Tse-tung's works. Four points in this editorial are of particular importance:

1. The Chinese communists reject every form of united front in the colonial and semi-colonial countries. That is to say they are opposed to the tactic forced on the communists of Iraq on Khrushchev's orders. This tactic aimed at establishing a 'united front' with General Kassem and the bourgeois and military forces behind him, and after temporary successes it ended in the defeat and destruction of the Communist Party of Iraq. In February 1961 even the international communist periodical *Problems of Peace and Socialism* was compelled to admit that the Communist Party of Iraq had suffered a defeat. In the view of the Chinese Communist Party 'united fronts' are permissible only if they guarantee 'the independence of the proletarian movement' and allow the communists independent control of their own *armed* forces, thus placing them in a position to extend their power.

2. Alliances with the imperialists (and this term includes the reactionary forces in the Afro-Asian countries) are of extremely limited value. To place any trust in the promises of the imperialists must, as the Chinese experience with Chiang Kai-shek in the twenties and in 1945-6 shows, create a dangerous situation for the revolutionary forces.

3. As the victory of the Chinese communists in 'a great Eastern country' proves, it is necessary to form 'innumerable small revolutionary bases (cells) . . . in the rural areas' and arm the people's forces. 'The existence and development of revolutionary armed forces and revolutionary bases (cells) will inevitably strengthen the revolutionary consciousness of the masses'.

4. The 'people's democratic dictatorship' in China had two phases of development:

'Before the founding of the People's Republic the people's democratic dictatorship in our country was in effect a dictatorship of a democratic revolution, the dictatorship of several revolutionary classes led by the proletariat and based on an alliance of the workers and peasants, a dictatorship of the Chinese people over the jackals of imperialism, the *compradore* class and the feudal class. After the founding of the Chinese People's Republic in 1949 the people's democratic dictatorship took on a new quality—it became a dictatorship of the socialist revolution, a real dictatorship of the proletariat. *But no dictatorship can be effective or even continue to exist unless it is based on force.* What is force? It is based on the armed forces, the police, the People's Courts, the prisons, etc.'[35]

In a direct attack on the thesis put forward by Khrushchev (and adopted by the Moscow conference in 1957), according to which there is in certain countries a non-violent, parliamentary way of taking over power, *Hung Ch'i* wrote, 'China found herself in a totally different situation. As comrade Mao Tse-tung said, there was no possibility in a semi-colonial, semi-feudal country like China of using the parliamentary way.' Only 'left-wing opportunists' in the Chinese C.P. had ignored this fact. In China the main way (to socialism) had consisted in 'the struggle of the communist armed forces in alliance with the peasants as the main contingent'.[36]

There can be no doubt about the great importance of this editorial, particularly because the quotations and ideas are all taken from volume IV of the works of Mao Tse-tung. To clinch the matter, since its appearance in October 1960 the Chinese communists have repeatedly informed the world that the book is not to be regarded merely as a collection of reminiscences but as 'a guide to action' for all revolutionary groups in the colonial and semi-colonial countries. 'Abandon your illusions and prepare yourselves for battle!' and 'In our actions we relied on our brains and on our rifles' are the two most important axioms of Mao's book; there is no doubt that today these axioms are directed at the left wing of the Afro-Asian liberation movement which, in the view of Peking, finds itself in a situation similar to that of the Chinese 'liberation movement, before its victory over Chiang Kai-shek and his colonialist wire-pullers'. This was made very clear during a number of open Sino-Soviet clashes. One took place in December 1961 at a meeting of the World Peace Council in Stockholm, which was being run by the Russians exclusively on the subject of disarmament. The Chinese representatives strongly opposed the view of the Soviet and other delegates that negotiation was essential for the maintenance of world peace, and the chief Chinese delegate, Liao Cheng-chi, insisted: 'The idea that we can come to an understanding with the imperialists and attain peaceful co-existence by negotiation merely demoralizes the fighting spirit of the people and damages the cause of world peace. We must stress that the struggle between the oppressed peoples and imperialism and colonialism is a life and death struggle.'[37] Another Chinese delegate, Liu Ning-yi, spoke even more plainly:

'Today disarmament is certainly not the most important problem for oppressed countries such as Laos, Algeria, Angola and the Cameroons. The important thing for them is the strengthening and building up of their armed forces. Neither Cuba nor any of the other young independent countries can be in favour of a reduction of the armed forces they have only just formed. On the contrary, in order to defend their independence they must strengthen their armies.'[38]

The dispute was continued at the conference of Afro-Asian authors held in Cairo from 12 to 15 February 1962:

'A proposal that the writers' conference should send a message to the World Peace Council and adopt a resolution on disarmament was opposed by the Chinese delegation, which was the largest at the conference. In his speech the leader of the Chinese group, Mao tun, Minister of Culture, stressed the difference between "unconditional" and what he called "principled" peaceful co-existence, adding that "sheep and wolves can never co-exist peacefully". He claimed that it was the struggle for national independence above all that helped "to create the necessary conditions for principled peaceful co-existence".[39] Mirzo Tursun-Zade, leader of the Soviet delegation, answered the following day with a plea for disarmament and peaceful co-existence, saying: "Only madmen and those who want a new world war do not, or are unwilling to, understand the enormous losses which could be inflicted on mankind by hydrogen warfare". Unlike the Stockholm conference, at which the Chinese were in the minority, the majority of the delegates to the Cairo meeting seem to have voted in support of the Chinese line.'[40]

It is significant that this clash was immediately made public by the Albanian friends of Peking; in a long, detailed statement Tirana accused the Kremlin of 'sinking ever deeper into the morass of anti-Marxism' particularly where the national liberation struggle was concerned, and of regarding the struggle against various forms of imperialism and colonialism as of secondary importance, while supporting 'bourgeois pacifist ideas'.[41]

The supporters of Moscow now came out into the open and at the beginning of 1962 the leading theorist of the Belgian Communist Party, Jean Terfve, published a series of articles in *Le Drapeau Rouge*, the official organ of the Belgian party, in which he accused the Chinese of making an idol of military might in the struggle against imperialism and colonialism. At the same time he drew the attention of the Chinese to a number of objective factors which still hampered the advance of communism in Africa, Asia and Latin America. Terfve charged the Chinese delegates at the Stockholm World Peace Conference with having tried to play off the idea of 'the arming of the colonial and dependent peoples against the communist aim of disarmament'. Between the lines, Terfve also condemned Peking's attempts to 'adjust' the national liberation movement to suit itself and to take over the leadership.[42]

Once again Peking returned to the charge, particularly over the question of disarmament or rearmament of the dependent and colonial peoples. *Jen Min Jih Pao* published an article again stressing the need for more militant policies in the colonial and dependent countries and for the use of methods derived from the Chinese revolution:

'Chairman Mao's writings are carrying more and more weight, and in very many countries people are eagerly studying them in the hope of finding something they can use in their own struggle for liberation . . . To put it bluntly, all oppressed nations and peoples will sooner or later rise in revolt and this is precisely why revolutionary experience and theories will naturally gain currency among such nations and peoples . . . That is why *pamphlets about guerilla warfare in China* enjoy such a wide circulation in Africa, Latin America and Asia, and are looked upon as precious documents, even after they are worn and tattered.'[43]

The main points of dispute in the 'colonial question' had already been clearly indicated and the statements which were published by the Russians and the Chinese later, in particular in the summer of 1963, were no more than a repetition. Nevertheless it is relevant to quote a few passages from one of the more recent documents in which Peking brands the Russians as 'apologists of neo-colonialism'. In the *Fourth Comment on the Open Letter of the Central Committee of the CPSU* by the editorial departments of *Jen Min Jih Pao* and *Hung Ch'i*, published on 22 October 1963, the following statements appear:

'In their words, the leaders of the CPSU dare not completely discard the slogans of support for the national-liberation movement, and at times, for the sake of their own interests, they even take certain measures which create the appearance of support. But if we probe to the essence and consider their views and policies over a number of years, we see clearly that their attitude towards the liberation struggles of the oppressed nations of Asia, Africa and Latin America is a passive or scornful or negative one, and that they serve as apologists for neo-colonialism.

'The leaders of the CPSU have also created the theory that the national-liberation movement has entered upon a "new stage" having economic tasks as its core. Their argument is that, whereas "formerly, the struggle was carried on mainly in the political sphere", today the economic question has become the "central task" and "the basic link in the further development of the revolution".

'The national-liberation movement has entered a new stage. But this is by no means the kind of "new stage" described by the leadership of the CPSU. In the new stage, the level of political consciousness of the Asian, African and Latin American peoples has risen higher than ever and the revolutionary movement is surging forward with unprecedented intensity. They urgently demand the thorough elimination of the forces of imperialism and its lackeys in their own countries and strive for complete political and economic independence. The primary and most urgent task facing these countries is still the further development of the struggle against imperialism, old and new colonialism and their lackeys. This struggle is still being waged fiercely in the political, economic, military, cultural, ideological and other spheres. And the struggles in all these spheres still find their most concentrated expression in political struggle, which often unavoidably develops into armed struggle when the imperialists resort to direct or indirect armed suppression.

'According to this theory of theirs, the fight against imperialism, old and new colonialism and their lackeys is, of course, no longer necessary, for colonialism is disappearing and economic development has become the central task of the national-liberation movement. Does it not follow that the national-liberation movement can be done away with altogether? Therefore the kind of "new stage" described by the leaders of the CPSU, in which economic tasks are in the centre of the picture, is clearly nothing but one of no opposition to imperialism, old and new colonialism, and their lackeys, a stage in which the national-liberation movement is no longer desired.'

The *Fourth Comment* then deals with Moscow's 'nostrums for all the ills of the oppressed nations'. Moscow's theory of 'peaceful co-existence' is attacked and Soviet economic aid to Asia and Africa is belittled; referring to Soviet disarmament proposals the Chinese comment says: 'This is not just the fostering of illusions, it is opium for the people'.

Even more serious are the following accusations:

'Although they talk about supporting the movements and wars of national liberation, the leaders of the CPSU have been trying by every means to make the people of Asia, Africa and Latin America abandon their revolutionary struggle, because they themselves are sorely afraid of the revolutionary storm.

'The leaders of the CPSU have the famous "theory that even a tiny spark can cause a world conflagration" and that a world war must necessarily be a thermonuclear war, which means the annihilation of mankind. Therefore, Khrushchev roars that " 'local wars' in our time are very dangerous", and that "we will work hard . . . to put out the sparks that may set off the flames of war". Here Khrushchev makes no distinction between just and unjust wars and betrays the communist stand of supporting just wars.

'The history of the eighteen years since World War II has shown that wars of national liberation are unavoidable so long as the imperialists and their lackeys try to maintain their brute rule by bayonets and use force to suppress the revolution of oppressed nations. These large-scale and small-scale revolutionary wars against the imperialists and their lackeys, which have never ceased, have hit hard at the imperialist forces of war, strengthened the forces defending world peace and effectively prevented the imperialists from realizing their plan of launching a world war. Frankly speaking, Khrushchev's clamour about the need to "put out" the sparks of revolution for the sake of peace is an attempt to oppose revolution in the name of safeguarding peace.'

Some concrete examples follow to strengthen the Chinese argument and the Soviet attitude to the Algerian war and Russia's policy in the Congo are particularly severely criticized:

'Take the example of the Algerian people's war of national liberation. The leadership of the CPSU not only withheld support for a long period but actually took the side of French imperialism. Khrushchev used to treat Algeria's national independence as an "internal affair" of France. Speaking on the Algerian question on 3 October 1955, he said, "I had and have in view, first of all, that the USSR does not interfere in the internal affairs of other States." Receiving a correspondent of *Le Figaro* on 27 March 1958 he said, "We do not want France to grow weaker, we want her to become still greater".

'To curry favour with the French imperialists, the leaders of the CPSU did not dare to recognize the Provisional Government of the Republic of Algeria for a long time; not until the victory of the Algerian people's war of resistance against French aggression was a foregone conclusion and France was compelled to agree to Algerian independence did they hurriedly recognize the Republic of Algeria. This unseemly attitude brought shame on the socialist countries. Yet the leaders of the CPSU glory in their shame and assert that the victory of the Algerian people paid for with their blood should also be credited to the policy of "peaceful co-existence".

'Again, let us examine the part played by the leaders of the CPSU in the Congo question. Not only did they refuse to give active support to the Congolese people's armed struggle against colonialism, but they were anxious to "co-operate" with US imperialism in putting out the spark in the Congo.

'On 13 July 1960, the Soviet Union joined with the United States in voting for the UN Security Council resolution on the dispatch of UN forces to the Congo; thus it helped the US imperialists to use the flag of the United Nations in their armed intervention in the Congo. The Soviet Union also provided the UN forces with means of transportation. In a cable to Kasavubu and Lumumba on 15 July, Khrushchev said that "the United Nations Security Council has done a useful thing". Thereafter, the Soviet press kept up a stream of praise for the United Nations for "helping the Government of the Congolese Republic to defend the independence and sovereignty of the country", and expressed the hope that the United Nations would adopt "resolute measures". In its statements of 21 August and 10 September, the Soviet Government continued to praise the United Nations, which was suppressing the Congolese people.

'In 1961 the leaders of the CPSU persuaded Gizenga to attend the Congolese parliament, which had been convened under the "protection" of UN troops, and to join the puppet government. The leadership of the CPSU falsely alleged that the convocation of the Congolese parliament was "an important event in the life of the young republic" and "a success of the national forces".

'Clearly these wrong policies of the leadership of the CPSU rendered US imperialism a great service in its aggression against the Congo. Lumumba was murdered, Gizenga was imprisoned, many other patriots were persecuted, and the Congolese struggle for national independence suffered a setback. Does the leadership of the CPSU feel no responsibility for all this?'

The Chinese point of view is then summarized, pointing out that 'the centre of the world contradictions of world political struggles' has shifted; 'Today the national liberation revolutions in Asia, Africa and Latin America are the most important forces dealing imperialism direct blows. The contradictions of the world are concentrated in Asia, Africa and Latin America'.[44]

There is detailed information in the following chapters on the practical policies of the USSR and China and to show that the attitudes of Moscow and Peking to the Third World are very different. It is important to note that what separates the two big communist Powers are irreconcilable differences of principle, but not of the ultimate aims of communist policy, in the under-developed countries. Neither Moscow nor Peking has abandoned the Messianic idea of world revolution and, now as before, both centres of communism relate their practical manoeuvres and operations to their profound eschatological beliefs. However, in the world of political reality, particularly in the world of communist reality, working methods can sometimes, even for long periods, take on a greater importance than objectives governed by matters of principle.

Soviet policy in Asia and Africa reflects the profound transformation of outlook and of the social system that has taken place in the Soviet Union. The result of these changes is that ideology counts for less in Soviet politics and in the behaviour of Soviet politicians. After forty years of a pragmatic domestic and foreign policy, the revolutionary core of the November Revolution has crumbled. The extension of Soviet imperialist power and the tremendous economic accumulation that has taken place in the Soviet Union have given rise to new strata of bureaucrats, technicians, skilled workmen, etc., and have led to the increasing adoption of 'bourgeois' ways of life; a state of affairs that is also reflected in the foreign policy of the Soviet Government. To pursue any kind of revolutionary (that is orthodox Marxist) policy at the moment would involve the risk of losing everything that has been gained, as it would provoke counter-action by the enemy. In the present stage of military development this risk would exist even if revolutionary policies were confined to peripheral zones. Even a local conflict, in Laos, in the Congo, or in any of the other trouble spots in Asia or Africa, could rapidly escalate into a global catastrophe.[45]

Secondly, because of this danger and because of the changed attitude of its rulers, the policy of the Soviet Union *vis-à-vis* the under-developed countries is, for the time being, not conditioned by any fundamental or specifically communist doctrine of social and national liberation, but seeks only to exploit the national-revolutionary movement empirically and opportunistically for its own ends. The domestic interests of the workers and peasants in these countries, who are allegedly represented by the communists, are secondary to the interests of the Soviet Union. At present the Soviet Union wants allies rather than proselytes and in this way hopes, for example, to weaken the West and strengthen the communist front in the United Nations. Such allies would take up a pro-Soviet (but not necessarily pro-communist) attitude. Soviet policy therefore seeks co-operation not so much with the embryonic communist movements in these countries as with their ruling classes, and the Russians seek to woo the existing régimes in Asia and Africa by giving them economic assistance. This new policy is clearly reflected in the Soviet attitude towards Iraq, India, Indonesia, the

United Arab Republic, Morocco, Ethiopia, Liberia and other independent countries. However, two qualifications are necessary: (a) this new line does not change the ultimate Soviet aim, which is still world communism; the young intelligentsia in the new countries, the third generation of the liberation movement, are still to be won over ideologically; (b) where régimes with left-wing tendencies exist, the Soviet Union naturally does not try to slow down the less social-revolutionary process. On the contrary, it invariably does its utmost to give it new impulse and to guide it into the desired revolutionary channels. Ghana, Guinea and Zanzibar are the best examples of this policy.

Thirdly, the Chinese communists, unlike their Soviet colleagues, are still unconditionally wedded to a revolutionary policy and to revolutionary tactics. Unlike the Soviet Union, China is not highly industrialized, and there is no comfortable neo-bourgeois stratum likely to inquire anxiously about the risks involved in important decisions. For twenty-eight years before coming to power the Chinese communists had to wage a constant war against both internal and external enemies. On two occasions during those years, from 1923 to 1927 and again in 1936, the Soviet Government exercised intense pressure on the Chinese communists to persuade them to enter into an alliance with Chiang Kai-shek, the leader of the Chinese bourgeoisie. The tangible result of this policy imposed by the Soviet communists was political disaster for the Chinese Communist Party, and its recovery was slow and difficult. It is understandable therefore that Mao Tse-tung is not greatly enamoured of strategy and tactics which in the past brought him to the verge of total destruction on two separate occasions.

In accordance with Maoism, China therefore prefers to support and encourage the communist forces, the predestined instruments of the revolutionary process, in the under-developed countries. The Chinese Communist Party is firmly convinced that its policy is correct because it believes it can see fundamental similarities between the social and economic situation of Africa and of pre-communist China. From this it concludes that complete decolonization is the first stage towards the establishment of a revolutionary socialist system in Africa and that this can be achieved only with the same *methods of violence* that proved so successful in China.

Finally, because of this Peking has developed a completely original programme of its own for 'the Eastern peoples'. This programme differs radically from Moscow's long-term proposals and seeks to bring about the eventual communist seizure of power in Africa and the establishment of a society of the Chinese communist pattern.

NOTES

[1] Pravda, 22 October 1947.
[2] World Marxist Review, II, No. 9 (September 1959), p. 72.
[3] Cf. Bolshaya Sovietskaya Entsiklopaediya (2nd ed.; Moscow, 1952), X, p. 203.
[4] Ibid., XV, p. 460.
[5] Sovietskoye vostokovodenye, Nos 5-6 (1955).
[6] World Marxist Review, II, No. 8 (August 1959), p. 66.
[7] Proceedings of the Twentieth Congress of the Communist Party of the Soviet Union, Current Digest of the Soviet Press, VIII, No. 10 (18 April 1956), p. 24.
[8] Ibid., VIII, No. 7 (28 March 1956), p. 20.
[9] World Marxist Review, II, No. 9 (September 1959), p. 68.
[10] Report of the conference in Mezhdunarodnaya Zhisn (Moscow), No. 3 (1959).
[11] Ibid.
[12] Pravda, 22 January 1957.
[13] Ibid., 6 December 1960.
[14] Kommunist (Moscow), No. 12 (1960).
[15] Mezhdunarodnaya Zhisn, No. 3 (1959).
[16] Asiya i Africa segodniya (Moscow), No. 9 (1961).
[17] Einheit ([East] Berlin), No. 11/12 (1961).
[18] Izvestia, 2 November 1961.
[19] Pravda, 1 November 1961.
[20] 'For A Lasting Peace. For A People's Democracy!' Bucharest, 27 January 1950.
[21] Ibid. Cf. Politika (Belgrade), 5 August 1951.
[22] Quoted from Mao Tse-tung and Liu Shao-chi, Lessons of the Chinese Revolution (Bombay, 1950).
[23] Liu Shao-chi, On the Party (Peking, 1954), p. 15.
[24] Ibid.
[25] Ibid.
[26] Ibid.
[27] Ibid.

[28] Ibid.

[29] Originally published in the Cominform journal; quoted here from A. M. Halpern, 'The Foreign Policy Uses of the Chinese Revolutionary Model', *The China Quarterly*, No. 7 (July-September 1961).

[30] Arthur A. Cohen, 'How Original is "Maoism"?', *Problems of Communism*, x, No. 6 (November-December 1961).

[31] Mao Tse-tung, *Selected Works* (New York, 1954), I, p. 304, n. 7.

[32] *Yen-min Yih-pao*, 10 December 1961.

[33] *Pravda*, 8 August 1960.

[34] *Daily Telegraph* (London), 31 August 1960.

[35] New China News Agency, 2 November 1960.

[36] Ibid.

[37] *Peking Review*, No. 51 (1961).

[38] Ibid., No. 52 (1961).

[39] 'Chinese Influence in the AAPSO', *The Interpreter* (London), March 1962.

[40] Ibid.

[41] *Zeri i Popullit*, 9 January 1962; quoted in *Ostprobleme* (Bonn), XIV, No. 6.

[42] *Le Drapeau Rouge* (Brussels), 5-17 January 1962.

[43] *Yen-min Yih-pao*, 10 December 1961.

[44] *Peking Review*, No. 43 (25 October 1963).

[45] Referring to this situation, the prominent Russian military expert Major General Talensky wrote in October 1960 in *Mezhdunarodnaya Zhisn* that even local wars had now become 'impossible' because there was always a dangerous tendency for them to escalate into world catastrophes. In consequence, the dictum of Clausewitz that 'war is the continuation of politics by other means' had lost its validity; modern warfare had become suicidal and therefore nonsensical.

Chapter VI

THE POLITICAL USES
OF AFRICAN STUDIES

IN the summer of 1920, at the Second Congress of the Communist International 'the colonial question' was for the first time discussed in principle, theoretically analysed and linked up with the world-revolutionary ideas and aims of Moscow. However zealously the delegates sought to clarify their standpoint and to arrive at a general practical plan of operations for Asia and Africa, they invariably found themselves grappling with a serious weakness in their position: their inadequate and inaccurate knowledge of the history, conditions and possibilities of Africa and Asia, while the little they did know was strongly coloured by wishful thinking.

That kind of vagueness and confusion in the communist camp no longer exists today. On the contrary, if the West were to try to understand and judge Soviet African policy today by the criteria of the early 1920s, when it was a highly theoretical affair based largely on illusions and ignorance, they would be guilty of short-sighted optimism and fatal smugness. The truth is that the Soviet offensive in Africa today is the most powerful attempt of any non-African power to secure a dominating influence over the development of the awakening black continent and to determine its future economic, political, social and cultural pattern. The ideological framework of communist actions in Africa is more than the general colonial-revolutionary theory worked out from 1918 to 1928 and further developed since 1955. It is based on very thorough research and analysis of the essential factors of African politics, economics, society, linguistics and culture. For years now hundreds of Soviet experts, working together with agents in the satellite countries, have been intensively engaged in exploring the political topography and in keeping up to date with the changes taking place. The results of their labours are harnessed to political aims and used for communist purposes. Soviet African studies play a special role in this general framework: they provide the basic material on which Soviet plans in Africa rest.

The decisive point in Soviet Africa policy was reached at the Twentieth Congress of the Communist Party of the Soviet Union which met in February 1956. In a self-critical mood, this congress recognized that a tremendous amount of energy was being generated and dissipated in the colonial and former colonial territories, particularly in Africa. Furthermore, it was realized that this energy was directed towards an independent process of emancipation over which communism exercised only marginal influence. Characteristically, the leading politicians were exonerated from all blame for Soviet errors and failures. Otto Kuusinen, the Finn, and Anastas Mikoyan, the Armenian, blamed the experts for the failure to intervene in this process earlier. Mikoyan declared mockingly: 'The Academy of Sciences does have an institute that studies the problems of the East, but all that can be said of it is that although in our day the whole East has awakened, this institute is still dozing. Isn't it time for it to rise to the level of current requirements?'[1]

Up to this time Soviet African studies certainly had been rather isolated from practical politics. The number of original works published was very small. Although a centre of African studies, under the direction of Professor Olderogge, had existed at the Ethnographical Institute of the University of Leningrad since 1946 and although there had been a joint research programme with the Moscow Africanist Professor Ivan Potekhin since 1949, the activities of the few experts on Africa were dull and academic—not that they differed greatly from their Western colleagues in this respect! However, after the Twentieth Party Congress there was a change: men from other branches of research were brought in while still others were newly trained in this field. The rather generalized view of Africa was now rapidly consolidated by increasing specialization. For example, North Africa was handed over to special oriental institutes, whilst black or Negro Africa became the sphere of the ethnographical departments of the Academy of Sciences; for special political aspects there was now a special Moscow Institute for Oriental Studies. Finally, in 1959, an independent Africa Institute was founded at the Academy of Sciences under the directorship of Professor Potekhin, so that Moscow now has a sound organizational framework for intensive study of African subjects. In February 1957 the first big research programme was drawn up. This programme had three main objectives:

1. An objective analysis of economic, social, ethnographical, cultural and linguistic problems relating to Africa with a view to providing the appropriate party and government departments with reliable, unbiased material on which to base their decisions;

2. A Marxist-Leninist interpretation of both the historical and present-day problems of Africa in order to allow the development of general communist theory and in particular of communist propaganda in Africa on a 'scientific' plane;

3. The drafting of Marxist-Leninist solutions to offer to the African élite in a way calculated to convince them of their logic and effectiveness.

The programme thus represents an intimate combination of objective scientific ideas with politically determined objectives and demonstrates graphically the important *political* role now being played by Soviet African studies in the formulation of foreign policies. Unlike African studies in the West, Soviet African studies are centrally controlled and governed by a uniform political approach (and, as we shall show later, this is so not only in the Soviet Union but also in the other countries of the Soviet bloc). Although there is good reason to doubt the scientific objectivity of some aspects of these studies, there can certainly be no doubt about the enormous advantages of this concentration of effort; the West would be well advised to take these activities very seriously indeed.

The Kremlin has never attempted to deny that the real aim of their African studies is political. Professor Gafurov, Director of the Moscow Oriental Institute, points out in an article[2] that in view of the 'growing political and world economic importance of Africa' the aim of his institute is 'to publish works of importance for the educational institutions and *government departments* engaged in the practical tasks in the East'. A little later another Russian publication stated: 'Our Orientalists regard it as a distinction to publish collections, monographs, pamphlets, articles, etc., whose content can be creatively utilized by *Soviet foreign policy* in its operations in the Eastern countries.'[3]

Similar statements have been repeatedly made by the late Professor Potekhin; what he said is particularly worthy of note as there was no one who personified the double task of communist African studies better than he. Professor Potekhin was not only director of the Moscow Africa Institute, he was also chairman of the Soviet Society for the Furtherance of Friendship with the Peoples of Africa, a member of the Soviet Committee for Solidarity with the Afro-Asian Peoples, and chief adviser to the Soviet Foreign Ministry on all African affairs. In an English-language broadcast to Africa, Potekhin, who died in 1964, declared:

'[Soviet] scientists concern themselves closely with all the new phenomena of the African historical process, such as the collapse of the colonial system, the rise of new States, the growing importance of Africa in world economics and world politics, the development of national [African] economic systems and a national African culture in those countries which have freed themselves from colonial oppression.'

Writing in *Izvestia*, Potekhin declared that his Africa Institute would

'deal with a wide range of problems directly connected with the struggle of the African peoples for independence, for emancipation from the chains of imperialism, and for the formation of sovereign independent States ... The activity of the institute will support the extension and consolidation of friendly relations between the Soviet Union and the countries of Africa, while at the same time acquainting the Soviet people more closely with the history and culture of the African continent, which is now advancing vigorously towards complete emancipation from the yoke of the imperialist colonialists.'[5]

Such a frank and outspoken admission of Soviet aims and motives should not, however, deceive the West into regarding Soviet African studies as a mere adjunct of Soviet political activities. Since the death of Stalin, it has progressively emancipated itself from this subordinate role and although it is true that even today Soviet science can hardly be separated from Soviet political objectives, nevertheless in recent years a reciprocal relationship has developed between science and politics in the Soviet Union. To give an example: the gradual rehabilitation of the national bourgeoisie and the more moderate and objective view now held of the embryonic working class in Africa were both to a large extent due to the recommendation of African specialists. A number of studies made it clear to the Soviet political leadership how weak the actual proletariat was, and still is, in Africa, whereas already after the Second World War Stalin was banking on their support. When Professor Potekhin wrote his contribution on Africa in the *Great Soviet Encyclopaedia* of 1950, he was still hamstrung by the stereotyped sterile formulae of classic Stalinism which permitted no deviation. As late as 1953 the essential Stalinist theses were formally repeated in a general work on 'The Imperialist Struggle for Africa, and the National-Revolutionary Emancipation Movement of the African Peoples'. But even this work pointed out that the national bourgeoisie, and even some tribal chiefs, were supporting the anti-imperialist united front. Earlier still, in October 1952, a Soviet periodical[6] published a devastating criticism by A. Orlova of S. Datlin's book, *Afrika podigom imperialisma* (*Africa under the Yoke of Imperialism*) a Stalinist work which had previously always been described as 'a masterpiece of Soviet African studies'. A typical passage of this criticism reads:

'It is also questionable whether the author has judged the role of the working class accurately. He is quite right when he says that the importance of the working class for the liberation movement of the African peoples is steadily growing, but it must not be forgotten that numerically the working class in Africa is *very weak* by comparison with the population as a whole, and that it is *very poorly organized*. Communist parties exist only in the French North-African colonies. Only a very small percentage of the proletariat is organized in trade unions. For example, in Madagascar, where the proletariat numbers 230,000, including 48,000 industrial workers, only 12,000 are members of trade unions.'

Writings of this kind contain an indirect but clear warning to the Soviet political leaders, and to those in charge of propaganda, not to rely exclusively on class conflicts nor to concentrate excessively on the class situation in Africa and to reconsider the role of the non-proletarian, anti-colonial forces. This warning was repeated after Stalin's death and in February 1955 was couched, for the first time, in quite unmistakable terms when the Soviet periodical *Sovietskoya*

Vostokovedenia analysed 'the anti-imperialist movement on the Gold Coast' (Ghana). Writing in the same periodical in January 1956, shortly before the Twentieth Congress of the Communist Party of the Soviet Union, Professor Potekhin frankly admitted the existence of a vigorous, all-national, liberation movement in Africa. For the first time he stressed the role of the African middle classes, and he no longer used the usual barren Stalinist formulae. He pointed out that the colonialists were seeking to win over the middle classes in the hope of creating a stabilizing factor which would preserve their own power; but he went on to say that the political aims of the national bourgeoisie drove them, willy-nilly, to the side of the people and that this transformed them objectively into an anti-imperialist force. This was the prologue to the astonishing change of tactics introduced at the Twentieth Party Congress. It was the cue for the new, more discriminating and elastic policy Moscow now put into operation in Africa.

In a number of ethnographical, linguistic and historical studies published in recent years similar, perhaps even greater, independence has been noticeable. Olderogge's work *The West Sudan from the Fifteenth to the Nineteenth Century*, which finally appeared in 1960, though it had been publicized a long time in advance, is said by Western experts to be, in many respects, highly expert and scientifically sound. The book is well documented, contains a number of facsimiles of ancient documents, some of them previously unknown, translations from the Hausa language, and so on. There are also a number of detailed and largely objective ethnographical maps of Africa, collections from Arab sources on the history of black Africa and, of course, from dictionaries and grammars of a number of the more modern African languages. Many Soviet works in this field cannot be denied their scientific seriousness. A number of works by Olderogge and (with some qualifications) Potekhin are of interest and value to Western students of Africa.

On the other hand, when they set out to provide an interpretation of social phenomena such works are completely subordinated to the general political objectives of communism. Even linguistic problems cannot always be treated with complete objectivity. For example, the Soviet periodical *Problemy vostokovedenia* writes: 'Our linguists must always remember that though their research work might at first glance seem to be quite abstract it should nevertheless aim to facilitate the struggle of the Eastern peoples against colonialism and its ideology.'

A case in point is the attitude of Soviet experts to the multi-language problem of Africa. According to them this is not a natural development, but was created artificially by (guess who?) 'the imperialists and colonialists'. With their policy of *divide et impera* and their colonial ideology, the imperialists, 'for obvious reasons', first created these great cultural divisions, isolation and language difficulties between the individual tribes.[7]

We have now arrived at a subject which is exercising the minds of Soviet Africanists, namely the rewriting of African history. Potekhin dealt with this problem in an interview published in *Izvestia*:

'Progressive scholars now have a very complicated but valuable task to perform, namely the writing of the *real* history of the century-old struggle of the African peoples . . . This is all the more important because the history of the African peoples has been distorted to the point of unrecognizability by bourgeois historians. In the works of the majority of the bourgeois historians the development of the African peoples is represented as a very small section of the histories of Great Britain, France, Belgium and other Western European powers. You will look in vain in such histories for any description of the obstinate and protracted struggle of the African peoples against the colonialists.'

In another contribution (the Moscow radio broadcast of 14 November 1959) Potekhin gave some idea of Soviet motives in these efforts to rewrite African history:

'The names of countries which existed in the Middle Ages are now beginning to reappear on the political maps of Africa. Gold Coast Colony, only a little while ago under British rule, is now Ghana, having adopted the name of one of these States. The Mali Federation was named after another. All this indicates that the peoples of Africa are becoming much more interested in their own history. They are properly proud of their own past and are anxious to know more about it . . . Up to the present, it is true that almost nothing has been done to study the history of the former mediaeval States of Ghana and Mali . . . There is, therefore, all the more reason why we should now make a serious study of the mediaeval epoch in Africa.'

Thus it is clear that the Russians are interested in rather more than a Marxist-Leninist interpretation of ancient Africa, because if its inquiries in this respect were strictly circumscribed by the canons of historical materialism they would arrive at a devastating denigration of the mediaeval epoch, whose social structure, being feudal, was (according to Marxist ideas), uncompromisingly hostile to progress. The real purpose of the new interpretation, as pointed out in a number of leading Soviet periodicals, is to serve the needs of Soviet foreign policy, which is anxious to exploit the historical consciousness of the nationalist élite. Hence the attempts to persuade this élite to accept the results of Soviet research. Similar motives are behind the demands of Potekhin, and other Soviet experts, for the rewriting of nineteenth-century African history. The first conference of Soviet African experts, which took place in February 1957, established two principles to facilitate this task:

1. The general heinousness of 'imperialist conquest, division and rule in Africa' must be constantly exposed in all its details and it must also be stressed that the so-called civilizing work of colonization was more apparent than real.

2. The revolts and insurrections against the colonists must be closely studied, presented *in extenso* and 'in harmony with the present-day national liberation movement'.

In 1957 certain subjects were chosen for full treatment. They included the Berlin Conference of 1894–5, Anglo-German rivalry in East Africa, the struggle of the Zulus and the Xhosas against British and Boer colonization, the struggle of the Matabele and the Mashona against the subjugation of Rhodesia. Some of these studies have since appeared and they have been supplemented by descriptions of the revolts in Tanganyika, Dahomey, Ghana, the Cameroons and other parts of Africa. Here too, as the texts indicate, the authors have been guided by the same motives that led to Soviet attempts to rewrite the history of Africa in the Middle Ages: Africans are to be persuaded that they have a glorious past characterized in particular by a ceaseless, heroic struggle first against feudalism and then against colonialism and, what is more important from the Soviet point of view, they are to be persuaded that only progressive Soviet scholars are able and willing to reveal this history to them.

The 1957 conference also planned a third group of research tasks under the heading, 'Africa's ethnic composition'. Two special problems were underlined:

1. African frontiers as they exist today were arbitrarily drawn by the colonial powers and are in contradiction to the natural settlement areas of the African peoples. Present-day African States are therefore multi- or part-national States which must be reorganized. These results of Soviet African studies comply to a remarkable degree with the demands of the Africans themselves, for example, with a resolution of the First All-Africa People's Conference in Accra in December 1958. Section 3 of that resolution on frontiers and federations declares:

'the artificial barriers and frontiers created by imperialism in order to carve up the African peoples must be abolished and re-examined . . . Frontiers which cut through the settlement area of any particular ethnic group, or which separate people of the same origin, are unnatural, and their maintenance can never lead to peace and stable conditions'.

The magazine *Sovietskaya etnografia* seized on this resolution to point out triumphantly that Soviet ethnographical scholars had already paid special attention to this problem, and that in order to show how ethnic groups had been separated by unnatural frontiers, the frontier demarcation in a number of areas had been especially studied—for example, in Kenya, Tanganyika, the Belgian Congo, South-West Africa, the Central African Federation, Angola, Mozambique and Nigeria. The periodical concluded that Soviet research offered a reliable basis for discussion of the more complex problems relating to the formation of African nations.

The *Bulletin of the Institute for the Study of the USSR* published an article by G. A. von Stackelberg on this point:

'The contention that the colonial frontiers of present-day Africa were arbitrarily drawn is of great practical importance to the Soviets. The obvious discrepancies between present-day political frontiers and ethnic lines of demarcation in Africa allow the Soviets to put forward the slogan of the unification of Africa on an ethnographical basis and thus to intervene in the internal affairs of the African countries. Present-day Soviet policy is to encourage the ex-colonial countries to unite within the framework of larger State structures. The formation of such bigger States with a central government could make it easier for pro-communist elements to take over and thus strengthen Soviet influence in Africa.'[9]

On the other hand, the formation of smaller States must necessarily, in Moscow's view, hamper the activity of pro-Soviet parties and trade unions and favour anti-communist elements. The Soviet periodical *Problemy vostokovedenia* also takes this view: 'The existence of a large number of single parties and the lack of unity between them weakens the anti-colonial front and prevents the establishment of a united front.'[10]

In contradiction to the classic maxim *divide et impera* the maxim of Soviet communist imperialism today is *unifica et impera*—unite and rule. Soviet foreign policy has sought to realize this conception both in the Congo, where from the start the Soviets backed the centralist group, and in the Cameroons, where—in the hope that in this way the extremist *Union des Populations du Cameroun* would be strengthened by amalgamation with the Cameroun Party—they came out in favour of a unification of the British and French mandate territories. All this despite the fact that even the *Great Soviet Encyclopaedia* had previously admitted the very great ethnic differences which still exist in the Congo territory today. The 1953 edition declared: 'The independent development of nationalities and States in the Congo area was violently interrupted in the fifteenth century by the arrival of European colonists.' If Soviet politicians see advantages in the large, centralized State, then quite clearly history must be rewritten to give support to this view. Potekhin and other Soviet experts carried out this task with great aplomb. Their present 'nationalities' ideology for Africa includes a theory of the development of the tribes (*plemeni*) into peoples (*narody*) and of peoples into nations (*natsii*). This last stage, it is pointed out, has not yet been reached everywhere, but it is an historical necessity which the African peoples will be unable to prevent. They once again argue that a linguistically united nation is a *sine qua non* for the political consciousness necessary for such supra-States. The areas involved in these calculations are indicated by Potekhin's reference to the

Nilotic peoples, whose settlement area extends from the Sudan over the former Belgian Congo, Uganda, and Kenya. It is not claimed that these groups already represent a united people, but it is pointed out that the Nilotic languages form a single stock of words and that three of them have an identical grammatical structure. This is apparently sufficient reason for Potekhin to conclude: 'it is by no means impossible that, given favourable circumstances, the Nilotic peoples will be in a position to form themselves into one united national people.'[11] For similar reasons the philological department has devoted itself for years now to the more widespread African languages such as Swahili, which is at least a trading and bartering medium for millions of people in East and Central Africa, and to Hausa, which is widespread in parts of West Africa. Treatment of the tribal problem has been guided by the same *arrière pensée*, with the result that the structure and behaviour of African tribal society has come in for some severe criticism. The campaign against tribalism began with the publication of a monograph, *The Peoples of Africa (Narody Afriki)*, in Moscow in 1954. Since then there has been a systematic, pseudo-scientific campaign to denigrate the idea of tribalism while the colonial powers are accused of having deliberately preserved tribal structures, tribal consciousness and tribal rituals 'in order to prevent the awakening of the African masses' or, at least, to delay and hamper it. A Moscow radio broadcast in English,[12] prepared by Soviet African experts, declared:

'One of the [negative] phenomena is tribalism, which stands in no relationship to the present stage of development of African society, and hampers natural progress. With the rise of the struggle for liberation the interest of the African in his past has naturally increased, but certain African leaders are now taking up a wrong attitude in this respect: they talk of a particular "African way of life", and say that it has developed on the basis of tribalism and the leadership of the tribal chiefs. In fact, they go even further, and declare that the tribes, the tribal chiefs, and tribal relations in general are an integral part of this "African way of life". This conclusion is due to a lack of insight into the laws of social development . . . Tribalism plays into the hands of colonialism . . . The tribal structure is so conservative and reactionary that it serves only anti-popular objectives.'

The frequent quoting of remarks by young, progressive Africans, who have allegedly recognized the hampering effect of tribalism and condemned it as 'a hindrance to social, economic and technical progress', clearly reveals the objectives of this 'scientific' propaganda. By attempting to establish a direct connection between tribalism and reactionary colonialism, it is hoped to awaken the resentment of young Africans and persuade them to destroy the integrating factors of African community life. The violent breaking-up of the existing social order in Africa and the social anarchy which results (a process which has already reached an explosive stage in the towns of West and Central Africa) favour those extremist tendencies in Africa which make for communism. How far this 'scientific' propaganda campaign against 'the remnants of feudalism and colonialism' has already gone can be seen from the growing number of Soviet attempts to denigrate Christianity as a non-African ideology. A symposium, entitled 'Problems of the History of Religions and Atheism' ('Voprossy istorii religii i ateisma'), and the Soviet periodicals *Sovietskaya etnografia* and *Voprossy vostokovedenia*, as well as Radio Moscow in its broadcasts to Africa, all deal exhaustively with the role of the Christian missions in Africa, and everything possible is done to create the impression that 'the chains of religion' fasten Africa 'to imperialism and backwardness'.

This investigation of certain aspects of the aims and methods of Soviet African studies leads to the following conclusions:

1. Soviet African studies are part of Moscow's political-propaganda programme for Africa. Its task is to provide an ideological and scientific-theoretical basis for Soviet policy in Africa.

2. At the same time it has a practical objective: by interpreting the past and present structure and consciousness of African society in the spirit of extreme African nationalism, to demonstrate the identity of its own views with those of the African élite—unlike similar studies in the West, which try to maintain high standards of objectivity.

3. It is intended to achieve the gradual indoctrination of the African élite with the ideas, formulations, and assumptions of dialectical and historical materialism, thus securing their ideological commitment to communism. As they are well aware of the importance of history and national aspirations as integrating factors in the development of political consciousness and national feeling, the

communists hope that this 'thorough, basic and scientific, cultural offensive' will sooner or later have the desired political effect.

NOTES

[1] *Current Digest of the Soviet Press*, VIII, No. 8 (4 April 1956), p. 10.
[2] In *Voprossi istorii*, No. 5 (1958).
[3] *Problemy vostokovedenia*, No. 1 (1959).
[4] Radio Moscow broadcast, 14 November 1959.
[5] *Izvestia*, 24 January 1960.
[6] *Sovietskaya etnografia*, No. 10 (1952).
[7] *Problemy vostokovodenia*, No. 1 (1959).
[8] *Izvestia*, 24 January 1960.
[9] *Bulletin of the Institute for the Study of the USSR* (Munich), No. 9 (1960).
[10] *Problemy vostokovodenia*, No.
[11] *Sovietskaya etnografia*, No. 4 (1957).
[12] Radio Moscow broadcast, 2 July 1960.

Chapter VII

THE OVERTURE:
FRIENDSHIP AND CO-EXISTENCE

THE ideological foundations of Soviet African policy of the Soviet Government were laid quite early and a systematic study of African affairs in the Soviet Union also began some time ago, but practical action, including political activity, diplomacy, propaganda, infiltration, economic and cultural contacts have a comparatively short history. There were certainly tentative attempts to infiltrate and form cadres as early as the twenties. The organizational instruments for this early Soviet activity were chiefly the Communist Party of Great Britain, the Communist Party of France, and one or two front organizations such as the International Union of Seamen and Dockers. But as both the Comintern and Profintern (the communist international trade union organization) repeatedly admitted, these attempts were very patchy; and in the last resort met with little success. The first efforts made after the Second World War were no more successful. The French Communist Party had proved itself incapable of exploiting the really big opportunity for successful communist activity and propaganda that existed in French-speaking Africa; the collapse of the *Rassemblement Démocratique Africain*, which was temporarily connected with the French Communist Party, and the spectacular defection of such prominent party supporters as Félix Houphouet-Boigny and Gabriel d'Arboussier spelt the collapse of the high hopes which Moscow had cherished with regard to French-speaking Africa. In the year of Stalin's death such vague Soviet hopes as still existed were pinned chiefly on a racial clash in the Union of South Africa and on the Mau-Mau movement in Kenya.[1]

Unconfirmed reports, zealously spread by some Western correspondents concerning 'communist intrigues' and 'powerful Soviet influence' in these areas turned out on closer examination to be little more than propaganda designed to compromise the independence movement of the coloured peoples by presenting it as a communist conspiracy. In the two or three years following the death of Stalin the men in the Kremlin were chiefly exercised by the ferment in the Near and Middle East, and it was not until Ghana and Guinea achieved their independence that Soviet interest in African nationalism was fully aroused. In fact it is only from this period onwards that one can talk of any really large-scale communist operations south of the Sahara. But it was only in 1959–60, on the eve of the radical changes in the political map of Africa, that after careful consideration and after studying the methods most likely to lead to success and making tentative approaches to the new Powers on the African continent, the Soviet Union really launched its African policy. The new departure was accompanied by a flood of pro-African declarations and publications and by personnel changes in two important Soviet diplomatic posts in Africa. On 12 October 1959 A. V. Budakov, who until then had been chief of the African Department of the Soviet Foreign Ministry, was appointed Ambassador Extraordinary to the Court at Addis Ababa, and on 2 January 1960, D. S. Solod, one of the best-known Orientalists of the Soviet Foreign Ministry, was appointed Soviet Ambassador to the new Republic of Guinea.

These appointments clearly indicated the scope of the forthcoming Soviet political offensive in Africa and demonstrated the special interest in Ethiopia and Guinea, two States fundamentally different in history, social structure, political outlook, and background. In fact, one might almost have been forgiven for supposing that co-operation and friendly relationships with one would have ruled out similar relations with the other. Soviet engagement in Ethiopia, for example, would be bound to call the honesty of Moscow's ambitions in Guinea into question. The dilemma was obvious and more than one naïve observer of the Soviet Union's African policy underlined this fact, questioning how the Soviet Government could, on the one hand, woo the feudalist ruler of a backward country and, on the other, make advances to the progressive leader of a quasi-socialist State. But obviously what the Soviet Government had in mind, with the appointment of two such prominent diplomats as Budakov and Solod, was an attempt to reconcile the apparently irreconcilable, to look both right and left, and to seek success in both directions. From the beginning, therefore, the Soviet Government was determined to allow no dogmatic rigidity to hamper its African policy. The friendly relationships with both Guinea and Ethiopia were intended to demonstrate the earnestness of the Soviet efforts to establish friendly relations with all the countries of Africa, whatever their social structures.

Neither Ethiopia nor Guinea offered ideal conditions for *direct* revolutionary activity. However, for the time being Soviet policy in Africa had to take three important negative factors into account, and the Soviet failure in the Congo underlined this:

1. The upheaval in Africa and its transformation from a mere object of colonial exploitation to a world-political force, particularly its scope and its speed, took the communists by surprise. As a result they were unprepared and not able to take advantage of the situation to obtain a firm foothold from the start.

2. Whereas most of the Asiatic countries had professional revolutionary élites or cadres trained in various countries of the Soviet bloc, and communism had become a traditional element in the political life of many such countries, Africa almost completely lacked organized communists. (Apart from Basutoland, where a communist party was founded in 1962, and Nigeria where a communist party was founded in November 1963, there were no communist parties in tropical Africa till the end of 1964, though in Senegal there is, for what it was worth, the crypto-communist PAI, whose influence has been confined to a small number of young intellectuals and in Cameroon the UPC.)

3. The infiltration by communists from outside, whether as diplomats or 'experts', their intervention in internal affairs, as in the Congo, or their support of guerilla groups, as in Cameroon, involved the risk of revealing to the Africans the real power-political objectives of the Soviet Union and rightly being regarded by them as a *direct* threat.

This review of the situation persuaded the Kremlin to adopt a different line, though one hardly less menacing to Africa in the long run. Guinea and Ethiopia were chosen as experimental fields for this, a long-term programme of infiltration and a demonstration of co-existence. In the first phase of this new policy (up to the middle of 1961), Soviet activity in Guinea was not greatly different from Soviet activity in Ethiopia. In Guinea, where communists found the ruling group and a great part of the youth psychologically and ideologically receptive to socialism, and where there were also very favourable opportunities for contacts with other extremist groups in Africa (especially of Cameroon and Angola), it was possible to eliminate the *first stage* of Soviet operations and aim more directly at the ultimate objective. Before long similar opportunities emerged in Ghana and Mali but on the whole they were, nevertheless, still very restricted, and the Kremlin therefore had to recognize that ideologically, Africa as a whole was still not ready to accept communism. This meant going through a *preliminary stage*. Ethiopia is a classic example of the strategy and tactics of this stage. It is an example of a grotesquely involved dialectical performance such as only Marxist-Leninists can put up when called upon to provide the theoretical justification for a policy which does not remotely fit into the pattern of their revolutionary ideas and principles. The party line first appeared in the controlled Press of the Soviet Union and the satellites. To take communist newspaper articles at their face value one might have supposed that ideal social and political conditions existed under Haile Selassie, 'The Lion of Judah', in a State which first arose in the early days of Christianity and which established Christianity as the State religion three hundred years later under the legendary King Azana. This State flourished until it broke up in the eighteenth century and was reconstituted on two occasions, after British pacification and after Italian occupation under Mussolini. Even the attempt to overthrow the régime in December 1960 did not stop the Press in the communist countries from continuing to praise the deeds of the Negus, while deliberately ignoring everything that did not fit in with their image. The fact that 'the progressive ruler' (Moscow Radio's description of the Negus) was doing little or nothing to encourage the development of his people, that one third of the arable land of Ethiopia was owned by the Coptic Church, while other big estates were still administered by the *Gultenya*, the Amharic landlords, 'under the auspices of the Crown'; that apart from 3–4 million Amharic tribesmen all the rest of Ethiopia's about twenty million people were without rights—all these and many other evils hardly existed for the communist Press, which was too busy criticizing evils in 'the reactionary West' to waste time on the evils in the 'progressive East'.

In the circumstances this paradoxical situation deserves more than summary treatment. In June 1960 an East German correspondent travelled through Ethiopia. The fruits of this journalistic visit were not, however, published until January 1961, a time when the events which had led to the serious political crisis and *putsch* against Haile Selassie in December 1960 were causing very frank discussion in the Western world about the deplorable aspects of his feudal policy. In a series of five articles entitled 'Journey into the Legendary Land of Ethiopia', the correspondent painted quite a different picture for his readers. As his reports enable us to draw certain conclusions about the domestic situation in Ethiopia and are an illustration of the methods of communist propaganda in Africa, a few quotations will not be out of place.

'Present-day Ethiopia is certainly a feudal State. It is ruled by the Negus Haile Selassie I, who, according to State tradition, is the 255th ruler of the Salomonic line, the "Lions of Judah". However, in forming a judgement on African social structure, caution is to be recommended. First of all, we must remember that many African republics have no more than a narrow bourgeois strip along the coast while their hinterlands are still way back in the feudal and even pre-feudal ages. For example, the Nigerians are ruled by the party of the Sultan of Sokoto (one of the biggest Fullani emirs to the south of the Sahara). And secondly, the Negus was not only one of the first anti-imperialist fighters and leaders of Africa, and one of the first victims of fascist preparations for war, but he is also a man who, despite tradition and dynastic outlook, is determined to lead his country out of the feudal middle ages into a bourgeois Africa of our own day.'

The following passages are even more interesting, completely ignoring the difference which existed between the wording of the constitution and its application in practice. The communist journalist describes what he regards as five 'particular advantages' of Haile Selassie's policy and administration.

'1. When he came to the throne in 1930 he introduced a constitution, and its provisions were extended in 1955 to include the general franchise for all men and women over the age of twenty-one.' (It should be pointed out here that no opposition party is permitted in Ethiopia, where the only political organization is Haile Selassie's own party of yes-men. Furthermore, all candidates are chosen by the Throne according to property and educational qualifications.) 'He (Haile Selassie) voluntarily restricts his own power as an absolute monarch in the following important aspect: war can be declared only with the approval of Parliament.' (This, by the way, is worth just about as much as a similar provision which existed in Hohenzollern Germany.) 'All territorial changes and all financial imposts on his subjects have first to be approved by both Houses of Parliament before they can be ratified by the Head of the State.' (All very fine, but in view of the composition of these two Houses of Parliament, an empty pretence.)

'2. The whole imperial family possesses bourgeois property: commercial undertakings, workshops, factories and shares in foreign-owned concerns . . . Against the opposition of the temporal and spiritual princes the Negus has introduced legislation to protect capitalist property.'[2]

Amazing though it may seem, no misunderstanding is possible: here is an official communist publication recording approvingly the interlocking of the economic interests of the imperial family with those of domestic and foreign capital and the extension of imperial family property (including estates, factories, mines, etc.) and representing all this as progressive; and this without the slightest criticism of the extension of the feudal property structure or the identification of the ruling stratum with the development of early capitalist profit-making enterprises.

It is the same with regard to the other two points the correspondent puts forward as indications of progressive development in Ethiopia: 'the head of the Ethiopian State is also in favour of land reform . . . the Negus is the inspiration behind a Five-Year Plan for the country and favours the investment of industrial capital.'[3]

People who read only the communist Press cannot discover that, in practice, Haile Selassie's 'land reform' is as useless to the people as the extension of the industrial sector on the basis of foreign-capital investment. However, readers are told why this feudal State should enjoy such considerate treatment:

'Ethiopia's foreign policy is developing rapidly, and the visit of Haile Selassie to Prague in 1959 gave a practical framework to the "alliance" policy on which it is admittedly based . . . The visit was an indication of political and economic far-sightedness . . . The fact that Ethiopia can now rely on the great and unfailing aid of the Soviet Union backed by its tremendous economic resources indicates a new orientation of Ethiopia's foreign policy and suggests a proper understanding of the changed power relationships in the world today.'⁴

This form of reporting, of which there are many other examples in Soviet journalism, is particularly interesting for its omissions. For example, the reader behind the Iron Curtain rarely if ever hears anything about the unusually high level of illiteracy in Ethiopia, nor about the impoverishment and misery of the masses of the people, particularly among the non-Amharic tribes. And of course the communist Press made no mention of the disagreeable incident in Dilla (in the Galla area) at the beginning of December 1960 when over two hundred natives were killed by a punitive imperial expedition. Nor have there been any reports about the 'mopping-up' operations carried out by Haile Selassie's imperial forces against the Somalis in the summer of 1960-1. The unsuccessful *putsch* which took place in Addis Ababa in December 1960 was widely reported in the Western Press. Obvious comparisons were drawn between early Tibet and contemporary Ethiopia and the archaic conditions existing in Ethiopia came in for a good deal of criticism. But the communist Press exaggerates the progressive aspects of Ethiopia while deliberately ignoring what might disturb the agreeable picture required by communist political interests. For more than once Ethiopia was heralded in the Soviet Press for the 'important role' it is playing in liberating and modernizing Africa. (See for instance *Yezhegodnik Bolshoy Sovietskoy Entsiklopedii*, 1962 [p. 405] or the book *Strany mira* [Moscow, 1962], p. 287.

This was not always the case. As late as 1955 the Soviet Press was denouncing the Negus as a 'reactionary autocrat' and feudal ruler, and the relations between Ethiopia and the West, particularly with the United States, were cited as a proof of an 'alliance between imperialism and colonialism'. Then came the Bandung conference and Moscow looked again at the role of Ethiopia. As a result the

Kremlin discovered that Haile Selassie's empire stood in good repute (despite certain reservations), with the young élite of Africa who were agitating for independence and sovereignty in British and French territories, because of its resistance to Italian fascist imperialism. One need only look at what Nkrumah has to say in his autobiography.[5] It was now remembered that friendly relations between Russia and Ethiopia had been traditional, and even though this had been in Tzarist Russia they saw no reason for not exploiting it now. Ethiopia was, in fact, the one country in Africa to which Tzarist Russia had paid particular attention, primarily because the Russian Orthodox Church felt it had common ground with the Coptic Church of Abyssinia and was in favour of union with its Abyssinian brothers in Christ. From 1888 onwards Russian visitors travelled to 'the roof of Africa' with the blessing of both the Russian government and the Orthodox Church: adventurers like the Cossack Ashinov, emissaries like the officer Mashkov, geographers like Yelisayev and Leontiev, the Archimandrite Yefrem, diplomats, and doctors who founded a hospital in Addis Ababa. Many of these Russians actually entered the service of the Emperor. Diplomatic relations established between Russia and Abyssinia in 1902 under the Tzars were renewed in 1943 by the Soviets and the present emissaries of Moscow in Addis Ababa never tire of stressing the 'friendly relationship' which, they say, 'has always existed' between the Emperor's palace in Addis Ababa and the Kremlin in Moscow. They prefer to ignore the fact that there are very different rulers in the Kremlin today from those in the old St Petersburg palace of the Tzar. Here, as elsewhere, the Soviet Union is acting as the legitimate successor to Tzarist Russia. In other words, Haile Selassie, Emperor of Abyssinia, is invited to look upon the Soviet Union not as a world revolutionary centre threatening all non-communist rulers with destruction, but as a loyal partner offering valuable economic benefits as the country which covers one-sixth of the world's surface, shoots *sputniks* and *luniks* into the sky and is the friend of all friendly people, in particular the friend of all Africans.

This was the atmosphere in which Haile Selassie's state visit to the Soviet Union took place in the summer of 1959. The Emperor was received by the Soviet leaders with unequalled pomp and accorded all the honours due to his high rank. In addition, he was presented with a splendidly equipped plane for his personal use by

Mr Khrushchev and Ethiopia was granted credits of 400 million old roubles (the equivalent of one hundred million dollars), the largest credit until then granted by the Soviet Union to any African country. On this state occasion very little was said about socialism, but a good deal about the traditional friendship between the two countries and the necessity for world-wide co-existence. The Negus was suitably impressed, and on his return to his capital declared:

'From the moment of Our arrival in the Soviet Union, the warm and wonderful reception accorded to Us by the people and their leaders, whose hospitality is well known, was beyond Our expectation . . . during Our fortnight's stay We were most impressed to see how the peoples of the Soviet Union have succeeded in recovering from the aftermath of a devastating war, have carried out full reconstruction within a very short period of time, and have at the same time achieved remarkable progress in the economic, industrial, scientific and social fields, thus establishing themselves, within the span of forty years, as one of the Great Powers of our time . . . We were able to make the personal acquaintance of Mr Voroshilov, the President of the Supreme Soviet, and Mr Khrushchev, the Prime Minister of the Soviet Union. A frank and friendly exchange of views on various matters resulted in full agreement being reached on all of them.'[6]

The naïve reader might imagine he was reading about a state occasion between the representatives of countries sharing a common ideology, something along the lines of the conventional state visits of monarchs in the nineteenth century.

Indeed, the representatives of the Soviet Union have referred as little as possible to the cardinal ideological differences between the two countries. This attitude inspires all the exhibitions arranged by the Soviet House of Culture in Addis Ababa and all the Soviet propaganda carried out in the interior. Some out-of-the-way village, consisting of tumbledown huts by the side of a road, will receive a visit from these Soviet cultural propagandists. The next village is perhaps twenty-five miles away and the capital, Addis Ababa, one hundred and thirty miles away. In the village there is no electric light, no telephone and no school; in fact nothing at all that could make the place worthy of notice by white men. Nevertheless the inhabitants of the village find themselves invited to an evening's entertainment. A film van parks in the small village square, a portable dynamo provides the projector with light, and a portable film screen is set up between two poles. On the screen every villager can see for himself just how warm and friendly are the feelings of the people of the Soviet Union for the subjects of Haile Selassie. Each stage of the state visit of the Negus to the Soviet Union in 1959 is recorded: there is the historic meeting between Haile Selassie and Nikita Khrushchev; the usual gala evening in the Bolshoi Opera House with *Swan Lake*; the Emperor talking to ordinary Soviet men and women; and, of course, a tremendous amount about the great achievements of the Soviet Union: huge tractors working on collective farms, hydraulic power stations, engineering works, schools, laboratories, universities, great blocks of flats in Moscow, Kiev and Leningrad, the special Ilyushin 14 plane, a personal gift from Mr Khrushchev to the Emperor. The presents from the Soviet Union to Ethiopia: a secondary school in Addis Ababa for 1,000 pupils, with a gymnasium, kitchen and dining hall; instruments and drugs for the old Russian hospital in Addis Ababa; and finally, the 400 million roubles of credit—the crowning proof of Soviet friendship. The effect of this unique confrontation on the dark-skinned audience is, of course, profound. Henceforth people up and down the country who have seen such films will automatically equate all ideas of higher civilization, greater economic strength, and unselfish friendship with the Soviet Union.

The only reference to socialism on such occasions is the phrase: 'The Great Union of Socialist Soviet Republics'. Little or nothing is said about communism and then only *sotto voce*. Soviet propaganda in Ethiopia is not interested in spreading an ideology; it is not intended to convert the Ethiopians to communism or used in order to form the usual communist cells. In fact it is quite different from the attitude of the Soviet Union to Western Europe, where behind a screen of normal diplomatic relations communist and crypto-communist groups are encouraged in every possible way to disturb or, if possible, undermine the social order in the host countries. Where Ethiopia is concerned the Soviet motto is 'honest co-existence whilst recognizing and even supporting the given domestic political order'.

What is going on here is a policy of long-term political speculation. Its aim is to dissipate psychological inhibitions and political reservations towards the Soviet Union, while at the same time gaining influence by force of example. So far the results of this policy have been highly satisfactory. It is true that Soviet-Ethiopian relations deteriorated temporarily when Moscow arranged to deliver arms to Somalia in 1963. But the Soviet arms deal with Somalia never materialized on its original scale, and as soon as the Soviet Union realized the increased continental importance of Addis Ababa as the capital in which the Organization of African Unity had been formed in May 1963, and that Addis Ababa had become the headquarters of the OAU, the Soviet campaign of friendship and co-existence towards Ethiopia was stepped up again.

NOTES

[1] See for instance Cyril Bryner, 'Russian Interest in Africa', *Current History*, July 1953.

[2] *Neues Deutschland* ([East] Berlin), 12-30 January 1961.

[3] Ibid.

[4] Ibid.

[5] *Ghana: The Autobiography of Kwame Nkrumah* (2nd ed.; Edinburgh, 1960), p. 22.

[6] *Speeches Delivered by His Imperial Majesty Haile Selassie I, Emperor of Ethiopia, on Various Occasions, May 1957 to December 1959* (Addis Ababa, 1960), p. 145.

Chapter VIII

REVOLUTIONARY UNITY AND NATIONAL RESERVATIONS: THE CASE OF GUINEA

So far the most favourable conditions for communism in Africa were to be found in Guinea, the country on the west coast which contemptuously rejected de Gaulle's *Communauté Française*. In September 1958, under the vigorous leadership of Sékou Touré, the people of Guinea dramatically defied de Gaulle and chose independence. Since the end of the Second World War there had been some contacts between communists and nationalists in Guinea. These contacts were zealously exploited and the countries of the Soviet bloc systematically extended and consolidated them. In addition, the spread of communist ideas was favoured by the extremely critical situation in which the young State found itself at that time. As Guinea was dropped by France and ignored by the West both economically and politically, the communist bloc was given an opportunity of breaking the international isolation in which Guinea thus found itself. The communist countries promptly signed trade agreements, granted credits, and sent technicians to save Guinea from ruin. From the spring of 1959 the communists were able to claim one success after another and it seemed only a question of time before Sékou Touré's country would be a mere satellite, bound hand and foot to communism. But at the last moment a dramatic change took place in Guinea and the triumph of communism was frustrated. In the late autumn of 1961 Touré uncovered a communist conspiracy, and as a result the Soviet Ambassador was compelled to leave Guinea rather hurriedly. Although it is not easy to unravel all the truth about events in this *état pilote* of

West Africa, it is necessary to examine the case of Guinea as closely as available information allows.

Guinea is a dictatorial State, the first and the most fully developed in Africa, with all the monotonous features of complete totalitarianism. The security forces, the police, the army, the officials of the party and the State exercise 'revolutionary vigilance' at all times and in a way familiar to anyone who has experienced the practices of fascist and communist countries. The model followed by the officials who lord it over the villages and rural areas is obviously a caricature of the behaviour of subordinate white colonial officials around 1898. The fact that all this is in contradiction to the much-lauded *Communaucratie* and the alleged 'complete solidarity of the people, the party, and the government' seems to disturb no one. If you want to be someone in Guinea you have to exercise whatever power you may possess as ostentatiously and blatantly as possible.

If this disagreeable aspect of 'the permanent revolution' is mentioned to anyone in authority in Guinea, he just shrugs his shoulders: 'What can we do about it? We can't control every subordinate official to make sure that he behaves himself.' That significant word 'control' is not used accidentally. Whoever glances at the decisions of the Political Bureau, or at the minutes of the congresses of the *Parti Démocratique de Guinée* (PDG), will repeatedly come across words like 'control', 'authority' and 'organization'. There is a great deal of talk about 'a merciless struggle against individualism, opportunism and egoism in all their forms'.[1] 'In what position would the Government or the Party be', demanded Sékou Touré at the Fifth Congress, 'if the leadership of the country had no authority? Wouldn't the country soon collapse in uproar and anarchy, and thus very soon lose its independence? When it is a question of authority there is no single problem, everything interlocks to form a whole.'[2]

The logical conclusion arrived at by Sékou Touré was that democratic centralism must be strengthened. In Guinea, as in the communist countries, this is the name for the process which safeguards the power of the bureaucracy and of the cadres. It replaces 'the revolution from below' by the guided and controlled 'revolution from above'. Sékou Touré constantly demanded that these cadres should be better trained, strengthened, and better prepared for leadership within the organization.[3] 'Organization' is the magic word in Guinea. It means 4,000 village cells of the *Parti Démo-*

cratique, thousands of subordinate part-time officials and a few hundred full-time officials in the main centres. It means not only a totalitarian party but a State trade union led and controlled by the party. Despite constitutionally guaranteed free trade unions this body jealously defends its monopolist position and has squeezed out the small group of Christian trade unionists, forcing them underground.

A big role is played by the *Jeunesse RDA*, also known as the Young Pioneers. The visitor will realize what power this organization possesses only when he comes across it in places far away from the urban centres; for example in one of the impoverished villages out in the bush where civilization has not yet penetrated. Among dilapidated, broken-down huts thatched with straw, he will find one newly whitewashed, barrack-style hut, above its entrance the green, yellow and red cockade in the shape of an elephant, the symbol of the new Guinea. (Sékou Touré's native title is 'Tilly' or 'big elephant'.) On the doors will be the initials PDG–JRDA. Inside the hall, under a picture of Sékou Touré, an official will be instructing the village youth. They will all be there sitting at his feet. Everything is highly disciplined and no one dares to complain. Instructions are issued briskly and smartly. The national programme known as *l'Investissement humain* is in full swing. On a Sunday the group may start building a permanent path to the capital—'voluntarily', of course, and without pay, encouraged only by the dull rhythmic thumping of the tom-tom and the new songs of the nation; it may well be '*Avant l'indépendance nous étions dans l'obscurité tels des aveugles cherchant leur chemin et, c'est pourquoi dans cette incompréhension, ses incidents sanglants nous divisaient*', or '*Salut à toi indépendance de la Guinée qui nous a ouvert definitivement la voie de la fraternité*'.

First we build the path, then a road, later a local schoolhouse, and after that a hospital; then perhaps a new market square—everything will come in good time. 'The party rightly demands', bellows the official, 'that we should not wait until progress comes to us. We must make it ourselves.' There is a good deal of talk about competitions between neighbouring villages and there are great national contests for the Gold Medal of the party. Everyone must feel responsible for everyone else, just as the organization is there for everyone—'Everything depends on organization . . .'

There are only a few men at the head of the organization; they are all members of the National Political Bureau of the party and most of them are also members of the Cabinet or leading officials. But the whole organization was created by one man, Sékou Touré, leader of the new Guinea, whose upright figure resembles that of an athlete rather than a politician. He is a passionate nationalist, a brilliant speaker and a persuasive agitator. But—particularly in African conditions—he is something more than that: he is a great, painstaking organizer. Under the noses of the French administrators, he built up a political machine which lends force to his nationalist slogans.

'You can't make politics with hopes alone,' he is once said to have exclaimed. When General de Gaulle presented his referendum in September 1958, this axiom was seen to be doubly true, both in Guinea and in France's other overseas territories. In the Niger territory, for example, all the leaders were firmly determined to reject de Gaulle's proposals, and yet two-thirds of the population voted 'yes' at the referendum.

The situation in Guinea was different. When de Gaulle arrived in Conakry shortly before the referendum in order to get support for the *Communauté Française*, Sékou Touré met him, not merely as the head of the administration, as a man filled with wishes, hopes and longings, but as the confident leader of a disciplined, efficient group of cadres, whose influence already extended into the farthest corners of the country. He did not allow himself to be intimidated either by the programme or the prestige of the general, still less by his pathos. 'Guinea prefers freedom in poverty to slavery in riches', he told de Gaulle bluntly. 'Then you will have to vote "no",' de Gaulle told him and, according to reports, he was more amused than angry. Sékou Touré saw to it that his people did, in fact, vote 'no'. He organized the referendum so efficiently that ninety-six per cent of the electors voted 'no', and Guinea was the only one of France's overseas territories to reject the *Communauté*. On 2 October 1958, Sékou Touré proclaimed the independence of Guinea, and the National Political Bureau of the PDG took power in the name of the people and for the people. Sékou Touré became President, Prime Minister, Defence Minister and, temporarily, Foreign Minister. In January 1961, when the first presidential elections were held, it appeared that the power of the party had not declined. There was only one candidate, and that was of course Sékou Touré, who won a victory which was overwhelming even if compared with what the Nazis and communists have been known to claim in similar circumstances: 1,576,747 votes were cast and of these 1,576,580, or 99·999 per cent, were for Touré. Of the million and a half people entitled to vote only ten thousand abstained.

Sékou Touré comes from an old clan of what is known as the sword nobility. When the whites first penetrated into Guinea in the 1880s, Touré's grandfather led his tribe against them and resisted vigorously, but their primitive weapons were useless against the firearms of the invaders and they were defeated and subjugated. Touré himself grew up in poverty and without social advantages. He eventually had some higher education, but was not able to complete his studies. Others, like him, remained dispossessed, but in Touré there was something of the fierce pride of his forefathers. As he was unable to complete his formal studies he taught himself and after a while managed to become a post office official. It was then that he began to show an interest in politics. At first he is reported to have veered first one way and then the other like a weathercock, but this ceased when he came into closer contact with Marxist ideas. He read the most important writings of Marx, Engels, Lenin and other communist theoreticians and towards the end of the Second World War, when the communist trade unions in France went in for missionary work in French West and Central Africa, he joined the *Confédération Générale des Travailleurs* (CGT), which was under communist control. Before long Touré was the leader of the CGT in Conakry. He also attended a number of courses run by the French CGT, and some at training-centres of the communist World Federation of Trade Unions (WFTU) on the other side of the Iron Curtain, though today the President of Guinea is disinclined to discuss these experiences and evades all questions on that subject. The evidence, including a report published in a Prague newspaper cannot, however, be disputed. This newspaper wrote: 'One day a young Negro came to our country to study . . . Since then twelve years—at least many years—have passed, and that young Negro has become the Prime Minister of his newly liberated country. A progressive Prime Minister, of course . . . He is Sékou Touré, the leader of the new African State of Guinea.'[4]

During the next stages of his career he held various official positions in the *Rassemblement Démocratique Africain* (RDA), founded in 1947, and the first mass organization to extend over the whole of French West Africa. Sékou Touré was one of its founders. Until the first split in 1950 the RDA followed a pro-communist line and provided the African representatives to the World Peace Movement and other front organizations run by the communists. Touré's own organization, the *Parti Démocratique de Guinée*, of which he is President, was first formed as a national section of the RDA. He first came to Conakry as mayor and in January 1956 he was elected deputy for Guinea in the French National Assembly.

During this period he engaged in a bitter struggle against what is known in Africa as the *chefferie*. He had long propagated the view that there was no hope of progress unless the chains of the past were broken and the country was liberated from the sterile traditionalism of tribal life. The rule of the old chiefs was, he declared, 'a totally unsuited instrument for bringing about the emancipation of Guinea'. Unlike most African politicians, Touré did not concentrate his attentions exclusively on the urban population and the officials. While mayor of Conakry and during the short period when he was a member of the French National Assembly he spent more time in the interior of Guinea than in Conakry or in Paris. He organized people everywhere, systematically and with unflagging vigour. He formed cadres in all areas and among all tribes and wherever he went he won supporters: the unemployed in Conakry, taxi-drivers, ex-soldiers, students, and above all women and peasants. He encouraged the peasants in their resistance to the feudal domination of the chiefs, who sought to reintroduce tribute and forced labour, and he promised the abolition of the worst social abuses.

The form and objectives of Sékou Touré's policy differed fundamentally from the organization and methods adopted elsewhere in Africa, but their success was not entirely due to his personality and undoubted ability. His movement and rise would have been inconceivable if the French had not first introduced various administrative reforms: labour legislation, the general franchise, municipal administration, and the *loi-cadre* introducing a measure of political and administrative autonomy. It was these French innovations that gave Touré his chance and prepared the way for his success. In particular his movement was never subjected to any particularly repressive measures on the part of the French colonial administration, which could easily have hampered, if not prevented, the growth of the PDG. If they had intervened, it would certainly have afforded Sékou Touré's enemies the opportunity of splitting the movement.

Of course, nowadays—and despite some reconciliation between Guinea and France in 1963—no one in Guinea mentions the tolerance shown by the French administration; no one has a good word to say for the civilizing achievements of the colonial era. In fact the legend is accepted that Touré was victorious only as the result of a hard, bitter struggle against colonial oppression, not to say terrorism. The truth is that he was strongly supported in his struggle against the *chefferie* by the French High Commissioner, Jean Ramadier, and the independence of Guinea is due solely to the fact that de Gaulle himself offered immediate and absolute independence as an alternative to the *Communauté Française* which he would have favoured. But Touré's propaganda goes very much farther than merely concealing these facts, and the people of Guinea are solemnly assured in numerous speeches and appeals that colonial bandits and imperialist agents are for ever threatening the independence of their country and that such plans and intrigues demand that they should 'intensify their revolutionary vigilance against foreign machinations', while at the same time waging 'a relentless struggle against the remnants of colonial behaviour and the colonial outlook' that have allegedly been left behind among the people.

As a government professing such an outlook could hardly continue to maintain friendly relations with 'the biggest and most ruthless colonial power in Africa' (which is France, of course), on 1 March 1960 Guinea withdrew from the French franc area. By this time, thanks to the intrigues of certain circles both in Conakry and in the French capital, relations between Conakry and Paris had sunk to a low level, although officially the step was explained by Conakry as 'an attempt to resolve the numerous economic difficulties facing Guinea since her independence'. The introduction of the Guinea franc was 'to make Guinea into one single economic area, a house open to all'. But the exact opposite occurred; the Guinea franc is up to now Touré's private currency and is unquoted outside Guinea; even banks in Liberia and other 'friendly countries' will not handle it. As the new Guinea franc is accepted only in Guinea and as the National Bank of Guinea has little or no foreign currency, and has to be very careful with any it has, the export and import trade has practically ceased since 1960. Another result of the currency change was an acute shortage of commodities; there are only empty shelves in the few shops still open in the capital, while the few remaining Europeans look back on the rationing period during the war as a relative paradise.

Far worse is the fact that, apart from the officials of the PDG, the people of Guinea are suffering from an acute shortage of staple goods. Gifts of rice from the United States and Red China have not gone very far and bad harvests have aggravated food shortages. Rigorous austerity measures, including close control of private trading in villages and areas, have done very little to remedy matters. The attempt to give local leaders of the PDG the responsibility for the distribution of foodstuffs in particularly short supply has merely resulted in a flourishing black market and caused nepotism and corruption.

Guinea's first Three-Year Plan, adopted in April 1960, was heralded as a guarantee of decisive changes in this situation. But this plan was mostly based on Soviet aid and on the then intimate relationship between Guinea and the communist countries. This relationship provides a typical example of communist policy—and failure—in the under-developed areas. In the case of Guinea, the troubles started in the late summer of 1959, when Saifoulaye Diallo, President of the Parliament of Guinea, went to the Soviet Union at the head of a government and party delegation on the first official visit to the Soviet Union. It was during this visit that negotiations between Anastas Mikoyan and Saifoulaye Diallo led to a credit of 140 million roubles being granted to Guinea.

On its return to Conakry the delegation was greeted with tremendous enthusiasm, but this soon gave way to depression when the expectations aroused by promises made in Moscow were not satisfied. Tension developed and discussions between Sékou Touré and Rashidov, then the Uzbekistan Prime Minister, and other members of the Soviet delegation at the Fifth National Congress of the PDG in Conakry, did nothing to clear up the situation. The countries of the Soviet bloc did at least take up the agreed banana and coffee quotas and, in return, modest supplies of sugar and grain arrived in Guinea; but the promised credits did not transpire.

The situation was not cleared up until November 1959, when

Touré paid his first state visit to Moscow. In an interview with Mr Khrushchev the Soviet Premier suggested that Soviet experts should visit Guinea to study, on the spot, the best way of utilizing the promised Soviet credits. Similar offers also came, either directly or through their Moscow embassies, from the People's Republic of China and from various Soviet satellite States. As Guinea's economic situation was deteriorating and as the extreme left wing of the Political Bureau of the PDG approved the communist proposals with enthusiasm, Sékou Touré had little alternative but to accept Mr Khrushchev's offer. With this the Soviet bloc secured the technical basis it required for exercising an even more powerful influence over developments in Guinea, which in any case were proceeding in its favour.

In 1960 there was a veritable invasion of Guinea by communist 'advisers' and 'experts', delegations from the Soviet Union, Czechoslovakia, Roumania, Poland, North Vietnam and Mao's China soon turned the only available hotel in Conakry, the Hôtel de France, into a dependency of the Savoy Hotel in Moscow. Experts on fisheries, soil erosion, veterinary science, broadcasting, and sport, bobbed up all over the place and in the background there were trade-union officials and military experts. In the spring of 1960 a 'trade delegation' of no fewer than seventy members arrived from Czechoslovakia to put the finishing touches to the Three-Year Plan. In the second half of the year, Chinese agricultural experts arrived from Peking; as a result of their investigations they proposed the formation of agricultural collectives along Chinese lines. The Political Bureau of the PDG had previously sent a delegation to Red China and it now declared itself in agreement with the Chinese proposals. However, the first attempts to found these collectives led to great unrest in the Kekedou-Kissidou area where the local agricultural population objected violently to the scheme. But the PDG leadership had gone too far in its enthusiastic acceptance of the Chinese proposals to draw back immediately and so, egged on by the Chinese guests, they used force against the restive peasants—announcing first that imperialist agents had stirred up the people and carried on anti-revolutionary agitation in the troubled areas. The troops sent in to 'pacify' the disaffected districted were able, for the first time, to make use of the weapons Guinea had obtained as a result of the military-aid agreement signed in Prague. Another result of this agreement was that groups of officers and NCOs from Guinea were to be sent to Czechoslovakia for training at communist military academies.

The evidence of large-scale political and propagandist infiltration was even more significant. Officials of the Soviet bloc countries delivered lectures in the State schools on DIAMAT (the communist abbreviation for 'dialectical materialism'), and on the principles and practice of current Soviet policy in Africa. Instructors of the communist-dominated World Federation of Trade Unions were active at the so-called trade-union university of Conakry and at the trade-union school in Dalaba. A sport exchange had also been organized with the countries of Eastern Europe and under the guidance of Hungarian trainers this increasingly took on the form of political support for the activist youth of Guinea. The bookshops and book depots run by the Youth League and the PDG were becoming centres for the distribution of vast quantities of communist literature. The works of Mao Tse-tung, Khrushchev's speeches, the works of Lenin, and the 'classics of socialist realism' were all to be had at low prices, and often even free. In the same way the *World Communist Review*, *Humanité*, and the various periodicals and publications of the WFTU were easily obtainable. The formulae and slogans of communist agitation were becoming more and more strongly impressed on public opinion in Guinea. Even the show trials that followed the suppression of unrest in April 1960 and led to a number of death sentences were held according to the same grotesque horror ritual with which Soviet Russia and its satellites have made us familiar. Guinea thus became a perfect replica: the counter-revolutionary agents, and the alleged discovery of imperialists in the background, invented evidence and forged exhibits.

Finally we must not omit to mention the furtive anti-clerical campaign conducted by the PDG against religion, with the ultimate aim of enthroning Marxist materialism in the minds of the people. Instructions issued by the PDG as part of this campaign had the illuminating title 'Pray less, work more!' In the summer of 1960, the Christian Working Youth, the Christian Country Youth, and the Scout organization were ordered to end their activities. On applying for an exit permit Catholics from Guinea who wished to take part in the Vatican Council found, to their surprise, that this Catholic religious assembly was, in reality, 'aimed at spiritually preparing neo-colonialism' and that therefore they could not attend it.

Guinea's foreign policy developed along much the same pro-communist lines as its domestic policy. At the time of the acute Congo crisis its attitude was hardly distinguishable from that of the Soviet Union. While even Ghana and the United Arab Republic both expressly supported the Lumumba and Gizenga régime, showed a certain reserve and discretion, deliberately delayed the withdrawal of their troops and, up to a point, even adopted a mediatory role in the United Nations between West and East, Guinea never shifted from its extreme anti-Western attitude. At first Guinea sent a contingent of its troops to form part of the UN force (as Lumumba had requested) and supported the policy of the United Nations, but later it changed its Congo policy in close accordance with the changes in Moscow's attitude. The culmination was reached with Sékou Touré's second visit to Moscow, in September 1960, shortly before Khrushchev's rowdy performance at the UN in New York. Khrushchev and Touré issued a joint communiqué stressing their 'complete agreement' on the Congo question and a little later, at the plenary session of the United Nations on 9 October 1960, Touré supported to the hilt the Soviet attack upon Hammerskjöld and the 'Western imperialists', declaring:

'It is impossible not to make the United Nations responsible for the dangerous situation in the Congo . . . The confusion that developed in the wake of Belgian aggression threatens everyone in the world today. Political oppression and economic exploitation still exist in all forms and every possible guise . . . Africa plays a dominating role in the expansionist ambitions of the imperialist powers, and they are co-ordinating their plans to secure the military bases (in Africa) that are essential for their expansionist lusts.'[5]

It was not surprising, therefore, that Guinea should withdraw its contingent (of 740 men) from the United Nations force in the Congo. Thereafter accusations and diplomatic protests synchronized completely with the attacks of the Soviet Union, whether against the late Secretary-General, Dag Hammerskjöld, the UN commanders and representatives in the Congo, the federalist Congo politicians, the Belgians, the Americans, the French, or 'the whole imperialist bloc'. Touré's Congo emissary, Tunkara, declared: 'The

UN command in Leopoldville has flagrantly interfered in the domestic affairs of the Congolese Republic and acted as an occupation force.'6 It is not surprising to find that exactly the same things were being said in Moscow: 'The troops of the United Nations have become an occupation power robbing the Congolese population of their freedom.'7 In connection with the alleged flight of a German plane carrying arms to Katanga, a Conakry radio broadcast declared: 'The coalition of the imperialist powers against the Congo is very obvious here, as also is the role of the German Federal Republic. The composition of Tshombe's forces is typical: West-German mercenaries, both officers and NCOs, and former SS men.'8 No one could therefore have been surprised to discover that the All-African People's Conference in Cairo accorded the German Federal Republic the honour of second place after the United States in the list of neo-colonialist powers.

Whoever examines the details of Guinea's development between 1958 and 1961 is forced to the conclusion (after making allowances for the claim of 'positive neutrality between the two blocs' of the Government and the PDG) that this neutrality really meant neutrality, if not hostility, towards the West only, and close, cordial relations with the East.

There is certainly no doubt that this was the conclusion drawn by the Soviet Government about the political situation in Guinea. It could not but feel confident; it was impossible to doubt that Sékou Touré's party had gone over whole-heartedly to its side and that this could soon be triumphantly confirmed in public.

From the beginning of 1960 the Soviet Government had a very clever operator at the head of its mission in Conakry: Daniel Semyonovitch Solod, a man whose diplomatic career had been a series of successes. This Ukrainian had been attached for a long time to the foreign-political department of the Soviet Foreign Office and he had occupied one post after another in the East. In 1944 Stalin sent him to the newly founded and already troubled States of Lebanon and Syria. In the six years that followed, Solod developed his mission so that it held a key communist position in the Levant and he won the reputation of being the most skilful communist representative in the Middle East. Speaking fluent Arabic, French and English, he persuasively put forward what appeared to be unconventional and undoctrinaire arguments and gradually suc-

ceeded in lessening resentment against the Soviet Union and intensifying resentments against the Western Powers. By the time Solod
was recalled to Moscow in 1950, his work was done and Syrian
representatives were negotiating with the Soviet Foreign Minister,
Vyshinsky, for the conclusion of trade and military agreements. At
the same time the Syrian Minister for National Economy, Maaruf
al-Davalibi, a close personal friend of Solod, was saying openly that
he would 'sooner see the Arab Republics become Soviet Republics
than victims of Zionism'. When Solod finally left Damascus to take
up a leading position in the Middle East Department in Moscow's
Foreign Ministry, he was accorded an honour that no Soviet representative before him had ever enjoyed in the Arab world: hundreds
of Syrian notables assembled to give him a warm ovation.[9]

Three years later, after the triumph of the revolutionary junta
over the corrupt but pro-Western régime of King Farouk in Egypt,
Solod appeared again outside the Soviet Union, this time as Ambassador in Cairo, where he repeated his successful Damascus and
Beirut performance. It was not long before he succeeded in improv-
ing the traditionally frosty relations between Moscow and Cairo and
in creating a warm and friendly atmosphere. When Nasser came to
the fore, Moscow's chances increased and Solod was actually
assisted at the birth of the policy of 'positive neutrality' formulated
in Cairo. Incidentally Western correspondents always referred to
him amongst themselves as 'Mr Troublemaker'. It was also Solod
who launched the large-scale trading deals between Egypt and the
Soviet Union and, as Nasser has told us, it was Solod who first
broached the possibility of Soviet arms deliveries to Egypt. In an
interview granted to an Egyptian newspaper, Nasser described
Solod's approach. It appears that at a diplomatic reception Solod
took him into a corner and asked him point-blank whether the
Egyptian Government would be prepared to consider buying arms
from the Soviet Union. Should Nasser's Government feel so inclined he, Solod, would see that this interesting information reached
the appropriate quarter. Nasser went on to say: 'I answered him in
the same tone, saying that I found his offer extremely interesting
and that I should be prepared to enter into negotiations in that
sense.'[10]

By February 1956, when Solod returned to Moscow to become
Deputy-Chief (for a while even Acting-Chief) of the Middle East

Department of the Foreign Office, the basis of the new relationship between Egypt and the Soviet Union had been well established. He was now in charge of Soviet operations in the United Republic, Iraq, the Lebanon, Jordan, the Sudan, Ethiopia, Libya, Tunisia, and Morocco, and he made use of his Cairo experiences in his dealings with the whole Arab world. But Solod's value to the Soviet Government was even greater: he had a keen eye for African developments and for the advance of African nationalism and in this capacity he was now invaluable to the Soviet Foreign Ministry, especially if one bears in mind the role played by Cairo in the extremist African nationalist movement. After the victory of the ambitious Nasser over the more moderate and conservative Neguib, Cairo became the centre for almost all the radical anti-colonial elements throughout Africa, and to some extent it still is. Jomo Kenyatta's successor party to Mau-Mau, the liberation groups in Angola, Mozambique, the Congo, and Tanganyika, the Uganda National Congress, and the terrorist *Union des Populations du Cameroun*, all established action centres in exile in Cairo. Their lack of money, arms, and tactical experience and their ardent longing for violent action drove these various groups into the arms of the Soviet representatives who were, of course, only too willing to assist them. Solod's close contact with such groups was clearly demonstrated at the second Afro-Asian Solidarity Conference in April 1960 at Conakry. Although he had no official connection with the conference it enabled him to renew his acquaintance with many African politicians and to make new friends, particularly amongst the Congolese and Angolan 'Friends of Peace'.

As Ambassador to Conakry, Solod's sphere of operations was by no means confined to Guinea. In fact his mission was a double one: first, to consolidate and extend the 'friendship between the Soviet Union and Guinea', and to guide the left-wing course of the Government of Guinea in the direction most favourable to the Kremlin. Second, in Moscow's interests he was to turn Conakry into the key West African centre for communist ideas and intrigues.

At first, as we have already shown, this policy was largely successful. Guinea's dependence on the Soviet bloc increased visibly and Soviet confidence grew to such an extent that in Soviet publicity Guinea was already regarded as a 'People's Democracy'.[11] In other words, in Soviet eyes Guinea had already reached the penultimate stage before the final transition to a fully developed socialist State. The award of the Lenin Prize of 1961 to Sékou Touré was therefore not surprising and it was followed by an invitation to the PDG to send a delegation to the Twenty-second Congress of the Communist Party of the Soviet Union—an honour shared by the totalitarian parties of Ghana and Mali. This congress took place in October 1961 and the guests from Guinea were invariably referred to as Tovarishchi, or Comrades. On 23 October, Saifoulaye Diallo, Political Secretary of the PDG and President of the Parliament of Guinea, addressed the congress as follows:

'The historic Twenty-second Congress of the Communist Party of the Soviet Union is of importance not only to the Communist Party of the Soviet Union, to all socialist countries, to the socialist or communist parties of those countries that are still under the dominance of capitalism, and to the progressive and anti-imperialist parties of the colonial and dependent territories,but also to the newly independent and under-developed countries of Africa, where neo-colonialism—a new aspect of transoceanic imperialism—is doing everything possible to stifle the proper efforts of our peoples to win freedom, justice, democracy, peace and happiness. The *Parti Démocratique de Guinée* fights unwaveringly on the basis of positive neutralism for peace and democracy and against colonialism and imperialism . . . In this way our positive neutralism does not mean indifference to the problems of peace and war, colonialism and the true independence of the peoples . . . In what circumstances could the *Parti Démocratique de Guinée* adopt the same attitude towards those who exploit and torment Africa as it adopts towards those who help Africa to free herself? Those who fight in a common cause against the same evil and for the victory of the same ideals are naturally in the same camp. Therefore we declare that co-operation between the socialist countries and the young countries of Africa is a perfectly natural thing. It cannot be weakened by any blackmail on the part of neo-colonialism . . . The socialist countries and the communist and working-class parties lend wings of hope to the peoples of Africa fighting for their independence and for the development of their countries; and, indeed, to the whole world . . . They (the delegates to the Party Congress) would understand better than others what significance Africa, exploited, colonialized and humiliated, must rightly attach to the glorious Revolution of 1917; and what hopes are raised among the peoples of Africa by your successes in the political, economic and social as well as technological spheres . . . Revolutionary Africa knows that it can rely on the socialist countries.'[12]

This last assurance must have been given with tongue in cheek, because during the months before the congress met it had become very clear to Guinea that it could not, in fact, rely on the 'selfless socialist support' promised. After the original priming operations and the grandiloquent promises of economic assistance, the Soviet-bloc countries did less and less for Guinea. The impoverished country and its one-party State staggered from crisis to crisis, while the Soviets and their satellites deliberately marked time instead of helping—obviously on the assumption that a worsening of the economic crisis in Guinea, having burnt its bridges to the West, would soon pitch the country completely into the arms of communism.

Promised supplies of foodstuffs either did not arrive, or when they reached Conakry they were rotten and no longer fit for human consumption. By the time a shipload of grain from Soviet Army stocks was unloaded in Conakry it was fermenting. And as though to make a mockery of their poor dupes, the Soviets sent consignments of snow-ploughs and large supplies of lavatory seats. At the same time Soviet and Czech technicians in Guinea were unable to make the water- and power-supply systems work satisfactorily, and the technical personnel sent to extend and improve the organization of the airfield at Conakry did no better. After violent disputes they were ultimately withdrawn and replaced by Egyptian technicians. A large printing plant financed and built by the East German Government, and which was intended to provide a technological basis for the propaganda infiltration of West Africa, had to suspend some of its operations shortly after it opened in the summer of 1961, because of constructional defects. Other important projects due to be carried out in accordance with Soviet plans for utilizing the credits granted in 1959 were repeatedly delayed and postponed.

While these and other defects and failures of Soviet aid were making themselves painfully felt, the unfortunate country also became aware of the drawbacks attached to the other less tangible forms of communist support. The hoped-for stream of foodstuffs, consumer goods, factory equipment and machine-tools from the Soviet bloc did not materialize, but the unflagging stream of communist propaganda continued unabated. It became such a problem that the authorities felt compelled to intervene, though only very cautiously. But the delegations still came, the instructors, the 'friendship groups', and the numbers of films, pamphlets, books and newspapers continued to grow bigger. As a result of this growing ideological infiltration, which was tolerated, if not actually encouraged, by the authorities, it is not surprising that an increasing number of party officials, particularly the younger men and youth officials, adopted the ideas pumped out from behind the Iron Curtain and that in consequence they decided optimistically that the acute difficulties affecting their country were 'natural crises of growth', brought about by the continued existence of 'class contradictions'—a situation aggravated, they decided, by a lack of ideological firmness on the part of the government. Obviously, if this were true, no improvement could be hoped for until the government abandoned its half-hearted attitude towards scientific socialism and went over whole-heartedly to orthodox socialism.

The trial which ended on 24 November 1961 with the conviction of five leading officials of the Teachers' Union of Guinea revealed the influence of these ideas. It also served as a signal for certain radical groups to launch a political offensive. In the capital and in a number of other towns throughout the country, students and young trade unionists marched through the streets demonstrating against the government. At first the slogans were confined to demands for the release of the convicted teachers, but before long they turned into general demands for socialism and communism. The government, which was being accused of indecisiveness, certainly reacted swiftly and vigorously to this offensive. It closed down all the schools and arrested a large number of the ringleaders, but two weeks passed before a sensational statement was made. Issued on 11 December 1961, it attributed the whole affair to 'a communist-inspired conspiracy'.[13] These were startling words for the Guinean public to hear. Meanwhile, Diallo Alpha, a Minister of State, was sent to Moscow with a special message from Sékou Touré. Received by Khrushchev and Gromyko on 18 December, he firmly demanded no less than the recall of the Soviet Ambassador to Guinea, the highly-prized Solod. Mr Khrushchev recalled him at once. What had Solod done to give such offence? Not surpringly, the Soviet Government had nothing to say about this and the Government of Guinea only made vague statements. In fact, Radio Conakry repeated the Moscow story, according to which Solod was recalled in order to take up 'another important post'. The only occasions on which the disagreeable word 'expulsion' was mentioned were during two speeches made by Sékou Touré in Susu, the native tongue. The reason given then was that the ambassador had interfered in the internal affairs of Guinea and his embassy had co-operated with the conspirators.[14]

But this charge was so general that it came to be widely assumed that there was no real evidence against Solod and that, in all probability, he had been made a scapegoat for the attitude of the Soviet Government towards Guinea and that he had been sacrificed to appease the Government of Guinea, which was understandably irritated by the many breakdowns, delays and postponements in the economic and credit agreements. According to information available in Conakry, Touré had made demarches on several occasions in the second half of 1961, and Solod is said to have lacked diplomatic finesse on these occasions, insisting bluntly that the responsibility for the delays and misunderstandings lay with the Government of Guinea and not with the Soviet Union. According to other reports, Sékou Touré had for several months refused to receive Solod, who finally expressed his annoyance in blunt, offensive terms. He is also alleged to have said that the trouble was that Guineans 'didn't want to work, and that they were ruining good Soviet equipment', and that in general it was difficult to take them seriously.[15]

The reaction of the Soviet Government to the Solod affair is an indication of the dismay it caused. If a Western State had dared to bundle out a Soviet Ambassador in this fashion, there is no doubt that the Soviet Government would have reacted in a no less dramatic fashion, but in the Solod affair Moscow adopted a policy of appeasement. Solod's expulsion was swallowed with as good a grace as possible and the Soviet Vice-Premier, Anastas Mikoyan, was sent off post-haste to Guinea. But when he arrived in Conakry his reception was anything but friendly, and Sékou Touré kept Mr Mikoyan kicking his heels in waiting-rooms on several occasions.[16] Mikoyan tried desperately to persuade the Government of Guinea that it was all a misunderstanding. At the opening of a Soviet exhibition in the capital he made the only public speech of his visit, though he was in Guinea for almost a week, from 5 to 10 January. He made a particular point of stressing that 'Soviet policy respects the sovereignty and independence of all peoples and does not interfere in their internal affairs', after which he turned with relief to the old story and put all the blame on the imperialists who had, it appeared, 'employed all sorts of devices . . . to sow doubts . . . on the various fields of our co-operation'. He concluded by assuring his hearers that 'our friendship is solidly based on equality and non-interference'.[17] But Touré was not so easily appeased and replied coldly and pointedly that other nations should not try to export revolutions to his country. He also told Mikoyan bluntly that Guinea would not tolerate interference in its internal affairs, even from countries lending it economic aid.[18]

Did this mean that communist hopes for a triumph in Guinea were illusory? Did it perhaps mean that this young West African State might turn towards the West? Despite the extraordinary events which provoked this question, the latter was too much to hope for. It is significant that in his statement of 11 December 1961, Touré included 'elements in Paris and Dakar' in the 'anti-Guinea conspiracy' in his attack, and declared that the French Mission in Conakry had played the role of a 'go-between' in what he described as an attempted *putsch*. There is, as the last years show, little room for much optimism in the West; even after this shake-up there are still prominent supporters of an orthodox socialist policy in the leading circles of the party and government and nothing has been done to get rid of them or to curb their political activities. Furthermore, during 1962 and 1963 both Guinea and the Soviet Union made some efforts to restore friendly relations, particularly in the economic field. It is also interesting to note that the relatively good relations between Guinea and the satellites survived the critical period at the end of 1961 and the beginning of 1962. When a Bulgarian government delegation arrived in Guinea in March 1962, Sékou Touré spoke of 'our joint socialist ideals'.[19] Finally, relations between Guinea and Mao's China (which we shall deal with later in connection with China's African policy) improved during this period. In fact, during conversations the author had with a number of politicians in Guinea, it was even suggested that the disputes in the communist world, and in particular the clash between the Soviet Union and Mao's China, had an important influence on the conflict between Guinea and the Soviet Union, and it is reported that in the period immediately preceding the Twenty-second Congress of the Communist Party of the Soviet Union, the PDG (Guinea's totalitarian party) made several attempts to interfere in the discussion in favour of the Chinese and Albanian standpoint. It is also reported to have been opposed to the Soviet policy of granting credits to non-socialist African States, to have expressed disapproval of the disarmament policy of the Soviet Union and to have declared itself in favour of the Chinese policy of supporting all revolutionary groups in African territories which are still in colonial hands. The ambiguous Soviet attitudes over the Cameroons rebellion, the Gizenga affair and the Angolan question, are said to have led to further disillusionment in Conakry over Soviet policy in the under-developed countries.

From any standpoint, the crisis in relations between Moscow and Conakry is significant. It clearly indicates two things:

1. Soviet African policy is by no means as successful as was hoped. In fact it is, to an astonishing extent, failing to exploit the very real chance for communism that exists in Africa; in particular it has failed to take immediate advantage of the situation in a country where, psychologically, conditions were unquestionably favourable. Confused by the great diversity and complexity of conditions in Africa and by the necessity of adopting different tactics towards each of the many groups, parties and régimes to be dealt with, hampered by the multifarious defects inherent in an over-centralized foreign trade structure, and relatively unpractised in the art of exploiting economic aid for the under-developed countries, Soviet African policy has persistently made the kind of blunders that have usually been ascribed exclusively to the legendary 'ugly Americans'.

2. Left-wing African socialism, even of Sékou Touré's variety, while ready and willing to co-operate with Marxist-Leninists and anxious to be recognized by the international communist movement as an equal partner, still has many reservations. These are due partly to nationalist fervour and partly to the personal vanity of its leaders (particularly Touré) who, like Tito, are keenly conscious that they too have accomplished something on their own. Like Yugoslav

Titoism, Guinean socialism is very proud of having won independence by its own efforts and of having created the organizational basis for its victory. Of course a parallel between Tito and Touré must not be pushed too far, but nevertheless it is quite clear that Yugoslavia and Guinea have certain things in common. And as in the case of Yugoslavia it is quite certain that there will be many ups and downs and unexpected changes before the position of Guinea becomes quite clear.

NOTES

[1] Cyclostyled Minutes of the Fifth National Congress of the *Parti Démocratique de Guinée* (PDG), 14–17 September 1959.

[2] Ibid.

[3] See, for instance, the cyclostyled Minutes of the Ninth National Congress of the *Parti Démocratique de Guinée*, September 1963.

[4] *Zemedelske Noviny* (Prague), 11 April 1959.

[5] United Press International, 9 October 1960.

[6] At a Press conference in Leopoldville, attended by the author.

[7] Radio Moscow, English-language broadcast for Africa, 23 September 1960.

[8] Radio Conakry broadcast, 14 April 1961.

[9] CRU (London), 20 October 1955.

[10] Quoted in Jean and Simone Lacouture, *L'Egypte au Mouvement* (Paris, 1956), p. 214.

[11] A. Arzumanyan, in *Pravda*, 17 December 1961.

[12] Report in *Pravda*, 26 October 1961.

[13] Radio Conakry broadcast, 11 December 1961.

[14] Information given in a private report to the author.

[15] Reported in *Le Soir* (Paris), 26 October 1961.

[16] Reported in the *New York Herald Tribune* (Paris ed.), 19 January 1962.

[17] Radio Conakry broadcasts, 6 and 10 January 1962.

[18] Reported in the *New York Herald Tribune* (Paris ed.), 19 January 1962.

[19] Radio Conakry broadcast, 23 March 1962.

Chapter IX

IN SEARCH OF PROSELYTES:
GHANA AND MALI

SOME observers have suggested, especially after the Soviet-Guinean crisis, that Ghana or Mali might ultimately play the role which Russia originally had in mind for Guinea, i.e. the role of a Soviet bridgehead distribution-centre for agitation and propaganda and of a base for infiltration in West Africa. Taking the long view, such fears, though they may seem exaggerated at the moment, are by no means without foundation. This somewhat pessimistic view is based, particularly where Ghana is concerned, not so much on the magnitude of communist successes so far achieved as on the internal ideological and constitutional crises.

The most surprising and alarming thing about Ghana is the extraordinary speed with which the old Gold Coast Colony (called by the name of the historic Ghana Empire since 7 March 1957) has been moving away from its original programme and the initial moderation of its leadership. The small group that made up the national élite of Ghana has suffered a steady process of erosion and disintegration, and in consequence the most intelligent and liberal personalities have gradually disappeared; they are now, as The *Guardian* stated in February 1964, 'in prison, in exile or muttering gloomily and doing nothing'.[1] The national life of the country also suffers: there is widespread and alarming corruption among members of the upper strata; State-run business and commerce is entangled in bureaucratic red tape; there is no effective opposition and such rival groups as existed originally, including the trade unions and the youth and women's associations have been swallowed up by the Convention People's Party (CPP). All healthy public opinion has been suppressed and individual, regional, tribal and ethnic differences are being flattened out.

These disturbing features unfortunately coincide with the increasing self-assertion and vanity of Kwame Nkrumah, the man who secured Ghana's independence from the British and has since been in control of the fate of its 6,300,000 people. The rather modest and likable young man who wrote the autobiography published in 1956 has since become 'Osagyefo' (which means Great Man, Redeemer, or All-powerful *Führer*), His Highness the President, 'Kukurundi' or Brave Hero, 'Kasapreko', He who has the Last Word, 'Nufeno' or Immortal Ruler over Life and Death, to quote a few of the obsequious titles showered upon him.

Wherever one goes in Ghana it is impossible to get away from his name—as it was with that of Stalin in the Soviet Union in the old days. There are Kwame Nkrumah roads, streets and avenues, Kwame Nkrumah training centres, schools and institutions—and everywhere there are his statues and pictures, many of them larger than life. True believers throughout the country learn the litanies of Nkrumahism by heart. For example:

'I believe in Kwame Nkrumah, the Creator of Ghana, the Founder and Benefactor of Ghana's schools and colleges; I believe in the revolutionary Convention People's Party, his imperishable organization and our salvation, granted to us by the inspiration of History, born of the masses, humbled, persecuted and repressed with harsh laws until they arose from their despair in the Third Month ...'[2]

The religious parallel is obvious and as though to dissipate any lingering doubts Nkrumah is lauded in the nationalist Press and party publications and in the government as 'Saviour', 'Messiah' and 'Transfigurer'. Objections by the Christian Churches to the use of such terms were rejected as hypocrisy and phrases were picked from the Oxford English Dictionary to show that, 'despite the arrogant clerical claim for a monopoly of sacred concepts', it is right and proper to praise Kwame Nkrumah as the 'Re-born' and the 'Saviour'.[3] The Young Pioneers of the Convention People's Party even pester visitors to buy picture postcards showing the President of the West African Republic of Ghana standing side by side with Jesus Christ.

This personality cult reached a first peak in the spring of 1960. Up to that time Ghana was still a member of the British Commonwealth of Nations under the Queen of Great Britain. This was, of course, only a matter of form, but Nkrumah and his followers attached great importance to formalities. They therefore staged a referendum to decide whether Ghana should continue to remain under the British Crown or adopt a new status in the British Commonwealth of Nations as a republic. The nominee for President of Ghana was, of course, Kwame Nkrumah.

There was not the slightest doubt about the outcome of this referendum, although the oppositional United Party did put up Doctor J. B. Danquah, the grand old man of Ghanaian politics, as a rival candidate. But just as it organizes everything else in Ghana, Nkrumah's State party, the Convention People's Party, organized the referendum, and did so very painstakingly and systematically. For weeks before the great day the population was steam-rollered into meetings, processions and mass demonstrations; special propaganda commandos of party members and youths flooded the countryside to make certain that every inhabitant of even the most remote villages was suitably housed and also to ensure that the local chiefs and headmen accepted the patronage of the campaign for Nkrumah in their localities. Leaflets bearing the picture of the 'Messiah' were distributed all over the country and anyone suspected of opposition to the campaign was persecuted with the African equivalent of 'rough music', personal insults, and baseless accusations in order to shame them in the eyes of their fellows. 'Who is it that in these great days does not stand behind our Government and our powerful Party, to which we owe everything, and behind our leader and protector Kwame Nkrumah? If there be such a one who stands aside, he can only be a traitor—a bought tool of Imperialism!'[4] But the Convention People's Party organizers did not rely exclusively on these methods; they announced that free food and drinks would be provided at meetings, adding that if anyone of goodwill were sick 'the gifts of the Saviour' would be brought to his bedside. Just before the referendum the government announced that 'in order to ensure a tranquil poll' voting would not take place simultaneously throughout the country, but with several days' pause between three separate voting areas. The idea behind this arrangement was obviously to give the CPP an opportunity of clinching the final victory by concentrating all its forces on each voting area in turn and, to be doubly certain, all opposition meetings were prohibited in order not to 'endanger public order and security'. Another reason advanced for this suppression of all opposition was that otherwise 'the lives of members of the opposition would be endangered'. The result was that on the days fixed for the polling only Nkrumah's men were on the streets, even in places known to be anti-Nkrumah, such as the stronghold of the opposition Ashanti tribe. Cars and lorries plastered with 'Yes' placards and with pictures of Nkrumah drove from village to village, their loud-speakers alternately cajoling and threatening and, as prophesied, the culmination of the campaign became 'a triumphal vote even before the poll'.

Similar methods of intimidation, cajoling and manipulation were used and even improved four years later, when a second referendum asked the Ghanaians to vote for a one-party State—at a time when only one party existed anyway in Ghana—Nkrumah's Convention People's Party. Again, the people voted as they were forced to vote; according to official figures released in Accra, over 2,500,000 people voted in support of one-party government; less than three thousand voted against it. *The Economist* commented on this result:

'President Nkrumah's one-man-one-vote-one-party State has been legitimized . . . Whom does the Osagyefo think he is fooling? Not the West: it has learned what to think about results like that. Not the East: it knows too well how such results are obtained. Not those of Ghana's people who oppose the régime: they know best of all why they felt it the better part of valour to acquiesce. Surely the answer is not Dr Nkrumah himself? A more hard-headed answer is probably this: in spite of Ghana's admirable economic, educational and technical progress since independence in 1957, the majority of the people have been left untouched by what can only be called the European mode of life. Dr Nkrumah, it now seems, intends to clutch his people by the lapels (or the kente cloths) and shake them once again, in the hope that they will sweat to create black Africa's first truly modern society in Ghana. This aim cannot be carped at: it is what all under-developed countries want. But the method—driving, deceiving, and regimenting the people—might turn out to be self-defeating.'[5]

But did the voters really have any idea of what was at stake—in 1960 as well as in 1964? The simple fact is that the great majority of the people of Ghana are neither able nor willing to take part in a rational political discussion, and in consequence the objections of the opposition to Nkrumah's proposed constitutional changes in 1960 and in 1964 came to nothing, for want of an audience capable of understanding them. The urban proletariat, the timber workers, plantation workers, fishermen and cattle drovers of the interior did not care whether according to the constitution of 1960 the President is at the same time the Prime Minister and has the power to veto any legislation of which he disapproves, or whether, if he thinks fit, he has power to prorogue parliament altogether, to quash any verdict of the Supreme Court of Ghana[6] and even to appoint its judges. For most Ghanaians Accra is so far away it might as well be on the moon, and in any case, had things not always been done that way in Accra and not merely since the CPP came to power?

As Peter Preston reported in The *Guardian* in February 1964:

'The men in the street selling gold watches, hairpins, and English chewing-gum don't care much about what happens in Flagstaff House . . . As one Ghanaian admitted: "We don't think much about politics really, as long as there is food and sunshine!" Few had much time for the delirious cant of the party Press. Dr Nkrumah's paternalistic image was tarnished still further by the pointlessness and stench of it all; only in the remoter regions, where new schools and water supplies are minor miracles, is his lustre undiminished.'[7]

The April 1960 referendum was synonymous with the complete emasculation of the people of Ghana. The 1964 referendum meant the complete emasculation of the last remnants of political individuality and opposition.

One of the few former leaders of the United Party who still dared to talk openly to foreigners told me bluntly in 1960:

'At the moment Ghana is ruled by fascism. Tomorrow it may be communism; and it will certainly be communism when Nkrumah leaves the stage—by natural causes or otherwise—because the left-wing leaders in the government camp are even worse than he is. They already have control of all the most important posts in the country. Nkrumah calls himself an "undogmatic Marxist," but the others—make no mistake about it—are orthodox Marxists.'[8]

By now this man is a detainee, his party is banned and the treatment meted out for the opposition by the leaders of the CPP has certainly demonstrated a thoroughly fascist outlook. Or should we rather say that the communist training of a number of its leading officials has borne fruit? Their methods are summed up in the Act which has become so well known today, the Preventive Detention Act, a symbol of repression in Ghana. This Act allows the authorities to take anyone into 'preventive custody' under mere suspicion of any act likely 'to endanger the security or authority of the State', or any 'predatory act', or any 'unworthy and criminal conduct'. The vague terminology gives the government a completely free hand to use the Act at any time to intimidate or hamstring active or potential opponents.

For a long time the government and its supporters tried to play down the implications of the Preventive Detention Act, but its operations were finally publicly admitted in an article published on 25 April 1960, by the official *Ghanaian Times*, which recorded that from the end of October 1958 no less than forty-nine leaders of the opposition, including the whole urban élite of the United Party, had been arrested and thrown into detention centres. In December 1960 the government arrested and imprisoned 118 people. According to information given by the leader of the United Party, Joseph Appiah, who was among those arrested, there were at least eighty members and officials of his party under arrest who, according to the provisions of the Preventive Detention Act, can be held in prison without trial for five years.[9] That Appiah was left at liberty for so long was perhaps due to the fact that he is the husband of the daughter of the late Sir Stafford Cripps, former Labour Chancellor of the Exchequer in Great Britain, and it was not possible to spirit him away without international public opinion showing some interest in his fate. However, in October 1960 Nkrumah abandoned these reservations and Appiah was arrested, together with forty-eight other members of the opposition, including J. B. Danquah. With this blow, the legal opposition (the United Party) ceased its *de facto* existence.[10] The *coup de grâce* was delivered a little later: on 13 November 1961 the parliamentary leader of the United Party, Diedjo Dombo, courageously informed the Press that within the past few days many hundreds of Nkrumah's opponents had been arrested, including 250 people in Kumasi, where the prisons were so overcrowded that the prisoners were unable to lie down at night. Among those arrested in this new wave of persecution were certain opposition elements within the Convention People's Party itself. A number of prospective victims escaped arrest by fleeing from the country. Meanwhile another decree lengthened the period during which a prisoner may be held without trial to twenty years. Among those lucky enough to make their escape in the spring of 1962 was Nkrumah's old confidant, K. A. Gbedemah, whose last post was that of Finance Minister. According to official calculations there were already, by the autumn of 1961, no fewer than 6,000 fugitives from Ghana in the neighbouring States of Togo and the Ivory Coast Republic.[11] In October 1961 a further law was passed introducing the crime of *lèse-majesté* for the person of Nkrumah and on 23 December 1961 the process was rounded off by a new State Security Law. The Nkrumah régime thus guarded itself by every possible legal device against any contingencies that might threaten to unseat it.

Despite this, there are still optimists in Ghana who have not altogether given up hope of a better future. They feel that the youth and the intelligentsia may still save Ghana and it is true that nowhere else in Africa are young people so politically wideawake and democratic in outlook as in Ghana. There is a sharp opposition at the University of Ghana in Legon, which is on the outskirts of Accra, and in the many colleges in the interior and even in the Ministry of Information and Education. The atmosphere around Nkrumah, the blatant political nepotism and patronage, the corruption in leading circles and the attempt to enforce complete political conformism are regarded with suspicion, disappointment and anger by many young intellectuals. The repressive actions taken by Nkrumah early in 1964 led to startling scenes of violence which caused considerable damage. Large crowds taken out to the university in CPP buses demonstrated against the students, whom they called 'saboteur intellectuals'. The students had earlier protested at the forced interruption of their studies for a seventeen-day period during the January 1964 referendum, and were discontented by the summary expulsion of six of their Western lecturers. Moreover, at a congress of the National Union of Ghana Students at Legon, resolutions were passed criticizing the attack on the judiciary, Sir Arku Korsah's dismissal, and 'creeping racial discrimination' against African students in Eastern Europe.[12] But Nkrumah's Convention People's Party had the upper hand. The *Ghanaian Times* published a formal warning that 'other nations have had to adopt sterner action . . . in order to obtain a reorientation of the élite',[13] and as most students are living on government grants, the intimidations of the CPP were not without effect. 'In the long run anyone in Ghana who tries to oppose Nkrumah is in a hopeless position,' a missionary told me in September 1964.

'Such a man is psychologically isolated, put under systematic pressure, and forced to confess his sins. If he does, and only then, he is allowed back into the community again. It must be remembered that these young intellectuals object mainly to Nkrumah's domestic policy; the opposition youth does not disapprove of his Pan-Africanism and certainly shares his favourable attitude towards the Soviet bloc.'

Extreme left-wing or radical socialism exercises a very strong attraction for the young intellectual élite of Ghana. Many discussions with students in Ghana have shown me that while they uncompromisingly reject colonialism—which they associate with the West—they regard socialism as a 'sensible solution' and accept it as a suitable 'third path' for Africa. At the same time their knowledge of communism and their ideas about it are usually based on the reading of one or two Marxist–Leninist books, reinforced by an uncritical acceptance of communist propaganda.

Broadcasts from Moscow and Peking can be quite well received along the whole of the West African coast and the Soviet Embassy in Accra, with its large staff, does its utmost to supplement these broadcasts with printed communist propaganda illustrating the happy life under socialism. In addition, the newspapers of the CPP are very susceptible to advertising pressure and the Soviet Embassy and representatives of other Soviet-bloc countries frequently pay for whole pages of the *Ghanaian Times*, the *Daily Graphic* and the *Evening News* in order to publish propaganda articles for the Ghanaian reader.

However it would be wrong to dismiss this paid propaganda as due exclusively to the corruptibility of newspapers, editors and advertising departments. The fact is that all means of influencing public opinion in Ghana are closely controlled by the government and the CPP and therefore such things could not happen without the toleration, if not encouragement, by official quarters. This is particularly true of radio broadcasts and these facilities are liberally placed at the disposal of Soviet representatives and of visitors from the Soviet bloc. As official exchanges of cultural groups, sports delegations, and scientific parties between Ghana and Eastern Europe are steadily growing there is nearly always some industrial or cultural exhibition in progress. It is quite clear that these matters are not arranged merely between minor communist officials and their Ghanaian counterparts, but are decided at government level with the blessing of the highest authorities in Ghana.

This may seem surprising because in the first phase of Ghana's independence it had not been greatly helped by the countries of the Soviet bloc. In accordance with rigid Stalinist doctrine, Nkrumah was automatically regarded as 'a marionette of neo-colonialism', quaintly abused as 'a representative of the compradore bourgeoisie' and considered unworthy of support or co-operation.[14] A change came about partly as a result of changes in Khrushchev's policy and partly as a result of the policy Nkrumah began to pursue both at home and abroad.

The essentials of Nkrumah's policy are Pan-Africanism and 'positive neutrality', the neutrality being reserved for the West and the positive side for the East. Nkrumah's relationship with the Soviet bloc has improved primarily because Pan-Africanism is now vigorously supported by Moscow, though (as we shall show elsewhere) Moscow was at first very cautious about this. However, Soviet Russia has now come to recognize that the Pan-African policy initiated in Accra is an excellent means of influencing African circles.

The dream of Pan-Africanism is older than the present clamour by African nationalists for independence. Like many similar movements it grew out of educational and cultural organizations, which were formed in London, Paris, and the United States in the early twenties, by African and American Negro students and writers. Although during his stay in London Nkrumah was for a time the secretary of an all-African students' group, he did not have much contact with these early idealistic endeavours.[15] His form of Pan-

Africanism is more elementary and political, and to some of his opponents and critics it appears to be nothing more than a cloak for egocentric dreams of African power.

So far very little has been done to put Nkrumah's political ideas into practice. In recent years the ostensible aim of Pan-Africanism —the establishment of an All-African Federation of States, or even of a United States of Africa—has not moved nearer to realization. The largest African State, Nigeria, without which there can be no united Africa, has firmly rejected the plans formulated in Accra. Even Ghana's immediate neighbours, Togo and the Ivory Coast Republic, are not enamoured of the idea of union with Kwame Nkrumah's State—particularly as Ghana has lodged territorial claims against both and, since 1957, there has been constant tension between Togo and Ghana over the problem of uniting the Ewe tribe. The tension was increased when Accra chose the very moment of Togo's declaration of independence to reveal its annexationist tendencies.

The only step towards the far-reaching ideal was the union with Guinea which Nkrumah brought about on 23 November 1958. The presidents of both countries made the following joint declaration:

'Inspired by the example of the thirteen American colonies that ultimately led to the formation of the United States of America, inspired by the efforts of the peoples of Europe, Asia and the Near East to come together on a rational basis, and, finally, inspired by the declaration of the Conference of Accra on African personality, we agree . . . that our two States shall form the core of the United States of West Africa.'[16]

This declaration has remained purely rhetorical, and an agreement signed by Nkrumah and Sékou Touré on 1 May 1959 materially restricted its scope. This second agreement did no more than refer to a 'co-ordination' of political, economic, military, and diplomatic measures. The union was to have a common anthem, a common flag and a common motto (Independence and Unity) but it was to have no supranational authority.[17]

Although no practical steps towards closer association were taken, both countries maintained the fiction of their 'union'. When the Sudan–Senegal Federation broke up in August 1960, both Conakry and Accra put out feelers in the hope of winning the left-wing, pro-Marxist politicians of Bamako (the former French Sudan is now known as Mali) for the idea of union. Nkrumah welcomed the first meeting with Modibo Keita of Mali, which took place in Bamako in November 1960, with the same exaggerated optimism which he had shown concerning his alliance with Touré two years previously. On his return he declared that their discussions had brought nearer the day when Mali and Ghana would have a 'common parliament'—the start of a new Pan-African Federation.

In fact the politicians of Bamako were more interested in Conakry than in distant Accra. Traditional attachments exist between Mali and Guinea, dating from the days of the *Rassemblement Démocratique Africain*, the first big supranational party in West Africa. (This organization sailed in the wake of communism until it was broken up by the defection of the Ivory Coast leader, Houphouet-Boigny.) In order not to be left out, Nkrumah immediately changed his ground: instead of a united Ghana-Mali he now urged a revival of the alliance with Conakry and the extension of the old union by the establishment of an Accra-Conakry-Bamako axis. In December 1960 the three national leaders met in Conakry and signed a declaration in favour of 'closely co-ordinating' their policies. Expressions like 'co-ordination' still meant no more than the fact that each party would be willing to surrender national sovereignty in order to establish a United States of West Africa, and this was not saying a great deal. In reality, their solidarity was already then being undermined by the jealousies and the mutual mistrust of the three leading men of the 'Union'.

To a certain extent this was also true of the relations of the Casablanca States, Egypt, Algeria, Morocco, Guinea, Mali and Ghana, whose governments were all associated. This union, established in Casablanca in January 1961, soon gave rise to the well-founded suspicion that it had been established chiefly in order to further the personal power aspirations of the various leaders. From the start both Nasser and Sékou Touré—with Nkrumah, who was not going to be outdone—did their utmost to put their own stamp on the Casablanca group and to exploit the propagandist declarations of the various sessions in their own national and Pan-African interests. Just how seriously the participants took their obligations could be seen from the obvious inconsistency between the voluble anti-Israeli declarations (forced through by Nasser) and the far-reaching economic co-operation between Israel and both Ghana and Mali. The oft-repeated announcement about their intention of forming a joint military command was also to be regarded as primarily propagandist, even though at its meeting in June 1961 the Casablanca group did adopt 'a definitive decision' to establish such a supreme command in Accra.

The unbridgeable gulf between the idea and the reality of a United States of Africa was soon recognized in Accra, but Nkrumah did not allow this to prevent him from taking advantage of the wave of nationalist enthusiasm throughout Africa. To increase Ghana's prestige, Nkrumah played yet another card: Accra was to be turned into a centre for all so-called liberation movements and all nationalist and anti-colonial forces throughout the African continent just as Cairo had been a centre for the Arab world until the trouble with Tunis and Baghdad, and was again striving to become such a centre.

How keen Nkrumah was on this can be seen from his invitation to Félix-Roland Moumié, exiled President of the *Union des Populations du Cameroun* (UPC), at the end of 1957, to move his headquarters from Cairo to Accra where he would be better placed to direct and organize the partisan war in the Cameroons. At that time Moumié was already receiving financial and 'technical' assistance from the Soviet bloc. Subsequently—first from Accra, then from Conakry—he broadcast spirited appeals to his guerilla units. It was also Moumié who persuaded the Government of Ghana of the advantage of establishing close relations with the Chinese People's Republic, which had been the chief source of support for the rebels in the latter phase of the civil war in the Cameroons. The successors of Moumié still have their headquarters in Accra, where they are praising Chinese revolutionary propaganda as well as Ghana's support for their 'anti-imperialist struggle'.[18]

Gradually more and more of the exiled extreme left-wing leaders of the African liberation movements in the Portuguese territories, East Africa, and some of the West and Central African Republics, had established their main headquarters in Accra, where, encouraged and financially supported by Nkrumah, they represented the hard core of the two organizations which had intensified the anti-colonial struggle in recent years: the Afro-Asian Solidarity Conference, which is definitely under communist leadership, and the All-African

157

People's Conference, whose leadership was controlled by Nkrumah, Touré and Nasser. For various reasons, the Solidarity Council, the executive of the Afro-Asian Solidarity Conference, stayed in Cairo, but the executive of the All-African People's Conference established itself in Accra and it was here, in December 1958, that the First All-African People's Conference took place and adopted a resolution condemning NATO and its 'economic auxiliary', the Organization for European Economic Co-operation (OEEC) and the European Common Market, as manifestations of 'military and economic colonialism'. Naturally no reference was made to the neo-colonialist intrigues and operations of the Soviet bloc.

It was during this conference that a friendship began which was soon to have a disastrous effect on developments in Africa—the friendship between Nkrumah and Patrice Lumumba, the nationalist Congo leader, who had founded his *Mouvement National Congolais* two months previously and was eagerly casting around abroad for advice and assistance. Nkrumah found a willing pupil for his Pan-African ideas in Lumumba, who assured him at once that as soon as he was head of an independent Congolese State, he would forthwith institute discussions with 'the already existing Union of West African States [Ghana and Guinea] in order to bring about a speedy unification of the three countries and thus lay the basis for a permanent edifice of the All-African State'. Even more sinister was the fact that Nkrumah confirmed and encouraged his Congolese pupil in the conviction that the way to power in the final phase of the struggle for liberation must necessarily be through spectacular, demonstrative actions. He assured Lumumba of 'every conceivable moral and practical support' when the time came for action.

It was not long before Lumumba was badly in need of the promised support. In January 1959—only a few weeks after his meeting with Nkrumah—a revolt broke out in Leopoldville, and in the following months, while independence for the Congo was drawing near, Lumumba had to ward off the attacks of numerous domestic opponents who resisted the ideas that he, the leader of the *Mouvement National Congolais*, had borrowed from Nkrumah—in particular, the idea that the coming, independent Congo State must be strictly centralist (along Ghanaian lines). Immediately prior to the declaration of independence, Nkrumah persuaded Lumumba that, in order to seize power and get his centralized State over its first hurdle, he must co-operate with his political opponent, Kasavubu, the 'king' of the Bakongo—although, of course, with the ulterior motive of getting rid of the awkward ruler of the Lower Congo at a later, more convenient stage. This, in any case, was the plan revealed in documents found at the time of Lumumba's arrest and made public by the Congolese military commander, Joseph Mobutu.[19]

In the spring of 1960 Nkrumah had reacted with cautious reserve to a Soviet offer of credits, but before long his attitude changed. In August 1960 a delegation from Accra travelled to the Soviet Union and an agreement was signed in Moscow for a 'far-reaching exchange' of scientific experience and of cultural delegations. In addition, the Soviet Union agreed to grant the West African State long-term credits to the tune of 160 million roubles. This was to finance the 'fraternal assistance' the Soviet Union proposed to give Ghana to help it exploit its natural resources, develop its industry, build hydraulic power stations and train technicians. The Soviet Union agreed to accept cocoa beans, coffee, rubber and fruit from Ghana in return.[20]

Towards the end of 1960 Nkrumah announced that over the next few years Ghana would send 3,000 students to the countries of the Soviet bloc for specialist training—a number far greater than in any previous agreements of this kind between Russia and African and Asian countries. More serious were the reports, which cropped up regularly from the middle of 1961, that Ghana intended to have the greater part of its officers and NCOs trained at Soviet military academies. The belief that there was to be close military co-operation between Ghana and the Eastern European countries was underlined, towards the end of June 1962, by the arrival of a Soviet military delegation in Accra. It was announced that the visit of the delegation, led by General Komarov, deputy-commander of Soviet land forces, was in return for the visit of Ghanaian military leaders to the Soviet Union; in fact, these military leaders had already made frequent visits to Eastern Europe, in particular in the spring of 1962.[21]

This close contact—particularly the military co-operation—was the result of talks between Nkrumah and representatives of the Soviet Government during his visits to the Soviet Union in July and September 1961. Nkrumah's first visit extended to other countries of the Soviet bloc as well and lasted several weeks, during which time he made dozens of pro-Soviet declarations in Moscow, Prague, East Berlin, Budapest and Bucharest. In a speech delivered at a banquet in his honour at the Kremlin on 11 July 1961 Nkrumah said that the future of Ghana was 'closely connected with the future of the Soviet Union'. After praising Lenin he concluded by saying: 'The new ideas of your country in this new era will, I am convinced, defeat the forces of reaction.'[22]

In East Berlin (which Nkrumah was the first representative of an African government to visit) and in Sofia and Budapest, the Ghanaian leader expressed approval of Soviet intentions towards Germany, stressing in particular the need for a peace treaty with 'the two German States' as set out in the proposals of the Soviet Government of 10 January 1959.[23]

Nkrumah's attitude at the Belgrade Conference of uncommitted nations, in September 1961, was no less clear. Of all the statesmen present he was the one who most staunchly supported the policy of the Soviet Government towards Germany and the one who, in the private sessions, called most vigorously for a joint recognition of the East German régime and the establishment of diplomatic relationships with its government.[24]

This attitude was further underlined during Nkrumah's subsequent visit to the Soviet Union and during the visit of Anastas Mikoyan to Accra in 1962. According to the reports of communist journalists, 'Ghanaian-Soviet harmony' was given 'overwhelming expression' during visits by the Soviet delegation to the house of the President of the Executive Bureau of the Convention People's Party and to the headquarters of the Ghanaian Trade-Union Federation. Everywhere the Soviet guests were greeted with the strains of the 'International'. The Secretary of the CPP declared: 'Nkrumah says that the aim of our party is socialism; and this is what binds us together.'[25] To clinch matters, Ghanaian leaders pointed out that like the ruling parties of Cuba, Guinea, and Mali, the CPP of Ghana had been treated as an equal at the Twenty-second Congress of the Communist Party of the Soviet Union, while its representatives had been made to feel 'the co-operation and friendship' that marked the relationship between the Communist Party of the Soviet Union and the CPP.[26]

This harmony between Soviet communism and Ghanaian social-ism, though neither complete nor without friction, naturally began to influence the day-to-day policy of Ghana, both at home and abroad. The language used by the leaders of Ghana was gradually becoming identical with communist phraseology. Eric Mettler, who as the London correspondent of the *Neue Zürcher Zeitung* has visited Ghana on several occasions, was quite right when he pointed out in December 1961:

'The new men who now wield influence with Nkrumah, the men who have been put in to replace his old comrades since he returned from his visits to the countries of the Soviet bloc [in 1961], talk in a pseudo-Marxist jargon, but they have digested the new ideas no better than they had previously assimilated the libertarian ideas of the West. They are impelled by an almost obsessive urge to shake off "Western tutelage".'

But Mettler exaggerated the practical effects of the American decision to finance the building of the Volta dam. The offer of American aid did not hamper pro-Soviet developments in Ghana. For example, the mere announcement of any proposed aid from the communist Powers was enough to send the controlled Press and Radio of Ghana into ecstasies of admiration and gratitude, but the late President Kennedy's decision to finance the Volta project with American dollars was coldly received and cynically denigrated. The *Evening News* of Accra, the official organ of the CPP, had only one thing to say about Kennedy's decision: 'Dollar Boss! Better late than never'—After which it immediately went on to publish a detailed report 'exposing the hostile policy of the United States' over the question of Red China's membership of the United Nations. The text of this article, incidentally, was provided by the Chinese embassy in Accra.[27] A Western correspondent in Accra aptly summed up the situation: 'The West pays, the East increases its influence.' The correspondent went on to say:

'Ghana already has a source from which it can obtain all the industrial plants it needs for making use of the surplus Volta power and making the whole Volta project viable. This source is the £38·1 million credits granted by various countries of the Soviet bloc. As a result of these credits Ghana is to receive an iron ore plant, a steel works, boot and shoe and textile factories, several shipbuilding yards, assembly works for Soviet tractors, sugar, rubber and yarn factories, a glass works, and so on. It will all be industrial plant that Ghana badly needs, and some of it will consume a great deal of power. Without the Volta project this power would simply not be available, so in the last resort, by financing the Volta project the United States is creating the basis on which the Soviet bloc can industrialize Ghana and dig itself in with its technical (and political) advisers, its experts, and all its usual methods . . .'[28]

In short, the Volta project will do nothing to dissuade Ghana from proceeding with economic measures designed to bring about fundamental social changes towards socialism. For some time now there has been a plan calculated to secure immediate economic benefits; it is based on a report drawn up at the beginning of 1962 by the communist Joseph Bognar, a Budapest professor of economics, and it lays down details for the stage-by-stage collectivization of Ghanaian agriculture. Ghanaian peasant farmers would, it was rightly assumed, oppose the plan, and an appropriate tax policy had been worked out to compel them to surrender their holdings. As a preliminary, they were warned in the summer of 1962 not to extend their activities, though they had been called upon to do just that the previous year.[29] The cocoa-bean growers were in any case in a precarious position; from the beginning of January 1961, when they were first compelled to sell half their production (Ghana is the world's biggest supplier of cocoa) through the state-controlled United Ghana Farmers' Council, which was in a position to depress prices and which is taking full advantage of this power. There was also the decree of July 1961, by which they are 'voluntarily' compelled to invest ten per cent of the guaranteed producer price in government bonds.

These measures stem from an economic policy directed against private initiative and property and in favour of collectivization and the establishment of a state economic sector; a policy vigorously supported by the propaganda of the CPP, which vociferously praises the communist economic system while bitterly attacking the European Economic Community. In 1962 Nkrumah joined in personally, in a vehement speech to an Accra conference of African

Freedom Fighters (most of whom have been subsidized by Ghana for years):

'The EEC serves the profit lust of the imperialists and is hostile to the independent and neutralist policy of the African States . . . The EEC represents an attempt to replace the old system of colonial exploitation by a new system of collective colonialism which will be stronger and more dangerous than the old evil from which we are seeking to liberate our continent.'[30]

But as an African Common Market had no hope of success, the only course left open to Nkrumah was still greater reliance on the economic system of the Soviet bloc.

With this we come to Ghana's cardinal difficulty, which is exacerbated by the rejection of all other possibilities and by the hasty adoption of measures decided upon in a highly emotional state. Constitutionally there is no longer any system of checks and balances that could help the country to maintain an even keel. On the one hand, the power of the old, conservative, traditionalist elements has been undermined; on the other hand, the new liberal forces have been hamstrung. A group of wild pseudo-Marxists is in control, though they still protest publicly that they have no intention of binding the country to either power bloc, but to Pan-Africanism and to a powerful Third Force based on a policy of non-alignment. It is possible that at first their assurances were honest, but today they are nothing but a camouflage for the truth. As neither Pan-Africanism nor a Third Force has hope of immediate success, the contradiction between words and deeds is becoming more obvious, and the way to a more moderate policy (and perhaps even to co-operation with the West) has been barred. The real beneficiary of this confused situation is the Soviet Union. *Not that communism has won the final victory in Ghana; far from it.* In fact, its practical successes and scope are not as great as they were in Guinea during 1960 and the first half of 1961. But public opinion in Ghana is being more and more bewildered and dominated by communist agitation and propaganda. The right to express unorthodox opinions is restricted and often suppressed. A thin stratum of pro-communists, entrenched in the various ministries and political organizations, is facilitating the infiltration of communist ideology and propaganda into the various groups and institutions.

The time is past when Ghana propagated 'African socialism', in contrast to 'Scientific socialism'. Early in 1963 *Spark*—the journal of the government-subsidized Bureau of African Affairs—came out in sharp contradiction to one of the basic tenets of African socialism, as expressed by Sékou Touré of Guinea, that 'the class struggle here is impossible for there are no classes but only social strata'. This *Spark* denied: 'Socialist parties in Africa must clearly realize their class struggle'.[31] At the beginning of January, 1964, the official *Ghanaian Times* wrote:

'Some of our political scientists have served us with the false doctrine that Ghana is fortunate to be starting its socialist revolution without basic class anatagonism. This is a dangerous fallacy . . . we underestimated the nature of the growing capitalist class and opened our ranks wide for them to infiltrate and subvert our revolution'.[32]

At the same time, CPP headquarters instructed party members that 'a real education in Nkrumahism must be preceded by an understanding of the principles of Marxism'. The staff of the Kwame Nkrumah Ideological Institute in Accra, most of them communist sympathizers and lecturers from bloc countries, has repeatedly made it clear that Marxism is to be understood as 'Marxism-Leninism'. Commenting on the January 1964 referendum in Ghana, Peter Preston wrote in *The Guardian*:

'Observers in Accra hold that the régime's current swing leftward eclipses all others . . . They either hold that the President, hidden perpetually in his white castle on the coast, ringed by militia and armoured cars, has lost all touch with reality, and dismiss him and his new batch of party advisers as "crackpots", or they find a pattern, tracing the sudden change of course to the conference of African leaders in Addis Ababa last year (May 1963). There, the argument goes, Nkrumah, who had not travelled abroad for a long time, found that his influence was negligible . . . He then decided that the only way to remain a power on the continent was to appeal to the extreme but influential minorities which exist in every African country . . . The belief is that communism is the Redeemer's means to his own ideological end.'[33]

Similar tendencies are present in Mali, the former French Sudan.

This State was established in August 1960 under the leadership of Modibo Keita, who proudly traces his origin back to the famous Keita dynasty which reigned in the early Middle Ages. After the break-up of the Mali Federation, which consisted of the former French Sudan and Senegal, the former adopted the name which had been given to the federation. The federation failed for a number of reasons: structural inadequacies, French intrigues and, in the last resort, the incompatible temperaments of the two partners, Léopold Sédar Senghor of Senegal and Modibo Keita. To put it bluntly, one might say that the Mali Federation broke up because it set out to reconcile the irreconcilable: a democratic spirit and constitution in Senegal, an authoritarian temperament and totalitarian conditions in the Sudan.

The constitution of the Sudan, headed by the Sudanese section of the old RDA under Modibo and Madeira Keita, revealed definite left-wing tendencies. Like Touré's *Parti Démocratique de Guinée* (PDG), the Sudanese State party still upholds the pro-communist ideas on which the RDA was originally based—not surprising when we recall that many of its leaders and officials were trained at various communist centres in the 1940s and 1950s.

In accordance with their communist training, the Sudanese leaders demanded all the decisive powers when the Mali Federation was officially founded in July 1960. They occupied the Ministries of the Interior and of Defence and opposed the election of Senghor as President of the Federation. When the Senegalese vigorously objected to such methods, Modibo Keita put the first phase of his 'seizure of power' campaign into action. It was his bad luck however that he had to operate in Dakar—the Senegalese city which had been chosen as the capital—because this meant that the slightest mis-calculation spelt failure. Details of the planned *coup* became known, the attempt to arrest various leading personalities was a failure, and the broadcasting station remained in Senegalese hands. Possession of the radio station enabled the Senegalese, led by Senghor and Mamadou Dia, to organize successful counter-action. The Sudanese were packed off to Bamako. They broke off relations with Dakar and proclaimed the Republic of Mali, which was now confined to the Sudan.

Since then, Sudanese Mali has become a staunch partner of Ghana and, in particular, of Guinea. Nkrumah, Touré and Keita established the three-State union of West Africa; at the beginning of 1961 the three, together with the United Arab Republic, Morocco and the Algerian GPRA, joined to form the Casablanca group. In a series of conferences a joint policy, particularly on the Congo, was worked out among Casablanca, Accra, Conakry and Cairo. This was chiefly characterized by wild attacks on Western colonial imperialism, full support for Lumumba, and later for the rebel movement in the Congo and in general the encouragement of communist agitation and propaganda. It was obvious, of course, that this alliance of the three West African States with the three North African States was a marriage of political convenience. The United Arab Republic was following its own interests and so were Ghana and Guinea, while Mali had unmistakably taken up its position alongside its two African brothers.

The nature of the policy pursued by Mali was first visible in the attitude of the Bamako representatives at the fifteenth session of the United Nations in the autumn of 1960. After Keita had established diplomatic relations with Peking in August 1960 Mali's demand for the admission of Red China as a member of the UN did not come as a surprise, particularly as most of the African States had taken a stand against the United States either by supporting the Soviet proposals or by withholding their votes. But on the Tibetan question, Mali and Guinea were the only two African States to support the Soviet Union when it angrily opposed a discussion of the tragic events in Tibet at the United Nations. Tunisia, Libya and Nigeria voted with the United States for a discussion of the Tibetan question, while the other African States (with the exception of Mali and Guinea) abstained. When voting took place on the proposal to put the Hungarian question on the agenda for discussion Mali was the only African State to vote with the Soviet Union against it. Tunisia and Liberia voted for the West, while the other African States abstained.

Mali's behaviour in the UN showed that the communists had a new potential ally in Africa. It is true that discussions are still going on within the Mali State Party concerning the particular degree of co-operation with communism, but the fact is that communist theses, arguments and propaganda are already playing a big role in Bamako, while various ministries, high party and trade union offices, and posts in the youth and women's organizations are (as in Ghana) already in the hands of orthodox Marxist elements, who have not only embraced communist ideology but have adopted communist methods and unscrupulousness and the communist technique of seizing and wielding political power. There is no doubt that the pro-communist elements in Mali have grown in strength since independence. In fact, as Soviet influence has tended to decline in Guinea, so it has increased in Mali; though Mali (particularly in economic matters, for example, on the question of co-operation with the EEC) has not yet burnt all its bridges to the West. On the other hand the representatives of the Mali State Party at the Twenty-second Congress of the Communist Party of the Soviet Union certainly outdid their colleagues from Ghana and Guinea in their pro-communist attitude.

Tidjani Traoré, a member of the Political Bureau of the *Union Soudanaise* and a deputy of the Mali National Assembly, declared at the Moscow Congress:

'Comrade Members of the Praesidium, Comrade guests, Comrade delegates to the Party Congress! Today with enthusiasm we observe the picture of the great prophecies of Lenin, who, because he presented the peoples with the methods of analysis and un-exampled, practical guidance to conscious, creative action, enriched Marxism and developed it into Marxist-Leninism, whose correctness and effectiveness is being confirmed every day by the successes of the Soviet Union in the scientific and technological sphere . . . Imperialism is digging its own grave. Yesterday, today, and at all times when peace-loving people anywhere throw off their chains, the colonialists immediately begin to whine: "Beware, this is the hand of Moscow, the hand of communism!" But this means that *communism has become synonymous with freedom*. Each time when an organization arises and does its best to abolish inequality and to secure a just distribution of the material goods of this world, the colonialists begin to shout: "Beware, this is the hand of Moscow, the hand of communism!" But this means that *communism is synonymous with justice, synonymous with equality*. Whenever any party exposes discrimination the imperialists and the colonialists start to rage: "Beware, they are agents of Moscow; they are communists!" But this means that *communism is synonymous with fraternity!* The peoples of Africa . . . know who their real friends are. And it is quite natural that the Soviet Union and the countries of the Socialist camp are amongst those friends, and that they give unlimited support to the powerful national revolutionary movements.'[34]

A few months later Modibo Keita himself talked in exactly the same tone. Speaking in the Lomonossov Institute in Moscow, the President of Mali declared:

'Unfortunately at the present time the experiment of neo-colonialism is being carried out in Africa, and its aim is to perpetuate capitalism under cover of talk about socialism. This is a great fraud, and we must fight against it unless we want to see the people of Africa deceived by such lies. How can one talk of socialism when foreign military bases are in one's country, and when the economic oppression of capitalism continues unchanged?'[35]

At a dinner given by Leonid Breshnev, then President of the Supreme Soviet, to the guest from Mali, Keita spoke even more clearly: 'You and we are both convinced of the victory of socialism. Precisely for this reason it was our desire to travel to the source of this idea, to see the life in your country with our own eyes and to witness your successes.'[36]

Nikita Khrushchev naturally welcomed talk of this kind and, at a demonstration of Soviet-Mali friendship held in the Kremlin he declared: 'Some of these countries [in Africa] have actually won their independence, and they can decide for themselves what they do. Others have for the time being won only a fictitious independence.' He went on to say that the peoples of these latter countries still had a hard fight ahead before they could win through to real independence, and in a number of cases this fight could take on 'very intense forms, including even armed struggle in conditions of existing national independence.'[37]

With these words Khrushchev was unmistakably laying down the guiding principle of Soviet policy in Africa: the Kremlin is to determine the nature of independence and thus the methods and the forms of the struggle—that is, by implication, the Soviet-communist form of action. Where forces favourable to communism are at work, as in Ghana and Mali, the Kremlin will wait for them to develop of their own accord. Nevertheless, there is a possibility, even in Ghana and Mali, that the ruling élite may still realize the dangers and penalties of co-operating with communism—as happened in Guinea in the late autumn of 1961. No prophetic vision is required to see that sooner or later a conflict will break out between the pro-communist nationalist forces and the pro-communist internationalist forces.

NOTES

[1] The *Guardian* (Manchester), 4 February 1964.

[2] Pamphlet issued by the Government of Ghana in early 1961; translated from the Twi.

[3] Editorial in the *Ghanaian Times* (Accra), 23 April 1960.

[4] Radio Accra broadcast, 18 April 1960.

[5] The *Economist* (London), 8 February 1964.

[6] As Dr Nkrumah did in February 1964 when he ordered the dismissal from office of the Chief Justice, Sir Arku Korsah.

[7] The *Guardian*, 4 February 1964.

[8] In conversation with the author, 26 April 1960.

[9] Information given in a conversation with the author, 24 April 1960.

[10] Reuters, 4 October 1961. Joseph Appiah and Dr Danquah were later released.

[11] *Neue Zürcher Zeitung*, 9 November 1961.

[12] *African Review* (London), March 1964, p. 5.

[13] Ibid.

[14] Cf. for example *Narody Afriki* (Moscow), 1954; *Neue Zeit* (Moscow), 14 February 1951.

[15] Cf. Nkrumah, op. cit., in particular, the remarks on Du Bois and Garvey.

[16] Radio Accra broadcast, 24 November 1958.

[17] Undated cyclostyled publication issued by the Government of Guinea (May 1959).

[18] See for instance the statement by Kingue Abel, Vice-President of the UPC, reported by (North) Korean News Agency (KCNA), 19 February 1964.

[19] *Neue Zürcher Zeitung*, 30 September 1960.

[20] *Vedemosti vershovnogo Soviets*, No. 51 (1960), pp. 1169-71.

[21] *Neue Zürcher Zeitung*, 1 July 1962.

[22] AFP (Moscow), 12 July 1961.

[23] *Neues Deutschland*, 13 August 1961.

[24] Cyclostyled reports of the Belgrade Conference.

[25] *Neues Deutschland*, 13 January 1962.

[26] Cf. the speech of E. Tsefas at the Twenty-second Congress of the CPSU, reported in *Pravda*, 25 October 1961.

[27] *Frankfurter Allgemeine Zeitung*, 27 December 1961.
[28] Ibid.
[29] *Neue Zürcher Zeitung*, 4 July 1962.
[30] *Neues Deutschland*, 17 June 1961.
[31] Cited in *African Review* (London), March 1964, p. 4.
[32] Ibid., p. 5.
[33] The *Guardian*, 4 February 1964.
[34] *Pravda*, 26 October 1961.
[35] Tass, 22 May 1962.
[36] Cf. *Neues Deutschland*, 24 May 1962.
[37] Tass, 30 May 1962.

Chapter X

THE ECONOMIC APPROACH

ECONOMIC factors play an important part in Soviet calculations concerning Africa. This is hardly surprising when we remember that Marxism is a 'science' based essentially on the determining role of the productive forces and the means of production in social life. Lenin even went so far as to describe politics as 'concentrated economics', thus underlining the dominant role of economics, its potentials and processes. Addressing the Twenty-first Congress of the Communist Party of the Soviet Union in January 1959, Mr Khrushchev described economics as 'the main sphere in which the peaceful competition between socialism and capitalism develops' and added: 'Our interest is to win this competition in the shortest possible historical space of time.'[1] The Soviet leader knew very well, of course, that in some respects the result of this competition will largely depend on whether capitalism or socialism can dominate the enormous natural resources and economic potential of Africa and harness them in its own interests. According to Lenin's theory capitalism must collapse when it loses its 'last reserves'—the colonial and semi-colonial countries—and it is therefore a significant indication of communist thinking that the political studies and propaganda writings of the Eastern bloc on Africa deal extensively with economic questions. For example, the February 1961 number of the international communist publication *Problems of Peace and Socialism* published a survey entitled 'Africa—Continent of the Future: Facts and Documents'. The survey noted that the natural resources of Africa included the biggest known deposits of uranium, 34·4 per cent of the iron-ore deposits, 74·9 per cent of the chromium, 51·4 per cent of the cobalt, 90·2 per cent of the diamonds, and

47·3 per cent of the copper in the capitalist world, in addition to vast oil deposits. The survey went on to say:

'According to a United Nations report, most of the minerals extracted in Africa (92 per cent) are still exported, and only eight per cent are left for internal consumption . . . Thus, though direct colonial rule has been abolished on the greater part of the continent, colonialism still exists. It relies mainly on *the economic positions of the imperialist powers* in Africa.'[2]

The Africans themselves had also realized this, the survey continued, and it quoted the President of Guinea, Sékou Touré, as follows:

'We have no grounds for saying that the imperialist States intend to relinquish voluntarily their economic, political and military power. Africa, despised and deprived of rights, now occupies the main place in their expansionist plans . . . Colonialism tends to acquire an international form which permits the banners and anthems of African nationalism but forbids any infringement of colonial interests. Political independence does not in itself signify complete national liberation. It is, of course, an important and decisive stage. Nevertheless, we must recognize that national independence presupposes not only political liberation but, and this is the main thing, economic liberation. Social progress is impossible without these two essential factors.'[3]

The ideas of Sékou Touré are shared by many African nationalists. The young African élite almost unanimously regards the traditionally one-sided economic relationships between the newly-independent countries and the West as a new form of colonialism that prevents full freedom of political decision and makes the welfare of the new African States dependent on the capitalist world market, with all its fluctuations, including the steady drop in prices of raw materials while prices of investment goods and technical apparatus are rising. There is a large measure of agreement between the Russians and many Africans when they regard the Soviet Union as an alternative to the West, and above all as an economic alternative, thus facilitating Russian attempts to influence the trading and industrialization policies of the African States. Communist propaganda tries to camouflage the imperialist core of this Soviet economico-political offensive, though it could be clearly detected in the Congo policy of the Soviet Union, which aimed at ending American and European exploitation of Katanga's enormous resources and thus depriving the West of its uranium and cobalt supplies.

But the ultimate aims of communist economic policy go much further: in practice, the balance of trade between most of the under-developed countries and the West is unfavourable to the former. Egypt is the best example of this. In 1959 the United States exported goods to the value of 30 million Egyptian pounds to Egypt and imported goods from Egypt to the value of only two million Egyptian pounds. On the other hand, the Soviet Union was prepared to accept an unfavourable balance in its 1959 trade with the United Arab Republic. The Soviet Union exported goods to the value of 26·8 million Egyptian pounds to the United Arab Republic and imported goods to the value of 28·3 million Egyptian pounds from the UAR.[4]

In other words, the commercial interests of the West are allowed to dominate its economic relations with the under-developed countries. This means that in African eyes the economic policy of the West bears a heavy psychological burden because it prevents the under-developed countries from balancing their imports by a corresponding volume of exports. A striking example of this situation is afforded by the trading relations between France and Guinea. When Sékou Touré defiantly led his country to political independence in 1958, France answered with draconian sanctions by immediately cancelling Guinea's exports of bananas to France, exports that were a matter of economic life and death for Guinea. This action of the French Government proved to be a grave error. The Soviet bloc (particularly East Germany) stepped in at once and offered to take Guinea's entire banana crop, though at a reduced price. Since then—and in spite of the Solod crisis and the following period of deterioration of the political relations—most of the countries of the Soviet bloc have concluded long-term trading agreements with Guinea, relieving it of its most immediate export problems.

Communist trade with Egypt and Guinea, as well as with Ghana, illustrates the political implications of economic relations with the new African States. Here was the beginning of a communist commercial offensive that would inevitably have political repercussions affecting both the internal order and the foreign policy of the under-developed countries. At the moment (and also it had been intensified in the early 1960s) this offensive is only in its preliminary stages, but it is already impossible to shut one's eyes to its inner dynamism and ultimate objectives. As early as 1959–60 the countries of the Soviet bloc were trying to do business with those African countries which were not yet independent. The Soviet Union, Czechoslovakia, China and East Germany all tried to establish relations with East Africa before independence; once sovereignty was achieved such relations could easily be extended. As late as 1958 the Soviet Union had no commercial relations with the three East African countries, Kenya, Uganda, and Tanganyika, but in 1959 the Russians imported goods from Uganda to the value of £2·48 million sterling.[5] In 1960 China and Czechoslovakia followed the example of the Soviet Union. The Soviet bloc also succeeded in increasing its trade turn-over with the former Rhodesian Federation and with Nyasaland. In 1959, African imports from these countries reached a total value of £482,000 sterling, and exports £4·86 million sterling, while the respective figures for the first half of 1960 were already £411,000 and £3·838 million respectively. Commercial relations with independent African States have developed in much the same proportions over the past seven years. The exports of Togo, only a small sum in 1959, had already risen to 19 million new francs in the first half of 1960, when Eastern Europe temporarily imported more goods from Togo than the West.[6] There had been no trade between Mali and the Soviet Union before 1960. By the end of September 1962, the Soviet Union was second only to France as an import market for Mali. Soviet shipments amounted to $8,844,000 against $15,136,000 for France.[7] In 1961 alone the Soviet Union expanded its trade (as compared with 1960) with Guinea by 293 per cent; with Algeria by 771 per cent; Sudan by 76 per cent, and Soviet exports to Ghana increased by 178 per cent.[8]

From the long-term point of view this development of commercial relations between Africa and the communist countries seems more important than Soviet technical aid and credits for Africa. Unlike the West, the communists are not, for the moment, attaching great importance to the sale of their own commodities on the African market, but are aiming primarily at 'liquidating the export difficulties' of the African countries. The communists' acceptance of an unusually unfavourable balance of trade is thus a political move which the national bourgeoisie of certain African countries approve since it enables them to consolidate their position as agents for foreign (mainly Western) goods within their own countries. This one-sided Soviet trade is facilitated by the favourable terms of payment which the Soviet-bloc countries are prepared to grant to their African trading partners. Unlike the West, which often demands payment for its goods in hard currencies, the communists will accept payment in any currency and pay for their imports from Africa in any desired form. The advantages for the Africans are so very great that the threat of dependence involved is often ignored.

It is hardly necessary to point out that African economic dependence on the Soviet bloc enables the communists to make political demands and to carry on political activity in the countries with which they have trading relations.

Another factor of inestimable importance enters into these commercial transactions and into the granting of credits and the placing of investments: the Soviet economic approach to Africa is essentially 'anti-capitalist'. Economic activities are conducted entirely through governmental channels, whereas those of the Western countries are primarily of a private capitalist and non-governmental nature. The Western businessman does not look for his business partners in government departments, but in the sphere of private enterprise. The Soviet-bloc countries have no private importers or exporters, no representatives of individual firms or concerns, but exclusively *officials* of a monolithic communist state economy. They are not interested in talking to, or doing business with private businessmen, but only with governments and government departments with whom they negotiate down to the last detail, and they encourage their African trading partners to implement their agreements. In this way they exert pressure on them to *organize* and plan their imports and exports.

The credit policy of the communist countries has the same aim. Credits are regarded as political instruments with which Africa's ties with the West can be disrupted, and economic measures introduced which will, in the long run, strengthen communism. Though the intentions of the Soviet bloc are perfectly clear, its activities do not, so far, appear to represent any real danger.

Firstly, the credits granted until now to African countries south of the Sahara have been on quite a small scale.

Secondly, although they are offered on very favourable terms (including low rates of interest), Soviet aid is often less attractive than Western aid. In a study in *Problems of Communism*, David L. Morrison deals with 'Moscow's first steps' (in Africa) and correctly points out that Soviet loans and credits are intended to be repaid, whereas this is by no means the case with all Western credits. In fact, when the West makes money available to the under-developed countries this is often not in the form of loans, but of direct grants.

For example, in the period 1 July 1957–30 June 1959, Western countries, independently and through the International Bank for Reconstruction and Development and other UN agencies, granted loans totalling $114·7 million to Africa, while in the same period non-repayable grants amounted to $296·3 million.[9] In their negotiations with Western finance agencies, African governments often proceed on the assumption that the 'credits' they are being granted will in the long run not be repayable. So far no major case of similar generosity is known on the part of the Soviet-bloc countries. It is well known that in 1961 the Soviet Union was pressing for the first repayment of credits granted to Guinea in 1959, although the credits had not yet been completely taken up.

The third factor of great importance in this matter is that Soviet credit grants are greatly inflated by propaganda. The formal declaration that a credit is to be granted is invariably made into a major item of publicity. During the negotiations, and above all when the agreement is signed, the Africans are given the most generous assurances concerning the rapidity and efficiency with which the arrangements will be implemented. (Invariably they include the construction of plants with the assistance of Soviet technicians.) Expectations are therefore very high and the African beneficiary visualizes gigantic factories, imposing sports stadiums and splendid school buildings literally shooting out of the ground like mushrooms. Before long, however, they face a reality which is usually less impressive. Many months, sometimes even years, pass before the projects for which Soviet aid has been promised emerge from the planning stage. Apart from one or two prestige buildings, it takes even longer before the various projects are actually completed. The result is subsequent disappointment and a loss of faith in the self-lessness of Soviet aid.

Guinea provides the best example of all this. During a visit to Moscow in August 1959, a delegation of the *Parti Démocratique de Guinée* were promised credits of 140 million roubles, or roughly the equivalent of $35 million. Announcements on 1 March and 8 September 1960 provided information as to how these credits were to be used. The first joint Soviet-Guinean announcement declared that the Soviet Union had promised technical assistance 'for the building of a cement works, a saw-mill for the production of railway sleepers, a combined leather and shoe factory, a canning factory for fruit and vegetables, refrigeration plant, a Polytechnic Institute for 1,500 students and a sports stadium in Conakry to seat 25,000 people'.[10] The communiqué also mentioned geological surveys for diamond and gold prospecting, the supply of machinery and equipment for diamond mining, the delivery of complete agricultural technical equipment, technical assistance for the development of Conakry airport, and for the building of the Conakry–Mamou railway line.[11] In the second announcement the Soviet Union promised technical assistance to help to build an industrial centre on the Konkouré river.

Up to the end of 1963 only a fraction of these and many other smaller projects had been realized. According to a statement made to the author by a highly-placed Guinean, by the beginning of 1963 various projects were at the planning stage and not one of them had been implemented. Dozens of projects had been allowed to fade out, particularly after the second half of 1961 when the crisis in the relations between Guinea and the Soviet Union was at its height. According to the same source, in the thirty-six months following the Soviet blanket assurances of August 1959 the Government of Guinea had been able to make use of, or had had placed at its disposal, only fifteen per cent of the promised Soviet credits. The 'generous and selfless assistance' offered by the Soviet Union, accompanied by widespread propaganda and publicity, turned out to be something of a fiasco—and was made more painful by the fact that, for a long period, the Government of Guinea had had to meet the expenses of innumerable Soviet experts, advisers, members of the planning staffs, and so on.

Taking into account such disappointing experiences and other disadvantages, the spectre of the 'rouble offensive' in Africa, which has been painted in such grisly colours by the Western Press, begins to look less menacing, even if we include the assistance provided by the other countries of the Soviet bloc.[12]

The following survey of communist credit policy towards some African States provides details of credits offered and credits actually made available. Up to the end of 1963 only six States had been offered any credits: Ethiopia, Guinea, Ghana, Mali, Somalia and Nigeria. When the communist Press publishes figures relating to Soviet aid, it departs from its usual custom of differentiating between North Africa and Black Africa. Thus when communists talk of 'Soviet aid to Africa' this includes, for example, all the arrangements between the Soviet Union and Egypt. In consequence the statement of the official Soviet foreign-trade publication that no less than 28·8 per cent of all foreign aid granted by the Soviet Union up to 15 March 1961[13] had gone to Africa appears much less impressive when one realizes that Soviet aid to Egypt, which represented a total of over $U.S. 600 million till then, is included in this amount When the details of Soviet aid to individual African countries south of the Sahara are examined they prove to be far less significant.

1. *Ethiopia*: The Empire of Haile Selassie was the first country in non-Arab Africa on the Soviet credit list. On 12 July 1959, during the visit of the Negus to the Soviet Union, the Kremlin granted Ethiopia credits totalling 400 million (old) roubles, representing a value of $U.S. 102 million. A joint statement published on 25 March 1960 recorded that the credits were to be used for building an oil refinery in Assab with a capacity for refining 500,000 tons per annum, and for geological prospecting, the construction of a caustic-soda factory in Massowa, gold mining and ore-dressing plant, and a small smelting works.[14] In addition, the Soviet Union promised to build a hospital and a technical high school for 1,200 students.

2. *Guinea*: We have already given details concerning the use of the credit of 140 million (old) roubles credit granted to Guinea in 1959. In addition, other communist countries also granted Guinea credits: the Chinese People's Republic ($U.S. 25 million), Czechoslovakia (commodity credits to the value of $U.S. 10 million), Poland ($U.S. 5 million), and Hungary ($U.S. 2·56 million). The grants and the financial and commodity credits made available by the

East German Government are not known in detail, but they are believed to amount to a total of about $u.s. 10 million. Part of this sum is known to have been spent on building a large printing works in Conakry. This was inaugurated in the summer of 1961, but within a few weeks it had to be partly closed because of grave technical defects.

3. *Ghana*: The first agreement for economic and technical co-operation between the Soviet Union and Ghana was signed on 4 August 1960.[15] Under this agreement Moscow granted Accra a first credit of 160 million (old) roubles, (about $u.s. 40 million), at $2\frac{1}{2}$ per cent interest per annum over an amortization period of twelve years. A programme for the use of this aid was published on 23 December 1960. Soviet aid was concentrated mainly on the following ten projects: the building of an hydraulic power station at Bui on the Black Volta (a project not to be confused with the other Volta River building operations financed by the West and about 60 miles away from the Soviet venture), the laying of about 150 miles of overland pipe lines, geological surveys, the building of a number of factories for the fishing industry, the establishment of three State farms, the experimental planting of cotton with a view to establishing a State cotton farm and a cotton mill, the building of domestic housing estates in Accra and Tema, a study of the practicability of building a smelting works, an iron-ore and manganese works, and a tractor-assembly plant.[16]

Between 1961 and 1963 there were reported negotiations concerning these credits, and the details were revised several times. It was not until 22 September 1961, that a definite agreement was arrived at for the building of the power station at Bui on the Black Volta river. And in June 1962 Ghana's Deputy Minister for Industry had to inform parliament that certain projects had been 'postponed' because it had been found that they were not in accordance with 'the present stage of Ghana's development'. This referred in particular to a project for a steel works, for which the Soviet Union had been pressing since 1959. A project to build a railway line from Kumasi to Ouagadougou in the Upper Volta Republic, which had been enthusiastically welcomed in the Ghanaian Press, was said by the Deputy Minister of Transport to exist solely in the imagination of Ghanaian editors influenced by the whispers of Soviet propaganda.[17]

There were long delays in Ghana before the agreed Soviet credits were made available. However, a correspondent in Accra[18] reported that by the middle of 1962 a good third of the credits granted to Ghana by the Soviet countries had been made available. But the doubt which still surrounded a second Soviet credit, said to have been promised to Nkrumah in 1961, has not been dissipated to this day. So far neither Soviet sources nor official sources in Ghana have said anything definite about the amount involved, or about the individual projects which the credit is to serve. The original announcement spoke only in general terms about institutions designed to train the 'national technical forces' of Ghana.[19] Apart from the Soviet Union the following communist States have also granted credits to Ghana so far:

Hungary	21 April 1961	£2·5 million
Czechoslovakia	22 May 1961	£5 million
Poland	25 May 1961	£1 million
People's Republic of China	8 August 1961	£7 million (free of interest)

The various credits granted by the East European States are to be used, among other things, for building a pharmaceutical works, an aluminium cable works, an electric-bulb factory (Hungary), a cane-sugar factory, a car-tyre factory (Czechoslovakia), an iron foundry, a machine-tool factory and a shipbuilding yard (Poland).[20] It has not yet been possible to discover whether the construction of various industrial enterprises (including furniture factories, mass-tailoring workshops, and technical-equipment factories) promised by Poland in an agreement signed on 18 December 1961, and representing an investment of £10 million in Ghanaian currency, is to be carried out on a credit basis.[21] On 20 April 1961 Poland had already signed an agreement with Ghana granting it commodity credits to the value of £5 million sterling.[22] However, a number of the projects promised by Poland, like some of the Soviet projects already mentioned, have been either deferred or abandoned altogether.[23]

4. *Mali*: On 18 March 1961 representatives of the Soviet Union and of Mali met in the Kremlin to sign agreements for economic and technical co-operation and for commercial and cultural exchanges. At the same time Mali was granted credits for 40 million new roubles (approximately $U.S. 44·5 million) at 2½ per cent per annum. The programme of Soviet projects for Mali included (1) geological

survey and prospecting operations, (2) the improvement of transport on the Niger, (3) the building of a sports stadium in Bamako to seat 25,000, (4) the building of a railway line between Bamako and Conakry (Guinea), (5) the building of a cement works with capacity for an annual production of 100,000 tons, and (6) the building of an educational institute for 300 students. The Soviet Union was also to provide Mali, as it did Guinea and Ghana, with planes to build a national air service.[24]

5. *Nigeria*: Nigeria, the biggest of the new African States and with pro-Western rather than neutralist policies, received a promise of Soviet credits (in June 1961) to a total of 40 million new roubles (approximately $U.S. 44·5 million), at 2½ per cent per annum. Up to the end of 1964 there were still no details available as to how this credit was to be used. In a joint communiqué issued by representatives of the Soviet Union and Nigeria, there was only a general reference to Soviet assistance in the founding of certain agricultural undertakings, factories for the preparation of agricultural produce, and the establishment of centres for training technical personnel for industry and agriculture.[25] Poland also agreed to advance credits to finance certain industrial projects,[26] and Czechoslovakia promised some credits but without a firm commitment.

6. *Somalia*: The Somali Government took advantage of a Soviet 'goodwill' mission to Somali in April 1961 to ask the Soviet Union for long-term credits.[27] During the visit of Premier Abdirashid Shermake to Moscow, the Soviet Government granted Somalia a credit of 40 million new roubles (approximately $U.S. 44·5 million), together with a five-year commodity credit of 7 million new roubles (approximately $U.S. 7·78 million). The Soviet Government also promised to provide assistance for the building of two hospitals, a high school, a broadcasting station, and a printing works. It also agreed to provide Soviet medical and teaching personnel and to train Somali doctors in the Soviet Union.

In granting these credits the Soviet Union intends to pave the way for Africa's greater dependence on the Soviet bloc. At the third session of the UN Economic Commission for Africa, held in Addis Ababa in February 1961, Soviet Minister V. S. Semenov declared that if the present expenditure on armaments could be diverted to the development of Africa it could catch up with Europe industrially in a very short time. He also declared that by 1965 the Soviet Union and the other socialist countries would together account for half the world's industrial production. He went on: 'Mr Khrushchev has pointed out that with the development of our own economy we shall progressively expand our co-operation with the African countries.'[28] This association of Soviet economic aid to Africa with the rising graph of Soviet economic development means conversely that any difficulties experienced by the Soviet economic system is bound to have an unfavourable effect on Soviet aid to Africa. This was already noticeable from the autumn of 1961 to the beginning of 1965 when the Soviet authorities closed their ears to African requests for financial and commodity credits, except the requests for military aid from Somalia.

Irrespective of the fluctuations of Soviet credit facilities and commodity deliveries, communist economic propaganda in Africa continues at high pressure. More than a third of the African broadcasts of Radio Moscow deal with socio-economic questions. The West and the motives of Western capital exports to, and investment in, Africa are played down, while the value of Soviet State aid is inflated. Thousands of communist publications, from weighty tomes to ephemeral pamphlets, sound the same note. In a study by Dr Ismailova Fruck, *State Capitalism in the Young African States*, published by the Institute for Economic Science in Moscow (a department of the Soviet Academy of Sciences) the young African States are strongly recommended to introduce nationalization measures, since this is the only way in which a State sector of the economic system can be created. At the same time the élite in the under-developed countries are urged to reject every form of industrialization by private enterprise. The study declares:

'The accumulation of capital in the hands of the national bourgeoisie is insufficient, and the still-powerful foreign monopolies often refuse to invest their capital in the national industries. In consequence the State *must* play an active role in the process of industrialization. In this respect the rise of State capitalism is of increasing importance.'

The study further points out that the recommended policy would be anti-imperialist, for a State sector in the economic system would automatically restrict the sphere of operations open to private capitalists. Moreover, the creation of State capitalism would have repercussions on the political structure of the country. In other words the advantage of State capitalism, in the eyes of the communists, is that it encourages the development of a socialist economic structure in the young national States and thus facilitates the transition to communism.[29]

This point of view is also reflected in an article written in 1962 by Jack Woddis, a member of the British Communist Party and a specialist on African affairs. For a symposium on 'Paths of Development of Newly Emergent Countries', Woddis wrote: 'The creation of a State sector of the economy is extremely important for the newly independent African countries where little industry exists and where the commanding heights of the economy are in the hands of foreign monopolies.'[30] He also points out that the creation of a State economic sector will greatly facilitate the direct transition of Africa from a colonial to a socialist State.

In May 1962 the Soviet Government began a special economic propaganda campaign for Africa. Launched on an unusually wide scale, it was directed chiefly against the EEC and the idea of the Common Market and it opposed any association between the EEC and the sixteen African States with European connections. Mr Khrushchev himself fired the first shot in the campaign at a reception on 30 May 1962, given in Moscow in honour of the President of Mali, Modibo Keita.

'Of late,' he declared, 'the imperialist monopolies have set great hopes on the so-called Common Market. This Common Market represents no danger to us, but the situation is different where the young States of Asia, Africa and Latin America are concerned, because they have only recently obtained their political independence and they do not yet enjoy economic independence. One of the main aims of the Common Market is to chain those countries which have obtained their political freedom to the economy of the imperialist States.'

Mr Khrushchev went on to say that everything possible should be done 'to free international trade from arrangements by which the stronger are enabled to enrich themselves at the expense of the weaker'. He described the EEC, or Common Market, as 'a State monopoly agreement of the Western European finance oligarchy' and declared that it threatened the vital interests of the people and of peace 'because aggressive imperialist circles are using it to strengthen NATO and to intensify the arms race'. The antidote he recommended—particularly to the African countries—was that they should create State monopolies for foreign trade and support the Soviet plan for holding an international conference under the auspices of the United Nations with a view to creating a world-wide trading organization.[31] The same line was adopted in an article by V. Tcherpakov in *Communist* of May 1962. In defiance of the practical experience of the EEC's African associates, Tcherpakov argued that any association with the Common Market 'will inevitably slow down their economic development . . . will to a great extent impede the solution of social problems and the introduction of socio-economic measures'.[32] The campaign was given further impetus at a Comecon conference in Moscow in June 1962, at which it was decided to revise the statutes of the Council for Mutual Economic Aid (COMECON), so that in future 'non-European countries' could become members. It is interesting to note that it did not say 'Asiatic countries', which would have included Mongolia and the other communist Asiatic States.

The Soviet Union's economic activity in Africa is only beginning, but its ultimate objectives are already quite clear. Despite all the propaganda to the contrary, the Soviet Government is much less interested in affording 'unselfish aid' to African countries than it is in creating a favourable atmosphere, or psychological climate, in which it would be easier to introduce communist economic principles. The Soviet call for complete economic independence from the West, the creation of a State-controlled economy and a collectivized agriculture falls on many sympathetic ears among the African political élite who believe in a socialist solution for their countries.

NOTES

[1] *Pravda*, 28 January 1959.
[2] *Probleme des Friedens und des Sozialismus*, IV/2 (30) (February 1961), pp. 139 ff.
[3] Ibid.
[4] *UAR Statistics* (Cairo, 1961).

[5] Trade and Revenue Report for Kenya, Uganda and Tanganyika for the month of August 1960, published by the East Africa High Commission.

[6] *Bulletin Mensuel du Togo*, July 1960.

[7] The *New York Times* (European ed.), 27 January 1964.

[8] *Neue Zürcher Zeitung*, 27 November 1962.

[9] *Problems of Communism*, x, No. 6 (November-December 1961), p. 12.

[10] Cf. 'Der Ostblock und die Entwicklungsländer', *Vierteljahresbericht der Friedrich-Ebert-Stiftung* (Hanover), No. 6 (December 1961), p. 10.

[11] *Pravda*, 3 March 1960.

[12] Soviet, East European Credits to Africa from 1958 to the end of 1962 (in million US dollars)

	Soviet aid	Bloc countries	USA
Ethiopia	102	12	117·8
Ghana	109	87	156·5
Guinea	78	47	14·3
Mali	44	54	5·1
Morocco	17	—	352·0
Somalia	57	6	26·4
Sudan	23	—	65·0
Tunisia	28	18	293·3

Source: *Hinter dem Eisernen Vorhang* (Munich), x, No. 1 (January 1964).

[13] *Vnezhnaya Torgovlia*, No. 4 (1961), p. 20.

[14] *Pravda*, 27 March 1960.

[15] *Vedomosti Verkhovnogo Sovieta SSSR*, No. 51 (1960), pp. 1169 ff.

[16] Ibid., No. 30 (1961), pp. 715 ff.

[17] *Neue Zürcher Zeitung*, 1 July 1962.

[18] Ibid.

[19] *Pravda*, 27 July 1962.

[20] Cf. 'Der Ostblock und die Entwicklungsländer', p. 10.

[21] Radio Accra broadcast, 18 December 1961; New China News Agency, 19 December 1961.

[22] *Neue Zürcher Zeitung*, 21 April 1961.

[23] Ibid., 1 July 1962.

[24] 'Der Ostblock und die Entwicklungsländer', p. 10.

[25] *Pravda*, 10 June 1961.

[26] Radio Warsaw broadcast, 13 June 1961.

[27] *Pravda*, 24 March 1961.

[28] *Problems of Communism*, x, No. 6 (November-December 1961), p. 12.

[29] *Neues Deutschland*, 7 February 1961.

[30] *Probleme des Friedens und des Sozialismus*, IV (44) (April 1962), pp. 348 ff.

[31] *Neues Deutschland*, 31 May 1962.

[32] *Neue Zürcher Zeitung*, 17 June 1962.

Chapter XI

THE CHINESE IN AFRICA

AFTER a decade dominated largely by the need to consolidate power at home, during which military and subversive ventures were confined to immediately adjoining areas, Mao Tse-tung's régime has in recent years embarked upon large-scale diplomatic offensives and attempts at infiltration in all the under-developed countries. As Chou En-lai's tour of ten African countries in December 1963 and January 1964 demonstrated, this continent is one of the main targets of the Chinese political 'leap forward'. As the Chinese prime minister said in Mogadishu at the end of his seven-week journey, 'revolutionary prospects are excellent throughout Africa.'[1] The continent is, in fact, in a state of great unrest and upheaval, and offers innumerable opportunities to the messianic world-political ambitions of Peking. The old-fashioned colonialism and paternalism of the white man is beating a precipitate retreat before the tumultuous advance of a nationalism based mainly on emotion and, on the whole, without clear-cut aims on all those decisive questions which will determine the future political, social, and economic shape of the continent. The young African élite lacks experience and there are no familiar models close at hand on which to base its strivings. It is equally opposed to traditionalism and to European liberalism. So far, their encounter with orthodox Marxism has not opened the eyes of many African leaders and men like Félix Houphouet-Boigny, President of the Ivory Coast Republic, are denounced by their more radical colleagues as reactionaries seeking conciliation with the colonialist régime.

In such a situation communism naturally exerts a strong attraction. In the view of some radical African leaders it has led to the social and economic development of backward countries despite the opposition of local reactionaries, and without foreign aid. Most Africans are not aware of the fact that these successes were bought at the price of tremendous suffering, including loss of life on a vast scale. When Westerners point this out they are regarded with mistrust, because many Africans are inclined to reject anything that comes from the West. And of course communist propaganda does its utmost to sustain them in this attitude by telling them that although many people did indeed lose their lives in this salutary process, it was entirely their own fault for opposing 'the march of history'. It would not be fair, however, to say that this propaganda has always been uncritically accepted in Africa. The Kremlin's version of the Hungarian tragedy of 1956 was regarded with great misgiving. On the other hand, Chinese communist aggression in Tibet is generally accepted and Westerners will be told by Africans that Peking was absolutely right in behaving as it did, since its action was obviously part of the general struggle against the same reactionary, entrenched feudal forces which are also seeking to stem the tide of progress in Africa and that they have to be defeated everywhere, whether in Africa or in Tibet.

These arguments reveal the many opportunities open to communism in Africa, opportunities which Peking has either created or which, if they existed, it has cleverly exploited. In this respect China has a great advantage over the Soviet Union in Africa, where Moscow's strength is at the same time its weakness. When the Russians boast about their *luniks*, *sputniks*, rockets and industrial achievements they are, in the eyes of many Africans, equating their country with the industrialized Western countries. Such boasting suggests that the Soviet Union has already achieved a stage of economic and industrial development far ahead of the underdeveloped countries—so far ahead as to be out of reach for all practical purposes. Its great achievements offer Africans no examples which they can follow now. An African visiting Moscow will undoubtedly be deeply impressed by the skyscrapers, the modern underground railway and the giant industrial plants, but they will also make him aware of the vast, the infinite, gulf that separates his own country from the Soviet Union.

If the same man visited communist China, he would experience something very different. Although, like the Russians, the Chinese take care in choosing what they show to foreign visitors, no member of any of the numerous delegations that have visited Mao's empire can have failed to notice the evidence that much is still unfinished and rudimentary.[2] The poverty of the Chinese people is as obvious as the primitive nature of many of their methods of work; in fact the reports of African visitors to China suggest that their Chinese guides made no attempt to conceal these things—on the contrary, they used them cleverly to impress their African visitors with alleged similarities between China's economic condition in 1950 and that of large parts of Africa today. A polite European may conceal a tolerant smile at the sight of China's 'back-yard' furnaces, but an African's reaction is different: he is filled with enthusiasm because this is something he could apply in his own country. He may be impressed, but he is much less stirred by ultra-modern, fully automatic blast furnaces and rolling mills, since this complicated industrial equipment is altogether out of reach for him and his fellow-countrymen and is likely to remain so for a long time. But China's back-yard furnaces can be constructed and manned by unskilled labourers in Guinea or in the Congo. In addition, and especially since the Moshi Conference in February 1963, Mao's propagandists set out to persuade their African visitors (with some success) that the Chinese and the Africans are 'brother races', as distinct from the Russians who are 'white'. Soviet propagandists do their best to counter this and try to curry favour with the Africans by pushing the representatives of their Asian minorities into the foreground. Nevertheless, the Soviet régime as such remains 'European' in African eyes, and at the end of the Geneva World Trade Conference in June 1964, for example, they did not succeed in persuading the Afro-Asians that the Soviet Union is a European and not an Asian country.

On the diplomatic level Peking found a uniquely favourable situation in Africa which still operates in China's favour. When the new African States emerged, Red China had already existed for about eight years. There were, of course, two Chinas, but for States which had just emerged from colonial tutelage, the choice between the island State of Formosa (or Taiwan, to give it its Chinese name) and the vast mainland empire under Mao's domination was not difficult. Moreover, at the Bandung Conference, communist China had already appeared as a potential ally of the African States, and the appeal of a communist State which had managed to free itself 'entirely by its own efforts and without foreign aid' from feudalism and semi-colonialism was much more powerful than the appeal of Chiang Kai-shek's régime in Formosa, which obviously relied for its existence on American support and patronage. From the beginning many Africans regarded 'People's China' as a possible model and example: 'I am convinced', said Ahmed Balafrej, a former premier of Morocco, 'that China's revolution has awakened the Africans.'[3]

Such views are by no means confined to extremist groups and can be found among the African bourgeoisie as well. In such circumstances therefore, it is not surprising that Mao's China found little difficulty in establishing friendly diplomatic relations with the new African States. Official relationships were established with the Egyptian Government on 30 May 1956, and a Chinese embassy was established in Cairo. This embassy is responsible for maintaining contacts throughout the Arab world and it also influenced exiled African groups and politicians who had established themselves in the Egyptian capital. An exchange of ambassadors was subsequently arranged with the Sudan (1 November 1958), with the new Algerian provisional government (20 December 1958), with Guinea (4 October 1959), and with Ghana (5 July 1960). At the end of 1965, full diplomatic relations between the Chinese People's Republic and the following African countries had been established: Algeria, Burundi, Central African Republic, Congo-Brazzaville, Dahomey, Ghana, Guinea, Kenya, Mali, Mauritania, Morocco, Somalia, Sudan, Tanzania, Tunisia, Uganda, the UAR and Zambia. Burundi suspended diplomatic relations with China in February 1965. This means that there were seventeen African countries at the end of 1965 with which Red China maintained official relationships, and this number is likely to increase. Only Madagascar, the ex-Belgian Congo, Liberia and the Ivory Coast Republic recognized the Formosa Government at that time. By comparison Red China was officially recognized by nine-non-communist States in Asia, and Chiang Kai-shek's Government by an equal number. For Europe (not including the countries of the Soviet bloc) the ratio was 7 : 8. In Latin America, Cuba was the only country which recognized the Peking Government.

THE FIRST STAGE

Those who regard the Chinese as the guardians of Marxist–Leninist orthodoxy will have to adjust their views where Africa is concerned. Peking's representatives there are quite prepared to let dogmatism go by the board whenever it suits them. They obviously attach considerable importance to persuading Africans to forget, at least in the beginning, that they are dealing with communists. This flexibility first paid dividends in Morocco, for example. When the Moroccan Communist Party was proscribed in September 1959 (a measure subsequently confirmed by the Moroccan Supreme Court) the Chinese Embassy in Rabat immediately severed all relations with members of the prohibited organization. It is also significant to note that neither Peking's African broadcasts nor the Chinese publications distributed in Morocco contain even a breath of criticism of the anti-communist measures taken by the Moroccan Government. Chinese wooing is now concentrated on the *Union Nationale des Forces Populaires*, the leader of which, Mahdi Ben Barka, former President of the Moroccan Consultative Assembly, visited China and on his return expressed warm sympathy for the Chinese People's Republic. The Moroccan Government has also repeatedly emphasized the importance of friendly relations with Peking and the desirability of increasing trade between the two countries. In fact, Red China has moved into fifth place in the list of Morocco's trading partners. The increasing importance of China in Morocco's trade was reflected at the industrial fair in Casablanca in 1964, where Peking had the largest pavilion of all the exhibitors. A good deal of literature was made available informing African visitors of the considerable amount of aid granted by Peking to the under-developed countries and drawing their attention to the bright prospects for all African countries which maintain good relations with China.

But there is, of course, more to all this than the mere desire to promote trade. Some attempt at indoctrination is made. The writings of Mao Tse-tung and other Chinese leaders are on sale in Casablanca, Rabat and Meknes. Special attention is given to the young Moroccan intelligentsia, and books and other publications are being distributed free to students.

Other African States are treated with a similar absence of dogmatism. While Moscow is constantly attacked for supporting the feudal, bourgeois and unprogressive elements, Peking does not hesitate to canvass the friendship of Ethiopian courtiers, Tanzanian businessmen, and Muslim dignitaries in Somalia and the Sudan. In fact Peking goes even further by establishing trading relations with countries with such governments as Rhodesia and Malawi, and even with the Union of South Africa.

It is interesting to see that Red China has made efforts to include Muslims in its friendship delegations and, through them, to get into touch with Muslims in Africa. The Russians have made one or two attempt to do the same, but without much success. The Chinese have been more successful and even Africans who are otherwise disillusioned with communism are convinced that Red China is friendly to Islam.

A China–Islam Association was officially formed in May 1953, and one of its main aims was to persuade Muslims outside China that the interests of their co-religionists in China are carefully safe-guarded. This is, of course, completely dishonest, because at various times in the past Muslim communities have been so dis-satisfied with their treatment at the hands of the communist régime in China that they have actually risen in revolt. In 1958 for example, even the Chinese Press printed reports of riots and up-risings by Muslim communities.

Since then however the Chinese communist Government has relaxed restrictions on Muslims, who are now given facilities to obtain the special supplies of food and oil they need to celebrate Id al-Fitr, the Festival of Bairam, which traditionally concludes the Ramadan fast.

In 1956, when a number of Islamic delegates were in Peking as guests at the May Day celebrations, the Chinese Government marked the event by organizing particularly elaborate festivities for that year's Id al-Fitr, and on 12 May a hundred Chinese Muslims celebrated the festival with co-religionists from Syria, Egypt, the Sudan and Indonesia. Later they attended a special dinner given by the China-Islam Association. Pakistani and Sudanese Muslims celebrated Id al-Fitr at the famous Nan Kuan mosque in Urumchi. The Chinese Government had good reason to be pleased with the results of its efforts; the delegates were enthusiastic about the special hospitality given to them as Muslims and assured their hosts that on their return to their own countries they would let everyone know of 'the free and happy life' led by their Muslim co-religionists in Red China.[4]

A similar show, accompanied by a good deal of publicity, was put on during the celebration of the Qurban festival by the Muslim community in China in May 1961. Chinese Muslims, diplomatic representatives from Muslim countries, and Muslim students joined in a special service in a mosque in the eastern part of Peking, and a special reception to celebrate the feast was given on 28 May by Burhan Shahidi, the chairman of the China–Islam Association. Once again diplomatic envoys were present from Islamic Asian and African countries. Addressing his guests, Burhan Shahidi observed that the friendship between the Muslims of China and those of other Asian and African countries had grown rapidly alongside the struggle of the peoples of Asia and Africa to attain and maintain their national independence; he assured them that Chinese Muslims laid great store by this friendship.[5]

In the following year the festivals of Qurban and Id al-Fitr were once again accompanied by a great deal of official publicity, and Peking Radio broadcast a message in Swahili from Mohammed Ali Chang, vice-chairman of the China–Islam Association, to the Muslims of Africa and the whole world on the occasion of the feast of Id al-Fitr. Ali Chang assured his listeners that Muslims in China enjoyed full political rights as citizens and were left perfectly free to practise their religion. They were, he declared, particularly gratified that Islamic peoples in various African and Asian countries had 'hoisted the banner of resistance to imperialism and colonialism'. This, he added with satisfaction, was a great blow to the imperialists and would help to bring about the promise of the prophet Muhammad that 'God will punish those who persecute others in this world'. He concluded by assuring his listeners that 'every passing day' would see the bonds of friendship and co-operation between the Muslims of China and those of Asia and Africa strengthened.[6]

Chinese Muslims celebrated the feast of Qurban on 15 May and there were religious services and celebrations in Peking and other parts of China. The celebrations in Peking were attended by diplomatic representatives from Guinea, the United Arab Republic, Pakistan, Afghanistan and Mali and by representatives of various other Muslim communities. In addition, according to the New China News Agency, the mosques in Yinchuan, the capital of the Ninghsia Hui Autonomous Region, were 'packed with Muslims' for the occasion.

Since 1955 Chinese Muslims have been allowed to make the annual pilgrimage to Mecca, but those who have taken part in the pilgrimages from Red China have impressed observers as being more interested in the opportunity of assuring everyone that China allows her Muslims freedom of worship than in the unique opportunity of practising their religion. Since 1960 Chinese Muslims on their way to and from Mecca have been breaking their journeys in the United Arab Republic, Morocco, Guinea, Mali, Somalia and other countries, for similar propaganda purposes.

Further evidence of Red China's efforts to establish contact with Muslims in Africa and the Middle East was provided in a Peking broadcast on 4 November 1960, which informed the world that two of the teachers at the Peking mosque had been seconded from the United Arab Republic.

Burhan Shahidi, chairman of the China-Islam Association, is also the deputy chairman of the Afro-Asian Society of China, vice-president of the Chinese-African People's Friendship Association (founded on 12 April 1960) and president of the joint Friendship Association of China and the United Arab Republic. Those Africans who have made his acquaintance would probably indignantly reject the suggestion that Burhan Shahidi is a communist and they do not realize that the China-Islam Association is just another communist-front organization.

THE SECOND STAGE

For some time many of Red China's African activities have been concentrated on Guinea, and Guinea has been Peking's first spearhead in Africa. Following the conclusion of a technical aid agreement in October 1959, the dispatch of a Chargé d'Affaires and the arrival of the first Chinese ambassador in Conakry, Mao's representatives had gained increasing influence on Guinea's political and economic life, in particular on the development of Guinea's agriculture—so much so, that in April 1960 the Three-Year plan adopted by Guinea embodied plans for the wide-scale collectivization of agriculture. After discussions which took place at the second Afro-Asian Solidarity Conference at Conakry, in April 1960, it was reported that Guinea had decided to take full advantage of 'the experiences of the great agrarian revolution in the People's Republic of China'. Following this, a large group of Chinese agrarian experts arrived in Conakry in the early summer of 1960. There were also unsubstantiated reports that several hundred Chinese rice-growers were to go to the West-African Republic to reorganize its rice production.

The climax of relations between Guinea and Red China was the visit of Sékou Touré to Peking in September 1960. Until then, no neutral Head of State had ever been received in the Chinese capital with as much pomp and ceremony. Liu Shao-chi, Chou En-lai and Mao Tse-tung had long discussions with their African guest. Enormous mass demonstrations formed an impressive background to the visit. To quote his own words, Sékou Touré was 'quite overwhelmed'. The two countries signed a number of friendship and trade agreements and Mao offered his guest credits amounting to 100 million roubles on terms which were more favourable than the 140-million-roubles credit granted to Guinea by the Moscow Government in 1959. China had previously granted similar credits, on very favourable terms, to other countries, including Indonesia, Ceylon and North Vietnam. These were at rates of interest of 1 to 1·5 per cent per annum. The Moscow credits bear interest at 2·5 per cent per annum but the Chinese credits to Guinea were free of interest. A second important concession made to Sékou Touré was that repayments were not to begin until 1970 and need not be completed before 1980. In addition it was agreed that Chinese experts sent to assist Guinea in its economic development should be paid at a rate not higher than that enjoyed by officials of equal standing in the service of the Republic of Guinea. The psychological importance of this provision can hardly be exaggerated. The Government of Guinea had usually had to foot the bill for the maintenance of Soviet, Czechoslovak and other Soviet-bloc experts and whoever knows anything about the style of living of these communist experts knows that it is at least as lavish as that enjoyed formerly by colonialists.

Sékou Touré's visit to China was not only an occasion for Chinese concessions. In his speeches and toasts the President of the Republic of Guinea dissipated all remaining doubts about his ideological and political allegiance. At a banquet given in his honour by Liu Shao-chi on 10 September, he declared: 'In the struggle between justice and injustice we have taken our place beside those who wage a just struggle for the well-being of all men and peoples', and he left no doubt in the minds of his hearers as to their identity. On another occasion he turned to his host and declared: 'We can assure you that we Africans know where truth is to be found, for Africans know that you had to fight against the same foes they are now fighting. They know that the great victory you have won is their victory too. Africans are also well able to learn the lessons your victory has taught them . . .' Speaking as official leader of an African State, Touré supported Peking's demand for the 'liberation' of Formosa and echoed the anti-American spirit of his hosts by referring to the 'imperialist States led by the USA', which had, he said, already been encircled by the 'people's forces' of the world and whose days were therefore numbered.[7]

Sékou Touré's remarks on so public an occasion made it clear that relations between the two countries were based on certain ideological affinities. A minor incident which took place towards the end of 1959 clearly indicated the pro-Chinese attitude of Guinea's leadership at that time: a lively clash of views took place in the Cairo Secretariat of the Afro-Asian Solidarity Committee over the exact formulation of a message of greeting to the forth-coming All-African People's Conference, which was to take place in Tunis from 25 to 31 January 1961. Some members of the secretariat proposed an uncontroversial text which did not attack the role of the national bourgeoisie in the movement for national liberation, referring to the programme of the Solidarity Committee in moderate terms in order to avoid giving offence. All the countries represented in the secretariat, including the Soviet Union but with the exception of China and Guinea, were in favour of the proposal. China and Guinea alone voted against it, and their representatives declared in concert that the attitude adopted by the majority was in contradiction to 'the revolutionary objectives' of the solidarity movement and would therefore do more harm than good.

It was also no coincidence that at the meeting of the World Peace Council in Stockholm in December 1961 Guinea's representative,

Diallo Seydou, sided with the Chinese communists against the Soviet Union on the question of disarmament and on the granting of active support to the armed national liberation struggle. (This incident has already been described in Chapter V.) In this connection it is also interesting to record that at the time of the Solod crisis in Conakry the Chinese Embassy was the only communist embassy allowed to continue distributing information and propaganda as before.

However, in my opinion, it would be an exaggeration to regard these incidents as proof that Maoism dominated ideology and politics in Guinea, or to regard the Solod affair—as some observers are apt to do—as another incident in the Sino-Soviet clash. It is certain, however, that irrespective of the question of communism as such, there is a large measure of agreement between Red China and Guinea on anti-colonialist policy. Inevitably this has its practical consequences, but it does not necessarily make Guinea a satellite of Red China. This is also true of the much-improved relationship between Ghana and China, particularly since 1961. In both these countries the Chinese have obtained a foothold which enables them to contact and influence the exiled leaders of various African extremist groups, now living in these countries, and in one or two cases they have succeeded in winning them over. This applies, in particular, to exiled politicians from the Ivory Coast Republic, the Portuguese territories, and some of the leaders of the terrorist wing of the UPC of Cameroon.

The promotion of co-existence with the Moroccan Government, the exploitation of China's apparent tolerance of Islam, the encouragement of trade relations with bourgeois régimes and the close contacts established with the leaders of Guinea and Ghana, all these can be properly understood only if seen as tactics preparing the way for the ultimate policy the Chinese communists envisage for Africa, as elsewhere, or as stages on the way to the armed struggles which, they believe, will end in the reorganization of Africa along Chinese lines. In three cases Peking has already tried to act in accordance with these ideas; in Algeria, Cameroon, and the Congo. As far as can be seen at present, Mao has not met with a great deal of success in any of these ventures. Algeria is now independent and, officially, is not in the least interested in introducing Chinese communism economically, culturally, or politically. The civil war in Cameroon has died down, though it could flare up again if the leaders of the terrorist UPC manage to gather their forces together, while in the Congo the Chinese and their African supporters have been excluded from any effective influence on events and their chances of a come-back are very slender. However, these three examples of Chinese communist influence in Africa are typical and what happened yesterday in Algeria, Cameroon, and the Congo could happen again in other parts of Africa if the circumstances were appropriate.

Let us return briefly to the Chinese-Moroccan relationship, which many observers regard as unusual. In my opinion, China was more interested in Algeria than Morocco. After a temporary clash with Cairo in 1959 (the Syrian communist leader, Bakdash, had made a sharp protest in Peking against the suppression of the Communist Party in the United Arab Republic and launched wild accusations against Nasser), and in view of the coolness of Tunisia, Morocco remained the only State in North Africa which offered Peking any chance of exerting influence on the Algerian war. In these circumstances it was hardly accidental that Chinese diplomatic activity was concentrated largely in the strategically placed Peking consulates in Tangiers, and in Oujda on the Moroccan-Algerian border.

Peking regarded the Algerian *Front de la Libération Nationale* (FLN) as an avant-garde anti-colonialist movement and sought to shape it, along the lines of the Viet-Minh movement in Indo-china, into an instrument of revolutionary strategy against France and against the West generally. When the Algerian Provisional Government was formed by Ferhat Abbas in the autumn of 1958, Red China was the first communist country to offer to establish official diplomatic relations with it, and in the following December the first Algerian delegation was received in Peking by the leaders of Red China. This delegation, led by Armaments Minister Sherif, and Social Minister Ben Chedda, had a number of discussions with prominent generals of the Peking Defence Ministry. Before long a second FLN delegation arrived in Peking. This time there were soldiers among its members, and it was led by the Secretary of State Amar U-Seddick, an experienced guerilla fighter who operated in the neighbourhood of Algiers. Two Algerian ministers then visited Peking during the tenth anniversary celebrations of the communist victory in China and after a visit by Krim Belkacem in the spring of 1960, Ferhat Abbas himself followed in August.

This visit of Ferhat Abbas, for which the Chinese communists had been pressing for some time, was repeatedly postponed as a result of the Algerian Government's indecision. The Government was divided into two camps and was unable to come to a decision. Those who favoured closer relationships between the FLN and the Chinese Communist Party insisted that the visit was absolutely necessary if the military aid promised by China towards the end of 1959 were to materialize, while others opposed it on the ground that communist influence on the FLN might grow too strong. Peking offered to send volunteers trained in guerilla warfare to North Africa to assist the FLN, and to provide 20 or 25 fighter-bombers, together with pilots and ground staff, large quantities of heavy and automatic weapons and munitions. For the time being, Abbas used this offer as a means of exerting pressure on de Gaulle, threatening to accept it unless Paris would agree to a solution of the conflict acceptable to the FLN. This attempted blackmail was successful and in the summer of 1960, under pressure from the other Western powers, (which were becoming alarmed at the possible consequences of Chinese intervention) France was compelled to back down on its conditions for a settlement, abandon the slogan *Algérie française*, and consider the alternative of *Algérie algérienne*. Discussions between representatives of the French Government and the Provisional Government of Ferhat Abbas began in Mélun. When these came to nothing the Algerian Provisional Government immediately sought closer contact with Red China; the long-delayed appointment of a Chinese ambassador took place, and the visit of Ferhat Abbas to China was decided upon. Although the tactics of Ferhat Abbas in this matter were designed to secure a political end, military aid from Peking ('its scope is a military secret'—Ferhat Abbas) began to take on more practical forms and the threat of direct Chinese military intervention in the Franco-Algerian war now became a possibility; in fact it was ultimately prevented only by de Gaulle's acceptance of *Algérie algérienne*, the referendum of January 1961 and the reopening of direct contacts between the French Government and the FLN in the spring of 1961.

There can be no doubt whatever about the intentions of the Chinese communists. They were not in the least interested in securing a peaceable solution of the Algerian problem, no matter how favourable the conditions. They did their utmost, by a vast flood of propaganda (including the holding of 'Algeria days' and even 'weeks') and by exerting all possible pressure on Algerian groups and leading personalities, to obtain the acceptance of their own revolutionary ideas. It is interesting to examine the difference between Moscow and Peking on the Algerian question. Moscow, of course, was not averse to making propaganda declarations of support for the FLN. During the meeting of the United Nations in New York in the autumn of 1960 Khrushchev ostentatiously received representatives of the Algerian Provisional Government and subsequently referred to these talks as 'an expression of our *de facto* recognition of the Algerian Provisional Government'. However, on several occasions, from the autumn of 1959 onwards, the Kremlin made it clear that it was interested in securing a *peaceable* understanding between de Gaulle and the Algerian insurrectionists. Addressing the Supreme Soviet on 31 October 1959, Khrushchev declared: 'The recent proposal of President de Gaulle for a solution of the Algerian question on the basis of self-determination and a people's referendum in Algeria can play an important role . . .' He also went out of his way to make it clear that there were, in fact, 'close historical ties between France and Algeria' and that if in the future these ties could be strengthened 'on the basis of a mutually acceptable arrangement voluntarily entered into and on a basis of equality' this could lead to the pacification of Algeria. The Soviet premier went on to make the idea of a peaceable settlement of the Algerian conflict more attractive to the French by a little flattery: 'It is not difficult to see that a peaceable solution of the Algerian question would greatly heighten the international prestige of France as a great power.'[8]

What had the Chinese to say on this point? On 17 October 1959, in a commentary issued by the Hsinhua Agency and broadcast by Radio Peking, they declared: 'French imperialism is now engaged in a dark conspiracy . . . The plan for "cease fire" negotiations and for a "people's referendum" in Algeria, proposed by President de Gaulle a month ago, is nothing but a *sugared poison draught* . . . There is merely a tactical difference in the situation: France is now trying to obtain by a trick what it has not been able to attain by force of arms.'[9]

The differing attitudes of the two communist powers were under-lined by a number of irreconcilable statements issued by Peking and Moscow, particularly in connection with the talks between de Gaulle and Bourguiba, the Tunisian president. Khrushchev had come to the conclusion that there was no chance of influencing the Algerian movement for liberation or of turning the 'revolution of arms' into a 'socialist revolution'. He therefore preferred to bide his time and hope for a future phase of internal conflict in Algeria, which would, he felt, inevitably arise out of structural problems. In the meantime, if he pleaded for 'the exclusion of war as a solution' in Algeria too, this attitude was calculated to increase his prestige as a 'prince of peace' and a prophet of peaceful co-existence.

On the other hand, the Chinese communists regarded war as inevitable for communism. Only so long as the armed conflict in Algeria continued could they have any hope of transforming an 'ideologically barren' fight into a real revolutionary struggle for a socialist revolution. In their eyes any other attitude to the Algerian conflict was an opportunistic deviation from the revolutionary strategy of Marxism-Leninism which, they maintain, implies effective, powerful intervention in any smouldering international conflict as the *conditio sine qua non* of ultimate communist victory.

It is not surprising therefore that when the final settlement was arrived at between de Gaulle and the Algerian Provisional Government, leading to the proclamation of independence on 1 July 1961, the Chinese reaction was very cool. At first the Evian Agreement was ignored altogether in the Chinese popular Press; finally it was reported without comment. An editorial on the subject in the Chinese newspaper *Jenmin Jih Pao* was typical of the Chinese attitude.[10] It admitted that if the agreement could be carried out without being sabotaged by the French colonialists, then peace and independence would be assured in Algeria. However, the cease-fire declaration did not mean the end of the struggle of the Algerian people, but rather the beginning of a new one—to make sure that France honoured its pledges. De Gaulle's government had connived at the OAS terror against the Algerian people and the OAS had been supported by the United States imperialists. There was also 'a new grave danger posed by the US neo-colonialists in Algeria'.

Evidence of continuing influence of Chinese propaganda, (par-ticularly on guerilla warfare) on events in Algeria has come with the publication of a report by a New China News Agency (NCNA) correspondent writing from Algiers. The report, dated 22 December 1963, was prepared after the correspondent had toured Algeria for over a year and described how he had been left with the impression that Mao's works enjoyed wide popularity among the people.

This popularity developed during the years of the 'revolutionary war', when, though banned, Mao's writings 'circulated underground often at the risk of lives, breaking through the blockade of the enemy'. According to an Algerian who was imprisoned at that time: 'All my fellow inmates read his works in prison. I read much of Mao Tse-tung's writings, which steeled my will to fight, and strengthened my confidence in Algeria's independence'.

Mao's works also circulated among guerillas in the Aures area. The officer commanding the insurgent troops in the Kabylia Mountains 'repeatedly quoted the theories of Mao Tse-tung to show how to arouse the peasants to fight the guerilla war'.

This account was said to have reminded the NCNA reporter of talks he had himself had with many officers of the Algerian National Liberation Army, who had testified, 'often with faces glowing with admiration', to the way they had been inspired by Mao's military theories to beat back the attacks of better-equipped troops. He also recalled how he had found four well-worn volumes of Mao's *Selected Works* in French and a copy of *Problems of Strategy in China's Revolutionary War*, copiously annotated in Arabic, in the political commissar's office in a barracks near the Moroccan border. On another tour he had been told that the experience of the Chinese revolution was 'a special course given in Algerian military training'.

These tributes to the inspiration and practical advice which Algerians found in Mao's writings during the years preceding the country's independence were echoed by the Algerian Minister of State Ammar Wizgan, who arrived in Peking on 29 September 1963 at the head of a delegation invited to join China's National Day celebrations. At a rally the following day Wizgan stated that liberty from 'French imperialism' had been won 'through people's struggle', and that Algerian officers and men fed themselves on Chairman Mao Tse-tung's works relating to the revolutionary strategy of guerilla warfare. But there is no proof of that from other sources. And at the end of 1965 one has to consider a remarkable deterioration of Chinese-Algerian relations, first because of the banning of the Algerian Communist Party only shortly after the country became independent; in contrast to the Soviet Union, Chinese propaganda did not hesitate to condemn this suppression. Secondly the relations cooled down necessarily after the overthrowing of Ben Bella by Colonel Boumedienne; the Chinese recognized the new government immediately, but only during the first weeks of Boumedienne's rule could one find friendly reactions to Algerian measures in the Chinese Press. How much the relations between Peking and Algiers had deteriorated was demonstrated later in 1965, when the Chinese government virtually boycotted the second Bandung Conference due to begin on 5 November 1965; the Chinese did not even consider Boumedienne's appeal to 'friendly governments' to act in favour of the meeting. They only had in mind their own ambitions and when they found out that a second Bandung Conference would not favour the Chinese position they took a firm stand against the meeting, which was then cancelled. No one can say now how and if China will be enabled to realize one of her ambitions —the still wider spread of Chinese influence in Africa by using Algerian help or Algerian proselytes.

This ambition is even more in evidence over the Cameroon question. Since 1955 this equatorial gateway to the African continent has been paralysed by chaos similar to that which disrupted Algeria, though perhaps not on the same scale. The Cameroon Government, under the leadership of Ahmadou Ahidjo (who asked the French to leave troops in the country even after the declaration of independence and for years depended heavily on this military assistance) soon found itself faced with increasing opposition from the insurrectionary *Union des Populations du Cameroun* (UPC) and with unpolitical banditry and powerful social discontent. This heterogeneous front against Paris and the Francophile administration was at first centred around Ruben Um Nyobé, who lost his life in the guerilla fighting in the autumn of 1958, and then around Félix-Roland Moumié, who died of poisoning in Switzerland in November 1960. Moumié was even more responsible than Um Nyobé for innumerable atrocities, massacres, banditry, arson, attacks on mission stations, government institutions and peaceful villages, and, unlike many other members of the UPC, he made no secret of his communist affiliations. In fact, he was the first *professional communist revolutionary* in Africa. As he told me, he was the son of a poor peasant of the Bamoun tribe in North Cameroon. He went to high school in Brazzaville and studied medicine in Dakar. While a student, he came into contact with the communist movement and from Dakar went as the vice-president of the students' organization of the *Rassemblement Démocratique Africain* on a visit to the East European countries in 1948. From the beginning he belonged to the extreme left wing of the UPC and the process of radicalization in this party was marked by his election as vice-president in 1949 and as president in 1952. In 1955 the movement went underground; as general secretary of the UPC Um Nyobé refused to emigrate, but Moumié wandered restlessly from country to country: first to the British Cameroons, then to Cairo, to Accra and finally, in 1958, to Conakry, the capital of Guinea, where he won admiration as 'the leader of the new anti-colonial Cameroon' and established a centre for Cameroon political exiles. In his last years he was present at all the important Pan-African conferences— and he visited Prague, Moscow and Peking. For a while he was a friend of Nasser's and he remained the personal friend of Kwame Nkrumah and Sékou Touré till the end of his days. He was received by Khrushchev and wooed by Mao Tse-tung—and not only wooed, but financed. He supplied his supporters in Cameroon with arms (chiefly Czech) and with increasingly violent slogans, and although he always described himself as a Cameroon nationalist, he began to play a more important international role. The red connecting threads to all radical and pro-communist groups in West Africa were gathered together in his UPC office in Conakry, which significantly was housed in the building of the National Assembly of Guinea. When the former Belgian Congo achieved its independence, Moumié went to the Congo as Lumumba's unofficial adviser. When the unrest began he founded a school for guerilla fighters, with Lumumba's approval and support, in the neighbourhood of Leopoldville, where young Congolese and Angolans were trained in the practice of guerilla warfare.[11] Powerful outside intervention and the victory of Mobutu in Leopoldville finally put a stop to this activity.

Who instigated and financed Moumié's actions? He seemed to have astonishing resources at his disposal. After his death, according to an official statement of the Cameroon Government, it was found that his bank account in Switzerland showed a credit of 771 million CFA francs (a sum equivalent to about a million pounds sterling!). Inquiries instituted by the Cameroon Government and other bodies cast some light on the question. As the result of a discussion with Sékou Touré on the Moumié affair, Cameroon's Foreign Minister, Charles Okala, informed the Yaoundé parliament on 9 December 1960 that Guinea had obviously supported the illegal UPC and was still doing so. It is also significant that Moumié was travelling on a passport issued to him by the Government of Guinea and that when he died his body was flown from Switzerland in a Guinean charter plane to Conakry, where he was given a state burial. President Nkrumah's attitude was also illuminating: on hearing of Moumié's assassination he announced publicly, 'Now the torch of freedom in Africa must be raised still higher'. On the other hand, President Nasser assured the Cameroon Government that his country had 'long since' ceased giving active support to the UPC—particularly as Moumié had tried to denigrate the Egyptian President in Pan-African circles. It is interesting that Cameroon's Foreign Minister, Okala, even discussed the Moumié affair with Khrushchev while they were both at the plenary meeting of the United Nations in New York. Reporting this interview to the Yaoundé parliament, Okala declared that Khrushchev had said: 'I told M. Moumié that revolutions cannot be organized from without . . . Go back to Cameroon to suffer with your fellow-countrymen, and win power *legally* by elections.'[12]

♦ These statements and this circumstantial evidence expose the existence of a considerable international system of common interests extending far beyond the narrow sphere of Cameroon's problems—a system in which Moscow, Conakry and Accra appeared as the wire-pullers of an extreme political radicalism uninhibited by any moral scruples, and this compromises them in the eyes of the genuinely democratic forces in Africa. Incidentally Khrushchev's statement to Cameroon's Foreign Minister should be taken with a pinch of salt: the former Soviet Premier admitted that he had had talks with Moumié and had given him advice. Obviously he could not admit to Okala that he had encouraged Moumié to persist in his extremist policies. Apart from this question, however, Khrushchev's statement was in accordance with the Soviet thesis, adopted at the

Twentieth Congress of the Communist Party of the Soviet Union and reaffirmed at the two Moscow meetings in November 1957 and 1960, which accepts the parliamentary method as one of two ways in which the still unfree peoples of Asia and Africa can achieve their independence. It is this alternative which is given weight by the Soviet policy of co-operation with the national bourgeoisie.

There is little doubt that, up to a certain point, the Kremlin gave more than mere propaganda support to the operations of the UPC in Cameroon. On the eve of the independence celebrations in Garoua on 3 January 1960, Ahidjo, then the Premier of Cameroon, gave a reception to local and foreign guests in the former Governor's palace. On this occasion he had a discussion lasting an hour with the Soviet representative at the celebrations, Nikolai Pavlovitch Firyubin. Up to this point the Soviet Government had not followed its usual practice of immediately offering to establish diplomatic relations with any new African State; indeed, because of the support the Soviets had given to the UPC they had been disavowed at all banquets and receptions. The long discussion between Ahidjo and Firyubin was therefore all the more remarkable, and the next day an official close to Ahidjo informed the author that this first official contact with the Soviet Government had been brought to a 'satisfactory conclusion' for Cameroon. According to later information from UPC circles, there seems little doubt that this 'satisfactory conclusion' involved an undertaking by the Soviet Government to cease its one-sided encouragement of the UPC and to use its influence to persuade the rebel leaders not to reject out of hand any proposals the Yaoundé Government might make for negotiations.

In any case, it is interesting to note that during an interview with the author, in Conakry in April 1960, Moumié very definitely changed his ground. During this interview, which lasted two hours, he did not even mention Moscow and the Russian communists to whom, up till then, he had always referred with great enthusiasm. Instead he spoke in great detail about his experiences during his stay in China, from which he had then just returned. With this we come to the decisive point of the Moumié affair. He frankly admitted that he had had personal talks with various Chinese communist leaders, including a discussion with Mao Tse-tung on Matworthy's classic book *Questions of Guerilla Strategy*, which appeared for the first time in 1938.[13] Almost triumphantly Moumié produced a

French edition of this book with a personal dedication written by Mao, saying: 'In this book you can read everything which is now going to happen in the Cameroons.'

After this there were further indications of Peking's keen interest in the civil war in Cameroon. These suggest that the Chinese communists were gaining increasing influence over the UPC, whose chief protector they now are. In the summer of 1960, Moumié again visited the Chinese People's Republic and his visit was followed by that of his deputy Ouandié and by at least three groups of alleged trade unionists from Cameroon. A special department for contacts with the UPC was then established in the Chinese Embassy on Conakry, and in addition to Chinese communist officials, there were two 'diplomats' from North Vietnam as advisers to the UPC centre in Conakry.

Further evidence was afforded by Byiavue Nicanor, the permanent representative of the UPC in Rabat, in an interview with the Morocco correspondent of the Chinese Hsinhua Agency. According to the account published in the English-language edition of *New China*, Nicanor declared: 'The Chinese people have never hesitated to support our struggle.' The tone suggests that he felt that this was not the case with other communist peoples:

'The daily growing interest of the Chinese people in our struggle is tangible proof of their attachment to the principle of the anti-imperialist struggle and of proletarian solidarity. *The great Chinese contribution* encourages the people of Cameroon to continue and intensify their revolutionary struggle. The rich experience of China amassed during twenty-eight years of victorious battle against imperialism and its lackeys, and China's great economic successes with "the great leap forward", and with the establishment of the People's Communes, add up to a valuable example for the peoples of Africa, particularly as the conditions of life and struggle in Africa do not differ greatly from those which existed in pre-revolutionary China.'[14]

There was thus complete adoption of Marxist phraseology, the unmistakable confirmation of the close relationship between the UPC and the Chinese people, the reference to the Chinese People's Communes, and finally a condemnation not quoted here of 'US and West German support for France in its aggression against the

Algerian and the Cameroon peoples'. All these already then spoke for themselves. The angry reaction of the Chinese Press and the Chinese Radio to the news of Moumié's death, a reaction which was very much more vehement than the treatment accorded to it in the non-Chinese communist Press, provided new evidence that the UPC owed its continued existence and ability to carry on to the Chinese, whose propaganda urged them to continue 'the war in Cameroon'.

How far it will prove possible for the UPC to carry out the Chinese plans is a matter of grave doubt. There was violent fighting in various parts of Cameroon in 1961, during which something like eighty per cent of all church and mission property was destroyed. In 1962 there was guerilla activity in various parts of the country, and in the following year the trials of captured terrorists suggested that the struggle was still smouldering, though the Cameroon authorities did their best to prevent news from leaking abroad. In the meantime, however, relations between the Ahidjo régime and some former UPC backers in Africa improved noticeably. Cairo, Accra and Conakry practically stopped their support for the exiled leaders of the UPC. The countries of the Soviet bloc also began to adopt a more friendly attitude to Ahidjo. The Soviet Union established diplomatic relations with Yaoundé in 1964 and only China, Albania, and the two Asian communist powers still support the UPC. In 1962 an official Cameroon Government delegation visited several Soviet-bloc countries, and between 19 and 30 September, Victor Kanga, the Cameroon National Economy Minister, had discussions with various prominent communist politicians in Warsaw, Prague and Moscow. In the Soviet capital he was demonstratively welcomed by Khrushchev.[15] At the same time, while Kanga was still behind the Iron Curtain, a delegation of the terrorist UPC, under the leadership of its vice-president, Abel Kingue, was being no less heartily welcomed in Peking by the Chinese Premier, Chou En-lai.[16] The presence of this delegation brought forth great praise in the Chinese Press and on the Chinese Radio for 'the battle-tested Cameroon National Liberation Army'.[17] Numerous reports from disillusioned trainees show that the programme organized by the Chinese for training Africans in guerilla warfare is still going on. In midsummer 1961 details were given of the experiences of six men from Cameroon who had undergone a ten-week course in China in 1960, during which the 'theory and practice of guerilla warfare' and combat tactics were well drilled into them both in the class room and during a battle course. During their stay in China they were taught how to make and use explosives, how to blow up bridges, houses, rails, tanks and lorries; how to sabotage airfields and telephone communications and how to destroy power stations and wireless stations. They were taught how to set ambushes, fortify villages, and deal with unsympathetic villagers and with sentries. They were taught that puppet agents and traitors should be killed off and that terrorist activities must be carried on. They were instructed in the ways in which to infiltrate vital concerns and organizations in order to reach positions from which their activities would have the maximum effect. On their return to the Cameroon Republic the six men carried documents giving detailed instructions for terrorist and guerilla activities and political action, together with binoculars, cameras, and transistor radio sets. These six men were arrested on their return to Africa. Another group of thirty 'students' came back to Cameroon after they had been expelled from China in August 1962. The students blamed this on racial discrimination by the Chinese. In the following months the leadership of the UPC became more and more subjected to pressures and manipulation by both the Russians and the Chinese, so that it seems to have reached a a point of almost complete disintegration. One of the first indications occurred in March 1964 when rival delegates, one supporting the Soviet Union, the other China, arrived at an Afro-Asian Solidarity meeting in Algiers. A couple of months later, in June 1964, the death in Cairo of Abel Kingue brought a stream of condolences from China and her sympathizers, but not from the Soviet Union. Then in September 1964 the UPC Revolutionary Committee declared after a meeting in Accra that the Chinese had 'assumed a hostile attitude towards them, had grossly interfered in the UPC's internal affairs and had supported opportunist elements which opposed its leadership'. This was followed by the news that Aloys-Marie Ndjog, former publicity and propaganda secretary of the UPC, had returned to Yaounde to make peace with President Ahidjo's government. Ndjog had been in exile for seven years, mostly in Cairo. His 'defection' from the exiles at this time suggested complete disillusionment with the present situation inside the Cameroon as well as in the UPC leadership. In 1965 the position of Ahidjo's government was stronger than ever before since independence was declared on 1 January 1960. The UPC is apparently split into several factions. But there is still a state of unrest in some parts of the country. And in September 1965 President Ahidjo told a Press conference in Paris that 'China has not completely stopped' interfering in Cameroon's internal affairs.[18]

In January 1959, when the insurrection took place in Leopold-ville and the Congo limped painfully forward to national sovereignty in a confused welter of personal, political, and tribal conflicts, the Chinese gleefully indicated that similar chances were opening up for them here as in Algeria and in Cameroon. At the end of January 1960, at a time when Independence Day for the Congo was being fixed at a round-table conference in Brussels, Congolese politicians and Chinese agents were meeting for important discussions against the background of the second All-Africa People's Congress in Tunis. Lumumba's representatives came to an agreement with the General Secretary of the Peking Afro-Asian Solidarity Committee, Chou Tzu-chi, on 'practical measures to support the Congolese people in their struggle against colonialism'. According to local information Peking then decided against one-sided support for the Congolese Socialist Party and provided Lumumba's party, the *Mouvement Nationale Congolais*, with large sums of money for its election campaign. Shortly before the declaration of independence several groups of Congolese politicians were in China, and on Independence Day Theodore Bengila, the General Secretary of the African Solidarity Party of the Congo, declared that China had given the peoples of Africa 'a shining example'. True independence, he declared (and he made it clear that this meant the complete exclusion of all Western, including economic, influences) could be attained in Africa only if the people took 'the Chinese lessons' to heart. Bengila also declared that 'the American imperialists' were planning 'a conspiracy against the independence of the Congo'. With this he gave the signal for an outburst of propaganda from Peking laced with violent threats. It was launched at the time of the *Force Publique* mutiny, and has not ceased since.[19]

Lumumba never visited China and neither did his deputy Antoine Gizenga. As a leading member of the *Parti Solidaire Africaine* (which, unlike Lumumba's MNC, openly proclaimed its extremist policy) Gizenga was always a potential ally of the communists. On 8 September 1960 he wrote a letter to the Peking Government:

'The Government of the Congo Republic would be very much obliged to learn to what extent your government would be in a position to support us in the following matters: personnel (volunteers); arms (various weapons with ammunition, fighter-planes, helicopters, artillery, tanks, armoured reconnaissance cars); finances (the sums necessary for certain urgent expenditure); and foodstuffs (rice, flour and tinned food). This urgently needed assistance would make it possible for the Government of the Congo to ensure the independence of its country, which is at the moment dangerously threatened. Signed on behalf of the Premier by the Deputy Premier, Antoine Gizenga.'[20]

Before long the friends of China in the Congo were compelled to realize that 'present conditions' were not favourable to their activities and that there was, for the moment, little hope of extending Chinese influence—as admitted by Mandungo, the Vice-President of the Congo-China Association in a Peking broadcast on 9 December 1960. The arrest of Lumumba, the vigorous action of Mobutu's troops, and the intervention of the United Nations force greatly diminished communist influence, and in October President Kasavubu closed down all the Soviet-bloc consulates in Leopoldville. China's Congo propaganda now became shriller, and Radio Peking, which is clearly received in the Congo, did its best to exacerbate the situation. With the murder of Lumumba it reached new heights. The Communist Party of China organized mass protest demonstrations; 500,000 people went on to the streets in Peking, 400,000 in Shanghai, 350,000 in Tientsin, and 200,000 in Canton, to protest against 'the imperialistic murder of Lumumba'. Addressing the demonstrators in the Chinese capital, Liao Chen-chi, Chairman of the Peking Afro-Asian Solidarity Committee, declared: 'The murder of Prime Minister Lumumba proves once more that the imperialists and the colonialists will never leave the stage of history of their own accord.' In other words, they must be driven from the stage by force in accordance with Chinese tactics; Soviet tactics won't do!

'The murder of Lumumba', Liao went on, 'teaches the Congolese people, all the peoples of Africa, and oppressed peoples everywhere that the imperialist bloc led by America must be regarded as a group of cannibalistic monsters who will never voluntarily grant the colonial peoples the boon of independence. True independence must therefore be won by a *people's struggle*. There is no other and less costly way.'

Referring to Moscow, he concluded:

'Many who have previously harboured illusions about the true character of imperialism because they have not faced all the facts are now being compelled by the crimes of imperialism to recognize the real situation . . . This is the logic of revolution. All the peoples of the Congo, of Africa and the whole world are now taking action. This is exactly what happened years ago in China.'[21]

These words raise once more the central problem in the dispute between Moscow and Peking. In Peking's view all attempts to come to any arrangement with the imperialists are just as hopeless as the chances of peaceful co-existence; no kind of conciliation is possible. The only alternative to the imperialism of Washington is that of an irreconcilable armed struggle, as exemplified by the case of China. There is no denying the fact that the murder of Lumumba greatly strengthened the hand of the Chinese communists and they lost no opportunity of reproaching Moscow with the 'hopelessness' of their 'soft' tactics in the under-developed countries. Incidentally Peking was the first of all the communist governments to recognize the Gizenga 'government' in Stanleyville as 'the only legal government of the Congo', and on 19 February 1961 it proposed the establish-ment of diplomatic relations. Even before that—on 16 January 1961—Gizenga's Foreign Minister, André Mendi, announced that Peking had promised 'all material assistance necessary for the victorious struggle of the Congolese people'. However, differences of opinion in the new capital, Stanleyville, delayed any effective Chinese intervention, as had similar differences of opinion in the Provisional Government in Algeria. Moreover, the practical basis of communist power in the Congo is weak; unlike the situation in Cameroon, there is very little of what might be termed virulent communism. Nevertheless together with Cameroon and Algeria, the Congo is still the main target of China's Africa policy and many reports refer to massive support by China for Pierre Mulele's movement (the *Jeunesse Mulele*), which terrorized several Congolese provinces in 1964.

Apart from these three areas, Algeria, Cameroon, and the Congo, which are receiving detailed attention, and Guinea and Ghana, Peking's efforts in Africa during recent years were largely concentrated on seeking to influence certain movements and groups in East Africa. Reports of infiltration in the ranks of the 'liberating elements' in Portuguese territory cannot be verified. On the other hand, reports from British sources concerning Chinese communist attempts to influence individual groups and publications in Uganda and Kenya seem to have some basis in fact. Incidentally Peking's embassy in Dar es Salaam is apparently being used more for representational purposes than for involved and devious underground machinations. The centre of Chinese communist activity in East Africa was Zanzibar and here Peking was banking on the Zanzibar Nationalist Party and its active general secretary, Abdul Rahman Mohamed, known as 'Babu'. Closely connected with his headquarters was *Zanews*, a cyclostyled publication completely taken up with Chinese agitation and propaganda and unquestionably controlled and financed by the New-China News Agency, some of its issues have contained only material provided by this agency. Numerous other publishing ventures were closely connected with *Zanews* and the objective behind this organization was to keep East Africa steadily supplied with Chinese communist propaganda material.

Babu's big moment came on 12 January 1964, when an armed group of anti-Arab nationalists succeeded in overthrowing the Sultan on the island. A new government was formed and declared the country a 'people's republic'. Shayk Abeid Karumé, quite neutral, was made President, and Hanga, who was known for having good contacts with the Soviet Union, became Vice-President. Abdul Rahman Mohamed 'Babu' took over the all-important Ministry of Foreign Affairs. He achieved rapid recognition for his country by the communist States, first and foremost by the Chinese People's Republic, for which he expressed particular sympathy in an official telegram. China immediately promised economic aid, and in a broadcast on 19 February 1964 Babu was able to announce the first fruits of this promise in the form of a grant of some

$U.S. 500,000.[22] While in the following weeks alarming reports circulated about the development of Zanzibar into an 'African Cuba' and Babu's name was linked with all these, President Julius Nyerere of Tanganyika was preparing the decisive neutralization of this danger. On 22 April 1964 he surprised Africa and the world with the announcement of political and economic fusion of Tanganyika and Zanzibar, which became a reality when it was accepted by both parliaments on 24 April 1964. Colin Legum commented on this sensational development in the London *Observer*, and with particular reference to Babu's position wrote as follows:[23]

'The decision by President Nyerere and President Karumé to merge Tanganyika and Zanzibar into a new union is as revolutionary an act as last January's *coup* which brought the Zanzibar Revolutionary Council to power.

'Everything now depends on the ability of these two leaders to hold their disparate countries together against the challenge of the extreme leftists.

'The struggle is not between moderates and militants, but between two sets of militants—the one committed to genuine non-alignment, the other using non-alignment as a façade to orientate Zanzibar in a communist direction.

'This conflict has been at the heart of the power struggle inside Zanzibar from the start of the revolution.'

And pointing to Babu's position, Legum wrote:

'Babu's strength came in large measure from his own superb abilities as an effective revolutionary leader. This gave him a clear advantage over the slow, unsure, defensive Karumé.

'But his natural capacity for leadership was heavily reinforced by two other circumstances. The first was the financial and moral support given to the revolution after its success by the communist countries: by the Russians no less than the Chinese. Chinese finance went not only to the Government but to Babu's group in a separate account. This gave him both prestige and financial resources.

'The second circumstance was the equivocal attitudes shown by the Western countries to the revolution. Babu exploited this fully to represent the British and the Americans as the enemies of the revolution.'

Only the future can tell how this fusion of the two countries will evolve and whether Western fears that it will open up new opportunities on the mainland for the communist elements in Zanzibar will materialize. Be that as it may: the role which Babu played during the short period of Zanzibar's revolutionary régime up to January 1964 is an indication of the close connections between China and some radical Africans, and of the effectiveness of the impact which Chinese radical policies have on certain strata of African society. A similar development could be observed in the former French Congo after the right-wing régime of Abbé Youlou was overthrown in a *coup d'état* in August 1963. Since the establishment of diplomatic relations in February 1954, the Chinese embassy in Brazzaville grew rapidly and Chinese influence was noted to be extraordinary, especially in the youth wing of the ruling *Mouvement National de la Révolution* (MNR). In its June 1965 issue the *African Review*, published in London, wrote:

'If the Chinese have been disappointed in the rebellion in Congo (Léopoldville), they are persisting in their attempts to gain a firm hold over Congo (Brazzaville). There are now more than 200 Chinese in Congo (Brazzaville). The Embassy has a staff of thirty and the rest are technical or military advisers, including some of their leading "experts". Colonel Kan Mei, the Embassy Counsellor, is an authority on subversive warfare, who has already figured as the main Chinese adviser to the Congolese rebels, while Kao Liang, head of the *New-China News Agency* arrived in Brazzaville from Dar es Salaam, where he had made contact with exiled African politicians and prepared the ground for the establishment of the Chinese Embassy in Burundi. Now the Chinese are concentrating on building up the army and the *Jeunesse* movement in Brazzaville with the help of other Communist and Arab States.

'The Chinese military mission consists of twenty officers, and liaison officers have been attached to every command of the new "People's Army", one of whose chief officers, Felix Mouzoubakani, has been sent to the Congo (Brazzaville) Embassy in Peking as military attaché.

'The Communists probably envisage Brazzaville as a model "Socialist" State with a one-party system, a policy of "scientific Socialism", a single trade union, and women's and youth movements closely tied to the ruling party on the Communist pattern. Thus the appointment of a number of young Communist-trained officials to Cabinet positions and the removal of the moderates is, as *Jeune Afrique* says, "a victory for those who are considered to be under the influence of the Chinese Communists".'

THE CHINESE RADIO OFFENSIVE

As a propaganda vehicle for reaching the illiterate, broadcasting has unlimited possibilities and the Chinese communists are taking full advantage of them. For one thing, the presence of Chinese communities overseas provides a ready-made audience for broadcasts in Kuoyu and Cantonese. The first available record of Chinese communist broadcasts to Africa dates from 1956, when broadcasts totalling three and a half hours a week were beamed to Egypt and Central Africa. Since then, and especially since 1958, Chinese broadcasts to Africa have steadily increased. But the following list gives some idea of the great expansion that has taken place since 1956:

Broadcasts in English
1956 Radio Peking inaugurated broadcasts in English to Egypt and Central Africa. Broadcasting time: 3½ hours weekly.
1958 A list of broadcasts in English published in December contained no mention of specific broadcasts to Africa.
1959 Peking broadcasts in English to South and East Africa. Total broadcasting time: 7 hours weekly.
1960 Peking broadcasts to South and East Africa. Broadcasting time: 7 hours weekly.
Peking broadcasts to West, Central and North-east Africa. Broadcasting time: 14 hours weekly.
Peking broadcasts to East Africa. Broadcasting time: 14 hours weekly.
1961 According to a list published in the *Peking Review* in October, broadcasts showed no increase.
1962 (January) Peking broadcasts to Africa (regions unspecified). Broadcasting time: 14 hours weekly.
West Africa: Broadcasting time totalled 7 hours weekly.
South-east Africa: Broadcasting time totalled 21 hours weekly.
1963 (April) Broadcasts to the whole of Africa totalled 63 hours weekly.

1964 (June) Peking broadcasts in English to Africa totalled 71 hours weekly.

Broadcasts in French

1961 Broadcasts in French totalled 12·50 hours ,weekly. In April 1963 they totalled 27 hours weekly. Prior to September 1961, broadcasts in French were increased to 21 hours weekly by the end of 1959, and to 28 hours weekly by the end of 1960. They were not designed specifically for African audiences but were transmitted on wave-lengths that could be heard in Africa. However, in September 1961 the broadcasting service was rearranged and there were two transmissions for Africa and two for Europe. From that date Peking catered specifically for African audiences and although previously there had been a greater number of broadcast hours the broadcasts themselves had been directed primarily at European listeners.

Broadcasts in Portuguese

1960 Peking broadcasts totalled 7 hours weekly. More recent information suggests that this time is divided equally into $3\frac{1}{2}$ hours for South Africa and $3\frac{1}{2}$ hours for West Africa.

Broadcasts in Kuoyu

1959 Peking broadcasts to North Africa totalled 7 hours weekly.

1961 Peking broadcasts to North Africa totalled 14 hours weekly. More recent information suggests that this time is divided equally into 7 hours for sub-Saharan Africa (regions unspecified) and 7 hours to North Africa.

Broadcasts in Cantonese

1958 Peking broadcasts to South-east Africa totalled 7 hours weekly.

1959 Peking broadcasts to South-east Africa totalled $3\frac{1}{2}$ hours weekly.

1960 Peking broadcasts to South-east Africa totalled 7 hours weekly.

Broadcasts in Swahili

1961 Peking broadcasts to East Africa totalled 7 hours weekly. These broadcasts were started on 1 September. On 20 October it was announced that as from 30 October two additional wave-lengths would be used when broadcasting each of the $2\frac{1}{2}$-hour-daily transmissions. However, it has not been possible to trace such broadcasts on any new wave-lengths and there is some doubt as to whether they are, in fact, being used.

Broadcasts in Arabic

1957 Peking broadcasts to North Africa totalled 7 hours weekly.

1958 Peking broadcasts to North Africa totalled 10½ hours weekly.
1959 Peking Radio broadcasts to North Africa totalled 14 hours
weekly.

The following list shows the weekly number of broadcast-hours
devoted by Peking Radio to transmissions beamed to one or more
parts of Africa (according to information available in January
1965)

English	82	Cantonese	7	French	38
Swahili	24·5	Portuguese	7	Arabic	24
Kuoyu	14				

making a total of 206·5 hours[24] as compared with about 150 broad-
casting-hours devoted to Africa by Moscow Radio.

The three main themes in these Chinese broadcasts are: 1. China
as an example: the methods by which China was freed from the
semi-colonialism of Chiang Kai-shek and the subsequent developments (economic, social, and cultural) in Mao's empire since 1949.
These are presented as a model for Africa to follow in its struggle
for freedom. 2. Decolonization: Africans are told that their liberation from Western domination must be quicker and more thorough;
and to this end it is most important that they should liquidate
Western capital possessions and reject all offers of aid from the West
as these are attempts to gain neo-colonial influence. Pride of place
is given to the exposure of American imperialism as 'the chief wire-
puller' behind all colonialist undertakings in Africa. In the summer
of 1960 Peking Radio began a special series of broadcasts designed
'to expose the criminal intentions of US imperialism' and to warn
Africans against 'the fatal consequences' likely to ensue if they
accepted 'so-called aid' from the United States. These propaganda
broadcasts were transmitted in several African languages. 3. The
complete identification of China with any and every form of African
emancipation: according to a Peking broadcast on 30 May 1960, Hu
Yu-chi, a member of the Political Bureau of the Chinese Communist
Party, declared at a reception for Congolese politicians: 'The
Chinese people, who won their victory in a long struggle against
imperialism and colonialism, regard the struggle of the Congolese
people as their own struggle, and the victory of the Congolese
people as their own victory.'

These three themes recur constantly in Chinese propaganda

material for Africa and in all Chinese demonstrations, etc., devoted to African questions, such as 'Kenya Day', 'Uganda Day', 'Help Algeria Week', 'Cameroon Solidarity Day', and so on. The unmistakable aim of Chinese propaganda in Africa is to present communist China as 'the natural ally of the awakening continent of Africa'. At the same time Africans are to be persuaded that by virtue of China's 'special experience' in the anti-colonial struggle for freedom and its subsequent economic reconstruction and class reorganization, that country is entitled to be the senior partner in the alliance. As such, it is called upon to lead the revolutionary forces and to protect Africa from all imperialist intervention. Denouncing alleged internal and external conspiracies against his government in a speech in Conakry on 10 May 1960, Sékou Touré declared that China, in particular among the Afro-Asian nations, had given an assurance that in the event of an imperialist attack on Guinea, it would mobilize its forces 'within forty-eight hours'. It is thus clear that Peking is not only anxious to present communist China as the protector of Africa, but also that these pretentions are being accepted in certain African circles.

THE ORGANIZATION

The strict centralization of China's Africa policy is intended to facilitate a more rapid and effective achievement of Peking's political ambitions in the future. At first the Peking branch of the Afro-Asian Solidarity Organization played an important part in the execution of China's Africa policy, but in the summer of 1960 a special Society for Chinese-African Friendship was founded. The next step came in December 1960 when Mao Tse-tung instituted a 'Special Committee for Africa' as part of the Political Bureau of the Chinese Communist Party, and appointed Li Keh-nu, former secretary of the Party Bureau for Social Affairs and an extreme member of the party leadership, to run it.

All relations with overseas friendship and cultural organizations are now under the joint supervision of the International Liaison and Organization Departments of the Central Committee of the Communist Party of China, and the State Council's Commission for Cultural Relations with Foriegn Countries. This body is responsible for the Association for Cultural Relations with Foreign

Countries together with the appropriate departments of the Ministry of Foreign Affairs, and wherever relevant the Chinese Institute for International Relations and the Chinese People's Institute for Foreign Affairs.

The following organizations are also concerned with African matters:

The Chinese People's Association for Cultural Relations with Foreign Countries. This association 'was founded in May 1954, with the aim of fostering friendly relations between the Chinese people and the peoples of other lands by increasing cultural contacts between them. It sponsors the exchange of cultural delegations, and the visits of writers, artists and scientists, the holding of exhibitions and commemoration meetings of outstanding cultural figures of different ages and different countries, and the staging of theatrical performances. Through these and other channels Chinese cultural achievements are introduced to the peoples of other countries whilst those of other peoples are introduced to China'.[25]

The Chinese People's Institute for Foreign Affairs. This institute 'was established in December 1949 as a people's organization devoted to the study of international affairs. It extends invitations to foreign political leaders to visit this country, and through personal contacts helps to promote international understanding and friendship.'[26]

The Chinese-African People's Friendship Association was founded in Peking on 12 April 1960 on the initiative of seventeen national people's organizations. On 17 April a rally was held to celebrate jointly the fifth anniversary of the Bandung Conference and the founding of the association.

Department of the State Council. The Friendship Association is one of the four departments set up under the aegis of the State Office of the Government of the Chinese People's Republic:

(a) *The Africa Office.* This department, which is also known as the General Africa Directorate, unlike the other three, is under the direction of the Ministry for Foreign Affairs.

(b) *The Research Commission for African Subjects*, which is responsible for the study and financial control of operations in African countries. It is in contact with the State Office, and controls the work of the other sections.

(c) *The Chinese-African People's Friendship Association*, whose most important undertaking to date has been the extensive four-month tour (from March 1961) of a Friendship Delegation led by the President of the Association, Liu Chang-sheng, to eight West-African countries. On his return Liu's comprehensive report on this tour was broadcast in Swahili in ten instalments.

(d) *The Commission for Social Relations with the Peoples of Africa*, which operates directly under the State Office and controls Chinese communists working in the various countries of Africa.

The China-Egypt Friendship Association was founded in Peking on 11 November 1956. In February 1958 it was amalgamated with the China-Syria Friendship Association to form the China and United Arab Republic Friendship Association. However in September 1959, the Syrian Minister for Social Affairs ordered the dissolution of certain organizations, including the China-Syria Friendship Association, and it is probable that the amalgamated organization now concerns itself only with Egypt, particularly as Syria and Egypt have since parted company.

The Asia-Africa Society. This is the latest organization formed in Peking for the promotion of interest in Africa and the propagation of communism. The society was founded on 19 April 1962 to promote academic research in China into the political, economic, religious, and cultural development of the Asian and African countries, and to intensify and extend China's contacts with these countries. The society, whose president is Chou Yang, has over five hundred members, most of whom are research workers and college professors.

Friendship Organizations in Africa: The Congo-China Association was founded in September 1960, with Alphonse Makwanbela as president; a Tunisia-China Association has been in existence since November 1960, and a Nigeria-China Friendship Society was founded in 1961, with C. Anozie as president.

Together with the very active Afro-Asian Solidarity Council (see the special chapter devoted to this organization) these bodies form a close network in Africa and in China dedicated to the propagation of communism. With them, communist China undoubtedly controls the strongest and most widespread organizational basis for African operations, far greater than anything set up by any other communist country.

NOTES

[1] Radio Mogadishu broadcast, 4 February 1964.

[2] In 1960 no less than 800 delegations from foreign countries visited Mao's China; of these, 270 were from Africa. For later years the figures from various sources disagree; cf. Ho Wei-yang, 'Communist China's Policy in Africa', *Aussenpolitik* (Stuttgart), XII, No. 3 (March 1961).

[3] C. Garratee, 'Peking's Star in Africa', *Far Eastern Economic Review*, 25 August 1960.

[4] New-China News Agency (hereinafter cited as NCNA), 12 and 13 May 1956.

[5] NCNA, 28 May 1961.

[6] Radio Peking, Swahili-language broadcast, 8 March 1962.

[7] NCNA, 10 September 1959.

[8] Radio Moscow broadcast, 31 October 1959.

[9] Two other quotations from different sources: on 15 July 1959 the Chinese newspaper *Ta Kung Pao* wrote: 'The Algerian people are simply compelled to continue their just war to a victorious end.' On 15 September 1959, the Moscow labour-union organ, *Trud*, wrote: 'The only realistic way to solve the Algerian problem is by the opening up of direct negotiations', i.e., between Paris and the leaders of the FLN.

[10] NCNA, 20 March 1961.

[11] Radio Yaoundé broadcast, 9 December 1960.

[12] Ibid.

[13] This book had a great influence on the strategy and tactics of the communist guerilla and liberation armies in Indo-China and was regarded as a textbook in Ho Chi-minh's movement.

[14] NCNA, 11 September 1960.

[15] Tass, 19 and 24 September 1962.

[16] NCNA, 3 October 1962.

[17] Radio Peking broadcast, 5 October 1962.

[18] Radio Yaoundé, 14 September 1965

[19] NCNA, 30 June 1960. See also the report by Radio Brazzaville on 23 October 1963 stating that during a Press conference on that day, M. Amany, Centre Defence Minister and Commissioner General Extraordinary for Leopoldville, referred to 'copies of Mao Tse-tung on guerilla warfare' which he said had been found in the abandoned hideouts of the followers of the Gizenga faction in Kwilu province.

[20] *Die Weltwoche* (Zurich), 11 November 1960.

[21] NCNA, 2 March 1961.

[22] Cf. *Newsweek*, 2 March 1964.

[23] The *Observer* (London), 26 April 1964.

[24] Monitoring reports of the Voice of America, the BBC, and the *Deutsche Welle* (Cologne).

[25] *China Handbook* (Peking), April 1957.

[26] Ibid.

Chapter XII

THE FRONT ORGANIZATIONS (1)

WHOEVER regards communism in action merely as a gigantic State machine and international party organization is overlooking one of the most important reasons for its success. Unlike conventional imperial systems and world political movements, communism breaks through the customary structure of organization and creates an additional sphere of activity on an international pattern—a third dimension of attack. This assumes decisive importance when traditional methods fail: when the communist parties are still embryonic or prohibited, when overt agitation is dangerous and any idea of penetrating into the State or sharing power is out of the question. Operations are then directed not so much at the converted as at the innocent, the undecided, the politically naïve. The snares in which they are caught and finally transformed into supporters differ according to circumstances and requirements: associations for the rights of mothers, trade unions, professional associations of lawyers, teachers, and artists; youth leagues and student groups, sports associations and peace committees—all these organizations offer excellent possibilities for camouflage. As front organizations, i.e. façades, they allow the communists to conceal their real intentions. In this way the true aims of communism are kept in the background, and potentially hostile reactions are forestalled.

Even in Lenin's day communism recognized the great value of these transmission belts, but it was not until after the Second World War that this political 'third dimension' offensive was organized on a big scale. Then communists everywhere set out to exploit the longing for peace and human solidarity, and finding supporters in the West, they founded the World Trade Union

Federation, the World League of Democratic Youth, the International Union of Students and innumerable auxiliary organizations, in which a variety of honest, if politically naïve people, reputable intellectuals, enthusiastic youngsters, dogged world reformers, empty-headed babblers, people in dire need of sympathy and comfort, came together to demonstrate 'the essential unity of the world' and to work for the realization of 'high ideals'. Although these organizations and associations rapidly lost much of their usefulness because of splits and exposures, they remained valuable to the communists in those areas where they were still weak and where people failed to recognize the front organizations for what they were. Particularly was this true in Africa and Asia. In Africa, front organizations are enjoying rapid growth and winning new adherents. Today not a single African country is without at least one of these 'humanitarian', 'pacifist', 'anti-imperialist' associations and, as time goes on, Africa is being increasingly covered with a network of the pink auxiliary organizations of communism. There is no shortage of African representatives at the various communist-organized and -controlled (though usually cleverly camouflaged) trade-union, peace, teachers, recreational, legal, and youth congresses; in fact their organizers always seem anxious for coloured faces to be prominent on the various praesidiums and special committees, and in particular at Press conferences. In this way Africans are used by these front organizations as a guarantee of 'neutrality' and as proof that they are 'non-party' and above board. They also serve to demonstrate the world-wide scope and 'growing support' the front organizations are receiving 'among the masses.'

The motives and objectives of this activity are as simple as they are effective:

1. The front organizations operate as a great dredger, scooping up neutral forces and gradually converting them into sympathizers, fellow-travellers or puppets. At first the intellectual bait seems relatively harmless and consists of very general ideas and conceptions, behind which one would not immediately suspect specifically communist ideas. But once the outlook of the victims has been focused in the desired direction, more sharply formulated slogans are introduced.

2. Contacts with like-minded people, who are also peace-loving and decent, even if they are in the communist camp, are intended to

persuade the approached people that they are not alone and can count on real friends in the socialist countries. In all this the communists are seeking to counteract a general unwillingness to enter into engagements and alliances with them, to dissipate coolness and distrust and to persuade the representatives of the national bourgeoisie and intelligentsia of the harmlessness and usefulness of the national people's fronts and unity programmes.

3. As long as there are only a few communist parties in Africa the front organizations serve as the disseminators of communist ideas and opinions and make the public familiar with them.

In different circumstances it might be possible to regard such efforts with indifference, but in Africa today there is a strong tendency, a psychological willingness, to enter into associations with all 'well-meaning' people, in fact, with almost anyone who is prepared to identify himself with the current slogans of African nationalism, provided (an essential condition this) that he is not 'in the camp of imperialism and colonialism'. Many Africans are prepared to risk the definite disadvantages to themselves of co-operation with, or membership of, such front organizations, provided it gives them a platform and a chance to address a sympathetic audience. To arrange this is simple for the communists; they can easily organize mass demonstrations and processions with bands and banners, and arrange appeals, resolutions, and so on. This ability is, in fact, the fundamental strength of communism, its tools for creating and exercising mass psychological influence, for keeping its followers in constant movement and in repeated emotional tension. It uses half the old recipe of 'bread and circuses', and the circuses happen to be the more important half.

Perhaps all this is only superficial and temporary. Even so, the founders of the science of mass psychology, particularly Tarde, Le Bon, and Sighele, have pointed out the profound emotional effect of even short-lived mass tension, and as far as our own particular problem is concerned it can hardly be denied. What satisfies the participant in such affairs, with their fanfares and drum-rolls, is an almost indefinable need for sympathy and contact. They help him to feel that he is no longer alone and on the fringe. He is now one of an applauding, cheering mass of people, all of whom obviously feel as he does and want the same things: national independence, freedom for the whole of Africa, the distribution of the best land among the coloured people instead of among the white exploiters, condemnation of Verwoerd's *apartheid* in South Africa, the right of Africans to a say in all important international affairs—and so on. It made a tremendous impression on Africans when, at the People's Congress for Peace in Vienna in December 1952, 2,000 delegates from a hundred countries sprang to their feet to cheer 23 delegations with 203 African members for their 'heroic struggle for freedom from the yoke of colonialism'; and when, on the communist Day of Colonial Youth, celebrated at every communist world youth festival, boys and girls from the 'free' countries of the world presented bouquets of flowers to their 'friends from Africa' in token of their 'heroic struggle for national independence'. And when, to quote another example, a subordinate official of a tiny break-away trade union in, say, Sierra Leone, finds himself a guest at a World Trade-Union Congress. Perhaps he is at first perplexed to hear himself introduced as 'an important African trade-union leader', but his doubts are dissipated quickly when he is invited to take his place among 'the guests of honour' on the platform and he hears the thunderous applause with which he is welcomed as 'a representative of the new Africa'. They seem almost to be vying for his favours. People from Czechoslovakian, Bulgarian, Russian, French and Italian brother-unions—people he has never seen before—surround him enthusiastically, shaking his hand and clapping him on the shoulder. Every evening he is the guest of this or that trade-union delegation. He is invited to report on his own country, his friends and comrades, and his struggle for freedom. Whatever he says is listened to attentively and received enthusiastically. He also discovers (how heart-warming and stimulating) that these strangers know a great deal about his troubles and what he should do about them. When the congress is over he finds that he now has innumerable 'real friends' and is warmly invited to accompany them forthwith to their own countries in order to get an objective picture of their many social achievements. Within a few weeks he has visited two or three socialist countries, shaken thousands of friendly hands and been shown all their 'socialist achievements': the exemplary health services, the people's factories and industrial undertakings, the 'fantastic social performance' of the collective farms, and the wonderful opportunities for youth. When he gets back to his own country he will babble enthusiastically about all he has seen in 'the lands of socialism'. When the next congress takes place he will not again go alone, but with a whole delegation from his union.

There is another bond that henceforth binds him to his new companions. The congress in which he took part adopted a resolution calling for the total economic independence of Sierra Leone from the West; and as everyone in the hall enthusiastically lifted his hand in favour, our African delegate could hardly refuse to raise his when his new-found friends put other resolutions to the vote, such as a demand for the 'liquidation of the West Berlin espionage network' and the transformation of West Berlin, about which he knows little or nothing, into a 'free, de-militarized' city. There were also other resolutions of a similar tenor: against American spy flights, against the treacherous plans of the imperialists in Vietnam, in Japan, or wherever else the heat was being turned on at that moment, and also resolutions thanking the leading men of the Kremlin for their peace policy. By this time he finds himself voting automatically for everything, no matter what. During his subsequent tour of the Soviet-bloc countries he will find himself surrounded by communist journalists anxious to hear what he thinks of the tremendous achievements of socialism. Next day their newspapers will contain a report (somewhat embellished if necessary) of his remarks under the headline 'Sierra Leone Trade-Union Leader enthusiastic about Socialist Construction in our Country'. On having it read to him he will find that he has said, 'Your deeds and achievements open up new perspectives for us'. There are quite a number of cases in which newspapers containing such reports have then found their way to Africa (or the communists have used such statements in their African propaganda broadcasts and publications) with the result that the unfortunate spokesman is called to account by his friends and fellow-workers at home. But that is his worry, and really not very important; the point is that once the man has made such statements and taken up this position he is psychologically branded and has a halter round his neck that is very difficult to get rid of. Thus an almost casual meeting has developed into an engagement. The next step takes place with inevitable logic: he becomes an agent, in the strict sense of the word. He is asked to collect signatures for this or that new communist peace appeal, for an anti-imperialist protest resolution, for the acceptance of Red China into the United Nations, and so on. Or perhaps he is asked to organize a 'solidarity demonstration' to give moral support to the Castro régime in Cuba. Before long he is on his way to attend a six-month training course at a World Federation of Trade Unions centre in East Europe.

This is not just a hypothetic example: one could quote many similar cases. I could mention the names of half a dozen Africans who have had similar experiences. The organizations in the background are not always big, well known, or easily identifiable, and the wire-pullers are well camouflaged. There is (one example among many) an organization known as the *Fédération Internationale Syndicale de l'Enseignement* (FISE). It sounds harmless: an international trade-union organization for teachers. Every year its members hold a World Teachers' Conference, and in 1960 its conference took place for the first time on African soil: from 27 July to 1 August at Conakry. The preliminary material and the invitations were not issued by a Soviet or Chinese vice-president, but by a French trade-union official named Paul Delanoue. No one was told anything about him; he is in fact a member of the French Communist Party and a leading official of the French communist *Confédération Générale du Travail* (CGT). Adroitly FISE persuaded the Federation of Coloured African Teachers, with which it has maintained close fraternal relations for a long time, to ask the African *governments* to choose the national delegations—a gesture that did not fail to please. In consequence, the President of Guinea, Sékou Touré, officially opened the conference and became a member of its præsidium, where he found himself hob-nobbing with the Soviet educational expert, Ivan Grivkov, with Alfred Wilke of East Germany, Fang Ming of Red China, Soebandri of Vietnam, old fellow-travellers and 'new friends', with Delanoue himself, with Oshilak of Denmark, Ballantini of Italy, Miss Azango of Liberia, and Leslie Rodriguez of Cuba. The mask, already slipping, was dropped completely when it came to drawing up the agenda and electing committees to work out 'a common attitude' to the following problems: 1. the development of culture, education and international solidarity; 2. international recreation and peace; 3. social security. In each case the communists and their supporters set the tone of the resolutions on these subjects. Not surprisingly, all the resolutions denounced Western principles and methods and Western 'imperialist educational aggression', while opting for 'socialist pedagogy'. However, although it was a teachers' conference, educational problems as such played a subordinate role; the political standpoint was what mattered and the correct standpoint was made clear in the first resolution adopted by the conference. It was entitled 'the participation of teachers in the struggle for full national independence' and declared: 'We vigorously condemn all the actions of the imperialists because they are leading to an intensification of international tension. We demand the immediate abandonment of atomic tests. We condemn the violation of the air space of sovereign national States and all other espionage.'[1] Another resolution called for support for the struggle of the Soviet Union against the 'provocative' policy of the United States.

The technique is always the same: first comes an invitation that looks harmless and seems to be without strings; then a programme is drawn up in such general terms that almost anyone could accept it. The programme is read at the opening session and various committees are formed in an outwardly democratic fashion to draw up the resolutions for the conference. In between, there are one or two public demonstrations to secure an emotional response from 'the masses', then the conference gets down to a guided discussion; finally, in addition to the generalized, non-binding formulations used as an introduction, deliberate and unmistakable pro-communist resolutions are pushed through. The success of such methods requires that the communists control the show from start to finish, and as they are invariably the only well-organized group with definite objectives (whereas the others are an amorphous mass with multifarious opinions) they find this easy enough. So the same trick succeeds again and again. Usually only a quite minor subterfuge is necessary in order to jockey a meeting or conference in the desired direction. In most cases it is enough to 'cook' the list of speakers who are to take part in the discussions, and to see that the right people are chosen as members of the various committees and commissions which deal with individual subjects behind the scenes. The results of their discussions are then presented to the full session of the conference for endorsement. To give two examples of how this gerrymandering works in practice: at the FISE conference in Conakry, the communist wire-pullers shunted off unreliable candidates into the unimportant committee dealing with social questions. The result was that the communists and their friends had complete

control of the two political commissions in which the really import-
and resolutions were drafted. At the Tashkent Conference of Afro-
Asian Writers in October 1958 the delegates, who came from almost
fifty countries, were asked to submit the text of their speeches and
contributions to the præsidium of the conference as soon as possible,
the ostensible reason being that this would allow time to supply
accurate translations into the various languages. The præsidium also
laid down the order in which the speakers were to address the
conference, and its tactics ensured that any unreliable speaker was
immediately followed by two or three committed men who would
efface the effect of anything unfortunate the first speaker might
have said. When these safe speakers had had their say, another
'doubtful' could be allowed to take the floor again . . . and so on.
In order to deceive public opinion, and even the delegates themselves, as to the number of communists present, and to make it
difficult to identify them, these front organization congresses never
mention to what party a speaker belongs. In consequence the
innocent delegates do not know who is addressing them or what his
background is.

The conference of Afro-Asian writers in Tashkent (which has
been followed by a number of similar ones arranged by a permanent organizing bureau) and the FISE Congress in Conakry, both
clearly revealed what the communists are aiming at in their struggle
on 'the cultural front'. The organizers of the conference in Tashkent, capital of the Uzbek S.S.R., naturally did not present the
196 delegates and the 22 guests at the conference with a cut-and-
dried communist programme. The main principle, a relatively
modest one, put forward by the conference was that the writer
must not 'lock himself up in an ivory tower' and behave as an
individualist. Instead, he must take an active part in the 'everyday
life of the people' and in 'the struggle of the people'. The important passages in the appeal adopted by the conference read: 'The
Tashkent Conference stresses the very important mutual inter-
actions of creative literature and the struggle of the peoples. As
writers we fully recognize that the great and joyful cause of literary
and cultural creation can thrive only in freedom. We also know that
our lives are indissolubly connected with the lives of our peoples.
Their aims are our aims, their struggle is our struggle, and we fight
determinedly by their side against the remains of colonial domi-

nance and against the threat of nuclear war, for freedom, unity and friendship between the peoples.'[2] In an article on the Afro-Asian Writers' Association, which was founded after the Tashkent Conference, the Soviet African official, Sharaf Rashidov, took as his motto the words of the Cameroonian writer, Benjamin Matip: 'The African writer is at once a sort of doctor who prescribes for the people a remedy against colonialism and a soldier who fights for national independence.'[3] Rashidov developed this idea further in writing on the Tashkent Conference:

'Perhaps the most widely discussed question at the conference was that of *the writer's place in the social struggles of his people*. Some writers tend to be suspicious of appeals to participate in such struggles and in public life generally. They still believe that art can be divorced from politics . . . Such prejudices, the reasons for which are quite clear, should be countered by thoughtful, convincing and tactful argument. The ideologists of imperialism seek to divert the Afro-Asian writers from the vital and urgent issues of our time and from participation in nation-wide movements for freedom and peace by trotting out the old argument that the writer is an artist not a politician. But no artist can be an indifferent bystander. The true artist is one whose art expresses the life of his people . . . In the course of informal talks and discussions, the writers who believe in the active, social significance of art succeeded as a rule in convincing the doubters.'[4]

The Afro-Asian Congress of the International Association of Democratic Jurists in Beirut in 1960, and the Twentieth Congress of the International Democratic Women's Federation in Cairo were held under similar auspices and with similar slogans.

Not to be overlooked were the efforts of the International Journalists' Organization (IJO) to get a foothold in Africa and to influence public opinion with the usual methods of communist Press policy. In pursuance of these efforts the IJO held a first African Regional Conference at the end of May 1961 in Bamako, the capital of Mali. Outwardly it was, supposedly, completely independent of the IJO, and its organizers had high hopes of an outstanding success, reckoning on the presence of about 600 deluded African journalists. The author was present as correspondent of the *Neue Zürcher Zeitung*, and was the only representative of the

Western Press. The gathering was not as successful as had been hoped and was attended by only thirty journalists and official government representatives. They came from Ghana, Guinea, Upper Volta, Mali, the United Arab Republic, and Algeria, and from certain left-wing opposition elements in Cameroon, Togo and Madagascar. The whole affair was organized and operated by the secretariat of the communist-controlled International Journalists' Organization, which had brought translators, interpreters and simultaneous translation apparatus from its headquarters in Prague.

The idea of the conference was first publicly mooted at an International Journalists' Day, organized by the IJO in Baden, near Vienna, in October 1960, at which a number of African guests were present. At the beginning of March 1961 the Ministries of Information of Ghana, Guinea and Mali held a preliminary meeting in Accra at which a secretariat was formed to organize the conference and send out invitations to African journalists throughout the continent. Doudou Guèye, a political adviser to Modibo Keita, the President of Mali, was put in charge of this secretariat. Guèye was no newcomer; he had been the vice-president of the IJO and had held various posts in the Senegalese movement for independence until the authorities in Dakar expelled him and sent him back to Bamako. Thereafter, he visited several Soviet-bloc countries. Thus the organizing arrangements for the African Regional Conference in Bamako were in safe hands. The few African visitors who did attend found themselves faced with a group of IJO representatives almost as numerous as themselves, culled from the various national organizations affiliated to the IJO and from the communist journalist organizations of the Soviet bloc. No journalist organizations in the West were represented; either they were not invited or their invitations were sent out too late for them to send even observers.

Under these circumstances the conference was completely controlled by pro-communists and so-called neutralists, and in any case, anti-Western elements. All the delegations from the countries of the Soviet bloc adopted declarations of solidarity for their coloured colleagues' struggle for freedom. There was, of course, no shortage of violent attacks on the colonial and neo-colonial policies of the West, which was said to be using its news agencies, Press services and 'monopoly position' in the African Press and Radio to wage an 'anti-African cultural offensive'. Representatives from the IJO, the International Radio Organization (IRO) (which is also, significantly, domiciled in Prague) and of various associations from other East European countries promised their 'unconditional aid' to the Africans to help them ward off this 'attack of intellectual colonialism' as quickly as possible. It was also announced that various measures had already been taken to this end: the participants were informed that East Germany had established in Conakry the biggest printing works in the whole of Africa, and had built radio studios in various African countries. It was stated that a solidarity meeting, held a short while earlier in East Germany, had collected 700,000 marks. In addition, the Polish Journalists' Association contributed 2·5 million zloty, which would be used to assist the publicity efforts of the young African national States. The Czechoslovak Journalists' Association was reported to be helping to establish Press facilities in Mali. Finally it was announced that the IJO and the IRO had generously contributed 'millions of roubles' in aid, and the leader of the IJO delegation, a Russian named Yefremov, assured his listeners that this was only a beginning and reminded them that the Soviet bloc had unlimited potential.

This undisguised propaganda by the Soviet representatives met with only an indirect response. The representatives of the United Arab Republic sought to persuade Africans to avail themselves of the services of the Cairo News Agency, and Ofori, a delegate from Ghana, announced that all facilities for establishing a Pan-African news agency were already in existence in Ghana, or could be set up immediately by the Nkrumah Government and placed at the disposal of the Pan-African scheme. However, these suggestions were turned down by the conference controllers, who also rejected certain timid attempts to tone down the vehemently anti-Western resolutions placed before the conference. These resolutions were largely the work of a committee including Jean Dean, from Guinea, Doudou Guèye, the Mali representative, and certain extreme left-wing delegates from Cameroon and Madagascar. Finally Dean was elected president, and Guèye general secretary of the Pan-African Journalists' Association in Bamako.

The note sounded by the Mali conference was, on the whole, discordant. The absence of both journalists and government representatives from the greater part of Africa clearly expressed a growing dislike of both violent language and communist influence; on the other hand, it revealed the extent to which the Press and publicity of some African countries were already under communist influence. In the circumstances it was not surprising that the newly formed association of journalists should proclaim its eagerness to co-operate actively with the IJO. In any case, the IJO had secured an instrument of its own for infiltration in Africa.[5]

In the meantime several declarations issued by the secretariat of this Pan-African journalists' organization, in connection with various international and African questions, have provided repeated confirmation of the real set-up.[6] This kind of activity by the secretariat of various communist-front organizations represents the follow-up and the conferences are only one aspect of the activities and efforts of the communist-front organizations. All the auxiliary organizations that they establish have their own executive committees and secretariats which carry out on a large scale pro-communist propaganda almost independently. Apart from the big World Peace Congresses, the World Peace Council (founded in 1948) has the following organizations at its disposal: a council, consisting of 400 representatives of all the individual organizations, trades, professions, and so on, affiliated to the council. As the countries of the Soviet bloc are not in the majority on this council, an executive bureau is necessary. This has only 60 members and is much easier to control. Outwardly it is represented by various Lenin-prize winners and it meets more often than the council, whose effective control it ensures. This is the case to an even greater extent with the decisive body, the secretariat, which consists of eight members only and is permanently established in Prague. The situation in other international organizations (for instance, the World Trade Union Federation; the World League of Democratic Youth; the International Union of Students; and the International Democratic Women's Federation) is the same. The secretariats of these various bodies are responsible for the editing and issuing of the various official publications, which appear in many languages. They are responsible for the ceaseless flood of resolutions and declarations on all possible questions. No opportunity for communist propaganda is ever lost by the World Peace Council, the Afro-Asian Solidarity Conference, the IDFF, the World Federation of Trade Unions, the IUS and so on—that is to say, in each case the communist-controlled secretariat of these bodies issues manifestos, decisions and appeals to world public opinion in the name of 'all friends of peace', 'all trade unionists', 'all peoples', and so on. The demands they put forward represent the comprehensive communist bag, from general disarmament and the admittance of Red China to the United Nations, to the condemnation of the imperialists over Suez, the Congo, Laos, Cuba, and the military bases in Africa. In a world so prone to propaganda, particularly in continents such as Asia and Africa, where ordinary people know little or nothing about the activity behind the scenes, this permanent propaganda cataract, which serves the communists and is, to put it mildly, anti-Western, must be taken very seriously, particularly as communism spares neither money nor effort to spread these manifestations into the farthest corners of Africa. At the same time it is disturbing to note that very rarely indeed do any of the great number of members or fellow-travellers of these communist-front organizations object to the misuse of their names in all the appeals, demands, etc. issued by the tiny minority of communists in control.

NOTES

[1] Cyclostyled report of the proceedings of the conference, issued at Conakry, 1 August 1960.

[2] *Die Presse der Sowjetunion* (Soviet German-language publication), No. 126 (1958).

[3] *World Marxist Review: Problems of Peace and Socialism*, IV, No. 3 (March 1961), p. 33.

[4] Ibid., p. 37.   [5] *Neue Zürcher Zeitung*, 2 June 1961.

[6] Special arrangements have been made between 1961 and 1965 to provide African newspapers and news agencies with material from East European sources. Africans are attending special journalist-training courses in East Europe. In his speech to the steering committee meeting of the Pan-African Union of Journalists held in Bamako on 10-11 April 1965, Sepp Fischer, IOJ Secretary, said that in the last six months alone the IOJ had organized or participated in eighty campaigns in support of the interests of the African nations. The International Solidarity Fund had given 10,000 dollars' worth of support in the first quarter of this year to journalists and their families persecuted by reaction. He recalled that many African journalists were studying in the various IOJ schools of journalism in East Europe and that in 1965 courses would be held in Africa itself. Four teachers, including Professor Treffkorn, the director of the School for African Journalists in East Berlin, would be sent to Accra. All this was part of the IOJ's Three-Year Plan. (*The Democratic Journalist* No. 6/7, July 1965.)

Chapter XIII

THE FRONT ORGANIZATIONS (11)

THERE are three front organizations that the communists find particularly valuable and all three are extremely active in Africa. These organizations are the World Federation of Democratic Youth (WFDY) the World Federation of Trade Unions (WFTU) and the Afro-Asian Solidarity Organization. The World Federation of Democratic Youth is the central communist instrument for selecting, consolidating and utilizing the future cadres of the West, and particularly of the colonial and former colonial countries. The organization was founded in November 1945 in London, and had its origins in the various international youth conferences held from 1941 onwards, when anti-fascism bound together the young people of the East and West. From its inception this organization, which was more vehemently anti-colonial than any of the other auxiliary communist organizations, aimed at being a reservoir of the 'progressive youth' of Asia and Africa. Afro-Asian students and young workers took part in the preliminary conferences which led to its formation; they were present, for example, at a conference in London in November 1941. A resolution adopted by the 1945 inaugural conference expressly declared: 'This conference supports the just struggle of the colonial and semi-colonial peoples for freedom and self-determination.'[1] A Western study devoted to the World Federation of Democratic Youth records: 'Subsequently the federation carried on widespread and successful activity in Asian, African and South-American countries. It was in these countries that it successfully broke into the ranks of the non-communist youth organizations.'[2] Elsewhere, referring to 'the basic rights' tabulated by the league, the study states: 'The basic rights proclaimed by the federation, the right to employment, education, recreation and medical attention, the right to organize, the right to belong to trade unions, and equality between the sexes, apply exclusively to the Western and *colonial* countries. All these rights are regarded as already firmly established in the countries of the Eastern bloc. The delegates of the communist unity organizations glorify political and social conditions in their countries, and invariably present them as exemplary. This means, of course, that the activity of the federation is exclusively directed to the West and to the colonial countries.'[3] However, the secession (from the federation) of many of the youth organizations in the West between 1948 and 1950 narrowed its activity in Europe and America. With the general emancipation of the colonial territories, the organizers and wire-pullers of the federation concentrated their activities more on Asia, Latin America and, of late, particularly on Africa. In the summer of 1964, the World Federation of Democratic Youth numbered the following affiliated organizations in Africa: *Fédération des Etudiants d'Afrique Noire en France* (FEANF); West African Students' Union (London); *Union Générale des Etudiants d'Afrique Occidentale*; *Union Générale des Etudiants Musulmans Algériens* (UGEMA); *Union de la Jeunesse de Dahomey*; *Ligue de la Jeunesse Africaine* (Ivory Coast); *Union de la Jeunesse Démocratique Gabonaise* (Gabon); Wasa Youth Association (Ghana); Takoradi Youth Association (Ghana); *Jeunesse Démocratique du Cameroun*; *Union Nationale des Etudiants Kamerunais* (UNEK, Paris); *Union de la Jeunesse du Congo*; *Jeunesse Populaire Africaine* (Leopoldville); *Alliance de la Jeunesse du Congo* (Leopoldville); *Union de la Jeunesse Congolaise* (Brazzaville); *Fikambanan 'my Tanora Demokration i Madagasikara*; *Association des Etudiants d'Origine Malgache* (AEOM, Paris); *Union Démocratique de la Jeunesse Marocaine*; *Union Démocratique de la Jeunesse Nigérienne* (Niger); Nigerian Youth Congress; Afro-Shirazi Youth League (Zanzibar); Youth's Own Union (Zanzibar); Somali Union of Democratic Youth; *Rassemblement des Jeunesses Démocratiques d'Afrique* (Senegal); Youth Action Committee (South Africa); *Ittihad al Shabab al Sudani* (Sudan); *Jeunesse Libre Togolaise*; *Union de la Jeunesse Tchadienne* (Chad); and the *Jeunesse Travailleuse Oubanguienne* (Central African Republic, formerly Oubangi-Chari).[4]

Apart from these directly affiliated organizations there are also a number of associated organizations which work closely with the federation, for example, the left-wing Council of African Youth, which has about 900 youth groups throughout the territories of former French West Africa. Close links also exist between the federation and the Pan-Africa Youth Conference. The idea of this particular organization was first mooted at a meeting of the non-communist World Assembly of Youth (WAY) at Bamako in August 1959. At a meeting in Conakry in March 1960 the Executive Committee of the World Federation of Democratic Youth decided to nominate a preparatory committee for such a conference, ostensibly in collaboration with Africans who had supported the idea at the WAY meeting. At a bureau meeting of the federation in Sofia, from 28 October to 2 November 1960, resolutions adopted on Africa included one supporting the establishment of an African Youth Congress as an 'autonomous organization' and a centre in Guinea to co-operate with all African youth organizations.

A preparatory meeting in Accra on 13–14 October 1961 was attended by Diallo Abdoulaye and 25 delegates from Ghana, Guinea, Mali, Niger, both Congos, Nigeria, Gambia, Tunisia, Angola, Basutoland, the Algerian revolutionary movement (FLN) and the exiled wing of the *Union des Populations du Cameroun* (UPC). The conference was scheduled to take place in January 1962, but it opened on 26 April. It was attended by delegates from 25 African States, extremist groups being well represented. Representatives from the two communist youth organizations, the World Federation of Democratic Youth and the International Union of Students (IUS), were present as observers. The conference adopted a number of resolutions condemning Western colonialism and neo-colonialism in Africa and supporting the struggle for liberation in Angola, Mozambique, and South Africa. Like other Pan-African organizations, this youth movement will ostensibly remain independent of other international organizations. This proviso will also apply to its affiliated organizations, though they will be entitled 'to maintain relations' with any international organizations they please. Soviet and Chinese Afro-Asian Solidarity committees and other youth organizations sent messages of greeting to the conference and stressed its value in uniting youth 'against Western imperialism'.

The headquarters of the new Pan-Africa Youth Movement (PAYM) are in Conakry and there are secretariats in Lagos and

Cairo. The general secretary of the PAYM is Kanfory Bangoura, who is also *directeur du cabinet* of the Guinean Ministry of Labour.

It is interesting to note that the first meeting of the executive committee of the World Federation of Democratic Youth, in March 1960, was held in Guinea, a country whose youth association was not formally affiliated to the federation. However, close links existed between the federation and the JRDA in Guinea, especially since the federation and the JRDA sections co-operated with other groups to organize the first Festival of African Youth in Bamako; for years Conakry served the federation as a distribution centre for its intensive propaganda in Africa, including such periodicals and bulletins as *Jeunesse du Monde; Nouvelles de la Fédération Mondiale Jeunesse Démocratique; Jeune Sportif; Jeunesse Travailleuse; Culture et Jeunesse; Bulletin d'Information*, etc.

Like all the propaganda publications of communist camouflage organizations, those of the WFDY take cover behind apparently harmless and innocent material, from sport to the 'Basic Rights of Youth', the announcement of meetings, and so on. Nevertheless, they do put forward a more specifically communist point of view than the publications of the teachers' organization, FISE, or the Democratic Association of Jurists. On the front pages of a pamphlet intended for distribution in Africa there is a representation of the famous Picasso dove of peace, while in the text readers are exhorted to take up arms in the struggle against the imperialists, and to drive the enemy out of Africa by force of arms. A typical example of the aggressive attitude adopted by the WFDY is a book published in 1960 in East Berlin and now being distributed in Africa, *United with Eighty-Seven Millions*. Among other things it contains a list of exemplary organizations and officials. There are 'the heroic youth of the Chinese People's Republic' and 'the young guerilla units in Vietnam'. It goes on to say: 'Among the most prominent fighters for the freedom and independence of Africa, from Algeria to the Cape of Good Hope, are the youth of Cameroon—the *Jeunesse Démocratique du Cameroun*. Every hour of their existence is filled with a struggle for the unity and the national independence of their country.' Cameroon is, of course, already independent. 'Its members [of the *Jeunesse Démocratique du Cameroun*] are fighters and commanders in the guerilla struggle in the jungle. They go from plantation to plantation to organize the young workers. Thousands of them have paid the supreme sacrifice for their burning love of freedom. In the long years of the underground struggle against the French colonial masters and under Ahidjo, the President of the independent Republic of Cameroon, the *Jeunesse Démocratique du Cameroun* has grown to be a powerful organization of 50,000 members.'[5] Side by side with the Budapest officers of the Hungarian communist security police, who fought 'heroically' against 'the Hungarian counter-revolutionaries', Paul Momo, a Cameroon WFDY official, is praised as 'a hero of the international youth movement'. Paul Momo, who is said to be 'a member of the National Council of the Cameroon Democratic Youth and Commander of the National Liberation Army in the Bamileke area' must be something of a 'scarlet pimpernel'. There is, we are told, a reward of 700,000 francs (CFA) on his head and 'gendarmes and five companies of French soldiers are searching for him; but although a whole company of soldiers is near his headquarters, two or three miles away he sits in a hut, the red flag with the black crab of free Cameroon on the wall, and discusses the next action with his fighters. For 400,000 out of the 500,000 inhabitants of the Bamileke area, Paul Momo's word is law.'[6]

With this, the conciliatory talk about peace, the mask of democracy and democratic methods is dropped and the ideological core comes nakedly into view: all the decent youth of Africa who love freedom are exhorted to think and act like Paul Momo and his friends of the Democratic Youth of Cameroon and to take up arms and achieve a revolutionary, rather than an evolutionary, solution. The same tone predominates at the 'world-wide' 'solidarity days' and 'solidarity weeks' organized by the WFDY and the International Union of Students every year; 21 February, Solidarity Day for the Fighters against Colonialism; 21–29 March, World Youth Week; 24 April, World Youth Day against Colonialism and for Peaceful Co-existence; 17 November, International Students' Day. A special Africa Commission attached to the secretariat of the WFDY in Budapest issues the appropriate slogans and instructions for these affairs and for the organization of demonstrations, mass meetings, and so on. The material issued in this connection is full of militant, aggressive exhortations to the youth in Africa and elsewhere about 'the struggle of youth against colonialism and neo-colonialism'.

The climax of communist efforts to win over the youth of Africa,

Asia, and Latin America is always the World Festival of Youth and Students which has been held every two years since 1947. Far too little attention has been paid to the fact that since 1955, at least, these affairs represent the biggest communist cadre-recruiting drive for the under-developed countries, and that the maintenance of 'friendly contacts' between the communist youth associations of the various Soviet-bloc countries with the communist-dominated youth organizations in Western Europe is a purely secondary matter. An unpublished study by a number of West German observers at the Vienna World Youth Festival in 1959 concludes: 'The political accent of the festival was undoubtedly on the under-developed countries, and the delegations present from these countries were generally stronger than they had been at the previous festival in Moscow in 1957. The "anti-colonialist" theme dominated the discussions and the various gatherings in connection with the festival. The coloured delegates were pushed into the forefront everywhere, and they were often appointed chairmen of the discussions and meetings. Some of the coloured delegations were communist, but the majority were not. The main objective of the festival was to get these non-communists interested in communism and to win them over to communism if possible. This intention was made perfectly clear in the preparatory phase, particularly in the matter of finance. As it would have been impossible for delegations coming from far-distant countries to pay their own expenses, the various youth associations in the Soviet-bloc countries sponsored the journeys of groups from Africa, Asia and Latin America. For example, in preparation for this Vienna Festival, the Free German Youth (the communist youth organization in East Germany) collected solidarity contributions on behalf of the Algerian, Iraqi and Sudanese delegations. Naturally these collections and the sums collected in the sponsor countries were utilized for intensive propaganda. A few weeks before the festival special friendship delegations from the Soviet-bloc countries visited the partner countries in order to bring them formal invitations and the cash necessary to comply with them. At the same time, of course, they made as much propaganda as possible for the World Youth Festival.'[7]

There are no accurate figures on the participation of Africans in these festivals. It was announced that 52 per cent of all the delegates present at the Budapest Festival of Youth in 1949 (a total of 10,371 delegates from 82 countries) came from 'capitalist and colonial countries'. It was reported that 2,592 delegates (out of a total of 34,000) at the Sixth Festival of Youth in Moscow in 1957 came from Africa and the Middle East. Some 18,000 delegates were present at the Vienna Festival of Youth in 1959, and 528 of them were said to be African (not including those from the United Arab Republic). The strongest delegations came from the Sudan (108 members); Algeria (55); Morocco (80); Ghana (39); Guinea (39); Senegal (41); Tunis (34); and Madagascar (25). Participation in the Helsinki Festival in August, 1962, was limited by the organizers, but most of the African countries were represented there. There were the following delegations: Algeria (157 participants); Angola (15); Ethiopia (2); Basutoland (2); Dahomey (7); Ivory Coast (4); Gabon (1); Gambia (3); Ghana (13); Guinea (78); Portuguese Guinea (4); Cameroon (7); Kenya (10); Congo–Leopoldville (9); Congo–Brazzaville (4); Liberia (4); Madagascar (17); Mali (68); Mauritania (26); Mauritius (3); Mozambique (2); Nigeria (24); Réunion (4); Rhodesia (1); Rwanda (1); Senegal (124); Sierra Leone (3); Somalia (14); Sudan (85); South Africa (17); Tanganyika (5); Togo (9); Chad (2); Tunisia (80); Uganda (11); Zanzibar (7).[8]

The opportunity afforded by these Festivals of Youth to influence the Afro-Asian delegates in favour of communism is described in the study on the Vienna Festival already quoted: 'The Free German Youth, which took part in the festival from East Germany, arranged friendship get-togethers with South American, British, Japanese and French delegates and delegates from the English-speaking parts of Africa. The well-appointed camp of the German delegates certainly made a good impression, and the generous hospitality extended to the visitors obviously had its effect too. In a discussion between an Algerian delegate and a student from East Germany, the Algerian (a nationalist, not a communist) asked about living conditions in East Germany, including grants for students and so on. He was particularly interested, he said, because he was thinking of studying in Germany. The East German student eagerly answered his questions and offered to help him. The Algerian student was obviously unacquainted with the political geography of modern Germany, and mentioned Marburg as a small university at which he would like to study. Whereupon the German student, who came from Leipzig in East Germany, informed the Algerian that Marburg was in West Germany and that West Germany supported the colonial powers, including de Gaulle. The East German then took advantage of the opportunity to persuade the Algerian to study in East Germany. In the special student gatherings at the festival the delegates from East Germany repeatedly stressed that the universities and high schools of their part of Germany would be glad to have students from the under-developed countries, and that grants were available to assist them to study there. A student from Jordan announced that he had studied for two and a half years in West Germany but was now studying in East Germany. He contrasted his experiences in the two Germanies and assured his listeners that he had found things better in East Germany, where, he said, both officialdom and the ordinary people were more frank and friendly than in the Federal Republic. The delegates from East Germany naturally exploited his remarks to the utmost in the subsequent discussion and did their best to influence the non-communists present . . . They sought to create the impression that by comparison with conditions in the Federal Republic the greatest possible freedom existed in their zone, while according to them the Federal Republic directly or indirectly suppressed freedom in its own territory and supported the last of the colonial powers.'[9]

This, it must be pointed out, is just one example of general communist tactics towards Afro-Asian delegations. The aim is to create a feeling of solidarity between the coloured delegates and the communists. There are friendship get-togethers in the various national camps, musical evenings and exhibitions, and coloured delegates are particularly favoured in the elections for presidents and members of the various committees formed in connection with the festival. In addition, the regular Colonial Youth Day ends in a celebration of friendship and solidarity with the youth from the colonial countries and from those States which have recently won their independence. There are also endless discussions and constant acts of friendly consideration towards the coloured delegates. Experience shows that this sort of thing is not without its effect, especially as the end of the festival is not the end of these high-pressure communist friendships. During the festival individual and group invitations to visit the countries of the Soviet bloc are freely distributed and many of the coloured delegates are taken in by these flatteries.

All these communist efforts to impress the youth of the developing countries, particularly at the World Youth Festivals, must be judged from a much broader angle. For one thing, only qualified (i.e. tried and trusted) members and officials of the Youth Leagues in the Soviet bloc are ever sent to these world festivals. Before they go they are specially trained for their job and their meetings and contacts with the young people from the West and the under-developed world are prepared in advance and carefully stage-managed. This activity has two main aims: the first is to create an impression of solidarity in favour of the East, to make propaganda for its 'socialist achievements' and at the same time to denigrate Western values and achievements. The second aim is to select likely young adherents both from the West and from the under-developed countries. Those considered 'capable of development' are invited to visit the countries of the Soviet bloc, where a more intensive attempt is made to win them over by grants, training and indoctrination.

These had also been the main aims for the proposed 9th Youth Festival scheduled for July 1965 in Algiers. About 25,000 people had been expected to take part in the first attempt to hold such a festival outside Europe. But after the *coup d'état* of Colonel Boumedienne against Ben Bella, the Soviet and East European members of the International Preparatory Committee, who had been living in Algiers for some time, hastily left, and on 10 July 1965 decided at a meeting in Tampere, Finland, to postpone the Algiers festival. The WFDY thus suffered a serious setback in Africa.

NOTES

[1] *World Youth and Peace* (Prague, 1945), pp. 27 ff.

[2] 'Aus Politik und Zeitgeschichte', supplement to the weekly *Das Parlament* (Bonn), 31 July 1957.

[3] Ibid.

[4] From various sources, especially World Federation of Democratic Youth publications.

[5] *Vereint mit 87 Millionen* ([East] Berlin), (1960), pp. 14 ff.

[6] Ibid., p. 102.

[7] This study is in the author's possession.

[8] *Frieden und Freundschaft? Weltjugendfestspiele, Funktion und Wirkung* (Bonn, 1964), pp. 50-6.

[9] Ibid.

Chapter XIV

COMMUNISM AND THE
TRADE UNIONS

THE most important of the communist front organization is undoubtedly the World Federation of Trade Unions (WFTU). It was
founded after the Second World War, ostensibly as an uncommitted
and non-party international organization of trade and labour unions
from both East and West, but despite the fact that the Western
affiliated organizations were represented in the præsidium and the
secretariat, it was not long before it degenerated into a mere tool
of the Kremlin and became the successor of the Profintern, the
international communist trade union federation of the Comintern
era. In 1949, when the cold war was at its height, disappointed and
embittered democratic trade unionists from the West turned their
backs on it and founded the International Confederation of Free
Trade Unions (ICFTU). This new organization quickly gained the
upper hand in the West and in the neutral countries and former
colonial territories, but despite impressive successes it has never
gained the upper hand in Africa. Attempts to draw trade-union
organizations in the European-dominated areas of Africa to the
ICFTU have not been successful and the communist WFTU has even
managed to worm its way into sections of the ICFTU in Africa.

This development was facilitated by a number of psychological
and tactical errors on the part of the ICFTU, which the WFTU, with its
clearer political and strategic objectives and more elastic tactics, was
able to exploit to the full. To begin with, the choice of Brussels as
the seat of the ICFTU Executive was a handicap as far as Africa was
concerned, because for the politically-conscious élite of Africa
Brussels was a centre of colonialism. Furthermore, the fact that

when socialist and labour parties were in power in the metropolitan countries, white trade-union leaders in Belgium and Britain, directly or indirectly, supported the policies of their governments and took no decisive steps to end the colonial régimes and abolish discrimination greatly damaged their credit in the eyes of their African colleagues. Moreover, the ICFTU hesitated for a long time before it appointed Africans to any responsible posts in its secretariat and executive organs, or before it gave any signs of taking Africans seriously. Initially, the ICFTU rarely made public condemnations of colonialism in general or of the Algerian policy of France and the racial terror in South Africa in particular; when it did so, its phraseology was felt by Africans to be tortuous and too generalized.

The facts show that the ICFTU lacked understanding of the symbiosis that exists between nationalism and trade unionism in Africa. The absence of a widespread industrial working class in Africa was regarded as an obstacle to serious trade-union activity. In other words, the ICFTU made the mistake of approaching African reality with European ideas; when in consequence it achieved nothing, it preferred to ignore a reality that refused to fit in with its preconceived notions. The situation was aggravated by sectarian ideas about the 'non-political' nature of trade-union tasks. For a while the West simply refused to co-operate with Africans who regarded trade unions as a spring-board for a political career, and under pressure of circumstances organized trade unions as a substitute for political parties, because the colonial authorities prohibited or hampered direct party-political activities.

On the other hand, the communists, with their keen eye for cadre policy and tactical manoeuvres, immediately recognized the favourable opportunities for infiltration offered by the African trade unions and realized that important political forces were crystallizing in these bodies. In all the independent governments in Africa today there are cabinet ministers who, at one time or another, were active in the trade unions—perhaps even founded them and certainly used them as a platform for the anti-colonial struggle. To mention only a few prominent personalities with trade-union backgrounds: Tom Mboya in Kenya, Sékou Touré in Guinea, and Cyrille Adoula in the Congo. As all these men harnessed the power of the trade unions into political channels during their anti-colonial struggle it is quite natural that now, in the post-colonial era, they should realize that the trade unions can fulfil important functions and carry out certain ideas on behalf of the government outside the socio-economic sphere. They are, in fact, using the trade unions as a 'transmission belt' and it is no coincidence that Nkrumah, the ambitious President of Ghana, makes a special point of using the trade unions in his campaign to achieve his Pan-African objectives. In a speech delivered on 14 March 1960 he declared:

'If the unity of our continent is to become a reality . . . the working class must take its place as the advance guard in the struggle against poverty, ignorance and sickness. A most important aspect of the establishment of African unity is the achievement of unity in the trade-union sphere by the formation of an All-Africa trade union federation.'[1]

Sékou Touré has declared: 'The path that Africa will take depends in no small measure on the African trade unions. Their decisions will be of decisive importance for the whole continent.'[2] Walter Ulbricht, the East German communist leader, has expressed similar ideas. Speaking at a reception to mark the twenty-second meeting of the executive committee of the communist WFTU on 3 February 1961 in East Berlin, he said: 'The time has come to give very active support to the free anti-imperialist trade-union movement, particularly in Africa. A strong, free trade-union movement in the African States is the most important guarantee of a democratic development.'[3]

This is not the first time that such ideas have influenced the African policy of the communists. As early as 1928 the Profintern established an International Committee of Coloured Workers, whose chief backing came from the Communist Party of South Africa, which was then a legal party.

From 1944 onwards, taking advantage of their position as partners in the French Popular Front Government, the French communists established branches of their *Confédération Générale du Travail* (CGT) in French West and Central Africa and in Madagascar. Some of these groups were still in existence in 1949. But at first it was the democratic ICFTU that made rapid progress, particularly in the English-speaking areas of Africa, partly because the various colonial administrations, particularly in East Africa, answered every attempt to affiliate to the communist WFTU by suppressing the groups in question. However, one way or the other, in the space of seven years the membership of the African sections affiliated to the ICFTU rose from 58,000 (in 1952) to 1·7 million (in 1959). Today the ICFTU in Africa is being seriously threatened from several directions. Pan-African, neutralist, and openly communist tendencies are growing, even in some organizations affiliated to the ICFTU, which had recently declared the Brussels executive to be a bulwark of free trade unionism.

Developments in Nigeria are typical: as recently as 1960 the Trade Union Congress of Nigeria (TUCN) was thought to be relatively immune to neutralist and left-wing influence, but since 1961 this body, which (with over 200,000 members) is easily the strongest affiliated organization of the ICFTU in Africa, has been hopelessly disrupted, and there is reason to fear that the rump organization—all that is left in the ICFTU and now known as the Nigerian Labour Congress (NLC)—will decline still further. The leaders of this rump, Adebola and Borha, insist that the majority of the Nigerian workers are behind them, but this can no more be proved than can the contrary contention of their opponents.

The first cracks in the TUCN edifice appeared in the autumn of 1959, when Imoudu, President of the TUCN and an active, popular personality, was invited to visit East Germany, the Soviet Union and Red China. Imoudu accepted without consulting his colleagues, and for several weeks he was passed from one Iron-Curtain host to another. He reported that he had been shown 'many impressive things' and given 'many proofs of sincere solidarity'. The result was that Imoudu allowed himself to be persuaded that only the Communist WFTU could offer African workers 'a future, and selfless assistance in their struggle for freedom'.[4]

When Imoudu returned to Lagos he made no attempt to deny holding views which the communists had, in the meantime, ascribed to him. He began to agitate at once for the withdrawal of the TUCN from the ICFTU, whereupon its general secretary, Borha, dismissed him from office. With this a split became unavoidable. The TUCN elected Adebola its new president and Imoudu and his friends founded the Nigerian Trade Union Congress (NTUC). However, this new body did not, as had been announced, formally affiliate itself to the communist WFTU. Instead Imoudu began to campaign vigorously for the affiliation of his organization to an 'independent All-African Trade Union Federation', whose initiators were the government-sponsored trade unions of Ghana and Guinea.

Borha and Adebola immediately took him up on this point. Although they were still loyal to the ICFTU they declared that they, too, were in favour of establishing an All-African Trade Union Federation, but that the affiliated bodies would have to decide whether to continue their association with the ICFTU or the WFTU. There would have to be firm guarantees that the federation would not be controlled by Ghana, Guinea or the WFTU. In particular the leaders of the TUCN accused the break-away leader, Imoudu, of having accepted at least £5,500 from John Tettegah, president of Ghana's government-sponsored trade union; these funds demonstrably came from the Government of Ghana and the WFTU. They also alleged that a Czechoslovak official of the WFTU had come from Ghana to Nigeria to give the Imoudu group practical instructions and that during the course of the previous year a number of Imoudu's followers had been sent, via Accra and Conakry, to training schools behind the Iron Curtain to take special courses for African trade-union leaders. Moreover, they declared, the WFTU had offered Imoudu 500 grants, through the Ghana and Guinea unions, to train his followers at various centres in the Soviet-bloc countries.[5]

Imoudu did not deny all these charges. He announced, for example, that in accordance with its declared neutrality his organization was prepared to accept training grants from both camps, from Britain as well as from Russia, from the United States as well as from East Germany. But he could hardly be blamed, he added, if the only grants that had been offered had been from the Soviet-bloc countries. Instead of blaming him, his detractors should complain to the 'neglectful' Western countries. Imoudu answered the charge that he had entered into close relations with the WFTU, although such a thing was clearly at odds with his expressed intention 'to build up a trade-union movement completely independent of the government, the employers, or foreign tutelage', by saying that the WFTU was not opposed to his programme, which was 'a completely autonomous matter'. He declared that he was not under the tutelage of Moscow or Peking, whereas the ICFTU was certainly subject to pressure from Washington and London.[6]

Unfortunately, as was proved during the strike in 1964, such attitudes meet with a good deal of approval from trade unionists in Nigeria. Talks with Nigerian working men indicate that the more radical attitude of Imoudu is often closer to their idea of what trade-union policy ought to be than the more cautious, prudent policy of Borha and Adebola. At a trade-union meeting in Lagos the audience booed every time Imoudu's speakers mentioned Washington, London or Brussels, and cheered whenever they talked about 'the peaceful policy' of Moscow, or 'the solidarity aid of the East-European working class'. There is another psychological factor which must be reckoned with: the cold, reserved and 'bourgeois' attitude of certain European and American trade-union leaders, their conventional habits, their constant appeals for moderation. To African workers this seems to suggest that Imoudu is right when he denounces the representatives of the ICFTU as 'disguised capitalists, bought and paid for by Western colonialism and neo-colonialism' in order to keep the bridle on the African workers.

Nevertheless, the democratic forces in the Nigerian trade-union movement succeeded in calling a general congress on 5 May 1962 in Ibadan, when 659 delegates supported their proposal for continued affiliation to the ICFTU. But no fewer than 407 delegates dissented, withdrew their previous consent to the organization of all the trade-union groups in the Nigerian Labour Congress and continued their old line in the NTUC, which, according to reports in the Lagos Press, is still based on close co-operation with the communist WFTU. The NTUC also sent a delegation to the Fifth Congress of the WFTU, which took place from 4 to 15 December 1961 in Moscow. Imoudu himself, and Ibrahim Nok, general secretary of the NTUC, were members of this delegation, and at the congress they both sharply attacked the ICFTU. Imoudu, chairman of the NTUC, called for international trade-union unity within the socialist camp and the victory of socialism throughout the world. It is interesting to note that at the beginning of 1963 the NTUC was conducting vigorous propaganda against the Common Market and Nigeria's association with it, in accordance with the line laid down in December 1962 at a conference on the consequences of the Common Market held by the WFTU in Leipzig.[7]

The leaders of the ICFTU might feel easier if developments in Nigeria were exceptional, but this is not the case: there are officials like Imoudu in almost all the African trade-union bodies affiliated to the ICFTU. Their slogan is 'Break with Brussels', and they make life very difficult for the moderate trade-union leaders by their demagogic, anti-colonial and class-struggle slogans. Not all of them betray their sympathy for the WFTU as openly as Imoudu. Many are just drifting along in the wake of the Pan-African ideas propagated by Accra and Conakry, and few are dismayed by the close relationship between some of the African and communist trade unions. However, it is precisely this relationship which provides the key to an understanding of recent events in African trade unions. The relationship has its history in the rise and decline of the first supranational trade-union link-up in the *Union Générale des Travailleurs de l'Afrique Noire* (UGTAN).

After a preliminary conference in 1957 in Cotonou, Dahomey, UGTAN was officially founded in Conakry in January 1959. It embraced trade-union groups in Guinea, Senegal, Mali, Nigeria, Togo, the Ivory Coast, Upper Volta, Dahomey, Cameroon, Congo–Brazzaville, Gabon, the Central African Republic and Mauritania. Most of these groups had been founded from 1944 onwards by French communists of the CGT, and their leading members had all been trained in communist trade-union schools in France, some even in training centres behind the Iron Curtain. Sékou Touré, who was elected president of UGTAN, had been a delegate to the third congress of the WFTU in Moscow. The second prominent man in UGTAN was Diallo Abdoulaye, later Guinea's Minister Resident in Accra. Until the formation of UGTAN, he was vice-president of the WFTU, and as late as the WFTU council meeting in Sofia in September 1956 it was he who presented the official report on 'the struggle against colonialism'. Diallo Seydou, who was elected general secretary of UGTAN, was frequently seen at meetings of the WFTU. He was present as an observer at its council meeting in June 1960 in Peking. Radio Peking and the New-China Agency both reported that he had 'extremely useful discussions with various highly-placed communist leaders'. Another prominent UGTAN official who was present at this council meeting was Yao Ngo Blaise, leader of the now illegal UGTAN organization in the Ivory Coast Republic. After his expulsion by Houphouet-Boigny he went to Conakry, where he is now active in the UGTAN central organization. It is interesting to note that at the meeting in Peking, Blaise was not thinly disguised as an observer (as was his general secretary) but was openly a delegate. Thus we have the odd situation that one of the UGTAN groups directed from Conakry is allowed to maintain its membership of the communist WFTU, whereas the central UGTAN organization in the same town is declared to be 'a completely independent body'.

This is by no means the only anomaly. After a short phase in which UGTAN sought to establish friendly relations with the West, it has now practically no contact at all with the democratic ICFTU and its affiliated organizations. On the other hand, 'mutual consultations' are constantly taking place between UGTAN and the labour organizations in the Soviet-bloc countries. The communist Press, from East Berlin to Peking, is continually publishing reports of the visits of UGTAN representatives to the communist countries and of return visits by representatives of the labour organizations in these countries to Conakry. The WFTU runs its liberal programme of grants through the UGTAN central organization and its subordinate body in Accra, where John Tettegah is one of the three UGTAN vice-presidents. It woos African trade unionists of all shades, including even the Christian organizations. The WFTU also uses Conakry for the distribution of books, pamphlets, films, technical equipment and money from the Solidarity Fund. The WFTU financed UGTAN's Central Training School in Dalaba (Guinea) and the African Workers' University in Conakry, where communist officials from the Soviet Union, Red China, Czechoslovakia and East Germany dominated the scene. No secret was made of this, for example, 'at a ceremony in Conakry on 4 November 1962 in connection with the opening of the sixth trade-union course run by the WFTU-sponsored African Workers' University, when Maurice Gastand, the director, thanked the WFTU and its member-organizations for their continued support'.[8]

However, after the inaugural congress in January 1959, this obvious link-up between UGTAN and the WFTU, and the use of UGTAN by the Guinea Government for its own purposes, resulted in much resentment outside Guinea. The UGTAN central organization in Conakry rather obviously ignored the 'national characteristics' and programmes of the affiliated West and Equatorial African sections. The differing tendencies in the States of the former *Communauté*, the growing independence of the African partners, and increasing resentment against Guinea resulted in 1959–61 in a crisis within UGTAN. UGTAN in Senegal split into three parts, an orthodox and two autonomous sections, under Cissé Alioune and Guèye Abbas respectively. The affiliated organization in the Ivory Coast Republic has no longer any legal standing. In these territories, and elsewhere throughout the West and Central African countries, the *Confédération Africaine des Syndicats Libres* (an organization founded by the French *Force Ouvrière*) made considerable progress until the new African governments began to force through their own preference for government-sponsored organizations. It proved impossible to check the decline of UGTAN, even by closer co-operation with the Ghana TUC, which had discontinued its original affiliation with the ICFTU, or even as a result of the break-up of the Mali Federation and the consequent re-establishment of closer relations between the Sudanese UNTS (now the *Confédération Nationale des Syndicats du Mali*—CNSM) and Conakry. In consequence, it became clear as early as the spring of 1960 that the old UGTAN was no longer viable. The hopes of the extreme Marxist initiators of UGTAN to establish a permanent, left-wing, anti-Western trade-union monolith in what had once been French West and Equatorial Africa were only partly fulfilled.

The left-wing forces now transferred their activities from regional bloc-building to the idea of Pan-African trade unionism. Even during UGTAN's inaugural congress in January 1959, discussions took place between representatives of UGTAN and trade-union officials from Ghana, Tunis, Morocco and Algeria; and these discussions resulted in a joint appeal for the speedy formation of an All-Africa Trade Union Federation. At Nkrumah's suggestion the central committee of the All-Africa People's Conference held a preparatory trade-union conference in Accra on 6 November 1959. A special commission under the leadership of Mahjoub Ben Seddik, general secretary of the Moroccan UMT, got in touch with trade-union organizations throughout Africa. Further discussions took place at the Second All-African People's Conference in Tunis at the end of January 1960. May 1960 was fixed as the provisional date and Casablanca the provisional venue for the proposed inaugural congress of the All-Africa Trade Union Federation.

However, this Tunis conference revealed considerable differences of opinion, and a number of organizations affiliated to the democratic ICFTU firmly rejected the proposed statutes of the new organization because they excluded the continued affiliation of any of the member-organizations to the ICFTU—or to the WFTU. Incidentally the WFTU had already instructed its African groups to bank completely on the Pan-Africa card and to oppose any form of double affiliation. In other words, the WFTU adopted a tactic completely in accord with Lenin's instructions: 'In order to get into the trade unions, to stay in them and be able under all circumstances to carry on communist work in them, we must be prepared to adopt all possible tricks, to use guile and illegal methods, to keep quiet if necessary and conceal the truth.'[9]

Still more vehement clashes between the 'neutralist' (i.e. pro-communist) elements and the democratic trade unionists took place at various meetings in the spring of 1960. This was particularly evident at a Seminar for African Youth, held in Tunis in April. There was a battle between the two leaders of the opposing factions, Diallo Seydou and Ahmed Tlili (UGTT, Tunisia). Tlili accused Diallo of being a tool of Moscow and Diallo accused Tlili of being a tool of 'international monopoly capitalism and Western colonialism'. Despite the pressure brought to bear on him, Tlili insisted that he and his followers would join the proposed Pan-African trade-union federation only if it were possible for their organization (the UGTT) to remain affiliated to the ICFTU. It proved impossible to come to any agreement. Some of the trade unions vacillated, adopting first one position then the other. The Casablanca inaugural congress had to be postponed, first until the following August, then for a whole year.

The most important of these vacillating trade-union organizations was the Moroccan Federation (UNT), with 600,000 members, and the Algerian *Union Générale des Travailleurs Algériens* (UGTA) with 110,000 members. Since the spring of 1960 both sides—the so-called neutralist, pro-communist organizations and the pro-Western organizations—have been doing their utmost to win them over. After tough negotiations the ICFTU succeeded in persuading UGTA, which sympathized with the FLN, to abandon its original position favouring the radical programme of Ghana and Guinea. Negotiations with the Moroccan representatives, in particular with Ben Seddik, were more difficult. Ben Seddik had meanwhile come into conflict with his own government and gone over to the opposition *Union Nationale des Forces Populaires* led by Mehdi Ben Barka.

Ben Seddik's zigzag policy is understandable in view of the fact that no other African trade-union organization is being so ardently wooed by the Soviet bloc as the UMT; and since the autumn of 1959 the East German, government-sponsored trade-union organization has concentrated its efforts on its Moroccan colleagues. At one time the Moroccans were regarded as being completely immune to communist influence, but the situation changed when Ben Seddik visited East Berlin in October 1959 as a guest at the celebration of the tenth anniversary of the foundation of the East German Republic. While in East Berlin he had discussions with members of the præsidium and secretariat of the FDGB, the East German trade-union organization, including its chairman, Herbert Warnke. Ben Seddik revisited East Berlin in July 1960 as the leader of a twelve-man 'students' delegation'. On this occasion, after further discussions with East German trade-union leaders, a decision was made to 'intensify trade-union co-operation' between the UMT and the FDGB. After this it was hardly surprising to learn that the UMT was sending 'an observer' to the council meeting of the WFTU in Peking, or to hear more anti-Western statements from its leaders.

The International Confederation of Arab Trade Unions (ICATU) is affiliated neither to the ICFTU nor to the WFTU, and on Nasser's instructions is steering a neutralist course. But for a long time after its formation in March 1956 it was under strong communist influence; in fact, its general secretary, Fathy Kamal, was present at the fourth congress of the communist WFTU in Leipzig in October 1957, where he delivered a fierce attack on the West and in particular on the ICFTU. In this situation Louis Saillant, general secretary of the WFTU, was able to report with satisfaction to the executive meeting in Prague in July 1958 that relations between the WFTU and the ICATU had developed into 'close co-operation'. He even assured the executive that from then on co-operation between the two organizations would be 'permanent and fruitful, and serve as a visible and exemplary instance of the development of that community of action which the WFTU has been striving for since its foundation.' However, things did not go so smoothly, and a few months later the communists had to moderate their hopes, when in April 1959 the ICATU replaced general secretary Kamal by Mohammed Assad Rejeh, who is much more moderate and less subject to left-wing extremism.

COMMUNISM AND THE TRADE UNIONS

Meanwhile the ICFTU had not been idle. Alarmed by the way things were going, it began to work of a re-alignment of its African forces, and in November 1959 a conference in Lagos adopted statutes for a new African regional organization. In June 1960 these were accepted with only minor alterations by the executive committee of the ICFTU. That summer a trade-union mission, of which the Tunisian, Ben Azzedine, was a member, toured several African countries to win the support of trade-union organizations for the inaugural congress of the new regional organization, which finally took place in Tunis from 7 to 11 November. Delegations from the following organizations were present: *Union Générale des Travailleurs Algériens*; Gambia Labour Union; *Confédération Congolaise des Syndicats Libres* (Brazzaville); *Union Nationale du Cameroun* (CASL); *Union des Syndicats Autonomes du Cameroun*; *Union Nationale Côte d'Ivoire* (CASL); Kenya Federation of Labour; Congress of Industrial Organizations of Liberia; Libyan General Workers' Union; *Confédération des Travailleurs de Madagascar*; the Mauritanian UNT; Mauritius Trade Union Congress; *Union Marocaine du Travail*; Trade Union of Nigeria; Northern Rhodesia Trade Union Congress; Nyasaland Trade Union Congress; Sierra Leone Council of Labour; *Confederazione Somala de Lavoratori*; Tanganyika Federation of Labour; *Union Générale Tunisienne du Travail;* Uganda Trade Union Congress; and Zanzibar and Pemba Federation of Labour.

The following organizations sent observers: Egyptian Confederation of Labour; Gambia Workers' Union; *Union des Travailleurs du Sénégal*; South African Trade Union Council; Southern Rhodesia African Trade Union Congress and *Union Nationale Travailleurs du Togo*.

Apart from the absence of the trade unions of Ghana and Guinea from this observer group, it is interesting to note that most trade-union groups in former French West and Equatorial Africa were also missing. In consequence, there was a clear preponderance of English-speaking organizations at the congress and this generally stamped its proceedings, a circumstance which led to some dissension by the French-speaking delegates, who at one time threatened to boycott the sessions.

More important was the attitude of Tom Mboya and Ben Seddik. In order to show his disapproval of the congress' not having taken

I   257

place sooner, and his annoyance at not having been promised the office of general secretary of the African regional organization in advance, Mboya (who was then perhaps the most outstanding representative of free trade unionism in Africa) did not attend the congress at all. Ben Seddik was present, but for one day only; and he was then careful not to take an open part in the proceedings. In fact, his behaviour as the leader of the largest African trade union suggested cautious reserve rather than approval.

The delegates did not hesitate to voice criticism and the executive of the ICFTU was bombarded with reproaches. It was accused of being lukewarm towards the principle of self-determination for Africa, of not having done enough to secure the release of arrested African trade unionists and of hampering initiative by its bureaucratic methods. At the same time there was an undercurrent of misgiving at the American preponderance in the ICFTU and some resentment at the rather brusque methods of its representatives, in particular of Irving Brown, the representative of the American Federation of Labor in Europe.

The success of the congress remained in the balance till the last moment, and the Africans repeatedly threatened to form their own independent regional organization. In the end, however, the ICFTU managed to attain its objective, but only because it agreed to accept an uncompromising African resolution on the colonial question and because a number of important questions were deliberately left vague. Ahmed Tlili, who was chairman of the congress, underlined the lack of positive obligations entered into when he described the congress as having 'put out feelers'. No working programme for the new organization was agreed to, and no budget was adopted. It was left to organizations which wished to remain in the ICFTU to affiliate to the proposed All-Africa Trade Union Federation if they so desired.

Subsequent discussions between representatives of the non-aligned African trade union organizations in December 1960 and again after the first African regional conference of the International Labour Organization (ILO) in Lagos, ended just as indecisively. Discussions with them did not give the impression that the Tunis congress and the discussions in Lagos had done much to consolidate the position of the ICFTU in Africa, or to create a clear understanding of the danger of a left-wing African trade union federation.

In the meantime, a different kind of activity was being carried on in Lagos by the so-called neutralists led by Diallo Seydou. They repeatedly met in separate conclave, and they did their best to win over the pro-Western trade unionists for the third All-African People's Conference, which was to be followed by a trade-union conference. All the ILO delegates and guests received a strongly anti-Western pamphlet in which the ICFTU was accused of 'neo-colonial' ideas and actions. The introduction to this pamphlet came from the pen of Gogo Chu Nzeribe, who took part in the council meeting of the WFTU in Peking in June 1960 as general secretary of the new left-wing Nigerian trade union, and who seems to have been thoroughly indoctrinated during his stay in Red China.

This pamphlet fulminated at length against 'the great conspiracy' which, it alleged, was directed by the West, with the assistance of the ICFTU, against Africa, in order to subjugate the continent once more. Naturally, there was no word about the communist conspiracy, with the assistance of African agents, to turn African trade unions into 'transmission belts' for revolutionary propaganda and action. This assistance is all the more important for communism in view of the fact that, at the moment, there are no communist parties working effectively anywhere in Africa, although communist publicists claim that while there were fewer than 3,000 communists in the whole of Africa in 1939, there were about 50,000 in 1959.[10]

Following the reconstruction of the executive committee of the WFTU at its Berlin meeting in 1951, the organizational centre of this conspiracy is now in the hands of a special section of the executive committee known as the Colonial Bureau. An African, Ibrahim Zakaria, is ostensibly in charge of this body. He comes from the Sudan Federation of Trade Unions and was present at the session of the WFTU Council in Peking in June 1960, when he made bitter attacks on the 'colonial and neo-colonial forces in Africa'. In reality, this Colonial Bureau is ultimately dependent on instructions from the Secretariat for African Affairs in the Soviet labour union, which is staffed primarily by officials from the Asian Soviet Republics. This was clearly seen in October 1960, at the first conference of the Afro-Asian Solidarity Committee of the Soviet Union, in Stalinabad, where the leading role was played by Salimgerei Toktamisov, a member of the Kazakhstan Labour Union Council and of the præsidium of the Central Labour Union Council of the Soviet Union.

From Peking to East Berlin the work of this body is furthered by the various 'national' African committees of the respective government-sponsored unions. In addition to Peking and Prague, a key role is played by East Berlin. From East Berlin alone African trade unions have received support, in cash and kind, out of solidarity and other funds, totalling ten million marks.

No less remarkable are the contributions of the WFTU and the individual labour-union organizations of the Soviet bloc for the indoctrination of African trade unionists at training centres behind the Iron Curtain. Since June 1960 a Seminary for Trade Unionists from Africa and the Arab World has been established in Leipzig as an annex to the Institute for Foreign Studies attached to the Karl Marx University. Special courses for Africans are held regularly at the Fritz Heckert East German Trade-Union High School in Berlin-Bernau.

Among the 70 trade-union officials from 18 countries attending the first course in Leipzig were officials from Ghana, Guinea, Nigeria, the Congo, Togo, Cameroon, Somalia, Angola, the Ivory Coast Republic, Senegal, Sierra Leone, Morocco, Mauritius, Zanzibar, and the Central African Republic. The curriculum of these eight-month courses, held in English and French, includes problems of international trade-union solidarity and problems of the political mass and youth work, etc. At the founding of this institution on 22 September 1960 the chairman of the East German State labour organization, Herbert Warnke, was perfectly clear about the objectives of the course of study laid down in the curriculum: 'The young African working-class movement needs cadres which are acquainted with the problems of trade-union work *and with the scientific outlook of the working class.*'[11]

The 'World Trade Union Movement' of November-December 1961 carried a detailed description of the trade-union school for trainees from Africa and certain Asian countries organized by the Central Council of Czechoslovak Labour Unions at its school near Prague the previous summer. The director of the course was Yaroslav Tehle, head of the Central School of the Czechoslovak revolutionary labour movement. He revealed that the East German FDGB High School at Bernau (which had already had a good deal of experience in the running of trade-union courses for Africans) had assisted in the preparations, which had lasted a year. 'We also took advantage of the wide experience gained by the international seminars organized by UNESCO, in which Czechoslovak trade unionists took part.' In consequence it proved possible for the Czechoslovak Labour Union Central School to prepare 30 specialized lectures six months in advance, to translate the texts of the basic lectures into French and English, and to provide two speakers for each lecture—one for the French-speaking and the other for the English-speaking group.

Twenty-five trade unionists from ten African and two Asian countries took part in the course; some from countries which had already achieved more or less complete independence, others from countries which were still dependent. Most of the students were between 20 and 30 years of age.

'The basic teaching consisted of 16 lectures on the following subjects: an outline of the development, experience and present problems of the Czech Republic; an outline of the development of human society; an analysis of imperialism; a description of the origin, present position, and significance of the world socialist system in international politics; and finally, a comparison of the fundamental principles of capitalist and socialist economics.

'A second series of lectures dealt with the following subjects: the origin and role of trade-union organizations under capitalism in the struggle for socio-economic rights, for social progress, and for peace; the origin and development, and the role of the WFTU and other international trade-union organizations (relating in particular to the need for trade-union unity in Africa); the development of the struggle for national liberation and the disintegration of the world colonial system; the world socialist system and the nature of the assistance it has granted to the economically less-developed countries; the problems of agriculture in Africa, and the role and tasks of the trade unions in close liaison with the peasantry in the efforts to solve these problems; and an analysis of class forces and their role in the national liberation movement.

'The following problems were dealt with in the final part of the course: the position and the role of the trade unions in the period of the building-up of socialism; the basic principles of the structure of the national economy, and the role of the trade unions in organizing the participation of the workers in the management of production; the participation and the role of the trade unions in raising living standards; and finally, the work of the trade unions in the field of culture and education.'

A central training school for the countries of the Soviet bloc was opened in Budapest in 1959 specially for the training of African trade unionists. The lecturers and instructors were provided by Czechoslovakia, Hungary, East Germany, the Soviet Union, and the communist trade unions of France and Belgium. At the end of the first course, the Secretary General of the WFTU, Louis Saillant, addressed the Africans who had taken part in it:

'See that you do not lose the ground under your feet when you return home. In your tremendous continent, where the young proletariat is rising and building up a young trade-union movement ... the bourgeoisie is anxious to spread obscurantism in certain vital questions, to intensify the contradictions and then to cloak these contradictions. Do not forget that the most important school for the working-class official is the *class struggle*, which he will wage side by side with his class brothers ... In the fire of the great anti-imperialist struggle, in which we join with all other sections of the people in all countries, we must always think of the necessity of *strengthening our own special class forces*.'[12]

These words unmistakably reveal the methods used and the aims pursued by the communists among the African trade unions. They are out to infiltrate the African trade-union cadres and create communists whose task will be to transform the national revolution in Africa into a socialist revolution and turn the anti-colonial, national struggle into a revolutionary class struggle. This intention was also clearly expressed at the twenty-second meeting of the executive committee of the WFTU which took place in East Berlin in February 1961, when Louis Saillant demanded that 'still greater attention' should be paid to developments in Africa. Thanks to its solidarity actions, he declared, the WFTU had succeeded in strengthening its influence in Africa.

At this meeting the executive committee also set out some of the aims which are to be propagated in Africa and form the basis for propaganda in the trade unions:

'Abolition of imperialist military bases throughout the whole world [a demand directed especially against Nigeria and one or two members of the *Communauté Française*, which had agreements with Britain and France for the use of African airfields and harbours]; the prohibition of nuclear armaments and a halt to the arms race carried on by the imperialist camp; general and complete disarmament; peaceful co-existence; the conclusion of peace treaties with both German States and thus the abolition of the most dangerous war flashpoint created and maintained by the aggressive NATO bloc under the leadership of the ruling circles of the United States; and the abolition of the American-Japanese Security Treaty.'

In conclusion Saillant declared:

'The movement for national independence has become a part of the movement for the defence of world peace. The working class and the trade unions must therefore give the peoples who have already won their independence constant and vigorous political, military and economic support.'[13]

Characteristically, nothing was said about the social problems of Africa, raising the living standards of African workers, social security, labour protection measures, agreements on working hours, and so on. Instead, as the executive meeting demonstrated, the WFTU has clearly put forward an aggressive programme with power-political aims. In the words of Victor Grischin, 'the friendly masses in the liberated countries must be enlisted in the tremendous and invincible front of the forces of peace'.[14]

The communist trade-union leaders believe they have come nearer to this aim since the long-prepared Pan-African concentration was achieved at the Casablanca congress in May 1961 by the foundation of the All-African Trade Union Federation (AATUF). For the moment the foundation of the AATUF has intensified the split between the various tendencies, particularly since January 1962, when, as an answer to Casablanca, those groups that remained loyal to the ICFTU came together in Dakar and founded the African Trade Union Confederation (ATUC).

The Casablanca congress which led to the foundation of the AATUF was a model example of a rigged meeting. The sponsors showed bias in extending invitations, and at the congress itself they pursued such undemocratic methods as voting by acclamation in order to get their way. Finally the wire-pullers gerrymandered the adoption—also by acclamation—of a charter embodying their ideas, but only after a number of important delegates, Tom Mboya among them, had left. The key clause of this charter prevents any member-union of the AATUF from affiliating to any other international trade-union organization and is, of course, aimed against affiliation to the ICFTU.

The ICFTU still claims that the great majority of the trade-union organizations throughout Africa are behind it. At first glance this would seem to be true, but the fact is that the connection of these African trade unions with the ICFTU is usually very loose and often involves no sort of obligation. Prominent trade unionists who are members of organizations formally affiliated to the ICFTU do not hesitate to take advantage of the propaganda and material support of the WFTU (for example, the Kenya Trade Union Congress, if one is to believe a report in the Nairobi *Daily Nation*)[15] or to send delegations to the Soviet-bloc countries and to receive the delegates of communist trade-unions in their own countries. The list of African countries whose trade unions were represented at the Fifth World Trade Union Congress in Moscow, in December 1961, is interesting. Amongst them were groups from the following African territories: Angola, Basutoland, Cameroon, Congo (Leopoldville), Dahomey, French Somaliland, Guinea, Kenya, Madagascar, Mali, Mauritania, Mauritius, Morocco, Niger, Nigeria, Portuguese Guinea, Senegal, South Africa, the Sudan, and Tanganyika.

Ibrahim Zakaria (Sudan), the WFTU secretary, delivered a lengthy report to the congress on 'The Development of Trade-Union Activities and Solidarity to aid Peoples Fighting to end Colonialism'. He stated that in the preceding four years '215 trade unionists from Asia, Africa, and Latin America have received trade-union education in schools organized by the WFTU and in some of its national centres. For two years now a permanent trade-union school has been run with the co-operation of UGTAN and the WFTU.'[16] Zakaria repeated the assurance of the WFTU that it 'considers the creation of the All-Africa Trade Union Federation to be a great success for the forces fighting for the unity of the trade-union movement in Africa . . . The AATUF and the African workers have . . . a sincere friend—the WFTU—which extends a helping hand to them.'[17]

There is nothing new in all this. As the communists themselves worked for the formation of the AATUF they can hardly regard it as a rival organization and so the propaganda put out by the countries of the Soviet bloc is full of approving references to the AATUF and its activities. For this reason, an article by the leader of the illegal Moroccan Communist Party, Ali Yata, in the *World Marxist Review*, December 1961, which expresses certain misgivings about the AATUF is particularly interesting. After a lengthy tribute to the federation's support for the struggle of the African workers against 'imperialism ... neo-colonialism ... and feudalism', the article goes on to say that this new anti-colonial 'weapon' was not without its faults. For example, it had not laid sufficient emphasis on the 'expansion of trade-union rights', on the need to 'end foreign monopoly domination' by urging nationalization, or on condemning those neutralist trade-union leaders who 'indiscriminately place the socialist and imperialist countries in the same category'. Ali Yata made his objective clear when he urged that the neutrality of such an organization as the AATUF should not preclude 'fraternal ties' with the international working-class movement, specifically with the World Federation of Trade Unions (WFTU).

Even more interesting from the standpoint of future communist tactics in Africa was Ali Yata's insistence that the trade unions alone could not lead 'the struggle for national and social liberation': such a role could be played only by 'the vanguard of the working class ... the communist parties'. It was logical, therefore, to strengthen the existing communist parties and to form new parties where necessary. Meanwhile communists everywhere were enjoined to link up with the workers in the AATUF and support the federation.

At least the executive bodies of the AATUF are acting in this respect and trying to use AATUF as an organization through which communist ideas and intentions can be channelled. Three officers in the original executive of AATUF had close links with WFTU: Seydou Diallo (Guinea), Wahab Goodluck (Nigeria) and Abdoulaya Guèye (Senegal). A former WFTU vice-president, Abdoulaye Diallo, also from Guinea, was instrumental in AATUF's formation. Membership of the committee formed at AATUF's second congress at Bamako (Mali) in June 1964 provides further evidence of communist penetration. Of the newly-elected vice-presidents, Goodluck, Kaba Mamady (Guinea), Mamadou Sissoko (Mali) and Thauley Ganga (Congo-Brazzaville) have had dealings with WFTU, some dating

I*

back to the late 1950s. The treasurer is Lazare Coulibaly (Mali), a former committee member of a WFTU trade department (TUI). The extent of AATUF's financial commitments clearly shows that WFTU channels money through AATUF.

The Bamako conference decided to establish a permanent secretariat in Ghana. It is headed by John Tettegah, a Ghanaian, and six secretaries, three of whom are newcomers to Pan-African trade unionism. They are Amlon (Dahomey), Kawambwa (Zambia), and Madia Diop (Senegal). Two other secretaries, who reflect AATUF's desire to influence and take over union activities in Central and East Africa, are John Reich of the Federation of Uganda Trade Unions, and O.O. Mak'anyengo of the Kenyan African Workers' Union. Both have communist connections and have formed splinter unions in their own countries. Mak'anyengo has publicly declared himself a supporter of the Marxist theory of class warfare, which he considers applicable to African conditions.

Since AATUF's earliest days, communist sympathizers in the federation's executive have aimed at strengthening their links with WFTU but without formal affiliation. The chief means of achieving closer co-operation have been through TUI. In addition to the significant number of TUI contacts on the AATUF Executive Committee, specifically African 'trade groupings' on the lines of WFTU, two trade departments have been formed in Accra, for agricultural, forestry and plantation workers, and for commercial, industrial, technical and clerical workers. The two groupings established after WFTU representatives had visited Accra, are closely supervised by WFTU officials and organize joint conferences, seminars, study courses and other group activities which provide opportunities for communist contact.

AATUF is a rich and well-organized federation. One wonders what will happen if and when the Organization of African Unity succeeds in sponsoring the formation of one Pan-African trade union organization to replace the AATUF and ATUC. At the beginning of 1960, AATUF's Executive Committee was already preparing for that moment and publicly declaring that AATUF could easily provide the infra-structure for the new organization.

NOTES

[1] Radio Accra broadcast, 14 March 1960.

[2] At the Fifth Congress of the *Parti Démocratique de Guinée*, September 1959.

[3] *Neues Deutschland*, 4 February 1961.

[4] In a discussion with the author in Lagos, December 1960.

[5] Information given to the author by Nigerian trade-union officials in Lagos, December 1960.

[6] Ibid.

[7] Cf. *Lagos Morning Post* and *Nigerian Tribune* of 1 March 1962; *Lagos Daily Telegraph*, 2 March 1962.

[8] *Horoya* (Conakry), 7 November 1962.

[9] Cf. Lenin, 'Left-Wing Communism, An Infantile Disorder', *Selected Works* (12 vols; New York, 1943), X, pp. 95-6.

[10] *World Marxist Review: Problems of Peace and Socialism*, II, No. 10 (October 1959), p. 51.

[11] *Tribune* ([East] Berlin), 23 September 1960.

[12] *Die Weltgewerkschaftsbewegung* ([East] Berlin), November 1959; quoted in *Ostprobleme* (Bonn), XII (1960), p. 101. Cf. also *Nepszava* (Budapest), 1 September 1959.

[13] Minutes of the executive meeting.

[14] Ibid.

[15] *Daily Nation* (Nairobi), 31 August 1962.

[16] *For the Abolition of Colonialism*, publication of the World Federation of Trade Unions (London, 1962), p. 16.

[17] Ibid., p. 37.

Chapter XV

THE AFRO-ASIAN
SOLIDARITY ORGANIZATION

ONLY a decade has passed since the historic Bandung Conference, but there are already many legends, fables and contradictory interpretations about this meeting at which the Heads of State and leading politicians of 24 African and Asian countries were present. Bandung has become a symbol and 'the spirit of Bandung' a shibboleth from Djakarta to Dakar. Nowadays even people and groups outside the Afro-Asian world claim to be legatees of the Bandung Conference and appeal to its principles.

The communists were not slow to realize the tremendous, almost magical attraction of Bandung. When the President of Senegal, Léopold Sédar Senghor, declared that 'no event of such historical importance' as the meeting at Java, in the spring of 1955, had taken place since the Renaissance, we may be sure that his remarks were carefully noted and soberly analysed, particularly in the Soviet countries.

This is understandable; the claim, first made by the coloured world at Bandung, that it should be able to go its own way independently of either of the great power blocs shocked not only the West, which up the late 1950s still cherished the delusion that anyone not definitely on its side must be against it. The communists also clung obstinately to the same idea in reverse and have never seen any reason to qualify it. For communism, which is less accustomed to ideological competition than the West, 'ideological coexistence', even after Stalin, is regarded as 'irreconcilable with the spirit of Marxist-Leninism', and a great deal depends (particularly in Asia and Africa) on whether it can succeed in forcing through the

268

ideological, social, and economic model of its own radical socialism, thereby securing a dominating role in the new community.

Leaving Africa out of consideration for the moment it can be said that until the Bandung Conference communism's chances of success in Asia were good. A systematic extension of the communist sphere of influence in Asia followed hard on the heels of Mao's triumph in China, but with the Korean War and the powerful intervention of the United States, the *status quo* was only maintained with difficulty, though the victory over the French at Dien Bien Phu in Vietnam clearly demonstrated the sinister power of a revolutionary movement over a great colonial empire. Throughout Asia the classic front organizations were active—from the World Peace Council to the World Youth League—busily infiltrating the ranks of the local élite and gaining influence over neutral governments. A number of spectacular propaganda congresses held under communist auspices drew the attention of the Asian intelligentsia to the communist programme and its slogans, which were made more acceptable by peaceable assurances.

The bare announcement by the five Colombo States—India, Pakistan, Ceylon, Indonesia and Burma—of their intention to meet at Bandung was in itself enough to arouse anxiety and fears in the communist camp, though the participation of the Chinese People's Republic and of North Vietnam seemed to offer some compensation. But when it came to the point, the ten principles laid down at the conference showed that it was the two communist delegations, not the neutrals, which had to make compromises under pressure.

It was not difficult to anticipate this, so before the Bandung Conference, which took place in April 1955, the communists used the Asian branches of their World Peace Movement to launch a rival conference in New Delhi, with the intention of prejudicing the results of the Bandung Conference and exerting pressure on those who were to attend it, or as the communists put it, of 'making the voice of the people heard'. This was given the ponderous name of Conference for the Relaxation of International Tensions and it, (and not, as the communists are so fond of saying, the Bandung Conference) was the origin of what became known as the Afro-Asian Solidarity Movement.

All the future characteristics of this 'solidarity organization' were clearly visible at the New Delhi Conference. Representation was limited to 'the true representatives of the peoples' and to 'the dedicated forces of peace and progress'—that is to say, exclusively to parties and groups of a decided 'left-wing neutralist' character. The communist countries of Asia had representatives at the conference, and the representatives of Soviet Asia were there too. Finally the initiators, stage managers, and wire-pullers of the conference were, beyond all question, either communists or thoroughly reliable fellow-travellers. Incidentally, one of the latter was Mrs Rameshvari Nehru, who was appointed chairman of the organizing committee and later played a leading role in the Afro-Asian Solidarity Organization.

The ideological background of this organization is obvious from the list of requirements put forward at the Conference for the Relaxation of International Tensions for work in the colonial and dependent countries. These included: the calling of a conference to solve the problems of Taiwan (Formosa) and Korea; the withdrawal of all United States forces from Formosa and Formosan waters; the ending of Portuguese rule in Goa, of Dutch rule in New Guinea, and of British rule in Malaya; the prohibition of all nuclear weapons; the admission of the Chinese People's Republic to the Security Council of the United Nations; the diplomatic recognition of the Chinese People's Republic by all other nations; and the removal of the trade embargo imposed on China by the Western Powers. It is interesting to note that the Chinese demand for membership of the United Nations was not even mentioned at the Bandung Conference.

Despite these and other slogans, the Conference for the Relaxation of International Tensions in New Delhi was a signal failure, particularly in comparison with the Bandung Conference.

There were two main reasons for this. First, the scope of the conference in New Delhi was extremely narrow in comparison with Bandung, which was attended by delegations from African countries, including Egypt, Ethiopia, Ghana, Liberia, Libya and the Sudan, in addition to the Asian delegations, and this meant that the importance and influence of Bandung extended far beyond the confines of Asia.

Secondly, as a protest against the obvious communist manipulation of the New Delhi Conference, numerous political representatives who really were neutral ostentatiously left the conference hall. One or two of the delegations so obviously lacked proper credentials that the organizers of the conference had reluctantly to refuse them. In addition, the Indian and Indonesian Governments went out of their way to make it quite clear that in no circumstances were they prepared to recognize the New Delhi meeting as 'a preliminary conference for Bandung' and that they were not prepared to allow any direct organizational, or other, relation between the two conferences. It was therefore not surprising that at the Bandung Conference there were one or two contemptuous references to 'the fictitious character' of the Conference for the Relaxation of International Tensions.

Even the communists were reluctantly compelled to recognize the difference in the quality and importance of the two conferences. The lack of influence secured by the New Delhi Conference was only too obvious, and the communist efforts at Bandung, which had a tremendous import throughout 'the Third World', were relatively unsuccessful. The communists were not slow to draw the conclusions. With one accord their publicists began to take the Bandung Conference very seriously (although they had at first adopted a reserved attitude towards it, being uncertain which way it would develop). From now on almost no reference was made to the Conference for the Relaxation of International Tensions. The old, stirring, and crude radical talk was toned down and communist propaganda in Afro-Asia took on more honeyed accents, with the hope of establishing friendly relations with the national bourgeoisie. The rigid Stalinist line became more flexible and in February 1954 the Twentieth Congress of the Communist Party of the Soviet Union inscribed the slogan 'co-operation with the broad masses of the people' on the communist banner for the anti-colonial struggle instead of, as previously, co-operation only with communist or crypto-communist organizations and groups. Gradually a new line emerged and this was certainly, to some extent, due to Bandung and its consequences. One result was the decision to wind up the Communist Information Bureau, better known as the Cominform.

In Asia and Africa this meant the tightening up of front organizations and determined efforts to create a special, unexceptionable front organization for all the African countries, in addition to the existing, compromised organizations and groups. For this purpose three conditions were laid down:

1. The new organization must exploit 'the Bandung image' and

extend the Bandung scope, without relying exclusively, as Bandung had done, on established governments, and without allowing itself to be restricted by the Bandung programme.

2. The new organization must be founded as 'the people's representation' of the two 'Eastern contingents' and embrace bourgeois as well as pro-communist groups—this in order that it should not be suspected of being a Soviet cat's paw.

3. The new organization must, from the beginning, recognize the right of the Soviet Union, as a member of the Asian people's community, to belong to it and enjoy equal rights within it.

The New Delhi Conference had already gone some way towards fulfilling this third condition by unconditionally accepting the representatives of the Soviet Asian republics as partners with equal rights. Later it constituted itself, with the inclusion of the Soviet representatives, as a preparatory Asian Solidarity Committee. The Soviet Union took the final step on 16 August 1956, when Mirzo Tursun-Zade, a Tadjik writer and president of a Peace Committee for the Asian Soviet Republics, formed a National Asian Solidarity Committee of the Soviet Union. This new body was immediately welcomed by the national committees that had in the meantime been formed in one or two Asian countries.

It was not long before the next step, and at the end of December 1956 the delegates to the New Delhi Conference decided to organize an inaugural conference of the new regional front organizations 'at an early date' in Cairo. This city was chosen as the venue because on account of the Suez affair (November 1956) it exercised a certain attraction. It was also decided to make an immediate start with the preparations. An Asian Writers' Conference, which took place in New Delhi in December 1956, and an Afro-Asian Jurists' Conference, held in Damascus in November 1957, afforded an opportunity of making close contact with various personalities and political groups from both continents, discussing which delegations should be sent, and drawing up the agenda of the proposed inaugural conference. Incidentally the so-called preparatory conferences in the Indian and Syrian capitals were naturally attended not only by writers and jurists. Both in New Delhi and in Damascus there were numerous officials of the Afro-Asian peace movement and the pro-communist labour and youth organizations. Indeed, political questions of a general nature clearly dominated the discussions and the resolutions despite the specialized subjects on the agendas. The resolutions adopted at Damascus were sharply directed against the 'imperialist-bloc policies' of NATO, SEATO, and the Baghdad Pact. Needless to say, Soviet military policy was not even mentioned, neither was the Hungarian question.

Despite the fact that all the preparations made it unmistakably clear that the future organization would be ideologically linked to communism and hostile to the West, in the last days of 1957, 39 delegations arrived in Cairo from almost all the African and Asian countries, to take part in the First Afro-Asian Solidarity Conference (AASC). Apart from the usual delegations from the communist countries of Asia (including the Soviet Union), there were official delegations from Egypt, Morocco and Tunis, semi-official delegations from other countries, and a number of groups (whose status would be difficult to describe) from the colonial areas of Africa. Although the Egyptian Government (through the Solidarity Council of the United Arab Republic) arranged the conference, the communist delegations ran it from the start. Rashidov, the chief Soviet delegate, who was President of the Supreme Soviet of Uzbekistan at the time and a leading official in charge of Soviet Eastern policy, lost no time in making the aims of the Kremlin clear when he promised all the delegations generous Soviet economic aid, assuring them that this would afford them an opportunity of breaking 'the grip of neo-colonial exploitation' and escaping from 'economic slavery at the hands of Western colonial capitalism'. He went on to declare: 'It would hardly be possible to exaggerate the importance of this conference, in which more than 40 Afro-Asian countries are taking part. At the Bandung Conference 29 countries condemned colonialism and proclaimed the principles of peaceful co-existence. These principles have since been adopted as the foreign policy of numerous countries all over the world, and they are fully supported by the Soviet Union. This Afro-Asian Solidarity Conference, its spirit, and its ideas are supported by all honest men throughout the world, because it is *anti-imperialist, anti-colonial and anti-militarist* and thus at the same time *just, progressive and humane.* The Soviet people support this consolidation of those forces in the Afro-Asian countries that will henceforth play an important role by *extending the zone of peace* in the struggle against the rotten system and piracy of imperialism.' Rashidov observed unblushingly that the oppression of other peoples and interference in their internal affairs 'are foreign to the true nature of the Soviet socialist state'. He described the Soviet Union as 'a tireless pioneer in the struggle for peace and an irreconcilable enemy of imperialism and colonialism'. He enumerated in detail the actions of the Soviet Union which, he declared, 'supported the struggle of the colonialized peoples for their freedom'. He concluded emphatically with the appeal: 'Brothers, comrades and friends, lift up your heads, the end of your enslavement is at hand!'[1]

Representatives of North Korea, North Vietnam, the Mongolian People's Republic and Red China sounded the same note and there was a good deal of talk about 'the unswerving solidarity of all African and Asian peoples', the 'glorious example' of the Asian people's democracies in the struggle 'to overcome the remnants of colonialist thought', and about the alleged attempts of the West ('the imperialist powers') to undermine the unity of the Eastern countries by intrigues, murderous weapons and provocations, and to keep the oppressed peoples in slavery for ever. To trained Western observers, the conference was clearly a communist set-up and its aims were manifestly communist, but what about the uncommitted groups and personalities present? John Kale, the general secretary of the Uganda National Congress (a man of goodwill and good faith who was elected a leading member of the permanent solidarity secretariat and was later killed in mysterious circumstances when the plane in which he was travelling crashed in the Soviet Union) told the author in a private conversation a few months before his death: 'For those of us who were taking part in such an important international conference for the first time and rubbing shoulders with cabinet ministers, presidents and prominent trade unionists, scientists, artists and writers from countries all over the world, Cairo was a tremendous experience. For the first time we felt that we were being taken seriously. They all treated us as equals, whether they had won their own independence 40 years ago or perhaps only a couple of years back. It seemed to us that a new force was coming together here, a force based on true solidarity and a common consciousness of a struggle against the old colonial order and against the obsolete social and economic system of our own countries in favour of something new and revolutionary. Although many of us instinctively, and some of us even consciously, rejected Soviet-communist interference in our work, and although many of us distrusted the communists, this mistrust was outweighed by a feeling of real gratitude that a great world Power should support our demands.'[2]

Kale's words illustrate the ideological and emotional trust of many of those who took part in the Cairo Conference and demonstrate the psychological success of communist initiative. It would be too easy to try to dismiss men like John Kale as communists, crypto-communists or fellow-travellers. Now that he is dead it is possible to reveal that during the second Afro-Asian Solidarity Conference he gave the author valuable information about communist manœuvres in the secretariat, although he knew perfectly well that his information would be used as proof that the communists had succeeded in infiltrating the Afro-Asian solidarity movement on a massive scale. As the representative of Uganda in the permanent secretariat, Kale constantly opposed communist efforts to gain complete control of the movement, and we may be sure that he did not stand alone in this.

His impressions of the activities of the communists in Cairo are therefore all the more valuable. They show how cunningly the communists take the political naïveté of their non-communist collaborators into account and how little even their crudest abuse of the West diminishes the willingness of these people to co-operate with them. It was therefore relatively easy for the communists to whip up anti-Western and anti-colonial resentment among the delegates by numerous emotional appeals, and subsequently to make them the basis of a completely anti-imperialist standpoint. The concluding declaration of the conference called upon the Western Powers to accept the Soviet proposal for the immediate abolition of nuclear tests; then followed a condemnation of 'imperialism in all its forms and manifestations', including all political pacts (not the Warsaw Pact, of course), military aid, economic aid 'with political strings', and 'the establishment of foreign military bases in Asia and Africa'. Great Britain was fiercely attacked for its 'innumerable brutalities' against the people of the Yemen and for its 'crimes in Kenya'; France was accused of pursuing a policy of 'cruelty and extermination' in Algeria; the United States was generally accused of continual interference in the internal affairs of the Arab countries. The conference demanded immediate and complete independence for all colonial countries and protectorates, the abolition of United

Nations trusteeships and the cession of West Guinea to Indonesia, of Portuguese Goa to India, and Okinawa to Japan. Finally it appealed for support on behalf of nationalist movements in Cameroon, Kenya, Uganda, Madagascar, Bahrein, Cyprus and Somaliland.[3]

This catalogue of aims, which was later endorsed by the permanent secretariat in innumerable declarations, was nothing but a rehash of the demands put forward by communist propaganda for Asia and Africa. The organizational work carried on in Cairo by the communists has been more important than these declarations—on the traditional communist principle that *propaganda is useless unless it is backed up by effective organization to give strength to the forces behind it*. And this is what the Cairo Conference was all about: a resolution put forward by the Committee for Organizational Questions which was, of course, dominated by the communists, called for the immediate establishment of two permanent organs, a solidarity council and a permanent secretariat. The resolution, unanimously adopted, declared that the task of these bodies would be to act as a liaison between the plenary sessions of the solidarity organization and to ensure the implementation of the decisions and recommendations of the conference. Representatives from the following countries were elected to this permanent secretariat: the Soviet Union, the Chinese People's Republic, Cameroon, Ghana, the Sudan, India, Japan, Indonesia, Iraq and Syria. Youssef el Sebay, an Egyptian, was elected general secretary.[4]

Superficially the secretariat has a preponderance of non-communist representatives, but in reality the situation is very different. For example, the Sudanese delegate elected to the secretariat was not a representative of the Sudanese Government but a member of the outlawed communist party, while the Cameroonian delegate represented only the terrorist *Union des Populations du Cameroun*. Further, the Indian, Japanese, Indonesian and Iraqi representatives in the secretariat were without exception left-wing politicians if not actually Communist Party members. This left only three neutrals in the secretariat: the members for Syria and Ghana were actually representatives of their governments, and the secretary general is an official of the 'peace movement' tolerated by both Nasser and Khrushchev. Thus, even when John Kale was made a member of the secretariat as the representative of the Uganda National Congress, there was still a preponderance of communists and crypto-communists in the executive body of the solidarity movement. This has remained the case. In my conversation with John Kale, he declared that these communist and pro-communist officials 'quite definitely dictated the work of the secretariat', though they had to show some outward consideration to the neutrals, and though the fear of secessions, which would have blunted the edge of the solidarity movement, caused them to steer 'a very careful course'.

It was in the nature of things—and altogether in the interests of the Soviet Union and its allies—that this Afro-Asian Solidarity Organization should occupy itself more with African problems. Apart from Indonesia, developments in Asia had lost their original revolutionary impetus, whereas the revolutionary upheaval in Africa was only just starting. It is not surprising therefore that in this situation the members of the secretariat felt it right to devote the greater part of their attention to Africa, as was pointed out in the joint declaration of the Guinean leaders and the general secretary, signed on 29 January 1960 in Tunis, announcing the convening of the second Solidarity Conference for April 1960 in Conakry, the capital of Guinea. In another passage the joint declaration states this even more plainly: 'Since it started its activities following the first Solidarity Conference, the secretariat has concerned itself primarily with African affairs. A review of the individual activities of the secretariat during the past two years shows very clearly what a vigorous part it has played in the struggle for African independence and unity.'[5]

This paraphrase hardly reflects the real situation accurately, and the truth is that during the 28 months between the conferences of Cairo and Conakry the problems of Asia hardly existed for the secretariat. *In fact it soon became very clear that the Asian interest was never intended to be anything but a platform which the Asian communist groups could exploit—'in the spirit of the fraternal solidarity of the masses of the peoples of the two continents'—in order to intervene in the process of African emancipation, in communist interests, and to influence and win over the neutral forces in Africa.*

This aim can be seen more clearly when we examine the three planes on which the Afro-Asian Solidarity movement operates—that is, the three planes on which communist infiltration is taking place:

1. *Propaganda infiltration*: From the beginning the communist States have emphasized three fundamental themes through the permanent secretariat and its subordinate national committees. The first was the demand for 'the unleashing of a continental struggle against the colonialists and imperialists'. At the same time all attempts to secure a peaceable settlement of outstanding issues with 'the colonial masters' were denounced as 'the manœuvres of collaborating and reactionary African politicians', while all revolutionary attempts at 'de-colonialization' were highly praised. This tendency was clearly seen in the attitude of the secretariat to the referendum organized by de Gaulle on 28 September 1958. All those who supported his proposed *Communauté Française* were denounced as unworthy 'to bear the honourable title of African', while the opposition to the *Communauté Française* led by Sékou Touré (and his subsequent success at the referendum) were acclaimed as 'a pledge of real African patriotism'.[6] In the case of Cameroon, the secretariat joined with the underground *Union des Populations du Cameroun* to denigrate the intention of the United Nations to grant independence to the trusteeship area from 1 January 1960. At the same time all attempts by the moderate elements in Cameroon to bring the rebellion to an end on the basis of a compromise and by negotiations before sovereignty was granted were vigorously rejected by the solidarity movement and denounced in fierce counter-propaganda.

The second theme advanced by the secretariat in its published propaganda was that after achieving political independence the African peoples must attain independence in all other fields as well, in particular economic independence. This campaign, which is conducted throughout the African continent was, and is still, directed against any and every form of Western economic aid, in particular against the continued existence of Western firms and undertakings in the politically sovereign African lands. Individual Western economic undertakings and Western economic activity in Africa in general are attacked in leaflets and pamphlets—'The Infiltration of Franco-American Economic Undertakings and Their Role in the Exploitation of Africa'; 'West-German Capital to support French Colonialism!'; 'Belgian Colonial Policy in the Congo—The Shareholders of the *Union Minière du Haut Katanga* in Action'; and so on. These propaganda tracts all finish with the same slogan: the African countries will not be 'really free' until they end the economic dominance of colonialism in their territories. Needless to say, all these publications advocate the economic principles of the communist countries as the proper model for 'a really independent economic development of the new Africa'.

The third theme in this propaganda infiltration is the defamation of the United States. America is constantly under attack in all the publications of the solidarity movement as 'the chief whipper-in of colonialist policy'. More recently a great deal of attention has been paid to 'Fidelism' in Cuba. Examples of 'America's interventionist policy' in Latin America are quoted in order to persuade the Africans that any dealings with the US imperialists will inevitably develop into 'a crushing and fatal embrace'. On this point the influence of Peking on the propaganda activity of the solidarity secretariat has noticeably increased.

2. *Solidarity actions and solidarity propaganda*: This is chiefly a matter of demonstrations and collections intended to attract general attention and is intended primarily for external consumption. Certain standard themes are worked out each time. The secretariat has fixed 1 December of each year as 'Quit-Africa Day' and this is celebrated with demonstrations in all communist countries 'to draw the attention of world public opinion to the colonial shame' in Africa and to stir the conscience of the world in order to compel the imperialists to liquidate their colonial bases in Africa. The solidarity secretariat has also fixed special Angola, Congo, and South Africa Days. The National Solidarity Committees in the Soviet Union, China, and other countries issue appropriate propaganda material for use in the Press and for broadcasting in connection with the special themes to be stressed on these various 'Days'. Throughout Soviet-controlled territory from Vladivostok to East Berlin any African who can be mobilized is pressed into service to persuade public opinion of the necessity for 'determined action against Africa's colonial masters'.

Often special solidarity collections are arranged in connection with these Days. For example, on Algeria Day members of the official labour organization in East Germany had to contribute a proportion of their pay to the Algerian Solidarity Fund. The use to which such money is put can be seen from the fact that the underground activity of the *Union des Populations du Cameroun* has been financed in part by the solidarity contributions of the various national solidarity committees—in this case chiefly the Chinese committee—channelled through the secretariat of the movement in Cairo.

Part of this activity was the communist attempt to obtain support for the formation of an International Algerian Brigade and to persuade the solidarity secretariat and the second Solidarity Conference in Conakry to adopt a decision to this end. If this communist manœuvre had succeeded, Asian volunteers (including, of course, volunteers from the Soviet Union, Red China and North Vietnam) would have arrived in North Africa to take an active part in the Algerian struggle on the side of the FLN. In fact the inner councils of the FLN were divided and it proved impossible to reach an agreement which would, in any case, have gone no further than calling for the establishment of an African Brigade. In consequence the communist manœuvre failed.

3. *Cadre formation and cadre training*: The Solidarity Council and the organizations affiliated to it represent the formal channels for a large-scale communist programme for Africa and fifty per cent of all African visitors to China during the past few years went at the invitation of the National Chinese Afro-Asian Solidarity Secretariat, though of late (outwardly at least) the special Chinese Solidarity Committee for Africa has been playing a more prominent role. Not that this really matters, because in fact it is the same institution under different names and both are controlled by the Chinese Communist Party. Grants to African students for courses in the Soviet Union and its satellite countries are distributed through the solidarity council and its subordinate bodies. The real aim of this activity is to recruit proselytes. The idea is to seed valuable and effective cadres for training at one or another of the various communist labour-union, youth, and women's schools, or universities, in order that they may return to their own countries and form communist or pro-communist cells (often in completely non-communist organizations) and generally act as a revolutionary yeast. In other words, the real purpose of the Solidarity Council is to serve as a central communist recruiting agency in Africa. An example of how this activity is carried out in practice can be seen from the behaviour of the delegations from the Soviet Union, the satellite States and Red China at the second Afro-Asian Solidarity Conference in Conakry, in April 1960. They not only distributed

propaganda pamphlets on behalf of the Moscow University of People's Friendship and the various Chinese training centres, but also issued personal invitations to dozens of African delegates to visit their countries and in many cases the airline ticket was handed over with the invitation. The same tactic was followed by the Soviet and Chinese delegations to the third Afro-Asian Solidarity Conference in February 1963, in Moshi, Tanganyika.

Communist solidarity propaganda and the communist cadre policy in the solidarity movement, with communist activity in the African branch organizations, are not universally welcomed. During the few months before the second Solidarity Conference there was a good deal of trouble in the leading bodies, some of it quite serious; and a number of African members handed in their resignations rather than continue to tolerate communist tactics. In the preparatory phase of the Conakry Conference there was similar trouble in the secretariat. This arose out of the temporary deterioration of relations between Peking and the United Arab Republic, the Sino-Indian border clash, and the obvious intention of the communist members to fix the conference venue and the future seat of the executive bodies in their own interests. However, the conflict between the Indian and Chinese representatives over the Sino-Indian clash was diminished by the announcement that there were to be direct talks between the Chinese Prime Minister, Chou En-lai, and Nehru. Moscow and Peking proposed Baghdad as the conference venue, and the final choice of Conakry was a compromise. The fact that Cairo is still the seat of the permanent secretariat— despite the protests of the communist and Iraqi delegations—was then regarded by the more moderate politicians of the Solidarity Movement as a clear victory for them. Some even went so far as to regard it as proof that the movement was freeing itself from communist entanglements and was on the way to becoming a completely neutral organization independent of communist control.

Thirty-nine groups were represented in Cairo, but at the Conakry Conference delegates attended from 68 African and Asian parties, associations, committees and trade unions, though some of them led an ambiguous and precarious political existence. A good many of the East African and South African delegates had been living for years in exile in Cairo, cut off from any real contact with their home countries. The only Cameroonian representatives were the extremist leaders of the *Union des Populations du Cameroun* headed by their late president, Félix-Roland Moumié. These men were permanently resident in Conakry. They had previously prevented Liberia from issuing an official invitation to a legal delegation from Cameroon. The Ivory Coast was represented by a so-called liberation committee which had no real following. A group from Cairo was accepted, without cavil, as representing Palestine. During the conference this group distributed violently anti-Semitic leaflets in the style of the notorious Nazi publication *Der Stürmer*. Together with other Arab delegates they also persuaded the conference to eject the Israeli ambassador, who was present as an unofficial observer.

The agenda of the Conakry Conference contained four familiar and characteristic points: 1. The complete liquidation of colonialism in Asia and Africa (sub-sections: independence, unity, co-existence, and disarmament). 2. The economic development of Asia and Africa. 3. Questions of cultural and social development. 4. The extension of the Afro-Asian Solidarity Movement. The delegation leaders were almost permanently in session and the main body of delegates was presented with a number of reports, of which only one—that drawn up by John Kale—broke away from the usual communist-inspired generalities so typical of all communist-controlled conferences. In his report Kale frankly admitted that the work of the Solidarity Movement was making no progress in a number of countries and was meeting with opposition from other political organizations. He recorded that the support which the movement was receiving from the various governments concerned was negligible. Since the last conference a number of areas had not even formed national solidarity committees in accordance with the decision of the Cairo Conference. Although there was a good deal of vehement discussion in the various commissions on these and other questions, the plenary sessions presented, on all five days, a completely harmonious picture of Afro-Asian solidarity and full agreement on all important questions. The denunciation of colonialism, Western imperialism, French nuclear tests in the Sahara and white racial policy in South Africa poured out monotonously, interrupted only by the equally stereotyped phraseology in praise of the Soviet disarmament plan and the principles of peaceful co-existence.[7]

Resolutions and proposals relating to cultural, social, and

economic problems in Africa and Asia, however, were of rather greater importance. The conference expressed itself whole-heartedly in favour of 'learning from socialist experiences' in the economic development of the individual countries concerned, and it was repeatedly stressed that 'the next stage of the struggle against colonialism' must achieve 'economic decolonization'. At the same time, it was proposed that historians, writers, sociologists and scientists from all Afro-Asian countries be invited to co-operate on various commissions, which would meet regularly. This programme for increasing co-operation in the intellectual sphere was initiated by the leader of the Soviet delegation, the Tadjik writer, Mirzo Tursun-Zade, a veteran organizer of many 'friendship conferences'.

One or two organizational changes made at the Conakry Conference were of some importance. In accordance with the growing interest in the development of Africa the permanent secretariat was extended by co-opting representatives of Algeria, Guinea and the former Belgian Congo. Apart from the general secretary, an Afro-Asian parity in the secretariat was established, with representatives of the Soviet Union, Red China, Japan, India, Indonesia, Iraq, Algeria, Ghana, Guinea, the former Belgian Congo, Cameroon (the illegal *Union des Populations du Cameroun*), and Uganda. In order to improve the political leadership and control of this instrument, a 27-member steering committee was established and was to meet twice a year. The committee was made completely responsible to a *conseil de l'organisation*, consisting of the leaders of all affiliated groups, which was to meet once after each conference. Finally it was decided to change the name of the Solidarity Movement, henceforth to be known as the *Organisation de Solidarité des Peuples Afro-Asiatiques*.

The subjects on the agenda of this second Afro-Asian Solidarity Conference indicated once again how directly the movement is communist-controlled and inspired. Since then further proof has been provided, if any were still necessary, that this solidarity movement is a front organization. An economic conference, held in May 1960 in Cairo, achieved little or nothing, but several measures on the part of the secretariat, particularly on the Congo question, underlined the complete ideological identity of the movement with the attitudes and actions of communist parties and governments. The list of resolutions adopted by the Afro-Asian Women's Conference, which took place in January 1961 in Cairo, obediently listed all the current propaganda themes of communism, from the denunciation of the neo-colonialism of the *Communauté Française* to approval of the rebels in Cameroon and Laos.

All communist-front organizations suffer from the same weakness: even before their methods and their objectives have been completely exposed, they begin to lose their attraction, become useless for the purpose for which they were formed, and have to be replaced by new organizations. The Afro-Asian Solidarity Movement is already facing this situation in Asia, but not yet in Africa. Discussions with African politicians show that many of them still do not realize that the solidarity movement is communist-controlled, while others either deny this or try to make light of it. Generally speaking, many Africans of goodwill still share the views of John Kale, which he expressed to the author shortly before his death. The experienced and cunning communist officials operating in the secretariat and its subordinate executive bodies are still able to deceive many well-meaning Africans, who are unaware of the real situation and are greatly impressed by the demonstrations of solidarity for their cause. In their innocence they are fair game and they become cat's paws of communism.

This situation obviously still existed when the third of these Afro-Asian solidarity conferences took place. After a number of postponements, it was held from 4 to 11 February 1963 in Moshi. The choice of Tanganyika as the host-country was no less pre-meditated than the previous choice of Egypt for the first conference and of Guinea for the second. In 1957 Cairo was an obvious choice on account of the recent events in Suez, which made it the ideal venue for an anti-imperialist and anti-colonialist demonstration. At that time Cairo was an excellent centre for making contacts throughout the Arab and African world. Three years later, in 1960, Conakry offered the wire-pullers of the Afro-Asian Solidarity Movement similar advantageous opportunities in West Africa, an area which at the time was in the decisive phase of its anti-colonial struggle. Now, at the beginning of 1963, conditions in the Arab countries and in West Africa had been consolidated—and not entirely in favour of communism. The main sphere of communist action had shifted to South Africa and East Africa, where Somalia, Uganda and Tanganyika had achieved full political independence. In

Zanzibar and Kenya the compass had been set for independence, but a critical phase within the disrupted African front was about to begin and there were, in consequence, many favourable opportunities for communist initiative. The collapse of the Central African Federation was obviously a matter of time, and of only a short time, and the likelihood of clashes between black and white in Southern Rhodesia was imminent. Finally the anti-Portuguese forces were massing in and around Mozambique for more determined action, while in South Africa antagonism between the white racial fanatics and African nationalism was assuming new intensity and bitterness. Tanganyika lies in the centre of this tremendous field of tension and Julius Nyerere had deliberately aligned his country in the vanguard of African nationalism. Since Tanganyika's independence, Dar es Salaam has become for East Africa and South Africa what Accra and Conakry were for West Africa—a centre of anti-colonial propaganda, a meeting place for groups of exiles from surrounding countries and a base of operations for the liberation of the neighbouring areas.

International communism therefore set out to make useful contacts, to play a role in the coming struggle against colonialism, obtain an influence on forces likely to be of importance in the future, win friends by making gestures of solidarity, and (this is true in particular of the Chinese communists) influence the nature and tactics of the coming struggle by advice, instructions and a supply of arms.

There were, and still are, many factors favourable to these communist aims and objectives. As in West Africa from 1958 to 1961, the anti-communist propaganda of the existing colonial administrations is often so gauche that it actually strengthens the communists. For a long time the British colonial authorities clung obstinately to the convenient axiom that all the followers of Mau-Mau could automatically be regarded as communists. At the same time the colonialist Press never loses an opportunity to denounce awkward African politicians and groups as communists or as paid agents of communism, as soon as it is able to point out the slightest similarity between their slogans and arguments and those used by the communists. The statements and charges given publicity on every conceivable occasion by the authorities in South Africa, Southern Rhodesia and Mozambique are even wilder and more extreme.

Anyone who is opposed to the dominance of the white race in Africa is automatically dubbed a communist. It is obvious that this stupid attitude must lead to exactly the opposite of what its propagandists hope to attain. The communists are denounced as the arch-enemies of colonialism, and in consequence Africans are automatically inclined to regard them as friends. And since no one in these areas has any practical experience of what communism is like in reality, and as the support by third groupings and elements is not particularly effective, communism finds almost ideal conditions ready-made for its operations. This is particularly the case when it is able to present itself to the ordinary African in the mask of well-meaning, helpful friend—as at the third Afro-Asian Solidarity Conference in Moshi in 1963. The situation becomes even more favourable when the wire-pullers of the various manœuvres succeed in keeping themselves in the background.

The Tanganyikan Government obviously hesitated for quite a while before it finally gave permission for the third Afro-Asian Solidarity Conference to be held on its territory. As a result of warnings of communist intrigues, received from various West African politicians, it attempted to delay the calling of the conference, and finally, when it did agree, it put forward various transparent pretexts for shifting the venue from Dar es Salaam to the more remote Moshi (which lies directly beneath Kilimanjaro) where public impact would be much less than in the capital. In fact, the 14,000 inhabitants of Moshi took hardly any notice of the conference. The posters and other propaganda put up in the streets and the squares of the town were already defaced by the second day of the conference and soon completely washed away by one or two heavy downpours. The conference itself was held in the building of a secondary school some distance from the town centre.

Thus the outward circumstances in which the conference was held were not impressive. The same was true of its composition, though the secretariat proudly announced that the conference was being attended by delegates from 58 affiliated organizations and by 40 other delegations as observers. Julius Nyerere and Jomo Kenyatta delivered the opening and closing speeches and the Russians and the Chinese attended in force. But neighbouring Kenya sent only a ten-man delegation, consisting entirely of officials of only one of the three main political parties, and even they were 'political unknowns, hand-picked by that communist-financed capitalist Oginga Odinga.'[8]

The biggest African country, Nigeria, was represented by only one delegate and he was there on behalf of the Youth Congress. Some comment was aroused by the fact that this 'youth delegate' had a grey beard. Exiles from Cameroon and delegates from Mali and Guinea were the only representatives of the French-speaking territories of West Africa. Ghana, which sent an enormous delegation to the second Afro-Asian Solidarity Conference, was represented at the third by only one politician, and he did not attend all the sessions and manifested a marked lack of interest in the proceedings. The group from Uganda consisted entirely of youthful unknowns. The head of the delegation, as he found himself called, was so astonished at this honour he thought they were playing a joke on him. There were the usual delegations from Palestine, Cameroon, and other parts of Africa, whose members as usual represented only themselves—little groups kept alive artificially by communist or Arab subsidies. There was at least one representative delegation, that from Malaysia, but in accordance with the anti-Malaysia line of the Russians and the Chinese, the credentials committee refused to accept it and it was unable to take part in the proceedings.

Two serious conflicts between members of the Afro-Asian Solidarity Movement formed the main background to the Moshi Conference. First, there was the question of the smouldering Sino-Indian frontier clash, the effects of which are still being felt throughout Asia and Africa. Secondly, there was the ideological dispute between Moscow and Peking, which was then reaching new heights with the Chinese denunciation of the 'Revisionists'. The Sino-Indian conflict was threatening to flare up at the second Afro-Asian Solidarity Conference in Conakry, but the fires were dampened by conciliatory gestures from both Peking and New Delhi, only to burst out with renewed vehemence two years later. The Sino-Soviet dispute echoed repeatedly through the Afro-Asian secretariat and at various meetings of the affiliated organs—for example, at the Gaza meeting in the spring of 1962. Unlike the Russians, the Chinese, in the period between Conakry and Moshi, had succeeded in extending and consolidating their influence over the various Afro-Asian solidarity organizations—for example, in the

Afro-Asian Solidarity Fund Organization, whose dominating committee member was Chu Tzu-chi, formerly chief Chinese delegate to the permanent secretariat of the movement, and in the permanent bureau of the Afro-Asian Writers' Association. Strong pro-Chinese tendencies also made themselves noticeable at an Economic Seminar held in Ceylon in October 1962, which was at first boycotted by Moscow. In view of the repeatedly sharp attacks by Peking against the allegedly soft attitude of Moscow on the question of intensifying the 'national liberation struggle', it was to be expected that Moshi would be the scene of more or less open Sino-Soviet controversy.

In fact, nothing of the kind took place, and this was perhaps the outstanding, though negative, feature of Moshi and the one and only success the Russians attained at the conference. At the preliminary meetings of the permanent secretariat they succeeded in persuading the Chinese, who arrived spoiling for a fight, that any open conflict at the conference between the hostile communist brothers would damage the general plans of communism, which both supported, and would have an unfavourable effect on their joint front organization in Africa.[9] An appeal issued by the World Peace Council not to debate differences of opinion in public and instead 'to stress the things all had in common' was handed, as a sort of address of welcome, to all the delegations arriving in Tanganyika.

But even this appeal could not prevent the Sino-Soviet conflict from expressing itself in Moshi in other ways. For example, the conference documents issued by the Russians stressed the urgent necessity for general disarmament and co-existence, while those issued by the Chinese pointedly made no reference either to disarmament or to co-existence; for the knowledgeable, the existence of the differences in the background was unmistakable. Behind the scenes both the Soviet and the Chinese delegations pursued what was described as tactics of 'fierce lobbying and currying for favour'. The author was present at smaller gatherings in which the Chinese did their utmost to persuade the African and Asian politicians that Khrushchev's attitude in the Cuban affair was proof that the Russians could not be relied on and that reliance could be placed only on 'really revolutionary countries', such as People's China. In addition, the Chinese never lost an opportunity of emphasizing that the Russians were 'whites' and not members of the 'Asian brother-race'. So the prophecy of the Nairobi *Daily Nation* on the opening day of the conference was borne out: many delegates did indeed find themselves 'dissipating their energies in a three-way stretch among the non-aligned, the Moscow-aligned, and the Peking-aligned.'[10] And in view of the struggle which was clearly going on behind the scenes, it can only be described as a breath-taking performance when, on the third day of the conference, Oginga Odinga rose and declared that the Sino-Soviet conflict was nothing but an invention of the Western imperialists.

Unfortunately for him, the facts made it impossible for him to adopt the same attitude towards the Sino-Indian conflict and so everything possible was done to bury this damaging dispute between two Asian countries under a welter of appeals for compromise and restraint. At the opening session of the conference the general secretary of the permanent secretariat, Yussuf El Sabai, urged the delegates not to give public expression to opinions which might lead to tension and disruption, and added: 'The delegations from India and China have agreed to treat their border dispute in the spirit of Bandung.' Awkwardly, however, Nehru's telegram of greeting to the conference contained the provocative word 'aggression', in referring to the action of the Chinese and therefore the least the Indian delegation could do was to ask the conference to include 'a special reference to the dispute in the final resolution'. The leader of the Indian delegation, Chaman Lal, declared that 'despite our adherence to the principles of peaceful co-existence a grave conflict has been thrust on India, and this conflict has endangered the very basis of Afro-Asian solidarity, the principles of non-alignment and world peace'. With a further indirect tilt at the Chinese, he declared: 'The dangerous world we live in is the *raison d'être* for the policy of peaceful co-existence. Let this be a warning to those who in their folly or arrogance persist in denying in word or action this policy of peaceful co-existence.'[11]

However, the Indian protests found little echo at the conference and the Chinese continued to blame India for the Himalayan frontier clash. The Indians even had to walk out of a meeting of the political committee of the conference on 7 February when they failed in their attempt to get a resolution accepted on the proposal of the Colombo States for the opening of negotiations on the Sino-Indian border dispute. This particular clash between the Indians and the Chinese was so heated that the committee chairman, Bhoke

Munanka, had to intervene repeatedly. Chaman Lal demanded that the Chinese accept the recommendation of the Colombo States without reservation, and when he was unable to get his point accepted he left the hall, declaring bluntly: 'The organization is killed, destroyed, ended. Without India there is no organization.'[12] Tremendous efforts were made to persuade the Indians to return, and after four days' absence the Indian delegation reappeared to endorse a compromise recommendation from which the words 'without reservation' had been deleted.

But that was not the end of the conference's troubles. Many of the delegates were more concerned with their own local problems than with world affairs and this opened up cracks in the façade of solidarity. The delegates from Kenya staged a walk-out of their own when the Somali delegates laid claim to the Northern Frontier District of Kenya. There were also bitter complaints by the delegates from Zanzibar that neither India nor Indonesia was buying their cloves. A heated altercation took place between the delegates from Aden and the Yemen. However, the much-vaunted feelings of 'solidarity' were able to express themselves happily in denouncing the West and 'neo-colonialism' in the usual stereotyped jargon. Even so, one of the Liberian delegates soberly pointed out: 'Talk about neo-colonialism, and the shouting of other disparaging slogans are merely abstract shibboleths to many minds. They are mere words, and their meaning has not yet been clearly defined.'[13] The Tanganyikan Minister of National Culture, acting as the leader of his delegation, also complained that the conference had heard 'too many words meaning too little in the way of practical action.'[14]

There was a good deal of substance to this; indeed, one got the impression that the work of the conference consisted of little more than the constant repetition of meaningless clichés. Most of the speeches sounded as though they had been run off the same gramophone record; grateful thanks to the host; references to the growing achievements of awakening nationalism in recent years; pledges of unswerving solidarity; attacks against colonialism, neo-colonialism, and imperialism; references to local problems in the homeland of the respective speaker; further denunciations of Western colonialism; grateful thanks to 'the real friends of the peoples of Africa and Asia', meaning, of course, the communist States, and so on.

Apart from all this talk there were ludicrous changes of front.

For example, after having conducted the friendliest talks with Golda Meir, Israel's Foreign Minister, and having agreed on close co-operation, the Tanganyikan and Ugandan delegates expressed their unqualified approval of the Arab attacks on Zionism and finally they all voted for an anti-Israel resolution. When Press representatives buttonholed Oscar Kambona, chairman of the conference and afterwards Tanganyika's first Foreign Minister, and pointed out the lack of logic in his attitude, he wriggled out of it by saying that there would be plenty of time 'later on' to discuss how this or that resolution adopted by the conference was to be put into practice. Delegates from member-States of the Pan-African organization PAFMECSA, which had invariably supported the legal authorities in the Congo, now unanimously applauded speeches and resolutions denouncing Cyrille Adoula, the Congolese Prime Minister, though as recently as December 1962 they had adopted a resolution expressing satisfaction at 'the clear policy the United States Government had recently adopted in the Congo'. Now they saw no harm or lack of logic in voting for a resolution which denounced the Congo policy of the selfsame government as devilish imperialist manœuvre.

After listening to this sort of thing for a few days the objective observer began to wonder whether he ought to take the conference seriously at all. The whole performance had little or nothing to do with solidarity. It was impossible to reconcile it either with the principle of strict neutrality and non-alignment or with the earnestly stressed dignity of representatives of the people of Asia and Africa. All in all, it is not surprising to record that the Moshi Conference achieved little if any practical significance: the Chinese distributed invitations to various African politicians to visit China; a special committee was formed to examine the advantages of a planning system for the economies of the former colonial countries; a good deal was said about the necessity for increasing the material assistance granted to the liberation movements in Asia and Africa; a list of denunciations was reeled off against Western colonialism; and once more the solidarity organization was given *carte blanche* to carry on endless propaganda activity between the conferences in the name of 'the peoples of Asia and Africa'.

The original communist plan (put forward chiefly by the Chinese) to extend the organization to Latin America had to be abandoned, probably because the only delegation from that part of the world came from Castro's Cuba. The conference did not succeed in persuading objective observers that it was either representative or powerful. Perhaps the most significant comment, and by no means an unfair one, was made by Ronald Ngala, former Chief Minister for Kenya, who declared forthrightly that the conference had been a failure. That opinion was undoubtedly shared by many other delegates.

This laconic judgement even found some support in the summary handed to the delegates by the general secretary, Yussuf El Sabai. His report confirmed that the chief activity of the permanent secretariat between the conferences consisted almost exclusively of propaganda, Press releases, denunciations, solidarity gestures and the issue of pamphlets. But even this propaganda campaign suffered, it appeared, not only from lack of support by the affiliated organizations, but also from an indifferent reception. The following passages from the report of the general secretary will show that this conclusion is not unfair:

'A circular letter was sent to the national solidarity committee calling on them to contribute material for these publications [a monthly bulletin, a quarterly publication, and various pamphlets on important questions], to make any proposals of their own to further the work and to help in the distribution. Unfortunately there was no response at all.'[15]

'The Quarterly was not published at all owing to lack of response on the part of the national committees to our appeal.[16]

'The efficiency of the Contacts Section reached a remarkably high level . . . Nevertheless, the fact remains that the response of the national committees and other organizations to our appeals and our letters is still irregular.'[17]

'The Research Section still stands in need of improvement. Unfortunately the critical financial situation of the secretariat constitutes the main obstacle to the establishment of a sound basis for the work of this section. The sub-sections for political, economic, social, and cultural research are similarly hampered in carrying out their tasks for the same reason: namely, lack of finance and the lack of response on the part of the committees and organizations to our appeals.'[18]

What are we to say to all this? How are we to sum up the significance of the whole movement? How effective is it as a channel for communist ideas and propaganda? How effectively does it further practical communist activities? It is not easy to give a satisfactory answer. Even at the second conference in Conakry I was still inclined to regard the movement as being of some importance—even indeed, as a threatening factor in African developments. But in Moshi, and before Moshi, I began to have doubts about the effectiveness of the organization as a communist instrument. Its original impetus seems to be largely exhausted. Apart from dramatic gestures and declarations which really do not mean very much, it seems to be finding no response. The fact that certain delegates took part in the conference does not even tell one much about their real political attitudes. Indeed, most of them seem to be using such platforms as an opportunity for putting forward their own egoistical wishes and plans, though there is always a point at which these coincide with the wishes and plans of the communist wire-pullers. This was certainly true of some of the delegations from still-subject areas in East, South, and Central Africa. Finally it must not be forgotten that in these days mere propaganda often has as much weight as practical action where Africa is concerned.

In the future we shall have to pay closer attention to the various branches and special organizations affiliated to the movement, most of which have not been long in existence. This is especially true of bodies such as the Afro-Asian Legal Consultative Committee; the Afro-Asian Organization for Economic Co-operation; the Afro-Asian Students' Organization; the Afro-Asian Reconstruction Organization; the Afro-Asian Youth Office; the Afro-Asian Sports Committee (which organized an Afro-Asian Table-Tennis Conference in December 1961); the International Committee for Aid to the Congo; the Afro-Asian Writers' Organization; and the Afro-Asian Solidarity Fund (with its seat in Conakry). It is beginning to look as though, in future, the communist wire-pullers behind the Afro-Asian Solidarity Movement intend to concentrate on the activities of such organizations, especially since the fourth conference of the AAPSO, held in Ghana from 9 to 16 May 1965, failed to attract prominent African and Asian politicians and became yet again an arena for the Sino-Soviet dispute, despite a ruling by AAPSO's permanent secretariat that ideological quarrels should be kept out of future meetings. Host for the meeting at the Winneba Ideological Institute was the Ghana Convention People's Party with President Nkrumah opening the conference. Moscow Radio commented that the conference's most important result was that the 'idea of unity of nations triumphed once more'. The Chinese, however, directly attacked the Russians—an editorial in the *Peking People's Daily* said that a 'struggle between two lines ran through the whole conference'. Lagos Radio said that the most surprising feature of the conference was its 'reluctance to address itself to certain practical problems facing African and Asian politics today'. It suggested that the delegates might have contributed 'their widow's mite' to the coffers of the OAU Liberation Fund, which 'could have been a more concrete and more convincing expression of solidarity than shouting anti-imperialist speeches'. Abidjan Radio (Ivory Coast) said that all that had been achieved was 'the customary verbiage of international communist dialectics which masks its active imperialism from those who do not share its devouring taste for domination'.[19]

However, the ultimate success or failure of the Afro-Asian Solidarity Movement and its various subordinate bodies depends largely on factors other than the activity of the communists themselves. Often the mistakes of the West unintentionally assist the communists to achieve their aims; and often, too, intransigent action on the part of the Western States where Africa is concerned drive the African nationalists to make common cause with the communists.

The stirring appeals of the Solidarity Council in the Lumumba case, its repeated protests against French nuclear tests in the Sahara, its constant condemnation of racialism in South Africa and of the reactionary policy of the white settlers in Rhodesia, its repeated exposure of co-operation between the democratic Western States and Portugal in Angola and Mozambique, the exposure of foolish neo-colonialist manœuvres on the part of capitalist undertakings in Africa, and many other such activities—which are taken very seriously by Africans—appeal to Africans, help to obscure the activity and aims of the communist wire-pullers and prevent African politicians from taking the movement into their own hands and turning it into a real instrument for the realization of their own ideas and aims.

NOTES

[1] Cyclostyled minutes of the First Afro-Asian People's Solidarity Conference, Cairo, January 1958.

[2] In Conakry, April 1960.

[3] Cyclostyled minutes of the First Afro-Asian People's Solidarity Conference.

[4] Ibid.

[5] Cyclostyled publication (Tunis, 29 January 1960).

[6] Declaration of the Permanent Secretariat of the AAPSO, Cairo, 4 October 1958.

[7] Based on the author's notes during the Conakry Conference.

[8] The *Daily Nation*, 4 February 1963.

[9] A year later, the Chinese and the Soviets clashed at an AAPSO secretariat meeting in Algiers.

[10] The *Daily Nation*, 4 February 1963.

[11] Cyclostyled minutes of the Moshi Conference.

[12] Witnessed by the author.

[13] Ibid.

[14] Ibid.

[15] Political-Organizational Report of the Permanent Secretariat for Afro-Asian People's Solidarity to the Third Afro-Asian People's Solidarity Conference.

[16] Ibid.

[17] Ibid.

[18] Ibid., p. 42.

[19] *African Review*, June 1965.

Chapter XVI

IT'S THE CADRES THAT COUNT

ALMOST every great political movement ultimately turns its back on reality and, always with the same arguments, seeks salvation in myths and legends. In the same way, African nationalism claims that the dissolution of the colonial system was its own achievement and ascribes it to the effects of 'the people' and 'the masses'. Yet the truth is clearly quite different. In Africa political emancipation was *primarily* the result of the emancipation of small élites—not of the masses. It was the élite who prepared the way for the upheaval, which was accelerated by a number of non-African factors. Trained and educated against a European background and at European universities in the spirit of liberalism and humanism, this intellectual minority succeeded in carrying through its programme, despite—and not because of—the masses, which remained largely lethargic.

The upheaval in Africa thus fits into the general historical tendency discussed and defined by Vilfredo Pareto and Gaetano Mosca. Their political sociology compares the fascination of the masses concept with the outstanding importance of the choice and distribution of the élite; and the validity of their theory has been confirmed by the history of both Soviet and Chinese communism.

There is thus a marked parallel between communism and African nationalism, and this is an important starting-point for communist infiltration into Africa, since the intellectual and organizational development of the leading strata of present-day Africa has been moulded on lines similar to that of the communist cadres in late-Tzarist Russia and revolutionary China. In each case the ideas that caused the revolutionary ferment were brought in as a mental pabulum from outside. Unlike Africa however, where the import was accidental rather than centrally organized, Leninism and Maoism systematically set about selecting and training their cadres, sending them abroad and giving them a uniform ideology. This created the essential condition for the communist seizure of power. It came about primarily as a result of the conscious, deliberate fashion in which communists treated the cadre problem, which as early as 1902 it regarded as decisive for defeat or victory.

For Marx, revolution was the task of a chosen 'class', the historic mission of *all* proletarians who, he was convinced, would organize themselves into this class and into a corresponding political party. The Communist Manifesto of 1848 declared: 'All previous historical movements were movements of minorities, or in the interests of minorities. The proletarian movement is the self-conscious, independent movement of the immense majority.'[1] In Russia at least this prophecy was not fulfilled. Tzarist Russia was a backward agricultural country, and the proletariat developed only late and as a minority class. In 1913 only 2,552,000 persons were engaged in Russian industry (and even that number included handicraft and home-workers), and this naturally represented an exceptionally weak basis for a class struggle.[2] Further, very few of these proletarians felt inclined to act, or were sufficiently knowledgeable to think, 'according to their class situation'; at the beginning of the great revolutionary year, 1917, the Russian Social Democratic Workers' Party, from which the Communist Party of the Soviet Union developed, had only 23,000 members.[3] In such circumstances, and on account of proscription and illegality, Lenin gave up all idea of leading the revolution to victory by winning over the 'proletarian masses' and making them politically active: and in his programmatic statement 'What is to be done?', written in 1902, he dismissed all thought of an 'appeal to the masses' as 'an attempt to drag us backwards'. If it tried to start from the basis of 'a large-scale working-class organization allegedly open to the masses' the Social Democratic Party would achieve nothing. Lenin's idea was very different: 'Let us begin with a sound organization of [professional] revolutionaries . . . A firm, small core of reliable, experienced and steeled workers . . . can, with the far-reaching co-operation of the masses, and without taking on any fixed form, carry out all functions a Social Democracy would wish.'[4]

These words, which sum up the communist cadre principle *in nuce* deserve to stand as a motto for the whole history of modern communism. They form the basic formula of the communist struggle for power and the secret of communist successes. However, they require an important addition. For Lenin the formula 'a firm small core' of professional revolutionaries implied a sound, uniform, dogmatic training according to centralized basic principles. As the conditions for this were very unfavourable in Tzarist Russia at the time, particularly after the failure of the Russian Revolution of 1905, he ordered the establishment of party schools abroad. The result was the formation of Bolshevist 'cadre smithies' in Longjumeau near Paris and on the island of Capri. Among other teachers, Lenin and Maxim Gorki lectured at these schools in which the 'advance guard of the Revolution' was trained for the decisive clash with Tzarism. In addition to these there were also itinerant schools, both in Russia and abroad, at which small groups worked according to a uniform curriculum on the basis of party ideological and practical themes.

As this method proved extraordinarily successful, it was a foregone conclusion that after the triumph of Bolshevism the idea would be mooted of trying the same method on a larger scale with foreign communists. Before long, special training centres for foreign communists were set up in the Soviet Union. The first of these started in Tashkent in May 1921, as the University of the Eastern Toilers. Then, as now, the Soviet concept of 'the East' was not confined solely to Asia, but included all colonial and semi-colonial countries, including Africa and Latin America. Thus as far back as 1921, not long after the victorious Bolshevik Revolution, Moscow began to select and train revolutionary cadres systematically for the whole sphere of communist colonial activity.

The enormous importance of this technique of 'exporting revolution' was first demonstrated in China and Korea. The Sun Yat-sen University was founded in Moscow in the early 1920s specially for the Chinese comrades, and up to 1949 most of the Chinese communist leaders and officials, the 'cadres', were trained there. Stefan Possony writes: 'The fact remains that when the time came for China, the communist midwives were prepared for it. They had thousands of trained experts experienced in the arts of revolutionary warfare and fully versed in Chinese affairs.'[5]

Between 1929 and 1939 about 800,000 Koreans were transferred from Outer Mongolia and the Amur district and settled in Turkestan, and every year between 600 and 700 reliable candidates were sent to the University of the Eastern Toilers in Tashkent to be trained for revolutionary activity. A special Korean Institute was subsequently founded in Fergana (Turkestan) and an additional 1,200 Koreans were trained there every year. Finally, about 700 selected Koreans received special training in the NKVD training centre in Tashkent. All men capable of bearing arms were called up for military service with the Red Army. When the Soviets took over North Korea after the Second World War, the élite of the Turkestan Koreans were resettled in their own country and entrusted with the establishment of "people's democratic rule". For example, the present Premier of North Korea, Kim Il-sung, who was also Commander-in-Chief of the North Korean Army during the Korean War, is known to have been one of those North Koreans who was trained in the Soviet Union for unspecified 'tasks in his own country'.[6]

Of course, this systematic organization and training of Korean cadres cannot be compared with the efforts of the communists to form and train an élite in Africa. Most of the students at the University of the Eastern Toilers were Asians and communists from the Near East. From Africa there were only Moroccans, Tunisians and Sudanese in any number, and in the 1920s only members of the communist groups and trade unions from South Africa, Senegal and Madagascar. However, the African ambitions of the Soviets were not forgotten at the fourth anniversary celebrations of the university in 1925. Stalin declared: 'There are about ten different groups of students at the Eastern University and they have come to us from colonial and semi-colonial countries . . . The task of the Eastern University is to forge them into *real revolutionaries*, equip them with the theory of Leninism and with practical experience of Leninism and thus enable them to carry out effectively the immediate tasks in the struggle for the liberation of the colonial and semi-colonial countries.'[7] Stalin gave the university students five tasks to accomplish on their return to their own countries: '1. To win the best elements of the working class for the revolutionary movement and found independent communist parties. 2. To form a national-revolutionary block of the workers, peasants and revolutionary intellectuals to oppose the alliance of the national bourgeoisie with imperialism. 3. To establish the hegemony of the proletariat in the national-revolutionary movement. 4. To wage a struggle to free the urban and rural petite-bourgeoisie from the influence of the national bourgeoisie and its ally imperialism. 5. To work for an alliance between the national-revolutionary movement and the proletarian movements in the progressive countries.'[8] Stalin appealed to his Asian and African listeners: 'The mission of the peoples of the East where the colonial and semi-colonial countries are concerned . . . is to take all the special features of the revolutionary development of these countries into account, and to guide the education and training of the cadres from these countries towards the fulfilment of the various immediate tasks I have enumerated.'[9]

The curriculum of the University of the Eastern Toilers was fashioned with these tasks in view; among the subjects taught were: the history of the Communist Party of the Soviet Union; the history of the Soviet Union; the history of the colonial peoples; the methods used in the revolutionary upheavals among the peoples of the East; historical and dialectical materialism; individual psychology and the psychology of the peoples of the East, and so on. In September 1955 the periodical *Ostprobleme* reported that all nationalities and groups of peoples—*including North, Central and South Africa*—had their own department in the faculties of Tashkent University—the university that developed from the original University of the Eastern Toilers—and that the curricula were specially adapted to the particular circumstances of their countries. 'For example, the history and dogma of Islam is an important subject for students from the Islamic countries. The course of study until the final examinations usually lasts from four to five years. Quite recently arrangements have been made to establish *special faculties for African questions* in order to train native Africans to become communist agents, at first chiefly for operations in North Africa, Nigeria, and the Gold Coast.'[10]

This development is obviously very closely connected with the increased activity of the communist-front organizations, particularly the World League of Democratic Youth, in selecting cadre candidates. Since the end of the Second World War thousands of Africans—often without realizing it—have been sifted by the central communist seeding apparatus in connection with international trade-union, women's, teachers' and youth congresses and world youth celebrations under communist auspices. The total number of

Africans who have been trained at the University of the Eastern Toilers or in Soviet or people's democratic youth and trade-union schools during the past ten years must now run into many thousands. They are still being trained according to the principles Stalin laid down in his Tashkent speech in May 1925; the revolutionary African advance guard are being schooled to become officials of the revolutionary class struggle, deeply versed in the spirit of communist Machiavellianism. An African course held at the high school of the Communist Youth League of the German Soviet Zone at Bogensee in central Germany in 1960, and run by officials of the Communist Youth League (FDJ) and the WFDY, included the following subjects in its curriculum: Marxist-Leninism, the formation of active youth cells at universities and schools in the colonial and semi-colonial countries, practical questions for active youth workers (including how to organize protest demonstrations, etc.), and the provision and distribution of literature (for 'literature' read propaganda material).[11] It is obvious that such a programme of training aims very definitely at communist objectives, as was made clear in a speech delivered by Louis Saillant at the Central Communist Trade Union School for African cadres in Budapest and reported in greater detail elsewhere in this book. The speaker left no room for doubt about the aims of the school when he stated: 'Do not forget that the most important school for working-class officials is the class struggle itself.'[12]

There are many training schools for coloured students (and in particular African students) in the countries of the Soviet bloc today and the situation is complicated by a flood of tendentious reports concerning 'thousands of African agents' who are alleged to be receiving training at the present time in those countries. The Paris newspaper *Le Monde* is probably right to describe the so-called Institute for Economic Studies, founded in Prague in 1958, as 'literally a military academy'. In the same report *Le Monde* mentions a number of special institutes for the training of coloured communist cadres in the Soviet Union, as well as others in Albania, Bulgaria, and East Germany. In addition there are said to be two such schools in the Chinese People's Republic.[13] There are also a number of military training centres in various countries behind the Iron Curtain; for example, in a private talk with the author in April 1960, a member of the Czech Embassy in Conakry confirmed the fact that NCOs of the Guinean Army are being trained at the

Prague Military Academy. In October 1961 the Ghanaian Government also decided to make use of military training schools in the countries of the Soviet bloc and announced that, for the time being, some 400 trainees would go to Iron Curtain countries to take part in communist officers' training courses.[14] According to a broadcast on Radio Accra the first 71 trainees left there in October 1961, on their way to Moscow to undergo such training.[15] Even where the training is frankly military there is little doubt that ideological indoctrination will be an important feature of the course.

Since 1955 communist cadre policy has undergone a noticeable change. In accordance with general Soviet policy towards Africa, which includes both revolutionary action and co-existentialist agreements and alliances, the Kremlin is laying less stress on the revolutionary aspect. Today cadre recruitment among the African élite pursues two distinct lines: there is the training of African professional revolutionaries completely devoted to communist doctrines and aims which is going on as usual, but at the same time Africans are being offered a supposedly academic and technological training, ostensibly without ideological strings. The large-scale programme of scholarship grants organized by the communist countries for Africa and in particular by the new Friendship University, founded in 1960 in Moscow, is aimed primarily at members of the bourgeoisie and intelligentsia who are not, or not yet, committed communists. In this connection the following aims are paramount: the dissipation of anti-communist feelings; the formation of influential groups of people who are at least amiably disposed to the Soviet Union and its satellites; and the exploitation of such persons later, when they return to their countries, as propagandists for a policy of co-existence, if not alliance, with the Soviet bloc.

Up to 1960 such students were recruited primarily on the basis of mutual agreement between the Soviet Union and the various African countries concerned or by means of scholarship grants to the United Nations through the (communist) International Students League or the Afro-Asian Solidarity Committee. Apart from free education, students were offered 900 roubles a month to live on plus a grant of 3,000 roubles for the purchase of winter clothing, fares to and from the Soviet Union, and specially arranged tours. What the student does not learn beforehand is that he will have to pay 90 roubles a month for his place in a common dormitory and over 500 roubles a month for food, books and fares. African students returning from the Soviet Union have also mentioned more important disadvantages: the continuous surveillance, the isolation from the Russian people and the constant if indirect indoctrination. Typical of these complaints is the account given by Andrew Richard Amar of Uganda, who in the autumn of 1960 left the Soviet Union in disgust and returned to his own country:

'Four students shared a room. Two of them were always Russians and they were in control. The students from Iraq were the only ones treated differently; sometimes they were left to themselves, or there was only one Russian in with them. To make this surveillance appear casual and not deliberate the Russian students were usually in residence before the foreign students arrived. Very often, but not always, these Russian students were in the uniform of the Soviet military security service. There were at least two such uniformed men to each floor. At first I, too, had to sleep in a room with one of these policemen, because that was really what these Russian students were. Soon after I arrived and before I had had much experience I asked the management of the institute why these men were present. I was told that they really had nothing to do with the institute at all and that they were there simply because there was a shortage of accommodation. The longer I stayed in Moscow the more I began to doubt this explanation, because, for one thing, these uniformed police-soldiers took part in all the activities of a university to which they allegedly did not belong.

'The surveillance system in Moscow covers all university students. It is quite effective and is being tightened up from year to year. The fact that it is obligatory to attend the various lectures is no cause for complaint, but the limitation of personal freedom is very onerous. I have already mentioned these uniformed policemen, or militiamen, who are always around in the main university buildings and whose presence is a source of resentment. There are two of the militiamen to each floor. The main building consists of six sectors, known as "zona", and these usually consist of nine floors. This means that there are a hundred policemen always around, and perhaps more, and the students can never get out of their sight. But these are only the external indications of power.

Each of us students had to suffer, in addition, from the attentions of Komsomol activists and spies, and this was true in particular of non-Russian and above all, African, students, who are practically put away in an institutional ghetto. There is a system of university passes, known as *propusks*, and this also greatly restricts the freedom of movement of all students. But worst of all was perhaps the interference and unfriendliness we had to suffer from our Russian fellow-students and room-mates. No one doubted that they were only there to spy on us, and in reality they were nothing but "student security police". On at least one occasion they were used by the university authorities to enforce discipline, and I witnessed at least one arrest . . .'[16]

Amar also describes the constant surveillance and the restriction of movement outside the university. Conducted tours were organized for the students in and around Moscow, but they were shown 'only the typical tourist attractions, and it was expressly forbidden to leave the party and go around on one's own. Whole days were often devoted to receptions and meetings with various organizations, such as the Communist Party, the Communist Youth and the Young Pioneers.' But even more important is what Amar has to say about the ideological indoctrination of the foreign students, and in particular the obligatory Russian lessons.

Amar writes:

'The first two or three months were devoted entirely to language lessons, and there were four full lessons every day, and, in addition, homework—as far as we were able to work at all in the inadequately heated and overcrowded rooms. Subsequently these language lessons were reduced to two a day. At first they were all given in the institute itself, later we went into the main building for courses and lectures. The Soviet authorities attach particular importance to the introductory lessons. When I was there all the language teachers were women. I was put into a class with students from Iraq. Right at the start our teacher told us: "Forget everything you ever learned before you came to Russia". Our first exercises were all to do with Russian popular heroes and people's leaders. Comparisons were made and parallels drawn with our own countries. Finally we were asked whether we would not wish such heroes and revolutionary leaders for our own countries, and it was made quite clear to us what reply was expected. This method of instruction was intended not only to indoctrinate and mould us, but also to discover our own ideas and tendencies. If we started to discuss things or to ask awkward questions, we were told that we were wasting valuable time and ought to apply for a transfer. The students were sifted according to political, not intellectual, criteria. All my friends experienced the same sort of thing. The teachers deliberately dragged out their lessons and never lost an opportunity to slip in little political homilies, at the same time studying our reactions in order to be able to sift and classify us. Once I realized this I pretended to be naïve. When I was asked a particularly provocative question I would answer innocently: "I haven't any idea" or "I really don't know much about the history of my country". After a month we were presented with carefully chosen extracts from the newspapers, all of which, of course, severely criticized and denounced the capitalist countries. One of our teachers, Valeria Dmitrievna, was particularly cunning: she admitted openly that our lessons were intended to educate us politically, and by her apparent frankness she hoped to win our confidence. She also assured us that the British, French and Americans did not want us to be educated and become free, whereas, on the other hand, all Russians were eager to help the Africans.'[17]

Similar stories were told at a Press conference in Frankfort-on-Main on 21 September 1960, at which three African students who had broken with Moscow vigorously denounced the establishment of a Soviet Friendship University specially for Africans, Asians and Latin Americans. They insisted that the founding of such an institution would be an insult to the peoples concerned, and that the idea violated the traditional concept of the university as an institution of learning open to all, irrespective of race, religion, or origin.[18]

Recently, and especially in 1963, Africans who have studied at institutions in the communist satellite States have reported similarly disappointing experiences on a par with those related by Richard Amar about the Soviet Union. Six Somalis who came from Prague in December 1961 had a particularly dramatic story to tell. They had been inveigled into Czechoslovakia with glittering promises and at first they found themselves treated in friendly fashion. The unpleasantness started when it came to buying some urgently needed winter clothing. Although they had been promised 'an adquate sum' for such purchases, all they were handed when they arrived in Prague was 500 crowns, and with clothing prices as high as they are behind the Iron Curtain this did not go far. Each of them had to 'borrow' from other grants to make up the deficiency, with the result that most of them spent their book allowance of 400 crowns on clothes. When they refused to join a very obviously communist-controlled Union of Somali Students in the socialist camp, the secretary of this organization warned them that if they persisted in their refusal it might entail 'disagreeable consequences', and buttressed his arguments by declaring that their 'socialist hosts' were entitled to demand 'a friendly attitude' on their part. After this, especially on arrival at a language school in Dobruska, the Somalis found themselves under suspicion and many irritating restrictions were placed on their personal freedom. Letters from home were opened and read before being handed to them and telegrams were often kept back for days before they received them—already opened. It was impossible for them to acquire any objective sources of information. The only newspapers they were allowed to see were those published behind the Iron Curtain or by communist parties abroad. All other Press material was confiscated before it reached them. Outside the institute, the students became aware of various forms of restriction and discrimination, all in flagrant contradiction to communist propaganda. They were not allowed to leave the Dobruska district without special permission. They also found that ordinary Czechs tended to avoid them, doubtless fearing the attentions of the secret police if they established contact with the Somalis. Even in dance halls and restaurants they found themselves cold-shouldered. Finally, they were made to suffer for their religious beliefs. They were ridiculed for upholding their religious observances and sometimes they were deliberately served with pork, although other kinds of meat were available and those responsible were well aware that Muslims are forbidden to eat pork. In the end, things got so bad that they decided to leave the country, but this they found far from easy and they had to suffer protracted and tiresome delays before they were finally able to obtain their exit permits. They stayed in Prague during this time and were kept under constant surveillance by relays of plain-clothes police. They were also made to endure continual chicanery: for example, they were unable to get hotel rooms and they had to spend the bitterly cold nights in the open.[19]

To what extent are such experiences typical? And do those who nevertheless persist to the end in their training behind the Iron Curtain—perhaps despite misgivings—share the disappointment of those who abandoned their studies, returned home and broke with communism? Or are these students who have returned home disappointed and discontented exceptions compared with the majority of coloured students behind the Iron Curtain? And are the latter content with their lot and perhaps even enthusiastic about their hosts? There are, of course, a few malcontents among the coloured students at Western universities too, though we know that they are exceptions.

Thus caution is advisable before coming to any final conclusions. In almost all cases where coloured students left, or were compelled to leave, training centres in Soviet-bloc countries, the associations of coloured students studying there adopted resolutions criticizing and denouncing them. This was the case with Richard Amar and with the six Somali students and with those who left Bulgaria in 1963 or the Soviet Union after the heavy clashes in December 1963. They were approached by other Africans, who sought to influence them and dissuade them from returning home prematurely.

Despite the mass demonstrations of African students in Moscow in December 1963, it seems that those Africans who go behind the Iron Curtain to study and are disappointed with what they find are in the minority, and there is much evidence to suggest that most of the African students behind the Iron Curtain are inclined—at least at first—to see advantages in the communist system. In fact, they are often fascinated by communism. The scale of the communist scholarship-grants programme and the intense propaganda that accompanies it have not failed to make a profound impression.

In particular, it would be foolish not to acknowledge the favourable reception given to Khrushchev's announcement, on 21 February 1960, that the Soviet Government intended to establish a great Friendship University (now named after Patrice Lumumba) and that after a short period it would be open to 4,000 coloured students. As soon as it was announced that the first 750 places were ready to be filled, no fewer than 43,500 applications poured in.[20] In short, the revelations of Amar and his friends have clearly not affected the flood of applicants, most of them from Africa, according to Moscow Press reports. Indeed, the Soviet authorities seem to attach particular importance to wooing coloured students, and during the first year 190 students were accepted from Africa, 145 from Asia and 130 from Latin America, so that Africa provides the biggest contingent.[21]

A number of points in connection with the founding of this new university deserve close attention:

1. Although Khrushchev and the Soviet Government were the first to announce the establishment of the new university (*Pravda*, 28 March 1960), Moscow still maintains the fiction that it is not a government institution and that it is being run primarily by the Afro-Asian Solidarity Committee, the Soviet labour unions, the Communist Committee, and the Communist Youth. These organizations, and not the Soviet Government, are said to have appointed the first Rector (S.W. Rumyantzev, formerly Deputy Minister for Soviet High Schools), chosen the university council and laid down arrangements for accepting students. *Pravda* has repeatedly stressed that the authorities will restrict their role in connection with the new university to providing quarters for the students, building laboratories and so on. This unusual—and patently hypocritical—attitude is intended to disguise the real state of affairs. Although Moscow Radio and Soviet propaganda publications instruct candidates to make their applications through their local Soviet embassies, the Russian authorities are able to disclaim all responsibility to the governments of the countries from which the students come. In this way they are able to side-step those governments with which they have cultural and educational agreements, and which would otherwise have a say in the choice of the students accepted for training.

2. The university has another important object in view, according to A. Sofronov, the Russian secretary of the Afro-Asian Solidarity Committee. It appears from his article that most of the students are to be recruited from strata of society from which youngsters would ordinarily find it impossible to attend 'capitalist high schools' abroad. This means an extension to other countries of the class educational monopoly as it exists in the countries of the Soviet bloc and the establishment of a monopoly for the education of the so-called 'workers' and peasants' children'. The communists hope that

when such students have completed their studies they will 'remain loyal to their class'. Thus Moscow intends to accept only applicants who are likely to serve the cause of communism in the African 'class struggle', as a result of their Soviet training and indoctrination.

3. The Russians have repeatedly sought to discount misgivings expressed in neutral countries that a course of study in the Soviet Union must automatically result in ideological indoctrination. At the opening of the university Khrushchev made a point of rejecting all responsibility for any 'cases of infection with that fashionable disease communism'. But it is quite clear that the spread of this disease is precisely what he and the university are aiming at. The students have to spend the whole period of their study in the Soviet Union—from three to four years. In addition there is the pre-liminary language instruction, and this takes a year. Furthermore, the university has not restricted applications to students who have already had a high-school education and are therefore ready for university training: it also takes younger students who need a period of 'preparatory training', and this will take another year or two. So that when one remembers that each student will spend between four and six years in the Soviet Union, out of touch with the non-communist world except by mail, and constantly influenced by Soviet newspapers, broadcasts and films, it is not difficult to imagine the ultimate effect of such surroundings and their direct and indirect indoctrination. It would be an illusion to suppose that all the graduates of the Friendship University will return to their own countries as diehard anti-communists, or disappointed and sobered. It is hardly to be expected that the Russians will abandon their practice of personal regimentation for the sake of a few thousand coloured students who may be embarrassed by it.

However, we can learn all we need to know from the Rector of the Friendship University himself. Writing in *Problems of Peace and Socialism*, Professor Rumyantsev says that there are six faculties in his university: economics, engineering, agriculture, medicine, history and philosophy, and international law. This sounds harmless enough, but he then goes on to stress the essential connection between study and 'social life' and quotes Lenin as having said that the under-developed countries must be helped in three ways: 'to go over to the use of machines, to lighten their labour, and to go forward to democracy and socialism.'[22]

Meanwhile, the many reports on the progress of the Friendship University all indicate the great importance the Soviet Government attaches to this educational institution. When the preliminary stage was completed the Rector had a staff of almost a thousand at his disposal, including 250 teachers of Russian. In addition there were a large number of full-time professors and over 700 younger lecturers; thus at the end of its first stage, the university had about 1,500 students, and there were two professors, lecturers or teachers for every three students—a proportion likely to be maintained as the university develops.[23]

Since its foundation the Friendship University has served as an example for similar foundations in a number of other countries of the Soviet bloc. In 1961 the University of 17 November was founded in Prague with four faculties: teachers' training, engineering, agronomy, and building.[24] In the following year 654 new students were enrolled.[25] The Polish Government also plans to concentrate all students from Asia, Africa, and Latin America in a single university. At the beginning of 1962 there were no fewer than 900 Africans studying in Poland on Patrice Lumumba scholarships.[26] And for a long time Leipzig has been the East German centre for training Asian and African students.

Since 1961 this cadre training has been supplemented by a new form of 'cadre export' to Africa from the countries of the Soviet bloc: one of the provisions of the so-called cultural agreements between many African States and the communist countries is that teachers should be sent to Africa from behind the Iron Curtain. As a case in point, the cultural agreement signed between the Soviet and Mali Governments in Bamako in February 1962 expressly provides for teachers from the Soviet Union to be sent to Mali. These Soviet educationalists will lecture on the Soviet system of higher and secondary education and the Bauman Higher Technical School in Moscow will assist the Technical Lycée in Bamako to arrange its curriculum.[27] From another source we learn that Czech experts have drafted a plan for a network of general and specialized schools in Mali and Somalia and that Czechoslovakia will provide the necessary text-books and help with the buildings and the supply of teachers.[28] These are only a few of many examples illustrating increased activity in the training of pro-communist cadres in Africa. For the sake of completeness we should not omit to mention communist broadcast propaganda which, where Africa is concerned, is concentrating more on educational and pseudo-educational 'lessons'—broadcasts for teaching Russian with illustrations taken from Soviet educational procedure, broadcasts from East Germany, and so on—not forgetting the broadcasts from Red China.

Naturally, these ambitious Soviet plans have not passed unnoticed in the West, but the general view is that it would be foolish to exaggerate either the extent or effect of these operations. After all, year after year thousands of Asians and Africans still come to the West for both university education and technological training. There are more Africans studying in France than in all the countries of the Soviet bloc together. But these reassuring arguments miss the core of the problem and they reveal a disturbing ignorance of communist propaganda techniques. All the West offers these Asian and African students is objective education and scientific training, and it does not make this easier for them by providing adequate grants. Apart from such education and training, the young student from Asia or Africa is left largely to his own devices. At best, he will strive to fit himself into the individualistic pattern of Western society and come to adopt similarly individualistic ideas and behaviour patterns. But in the Western world ideological factors play a minor role, and generally speaking there will be no specific attempt to mould his views in any particular direction—though admittedly the general environment of bourgeois democracy may be regarded as a factor tending to inculcate a certain ideology in the student. Socially and politically, the whole Western high-school system and environment tend in the last resort to result in intense individualism. The African who studies medicine at Oxford or Harvard will probably become a good doctor, but very little will be done to encourage him to take any particular social and political line outside his practice. On the other hand, the activity of communist student groups in Paris, which have many African members, suggests that the African student is inclined to counter the threat of excessive individualization and satisfy his instinctive objection to the antisocial environment of the West by turning to left-wing radical groups. At least they offer him an attachment and a 'solution'.

In the countries of the Soviet bloc, the communists do their best to persuade the student to regard his scientific training and his work as only one side of his 'service to the community'; and they often succeed. According to communist calculations, when the African doctor trained in Moscow or Prague returns to his own country he will be something more than a doctor; he will be an 'agent' (in the strictest sense of the word). He will not regard it as his task merely to heal his patients physically, he will also try to heal them ideologically. At best, from the communist standpoint, foreign students who have been trained in the Soviet bloc will return to their own countries as 'missionaries' and agents of a world-wide ideological movement with a 'historical task' to perform. Whether they know it or not they will have become communist cadres in their own countries.

This picture is, of course, over-simplified. The reality, both in the West and in the East, is far more complicated—as shown by the example of many Africans who fled from Eastern Europe. However, the really dangerous omission at the moment is the lack of any systematic élite programme by the West in an effort to give its Afro-Asian students something more than an objective education or scientific training, in order to counterbalance the systematic, large-scale and effective programme being operated behind the Iron Curtain. The plans of the communist universities in Tashkent, Moscow, Prague and Budapest are a clear warning. They may differ slightly in detail, but they are at one in their fundamental objective based on the Stalin principle, 'It's the cadres that count!'

NOTES

[1] Karl Marx and Frederick Engels, *Communist Manifesto* (London, 1934).

[2] B. Gukhman, *The Size of the Proletariat and Wages in the USSR* (Moscow, 1926); cited by Solomon M. Schwartz in *Labor in the Soviet Union* (New York, 1951), p. 6.

[3] According to a statistical table drawn by A. Bubnov for the *Great Soviet Encyclopaedia* (Moscow, 1930); cited by Merle Fainsod in *How Russia Is Ruled* (Cambridge, Mass., 1953), p. 60.

[4] Lenin, '*Chto delat?*' Sochineniya IV, p. 452.

[5] Stefan T. Possony, *A Century of Conflict: Communist Techniques of World Revolution* (Chicago, 1953), pp. 350-1.

[6] *Ostprobleme*, II, No. 50 (December 1950).

[7] *Pravda*, 22 May 1925.

[8] Ibid.

[9] Ibid.

[10] *Ostprobleme*, VII, No. 39 (September 1955), p. 1505.

[11] Information given to the author by a communist official who fled from East Germany.

[12] *Die Weltgewerkschaftsbewegung*, November 1959.

[13] *Le Monde*, 18 July 1960.

[14] The *Guardian*, 11 October 1961.

[15] Radio Accra broadcast, 10 October 1961.

[16] *Neue Zürcher Zeitung*, 6 and 12 December 1960.

[17] Ibid.

[18] *East Europe*, IX, No. 12 (December 1960), p. 48.

[19] *Forum Service* (London), No. 461 (February 1962).

[20] *Pravda*, 17 November 1960.

[21] *Politika*, 5 November 1960.

[22] *World Marxist Review: Problems of Peace and Socialism*, III, No. 8 (August 1960), p. 86.

[23] *Neue Zürcher Zeitung*, 23 January 1962.

[24] The *Ethiopian Herald*, 23 January 1961.

[25] CTK, 16 and 19 February 1962.

[26] Warsaw Radio broadcast, 21 February 1962.

[27] Tass, 16 February 1962.

[28] The *Ethiopian Herald*, 23 January 1962.

Chapter XVII

SOME CONCLUSIONS

HARDLY a month goes by without newspaper headlines proclaiming some dramatic new event in Africa. The revolution of this continent has, in fact, become one of the main themes of our time and is likely to remain so for many years to come. But although the West is unamimous in agreeing on the importance of this revolution, views differ widely when it comes to judging the motives behind it and the results which are likely to emerge. Has the West any chance in Africa? Can African nationalism take its place as an independent force in a new system of international relationships between West and East? How far does communist influence in Africa already extend? Is communism a real danger in Africa today, is it likely to engulf the African continent and turn it into a new geo-political base for its struggle for world power? Western views on these and other points are often diametrically opposed and it is difficult to arrive at any objective conclusion because the debate is so often dominated by two extreme attitudes.

One group declares that African nationalism is nothing but a cover for communism and that one should look for the real wire-pullers not in Cairo, Accra or Leopoldville, but in Moscow, Peking, and Prague. This group would have us believe that the Red dominion over the black thrones has already taken place. The conclusion we are asked to draw from this presents us with dangerous alternatives: either the West should defend its remaining positions in Africa to the bitter end and with all possible means, including the use of brute force, or it should leave the field to the 'Bolshies and the Niggers'. The main upholders of this stark, unimaginative attitude are the former Algerian ultras, the colonial officers of Portugal, and the *apartheid* fanatics of Pretoria and Salisbury—people who are anxious to force the West into 'colonial solidarity' with them, thus buttressing their own weak positions.

The other extreme group consists of the one-eyed or politically blind, who have long assured us that 'communist aggression' is largely an invention of the West to discredit and halt 'progress'. They regard warnings against communist activities as political hysteria and attempt to examine this running sore of our times and diagnose the creeping communist infection as McCarthyism and a conspiracy on the part of 'the right' to destroy 'progress'. The gist of their argument is that the West should regard the hostile policy of radical African nationalism as a 'natural reaction' to its own centuries-long system of colonial oppression and make no attempt to counter it. Instead of examining colonial history objectively and acknowledging the long tale of slave-trading, slaughter and repression, they prefer to accept the anti-Western outbursts of black extremists—a mixture of practical calculation and emotion—at face value. The bad conscience from which these intellectual worshippers of progress suffer at the thought that they themselves are part of the 'gang of exploiters' (part of the West, which has in their view been 'poisoned by colonialism') leads them to over-compensate for their feelings by a rather touching but pathological Negrophilia which draws sustenance from artificial pictures of both the 'wicked white' and the 'good Negro'. And they do just as much damage as the other extremists with their Negrophobia.

The psychological interaction between these two extremist groups goes even further: the louder the one shouts 'Hosannah!', the louder the other shouts 'Crucify him!'. The more incredible the arguments of one side, the more credible—temporarily at least—become the arguments of the other. All this would not matter very much but for the fact that the whole discussion on Africa in the West is being constantly distorted by these radical and ultra-radical poles. If only we could free our minds from the whirlpool of prejudices, self-deception, ideologies and baseless illusions and analyse the situation objectively, instead of allowing ourselves to be sidetracked by wishful thinking and a self-destructive '*peccavi*'.

Before this can be done, the West will have to eschew these isolated notions of the situation and make an objective analysis of African nationalism, of the success achieved by the communists and of its own present and future role in Africa. It is the interrelation of these three factors which determines the present and will determine the future of Africa. The fate of the continent does not lie entirely in the hands of the Africans themselves; to a great extent it will be determined by the East and the West. In the same way, the successes of communism are not exclusively due to communist activity and initiative, but to the willingness of Africans to adopt communist slogans, plus the failures and mistakes of the West. Finally the strength or weakness of the West in Africa will depend on whether it is able to overcome its own failings and find a constructive answer to the challenge of present-day Africa and to the destructive provocation of communism, which will not be defeated in Africa by conventional means.

African nationalism, communist activities, and the position of the West—let us consider once again the interaction and some specific characteristics of these three factors before drawing conclusions.

First, African nationalism: its present strength derives primarily from the fact that it has succeeded in attaining its original aim—the liquidation of colonialism and the achievement of political independence—in an extraordinarily short time, so short that historically it is hardly measurable. But here lies its innate weakness and the source of its enormous difficulties and present complicated disputes. Africans were prepared for a long struggle to attain sovereignty; instead, victory fell into their laps before they had a chance to consider, even theoretically, the complicated internal and external problems of government. It was not difficult to mobilize the African élite *against* something and occasionally it was even possible to mobilize the lethargic African masses against colonialism. But what now? What constructive slogans and objectives are best calculated to attract them after independence has been won? What constructive programme is best calculated to hold the élite together? But before these questions can be answered, others are piling up and they all demand a speedy answer. The nationalist leadership of the new African States finds itself faced with a disrupting and disintegrating social and economic situation. For the first time the African leaders are beginning to realize the full magnitude of the problems they are up against: lack of an internal market, of capital, and of industrial plant. They are saddled with the single-crop cultivation that was in the best interests of colonialism but which does not accord with their present interests and involves them in the growing raw-material crisis on the world market. This crisis hits Africa particularly hard because it occasions a constant fluctuation of raw-material prices. And this is only a part of the urgent economic problems facing them. Even more dangerous is the social unrest which is spreading over the whole continent. The ancient harmony and integration of African tribal society has been violently disrupted, and in some places destroyed, by the break-through of European standards and values, the emergence of an anti-traditionalist élite, and the general and increasing Westernization of African life. The more profoundly this process of dissolution affects African society the more rapid becomes the process of social differentiation. Once homogeneous groups and associations begin to split up, minority groups aggressively press forward their own special interests; and radical and ultra-radical slogans are adopted. During the era of colonialism it was relatively easy for the young nationalist movement to place the responsibility for growing economic and social conflict on the broad shoulders of whatever foreign régime was involved; and in so doing it greatly strengthened its own psychological basis and appeal. But now Africans must tackle these problems for themselves. It is no longer colonialism but African nationalism which has the task of working out solutions and making them acceptable to those directly concerned.

But the fact is, whoever talks to leading African nationalists, or reads their speeches and writings, soon discovers that they are in deep perplexity and do not know what to do. Most of them have some general ideas about the difficulties and the requirements of their countries, but their plans do not add up to a coherent programme based on any specifically African conceptions. To say this is not to reproach them or to gloat over their condition. Their perplexity is general, even a man like Sékou Touré, a leading apologist of black nationalism, has little more than a collection of slogans and generalities to offer—which is not much good when it comes to dealing with harsh realities. Time is pressing! In almost all the independent States opposition groups are forming, recruited from among the sullen and dissatisfied people who expected too much from their leaders, people who were passed over in the distribution of privileges and are now disappointed. In Ghana, opposition liberals are putting every possible pressure on Kwame Nkrumah to adopt a programme of European liberalism; the conservatives would like to see the power and authority of the tribal chiefs restored; while the National Association of Socialist Student Organizations (NASSO), or the weekly *Spark*, whose influence is steadily increasing, demand the complete nationalization of the economy and a total, Marxist-inspired, over-all plan for economic and social development. A similar process, different only in degree and local conditions, is taking place in other African States. In East Africa, arguments about economic and social ideas were vehement even before independence was achieved, as internal dissensions in Kenya, Uganda, and Tanzania clearly showed. The crisis in January 1964 did not come as a surprise. Almost everywhere, the leaders of the anti-colonial struggle are now beginning to find their prestige and power seriously threatened; in some African countries there is a masked antipathy to deliberation and discussion and this contributes to the progressive poisoning of the political atmosphere. (In 1963 alone, no fewer than seven of the twelve countries belonging to the *Union Africaine et Malgache* (now OCAM) were involved in serious internal upheavals.)

The way of escape from this situation which the new masters of the African continent are choosing is one which is tragic for Africa and a threat to the West. Freedom from outside rule has been won, but now the African leaders are, almost without exception, turning against the internal freedom of the African people, while simultaneously inveighing in a new emotional outburst against the alleged neo-colonialism of the West. Many reasons are being put forward to explain this rejection of democracy and the establishment of dictatorial or semi-authoritarian régimes, and they cannot all be dismissed as being groundless. It is, of course, perfectly true that early African society knew little about democratic forms and techniques and the undemocratic ways of the various colonial administrations were hardly calculated to create confidence in the democratic principles of the West. However, the contention of many Africans that the short history of African independence has already exposed democracy as a destructive system rings hollow and suspect. With smug indignation, the new African dictators justify this attitude by pointing to the Congo. But the Congo exposes the falsity of this attitude; the confusion and chaos there were due not only to a failure of democracy, but to the fact that the party of Patrice

Lumumba (which certainly secured no mandate at the elections) sought to impose its policy on the country in defiance of the most elementary democratic principles.

Unlike his allies in Ghana, Guinea, and Mali, Lumumba let his real intentions be seen only incidentally and fortuitously. For example, in March 1960, Madeira Keita, Bamako's Minister of the Interior, wrote in the periodical *Présence Africaine* that in the circumstances a strong central administration was necessary because regional and tribal dissensions had to be suppressed with a firm hand. Authoritarianism was therefore preferable to Western-type democracy. Keita went on to argue that differences over the functions and tasks of the administration, which would justify the existence of opposition groups, were simply unthinkable in the young African States. Everyone, he insisted, had the same high aims and ideals, and, as time was pressing and the great problems which faced them had to be swiftly settled, the new African States could not afford 'a ministerial crisis every six months or so'.

No one can expect the young African States to become carbon copies of Western democracies, which are not in any case always ideal themselves. No one expects the new African rulers not to govern firmly in a difficult situation, or to undermine their own position by showing excessive consideration to every opposition tendency—provided, however, that their régime is amenable to reasonable influence in tackling its problems and that freedom of discussion is constitutionally safeguarded. Certainly one can readily imagine moments of crisis when it might become necessary to introduce moderate and reasonable restrictions on democratic liberties. Despite misgivings, one could hardly deny President Olympio of Togo (who was murdered in 1963) the right to introduce a one-party régime in April 1961 and to establish certain special presidential rights, as his small country was under heavy pressure from its more powerful neighbour Ghana, an expansionist State. But the situation is very different when Kwame Nkrumah, relying on his all-powerful State party, arrests the last minor leaders and supporters of the crushed and impotent opposition party and thrusts them into concentration camps for an indefinite period without trial. Or where they are tortured to death as happened to the 'Grand Old Man' of Ghanaian nationalism, J. B. Danquah, in February 1965.

In each case the suppression of the opposition, the restriction of fundamental human rights, and the general advance towards authoritarianism represent the disruption of the national unity achieved in the anti-colonialist struggle—although those responsible still praise this national unity *ad nauseam*. The techniques of dictatorial rule poison the political atmosphere, arouse resentment, and lead to a strengthening of extremist forces. In this connection one should remember and be clear about two things: (1) communism unquestionably has a highly developed technique of opposition and underground struggle at its disposal and the means to infiltrate. If the communists succeed in influencing and winning over the opposition groups in the right-wing African States, then sooner or later we shall see the formation of a pro-communist united front reaching from the left-wing ruling groups in some West African countries to the opposition forces of large sections of the liberal and right-wing elements in Africa. (2) The right-wing dictatorial régimes in Africa have no really effective power behind them, as was demonstrated by the revolt against Abbé Youlou in Brazzaville in August 1963. There is hardly a single African State today which has a numerically strong, well-trained, well-equipped and efficient army on which the régime could rely with confidence in times of acute trouble. The successor States of the French *Communauté*, which have military arrangements with France, could call on Paris to aid them in times of trouble, but what happened in Gabon in February 1964, when French troops intervened in a *coup d'état* in favour of the régime, shows the serious psychological difficulties involved in such appeals to the former colonial power for military assistance. The presence of French troops on Gabon territory has driven into opposition even those groups who were formerly loyal to the Government. At the same time, the civil service, which has been the last bulwark against anarchy and chaos for many countries in Asia, the Near East, and Latin America, is still too weak, inexperienced and heterogeneous, to play that saving role in Africa, and in consequence it is no more reliable than the army.

One or two of the right-wing African dictatorships already have some conception of the difficulties and dangers involved in the political structure they have adopted. The radical agitation of their oppositions (all more or less violently repressed) is carried on with all the standard theses of communist propaganda, and this results in growing popular unrest, which is constantly intensified by attacks from extreme nationalist and left-wing countries outside. The reproaches and attacks culminate in the argument that although political independence has been won there has been no fundamental change in the economic and social policy of the new State. The situation of the masses of the people has not improved; on the contrary, owing to the absence of foreign capital investments and credits, constant fluctuations on the raw-material markets, and the increase in prices and taxation that these involve, it has grown steadily worse. Further, the 'reactionary' governments of Africa still have as their foreign advisers the very same men who before independence played the role of colonial masters; and finally, the economic power of colonialism is still unbroken. These governments are accused of being 'puppet governments' and every new economic agreement with the former colonial power is taken as further evidence in support of the opposition charge that the change of administration has been more apparent than real, and that the sovereignty of the new African States under such reactionary government is a sham. The opposition loudly insists that such decolonization is nothing more than an 'imperialist trick'. At the same time any delay by a government in establishing diplomatic relations with the Soviet bloc, the failure to encourage trading relations with the countries of the socialist camp and the absence of any cultural agreements with the Kremlin are all cited by the opposition as evidence of an un-African foreign policy serving the interests of the imperialist camp. These accusations are not confined to the pro-communist opponents of such African governments.

What is the result? 1. A political minority denigrates the new régime, denounces it as 'dishonest', 'treacherous' and 'incompetent', and claims for itself alone the true custodianship of sincere and uncompromising nationalism. 2. Naturally when attacked in this way governments do their best to defend themselves, and a number of right-wing African régimes have endeavoured to increase their popularity by outdoing the opposition with even more radical nationalistic slogans. Cautiously, some of these régimes are taking up certain demands of the opposition and trying to satisfy them. The best example of this can be seen in Nigeria where, especially since the electoral farce in 1964, the régime is constantly under attack from its radical opposition, trade unions, and various youth and student organizations. In order to reduce this pressure, the Lagos régime established diplomatic relations with nearly all the communist countries including Red China. Furthermore, the Nigerian Government was the only African administration that responded to the third French nuclear test in the Sahara by breaking off diplomatic relations with France. The premier saw no other way of rebutting the charge that his cabinet was deliberately delaying the 'Nigerianization' of the administration than by making concessions to the opposition, and it is a fact that since then the agitation of the opposition (which is supported by Ghana and the countries of the Soviet bloc) has lost a good deal of its sting. On the other hand, even the Nigerian Government is now gradually adopting a policy of 'neutrality' and professing to struggle against 'neo-colonialist intrigues'—the sort of thing which in practice favours the left. Developments in this direction have already gone so far that one wonders what further concessions the Nigerian Government will make to the opposition if its internal and external enemies put on the pressure again.

The communists are observing this trend with unconcealed satisfaction, as their Africa propaganda quite clearly reveals. The helplessness and perplexity of the Africans in the face of their economic and social difficulties, and the growing tendency towards disruption in the nationalist movement itself, confirms the communists in their belief that African nationalism is essentially a transitional phase, a part of the inevitable historical process which must finally lead to socialism. The communist position in Africa is greatly strengthened by a number of other factors, and in particular by the psychologically important fact that communism had nothing to do with the clash between black and white which led to the present upheaval in Africa. Communism has always, in its propaganda at least, been on the side of the black élite. In the Trusteeship Commission of the United Nations, for example, the Soviet Union exceeded all other Powers in the vigour of its demands for the release of the mandated areas from European control. Another great advantage for the communists is that Africans came into touch with communism relatively late and at a time when Stalinism, with its terrorism, had already undergone modifications. Apart from the Arab Northern region and South Africa, which were in any case always isolated from the rest of Africa, there was not a communist party anywhere south of the Sahara until the early 1960s. In consequence, the Africans never had the salutary experience of witnessing the wrigglings of a political body completely dependent on Kremlin orders and subject to brutal purges and fierce campaigns of 'self-criticism', initiated and controlled from outside. Today communism is able to present itself in Africa as the opposite of its old traditional image of a bloodthirsty, oppressive and fanatical organization, bent on securing power at all costs. For Africans, Soviet-communism is first of all a mighty international bloc led by the Soviet Union, which is the biggest counterblast to the highly industrialized West. Furthermore, in an extraordinarily short space of time the Soviet Union has performed economic and technical miracles, including sending up the first *sputnik*, the first *lunik*, and the first manned space-ship. In African eyes, the mere existence of this powerful State did much to force the West to abandon its colonial policy and give Africa its independence. *This* is the communism the Africans know—a tremendous concentration of power, progress and moral force.

Naturally the communist countries do their utmost to consolidate and strengthen this favourable interpretation, using all the powerful propaganda at their disposal—broadcasts, written propaganda, invitations, cultural festivals, and so on—to underline their self-styled role as unselfish friends and helpers of all Africans. The never-ending spate of pro-African declarations, which are an essential part of this propaganda, seek to persuade the Africans that communism has no expansionist plans in Africa, since it has sufficient room for expansion within its own frontiers, and that—unlike the West—it does not depend on Africa's great natural resources, since the Soviet bloc has its own enormous deposits of uranium, cobalt, ores and so on. Moreover, it claims to be in favour of total and unconditional international disarmament and the political neutralization of Africa, whereas the West still maintains a large number of military establishments and bases on African soil and has concluded defence and military-aid agreements with a number of African countries. Communism also claims, though with rather less cogency, that it upholds the right of self-determination for all peoples everywhere in the world, whereas the United States organized and financed the invasion of Cuba, France and Great

Britain went to war over Suez, and Portugal, a NATO member, carries on a ruthless campaign of extermination in Angola against a people longing for its liberty.

The economic, social and political techniques of communism are particularly attractive to Africans. The solutions proposed by the West for Africa's difficulties are rejected by many Africans either instinctively, as 'colonial' or 'neo-colonial' deceptions, or as impracticable, whereas communism appears to them as the practical and useful model to overcome their acute economic and social misery. After all, forty years ago Russia itself was as little developed as are many African States today. While after their victory over 'the feudal régime of the Chiang Kai-shek clique and the camouflaged colonialism of the United States', the Chinese had found themselves faced with difficulties similar to those the Africans are facing today. And how quickly and progressively the Russians and the Chinese developed their countries and consolidated the power of the revolutionary groups!

This is the glowing picture presented by communist propaganda in hours of daily broadcasting in English, French, Portuguese, Arabic, and Swahili. Meanwhile most of the naïve African visitors to the countries of the Soviet bloc come back confirming much of this and (since no other solution promises rapid success and any attempt to co-operate with the imperialist West would compromise them) they are prepared to use communist know-how and to try communist methods to tackle the economic, social, and political problems of Africa. This means, in effect, the establishment of an authoritarian, one-party State with a hierarchic structure of command and obedience, the quickest possible methods of industrialization based on concentration of labour, and the complete control of labour for 'collective social uses'. The Africans do not realize how great the risk is, because not only do the Chinese, the Russians, the Czechs, and the leaders of all the other communist States promise them material and personnel assistance, but they guarantee the automatic success of the experiment. The proposition is made even more attractive because certain of the communist assumptions are in complete harmony with the ideas and the desires of the African élite.

We know that communism is something more, and something very much more dangerous, than the idealized and harmless image cooked up by communists for the benefit of Africans and accepted by many at its face value. *We* know, but they do not, that communism is a highly developed compound of promises, of dogmatic interpretation of the past and the present, and the incarnation of Machiavellianism: a gigantic power-political compound that subordinates all its measures, pronouncements, and plans to the one aim of securing total dominance of the whole world. The proclamation of the policy of co-existence with ideological infiltration, the support of feudal régime and the creation of a revolutionary élite to overthrow it; Peking's open and aggressive attitude to the national bourgeoisie and Moscow's readiness to conclude a temporary fraternal alliance with this same group; the granting of credits and the acceptance of an unfavourable balance of trade with the new States of Africa; the game of hide-and-seek in the front organizations and at the same time the arming, equipping and training of cadre troops for jungle warfare in Cameroon, the Congo, and Angola —all these are but variations on the same basic theme—power. For communism in Africa, the greatest advantage, which it does its best to consolidate and extend, lies in the fact that this power complex and the imminent danger it represents to the whole African continent is as yet hardly discerned. Almost without exception African nationalists harbour the illusion that the negative and unfavourable phenomena they do recognize can be readily dealt with as long as there are no official communist parties in existence.

Fortunately there are limits to what the communists can realistically hope for in Africa. In the first phase of their operations, the Russians, in particular, made glaring mistakes: (a) They overestimated their strength and popularity among the Africans and relied too much on the widespread but superficial identity of their slogans with those of the Africans. (b) They underestimated the Africans, misjudged them and often found themselves backing the wrong horse. The difficulties in which they became entangled were especially obvious in Guinea and the Congo. I am of the opinion that the Russians had such a flying start in Guinea in 1959–60 that with a little adroitness, tact, and economic aid on a really effective scale, they could have turned Sékou Touré into an African Castro and Guinea into an African Cuba. They failed because they omitted to make proper allowance for the natural dignity of a man like Sékou Touré, (which, to some extent, they also did with Castro), because they talked about aid instead of giving it effectively, and because what they really wanted was an African satellite, not an African ally. If they had treated Touré as a real comrade on an equal footing and had conceded him the right to make his own national way towards socialism they would be in a much better position in Guinea than they are today.

They behaved even more foolishly in the Congo. Thanks to their clumsy tactics—which might not have mattered had well-trained communist cadres existed in the territory—they played right into the hands of the United Nations and the United States. Thus the whole edifice of their Congolese propaganda collapsed like a pack of cards as soon as Americans and the United Nations seriously tackled the problem of Katanga separation. In February 1963 the communists did secure the adoption of a resolution by the third Afro-Asian Solidarity Conference criticizing the Congo policy of the United States and the United Nations. But by that time it was too late to remedy the situation and the fiasco of Russia's Congo policy was obvious to everyone in Africa.

It was certainly clear by this time that the communists erred in thinking that nationalism in the new Africa would be easy game for them. One of the chief reasons for their error is the egocentricity, common to communist leaders, who draw conclusions from themselves to others and firmly believe that they have a theory which will explain anything anywhere in the world. They fail to realize that the Africans they are wooing, including those who appear to be willing to come to terms with them, are people with a variety of different mentalities. Instead of trying to understand this, they too readily assume that the obvious willingness of many Africans to go part of the way with them means that they are ready to go all the way and take over orthodox Marxist-Leninist philosophy *in toto*.

This misconception dates back to the early 1920s, when the first contacts were established between African nationalists and communists. Even in those days African students were privileged guests at communist meetings and demonstrations in France, Britain and the United States. They served to underline the internationalism of the communist parties of those countries. In the meantime, however, the communist parties of Great Britain and France, who had been given the task of carrying out the instructions on Africa of the Second Congress of the Communist International, made little or no progress and finally landed in a blind alley, because of the natural contradiction between communism and British and French nationalism. The attitude of the communist parties of Great Britain and France to the colonies' struggle for liberation was far from clear. Speaking at the Fifth Congress of the Communist International on 30 June 1924, Manuilski observed reproachfully:

'About a year ago the Communist International directed an appeal to the colonial slaves to rise in revolt against their masters. When a copy of this appeal got as far as one of the branches of the French Communist Party—Sidi bel Abbès in Algeria—the branch actually adopted a resolution condemning the attitude of the Communist International . . . I will also take the liberty of asking the French comrades what documents they can produce to show that the French Communist Party has very clearly demanded in the hearing of the whole world that the colonial countries should be given their freedom . . . Our British comrades have earned just as serious a reproach for their passivity in this same matter . . . In none of the documents that have come to our notice concerning the British Communist Party's attitude to the colonies do we find one single clear and definite statement that our British comrades are uncomprisingly in favour of the separation of the colonies from the British Empire.'[1]

Even in 1947, Maurice Thorez was talking at the Eleventh Congress of the French Communist Party in ambiguous terms about the policy of the French communists towards the colonies; both he and Etienne Fajon described the *Union Française*—the policy of a French assimilation of the colonial peoples—as 'the most favourable framework' for the activities of the overseas territories.[2]

In such circumstances even those Africans who had at first felt drawn towards communism were repulsed instead of being won over. The result was evident in French-speaking Africa in the collapse of the *Rassemblement Démocratique Africain* in 1950, though there were certainly other, deeper-lying reasons for what happened in the RDA. All in all, one can say that the secession of such prominent party men as Félix Houphouet-Boigny in the Ivory Coast and Gabriel d'Arboussier in Senegal was the result of profound emotional and psychological misgiving. Communism expected its African followers to rally unconditionally round the aims and actions of the metropolitan parties, but it refused to take into consideration the particular conditions, requirements, desires and longings of the Africans. Blindly the traditional class pattern of communism was transferred quite arbitrarily to African conditions. In strict logic, though in crass stupidity, all 'non-proletarian' Africans were condemned as 'secret lackeys of colonialism', even when they were clearly engaged in fighting against colonialism. Evidence of this is provided in *Narody Afriki* (*The Peoples of Africa*), published in Moscow in 1954. It roundly denounced Kwame Nkrumah and his Convention People's Party as 'a screen behind which the reality of British imperialist dominance is hidden'. Even as late as 1955 an official Soviet publication[3] declared: 'the anti-imperialist and anti-feudal revolution in Africa' can never be carried out in alliance with the national bourgeoisie 'but only on the basis of an alliance of the workers and peasants led by the communists'. Four years later the British communist, Idris Cox, finally had to admit that after the Second World War political independence has been won by India, Indonesia, Ghana and other countries under the leadership of their national bourgeoisies.[4] Thus, at first, communism largely ignored the genuine national movement in Africa, though it was obviously growing rapidly. The communist leaders also failed to understand that most of the Africans who were co-operating with them (especially those in the *Rassemblement Démocratique Africain*) were seeking association with them, not full commitment; they had their own ideas and were pursuing their own interests.

This attitude involved, and still involves, a very important reservation, a matter of principle which precludes any total commitment. In the past, many African politicians in close touch with radical continental socialism have drawn attention to this particular point, which is primarily of an ideological-religious nature. Sékou Touré put it pertinently to Fernand Gigon:

'In my view Marxism offers us important ideas concerning the history of mankind. Dialectical and philosophical materialism offers us a possibility of interpreting social and economic reality, but it involves the denial of the existence of God. Now nowhere in any African country, and particularly not in Guinea, will you find a single man or woman who does not believe in the existence of God.

Even if you find someone who tells you that he is a fetishist, or that he hasn't any religion, nevertheless he is a believer.'[5]

In a lecture entitled 'Ghana's Conception of Socialism', the Ghanaian politician, Kofi Baako, said much the same thing:

'I should like to draw your attention to the religious feelings of our people. No native of Ghana, or of any other African country, is an atheist. Deep down within him there are hidden spiritual forces which move him to honour the gods of his ancestors . . . No matter how educated or intelligent he may be, his whole being instinctively rejects the idea that the beginning and end of all life is in this world alone . . . It would therefore be well to bear in mind that no political ideology that fails to take these basic facts into account can be regarded as acceptable, and that if it is nevertheless imposed on the people it will lead to nothing but trouble and social revolt. You will therefore understand that the type of society we are trying to build in Ghana will be permanent and bring peace only if it takes the given conditions and traditions into account.'[6]

With this it is clear that the all-embracing monopoly claimed by communist ideology is breached at a most decisive point, and this often gives rise to serious conflict between orthodox communists and their African comrades. Students who have broken off their studies in the countries of the Soviet bloc and returned home are a living proof of this. Most of these men were Africans who were officials in communist groups or front organizations before going behind the Iron Curtain. One of them, who may serve as a typical example, is Mahdi Ismael of Somalia. He studied in Soviet-bloc countries for four years and for a while represented a radical Somali trade union there. At one time he was even a member of the Communist Party of Great Britain. One of the reasons for his breach with communism was, he explained, that 'communist officials think coldly and abstractly, and are quite unable to satisfy the spiritual needs of African students.' In Ismael's opinion, their contempt for religious feelings and their cold, calculated reasoning put them on a level with 'the representatives of the capitalist West, who are just as cold and unspiritual in their hunt for profits and who worship God without believing in Him.'[7]

Walter Kolarz, who has also analysed this phenomenon,[8] draws a parallel with certain forms of Asian communism when he writes: 'Like the Buddhist Marxist in Burma, the Afro-Asian Marxist has no use for Marxism as a universal materialist ideology dominating all aspects of life, as it is usually understood in Europe.'

Another and no less important factor is the quite different attitude of African socialists to the world situation. The upheaval brought about by the African struggle for liberation has not carried the African socialist beyond the confines of his own continent. He is interested only in Africa: Africa is the scene of his desires and the aim of his struggles and he is not particularly interested in an abstract world proletariat, which means very little to him; in fact he is completely in agreement with Kwame Nkrumah, who has replaced the slogan 'Workers of the World Unite!' by the slogan 'Peoples of Africa Unite!' This slogan embraces the peoples of all colonial territories and more often than not has a definitely racial tendency. For the African the world is not so much divided into capitalists and proletarians as into rich whites and poor blacks. Similarly, the ideal of many Africans is not an 'international of the toilers', but an 'international of the coloured peoples'. The Soviet leaders have now recognized this phenomenon and are doing their best to take it into account by making use of officials and experts from their own Asian republics in their African policy. Often, however, this has had much the same effect as the similar tactics of the US State Department in appointing coloured US citizens to diplomatic posts in Asia and Africa. The manœuvre met with little success because the motive behind it was too transparent.

Despite all this however, Africans are susceptible to the fascination of communism. Its attraction is powerful when there are obvious parallels with the situation in Africa—which means that it is less powerful where the Soviet Union and its European satellites are concerned and more powerful where China and Yugoslavia are concerned. It is obvious that Africans see very distinct differences between these three models and this approach to communism is taking place at a time when 'the Third Rome' has already lost a great deal of its prestige as the exclusive centre of world communism. One might say that the modern African has been born, politically, into a polycentric communist world which no longer offers only one way, but a number of quite different ways of socialist development.

The success of communism in Africa depends on the extent to which it can take these fundamental facts into consideration in its plans, thus giving itself the opportunity to operate unconventionally and we have given a number of examples that suggest that it now understands the situation, which it exploits with suppleness.

It will succeed all the more rapidly if the West persists in its failure to recognize the changed face of Africa and in harbouring illusions about its own potential there. The West has already suffered a heavy defeat in Africa and by this I do not mean the fact that it has abandoned, or been compelled to abandon, its former colonial territories. This was inevitable and foreseeable and was in any case welcome on moral grounds. The real defeat of the West lies in the fact that it did not encourage this development from the beginning, guiding it harmoniously and without violence or bloodshed; it lies also in the fact that the departure of the white man from Africa coincided with a profound shattering of confidence in him and in his way of life.

It is not the task of this book to write the history of colonialism and to list the benefits it brought to Africa and the crimes it committed in the name of Europe. Perhaps one day the science of history will be in a position to provide a sober, objective picture of the part-contact, part-collision which has taken place between Europe and Africa. But what must be exposed and explained here are the direct causes which led to the weakening of the Western position in Africa and facilitated the rise of extremists, radical, anti-European and anti-white movements, and which made communist infiltration so easy. We cannot afford to hide our heads in the sand and refuse to recognize that the popular attitude in present-day Africa is sharply anti-Western, and that many Africans regard communism as an attractive alternative to the political, economic, social, and moral principles of the Western world. This is a situation that must be faced.

The errors, omissions and failures of the African policy of the West can be summed up in five points:

1. Despite the repeatedly proclaimed moral principles of Western policy, the ultimate recognition of Africa's right to self-determination was not, in fact, a matter of moral principle but primarily a matter of political expediency. Even then, recognition was granted reluctantly and only under increasing pressure from black national-

ism, when the West was increasingly harassed by actual or threatened risings and when its position had become untenable in the face of a hostile public opinion. The demand for the right of self-determination for the nations of Eastern Europe and the refusal or restriction of this same right for the peoples of Africa made the representatives of the West appear as hypocrites and demagogues in African eyes. The tactics, adopted by the West, of making concessions only in answer to nationalist pressures, attacks and reproaches, instead of forestalling them by voluntary concessions in the first place, meant the surrender of the *moral initiative* to the African liberation movement and thus indirectly to the hypocritical forces, particularly communism, that supported it. The surrender, when it came, was the result of precipitate, panic-stricken decisions—as in the Belgian Congo, which was surrendered without a reasonable period of transition and planning and was abandoned to a sovereignty shaped by the centralist ideas of the local radicals.

2. The moral and material support granted by the West—though not uniformly—to France in the Algerian war, to the South African racial fanatics in their policy of *apartheid* and to the small, obstinate groups of white settlers in Kenya, Rhodesia and Nyasaland, grievously compromised the cause of the West as a whole, particularly since African nationalism, inspired and encouraged by the communists, deliberately exploited this attitude as a cardinal issue. Declarations by certain Western politicians that the fate of the Western world was at stake in Algeria, the invitation extended to South African Premier Verwoerd to visit the West, and the official and officious expressions of sympathy for Spain and Portugal, all contributed to discredit the West in Africa. Until Kennedy took office, in January 1961, the African policy of the United States, which for years supported the most reactionary régimes in Africa (those in Liberia and Ethiopia) vacillated first one way and then the other, without any firm, guiding policy. The still unresolved racial problem in the United States represents an extra burden in Africa. When African delegates to the United Nations find it almost impossible to obtain accommodation in New York and discover that because they are coloured they have to pay much more than the normal price for houses and leases, the consequences can hardly be overestimated. This sort of thing makes Africans wonder whether United States African policy really is unprejudiced after all.

Even worse for the prestige of the West in Africa was its policy of material self-interest in the Congo, where Belgium, South Africa and one or two other countries intervened—against the decisions and behind the back of the United Nations—in support of a separatist Katanga (the President of which, Tshombe, was regarded, probably rightly, as a mere puppet of the Belgian *Union Minière du Haut Katanga*), and where a year passed after the creation of the Congo State before the 'Belgian advisers' could be moved out of Elisabethville—and then only under strong United Nations pressure. Making allowances for the responsibility borne by such men as Lumumba and Gizenga, fairness demands that the destructive, un-African role of Tshombe and his supporters should not be forgotten. In view of the fact that the Katanga group did not enjoy the slightest respect, even among the friends of the West in Africa, whereas Lumumba (allowing for misgivings on account of his demagogy and indolence) was and is regarded as a typical representative of the young, dynamic, fighting Africa, the consequences of such blatantly selfish, behind-the-scenes intrigues can readily be imagined.

3. Another important disadvantage of the West is that Africans are accustomed (and encouraged by communist propaganda) to regard the actions and behaviour of individual Western countries as reflecting the general attitude of the West, although, of course, this assumption that there is a general solidarity and co-ordination of the African policies of the various Western Powers is quite unfounded. The ambiguity and the conflicts of Western policy in Africa have a long history. Europe always exported to Africa not only those things it had in common but also those things which divided it: Flemings and Walloons did not cease to rub each other the wrong way in the Congo just because 'Belgium's black children' were looking on at the spectacle; Catholics and Protestants, Baptists and Anglicans, blindly carried their religious differences into the colonies and there were the power-political struggles of the European governments and the intense economic competition of the European countries. Today in the United Nations the characteristic features of the Western policy towards Africa are disunity, antagonism, disharmony, and the absence of any will to solidarity. This has its effect in frequent, almost grotesque changes of front, which do further damage to the image of the West in Africa. For example, the United States votes with the Soviet Union for a programme of

333

complete de-colonization, while at the same time some of the NATO allies of the United States (such as France, Portugal and Spain) either abstain from voting or vote against the United States.

This lack of co-ordination and co-operation is particularly obvious in connection with the discussions, planning and execution of Western aid programmes for Africa. The damaging dividing line between the Common Market (EEC) countries and the countries of the European Free Trade Association (EFTA) extends into Africa. France and Belgium have secured the association of their former African territories in the Common Market, with the consequent benefits for them of preferences and import facilities and with consequent disadvantages for the non-associated African countries. Apart from this there are at least seven different Western aid programmes for Africa (apart from the aid programmes of the United Nations, the World Bank, the International Monetary Fund, and many private institutions). This confusion, which is rendered worse by selfish interests and rivalries, is all the more harmful at a time when concentrated aid is so necessary. But so far, neither on a national nor an inter-allied scale has the West any central, co-ordinating bodies which could give its Africa policy a uniform front and create the impression that there really is some effective control and understanding of the immense problems of the under-developed countries. On the contrary, new rivalries have lately developed which make for further confusion and conflict and their aim is obviously to secure a market monopoly in Africa for the former colonial Powers while keeping out 'foreign' countries and competitors.

4. The aid policy of the West in Africa lacks clear, cogent, long-term, productive ideas. Even today, the initiative for individual projects is usually taken by the Africans themselves. They approach their bi-lateral and multi-lateral partners in the West with proposals which their Western partners proceed to examine, discuss and eventually approve. But there are two important disadvantages in this process: the investigation is restricted to the individual project concerned and delay and procrastination are an inevitable part of the system. According to information given by Schleswig-Holstein's Premier, von Hassel, it usually takes eighteen months before a decision can be arrived at on any proposal made to the Federal Government. A French Deputy to the Council of Europe at

Strasbourg reports that it can take two years before a request from one of the African States associated with the Common Market for an aid project can be dealt with in the general framework of the aid programme and advanced to the point where instructions can be given to start the job. President Olympio of Togo, during a visit in May 1961, stated that he had been waiting for months for the arrival of a hydrographical commission from the German Federal Republic which was to make a preliminary survey before work on an all-important harbour for Togo could be started. Olympio, who has since been murdered, was a friend of the West, but he hinted that 'certain promises' made by Tito while he was in Lomé had received much prompter attention from the Yugoslav communists. In many cases the requests reflect the prestige requirements of the ruling élite rather than the real needs of the country. Thus certain African régimes have a passion for large-scale industrial projects, including atomic reactors and fully automatic steel works. Such projects incidentally favour the State economic sector, and further centralist ideas of State economic control. But according to the unanimous opinion of most economic experts, what Africa really needs is economic aid which will encourage not only the infrastructure but also intensive labour forms, a network of small industries and handicrafts, and above all, agricultural units producing for market needs. In this way a large section of the population could be painlessly introduced to sound economic principles (based on a market economy rather than on self-sufficiency) and educated to sensible economic thinking. As a result there would be a wider and fairer distribution of the national income, coupled with social amelioration for a broad section of the population.

But two fundamental requirements must be fulfilled: the West must always bear in mind that the best possible results from economic aid will be secured only if the social and economic conditions of the country being helped are largely accepted and if no attempt is made to encourage any particular development merely because it happens to favour the current social and economic interests of the country providing the aid. In other words, a free capitalist economic policy for Africa is not possible today, and any attempt to impose it would only do damage because it would force the Africans to abandon the traditional communal and co-operative principles by which they have always lived and worked. One must take into account the fact that for hundreds of years agriculture, trade, and handicraft in Africa have been carried on collectively and that large areas of the continent have never known anything but communal ownership of land. Traditionally, social and economic thought in Africa has been directed at the communal satisfaction of needs; and the West will ignore this at its peril. In such matters, the Israelis are far ahead of the Europeans and Americans in Africa, because with their *kibbutzim* they go a long way towards meeting traditional African ideas and desires. They are thus in a position to offer Africans an effective way of adapting their centuries-old social and economic institutions to modern requirements, without in any way encroaching on the voluntary principle which is so deplorably lacking in Soviet and Chinese collectivism. If Israel were not a small country wrestling desperately with tremendous problems of its own and if its every initiative did not automatically provoke counter-measures on the part of Cairo, it would be in a position to make a valuable contribution to the development of Africa which would have an effect far beyond the African continent. With certain provisos this is also true of Yugoslavia, which first established close contact with Africa when Tito made his West-African journey in the spring of 1961. Yugoslav 'national communism' is respected and admired among the native élite of Africa, primarily because the Yugoslav forms of property and economic activity, with their relative liberalism and collectivist trend, are more in accordance with African social feeling.

But the possibilities at the disposal of Israel and Yugoslavia are limited, and in consequence African eyes are still chiefly directed at the great models offered by West and East. Unfortunately, Africans are soon compelled to recognize by experience that whereas the East *is* prepared to compromise and adapt itself to African ideas, the West is seldom willing to do so. The first condition Western countries usually make when Africans apply for credits and technical assistance is that there should be some sort of investment and credit guarantee; immediately afterwards comes the demand that the preliminary investigations before the investment of the proposed credits, and then the actual investment itself, should be carried out by private investors and producers. This automatically makes Africans suspect that the motive behind this is not an unselfish desire to assist an under-developed country but an attempt to use economic aid as a lever to secure profits and returns from the African market. Yet the countries of the West are not without economic models and solutions which could appeal to Africans and arouse their enthusiasm. Throughout Western Europe there are co-operative organizations in trade and handicraft, and particularly in agriculture, with a long tradition of strict voluntarism. The West should mobilize these experiences and adapt them to African needs and desires. But as long as it fails to do this, it must not wonder and complain when Africans gaze in fascination at the Potemkin villages of communist collectives.

5. More important than economic or technical aid is generous educational assistance. A large-scale programme to develop broad educated strata in Africa is necessary. The worst omissions of the West lie here. Nine-tenths of all Africans are still illiterate and for a long time Africa will be short of skilled workers, agricultural experts, doctors, elementary school teachers, businessmen, trade-union officials, civil servants, mechanics and technicians. One of the first requirements for a large-scale educational programme for Africa is the abandonment of the unsatisfactory practice of sending Africans to Europe for their studies, since this makes their training more difficult by erecting artificial barriers of language, customs, and ideas, while forcing Africans to adapt themselves to Western habits. Secondary training schools, training workshops, trade schools, technical schools and universities must grow up in Africa itself. Europeans must go to Africa as teachers instead of making Africans come to Europe to be educated and trained in an atmosphere which is completely foreign and inhibiting to them and inevitably leads to unnecessary conflicts. In this respect, there is a further disadvantage under which the West labours; the personal and professional inadequacy of too many of the political, diplomatic, technical and teaching personnel that the West sends out to Africa. In general, they lack a sense of mission, which their sometimes clumsy communist rivals have in abundance. What most hampers the work of these Western representatives is that, almost to a man, they feel a sense of superiority towards Africans, whose language, culture and customs they despise. Africa must no longer be regarded as a place to which the second-best can safely be sent, a backwater for personnel not good enough to be used elsewhere. Africa must become the field for a new altruistic idealism on the part of our young people,

who should be made to realize the enormously important fact that the struggle for the real emancipation and the liberation of Africa will be decided by the 'third generation' of African nationalists now growing up in Africa. This is the generation which will pass judgement, and a great deal indeed will depend on their decision—not only for Africa but for the whole world. It would mean nothing less than total surrender if the West failed to recognize and meet the constructive appeal and challenge of Africa, and refused to mobilize its spiritual and material forces for a great and altruistic programme of development. Failure would clear the way for communism.

There is no point in indulging in a fruitless discussion of our errors, especially as there is now increasing recognition of the European-Atlantic obligation towards Africa, and the policy of the West is beginning to show signs of a real change.

An important factor is the immense psychological and political progress made in Africa by the United States under President Kennedy. This resulted not only from his inspiring plan to set up a Peace Corps, but also from the spirit of the New Frontier, which now determines America's relationship with the Third World. Where Africa is concerned, this culminates in the unqualified recognition of the right of its new States to go their own way between the great power blocs in a spirit of real political neutrality. Under Kennedy's leadership the us administration broke with the dangerous tendency to blame communism for any and every trouble anywhere in the world—an attitude which involved granting aid only where it would seem to reinforce the basic principle of American strategy, namely, a sterile anti-communism. In all this, the constitutional structure and political tendency of the country receiving aid was largely ignored. At first this policy paid no attention whatever to the political constitution or moral attitude of the régime concerned: any régime was automatically worthy of aid if it had the power and the will to crush any incipient social revolts. In consequence, men like Trujillo, Batista, and one or two reactionary African potentates were able to enjoy American support for a long time without any pressure being exerted to persuade them to introduce just and civilized measures in their countries. Mere anti-communism frequently triumphed over the principle of liberty, and it was therefore a very good thing when, on 6 June 1961, after his Vienna meeting with Khrushchev, President Kennedy told the

American people that he proposed to discontinue this policy and that henceforth aid to the under-developed countries would not be granted merely on the grounds of anti-communism. 'Aid', Kennedy declared, 'represents the recognition of both our opportunity and our duty to help these people to live in freedom.' In another speech he referred to a remark Khrushchev had made to him, to the effect that communism should not be held responsible for *all* the unrest in the world, and he frankly admitted that this was quite right. He added that it was too easy to dismiss every anti-governmental or anti-American movement, every revolt against a corrupt régime, and every mass protest against misery and despair, as being communist-inspired. The communists certainly exploited events for their own purposes, but they had not created the conditions which had led to the events. With this, President Kennedy decisively broke through a taboo which, until then, had been carefully preserved in Washington and the West. The first consideration of the West, particularly in Africa, should not be the struggle against communism. The communists should not necessarily be suspected of being behind every anti-Western move. The West should aim at an improvement of the objective conditions and *at changing the existing circumstances in such a way that they no longer favour the growth and spread of communism.*

The progress which has already been achieved in the analysis of the African situation, and in the West's practical African policy is not enough in itself. The fact is that the West finds itself, particularly in Africa, still in the position of merely reacting to the attacks of an active and virulent communism. The result is that many of the measures taken by the West are triggered off in the first place by actions taken by the communists and their followers. As things stand, a summary of the whole situation, dealing with the interaction of all the various relevant factors (and in particular with the interrelations of black nationalism, communism and Western policy in Africa) can hardly prove favourable to the West. In the continuing economic, social, and political upheaval on the African continent, African nationalism is obviously divided. It is unstable and it is particularly subject to crises. Above all, it has no clearly formulated ideas of its own. In this situation the communists are waging a determined offensive behind a grinning mask of friendship, and making attractive offers of assistance. Unfortunately the

339

West still lacks the necessary moral force and a clear and convincing programme adapted to African conditions and requirements; in fact, it often seems to have no real idea of the direct threat to the idea of freedom represented by the co-operation of Africans and communists.

Over and above this, the West lacks a clear insight into what it can and should do in Africa. A similar problem has already existed for some time in Asia and Latin America, and it is therefore of great importance that it should be solved now. The basic question is whether the alternative to communism should be a political, economic and even military alliance with the West and the adoption of strictly Western ideas, customs and standards in these areas, or whether there is not a 'third way' which could be permitted to these countries and peoples on their own responsibility. At least as far as Africa is concerned, it is already clear that in view of the continuing upheaval there, the alternatives cannot be East or West; there is indeed a third possibility, the establishment of a stable African power, an independent and free Africa as the best answer to communist attempts at infiltration and domination. In reality, the West has no alternative but to do its utmost to see that the slogan of African nationalism—'Africa for the Africans!'—becomes a reality in the shortest possible time and that the new Africa develops into a respected factor in the world political situation. The West hesitated and procrastinated before allowing Africa to plunge into the in-security of political sovereignty, but it should not hesitate to encourage Africa to attain its complete political, economic, and spiritual independence. This is the only way in which communism and the extreme, brutally anti-libertarian wing of African national-ism can be thwarted, and in which the resistance of the African continent to totalitarian solutions and practices can be built up.

No one who thinks in terms of practical politics can imagine that it is possible for all this to be carried out swiftly and smoothly. But since Africa and the whole of the free world is faced with great dangers, the West will finally have to recognize that desperate diseases require desperate remedies, that it must come forward with new and original ideas, make new and greater efforts, and even take considerable risks. Meanwhile, communists will do their utmost to denigrate and sabotage any pro-African policy on the part of the

West and it will not be easy to convince the suspicious Africans that such a policy is, in fact, pro-African.

It is not the aim of this book to provide detailed solutions to these problems or to reshape the West's African policy. But the material we have examined and the objective comments we have made do, of themselves, suggest a number of possibilities and we propose to summarize them under five headings.

1. The West should solemnly and convincingly proclaim that it aims at the abolition of all colonial and semi-colonial survivals anywhere in the world and it should not hesitate to exert really strong pressure on any members of the Western alliance if they attempt to flout this proclaimed intention. At the same time the West should stress that its own pro-African attitude is not influenced by any form of political self-interest or *arrière pensée*, but is based solely on the categoric imperatives of liberty, social justice, and democracy.

2. A uniform programme of African development should be worked out—one that could be followed by the West as a whole. It should be determined and implemented largely by Africans themselves. The first matter requiring attention is the establishment of a world-wide raw-materials fund from which the steady losses incurred by the under-developed countries through the creeping depreciation of raw-material prices on the world market can be made good. The greatest importance should be attached to the programme for training and educating wide sections of the population. The degree of aid offered to the individual under-developed countries should not be made dependent on the régime's attitude to the West but on the degree to which they are clearly striving to establish liberty and social justice in their countries.

3. The West should solemnly proclaim that it will oppose any attempt, no matter from what quarter, to intervene in the internal affairs of Africa and that with a view to reducing international tensions it will make no attempt to involve any African State in any military alliance provided the East will agree to exercise similar restraint. This would mean the evacuation of its military bases in Africa, but they are in any case of limited strategic importance.

4. The West should make it unmistakably clear that in order to keep the cold war out of the African continent it will reject any ideological propaganda rivalry between communism and Western

libertarian ideas there, but that if there is a continuation of communist agitation and propaganda it will take measures to counteract such activities. In this event the West should ascertain that Africans realize from the start that, in such circumstances, the West will not be acting on its own initiative, but simply reacting to communist provocation; that it will be defending itself and not launching an attack.

5. Even in African countries the constitutions of which conflict with Western principles or which already co-operate with the communists, the West should not lose heart or allow itself to be forced out completely despite its weak position, nor must it hold itself aloof, as so often in the past, from left-wing Pan-African or regional projects, or allow itself to be excluded from them. On the other hand, it must also make it quite clear that it will evince the greatest respect and sympathy for such countries, groups and elements as acknowledge the basic principles of human liberty.

The West must now try to recover the moral initiative in Africa and turn the whole continent into a demonstrating theatre for its ethical, spiritual, social, and economic values and abilities, though its aim should not and cannot be to bind Africa to Europe again, or to make Africa dependent on Europe, or turn it into a satellite. On the contrary, the West must help Africa to attain its own independent and free existence.

NOTES

[1] *Protokoll des V. Kongresses des Kommunistischen Internationale* (Hamburg, n.d.), pp. 630-2.

[2] *L'Humanité* (Paris), 26 and 27 June 1947.

[3] *Sovietskoya Vostokovodenie* (Moscow), Nos 5 and 6 (1955).

[4] 'New Features of the National-Liberation Movement', *World Marxist Review: Problems of Peace and Socialism*, II, No. 9 (September 1959), pp. 77-8. A discussion of the role of the bourgeoisie in the national struggle for liberation.

[5] Fernand Gigon, *Guinée Etat-pilote*; quoted in Franz Ansprenger, *Politik im Schwarzen Afrika* (Cologne, 1961), p. 292.

[6] Kofi Baako, 'Ghana's Conception of Socialism', lecture to an international seminar of Christian students in Accra, 19 August 1961. Typescript in the possession of the author.

[7] Statement made in a conversation with the author, in Bonn, 30 December 1961.

[8] Walter Kolarz, 'Communism in Africa—The West African Scene', *Problems of Communism*, No. 6 (1961).

INDEX

Abbas, Ferhat, 18, 198; visit to China, 199

Abyssinia: *see* Ethiopia

Adoula, Cyrille, 45, 247–8, 291

Afghanistan, Stalin on independence struggle of, 63–4

Africa Institute (USSR Academy of Sciences), 102–4

African students, Soviet indoctrination of, 303, 304

African Unity, Congress for, 51

African Workers' University, 253

Afro-Asian Authors' Conference (1962), 91

Afro-Asian Jurists' Conference (1957), 272

Afro-Asian Society of China, 194

Afro-Asian Solidarity Organization (AASO), 210, 211, 221, 237, 268–94, 308. Conferences, 138, 158, 195, 196, 273–6, 281–93

Afro-Asian Women's Conference (1961), 283–4

Afro-Asian Writers' Association, 231–2

Ahidjo, Ahmadou, 203, 206, 208

Albania and China, 91–2

alcohol, effects of, on Africans, 31, 32–3

Algeria, 12, 156, 166; and AASO, 279–80; Chinese infiltration, 198–203; Ferhat Abbas on, 18–19; Khrushchev's views attacked by China, 95

Alioune, Cissé, 254

All-Africa People's Conference and Congress, 157–8, 210

All-Africa Trade Union Federation, 254–5, 258, 263–5

Amar, Andrew Richard, 303–5

American Federation of Labor in Europe, 258

Americo-Liberians, 42–3

Angola, 117

Appiah, Joseph, 151

Arboussier, Gabriel d', 114

Asia, European colonialism in, 18

Asian Writers' Conference (1956), 272

Atlantic Charter and the colonial areas, 12

Azikiwe, Nnamdi, 19, 20

Baako, Kofi, 329

Babu: *see* Mohamed, Abdul Rahman

Balafrej, Ahmed, 190

Bandung Conference, 74, 120, 189, 268–9; colonialism and, 273; importance of, 270–2

Barbusse, Henri, 65

Basutoland, communist party in, 116

Belgium and the Congo, 15–17

Belkacem, Krim, 199

Ben Azzedine, 257

Ben Barka, Mehdi, 191, 255

Ben Bella, 51

Ben Chedda, 198

Ben Seddik, Mahjoub, 254–8

Bidonvilles (shack dwellings), 31, 32

black marketeering, 44, 132

Blaize, Yao Ngo, 252–3

Borha (of Nigerian Labour Congress), 249, 251

bourgeoisie, the and the 'colonial struggle', 72–9, 82–3, 104–5, 271, 328; communists' wooing of the, 302

347